Development after Statism

How can industrial production be managed without the guidance of the state? Adnan Naseemullah discusses industrial development in a new era of drastically constricted state capacity, from the perspective of the manufacturing firm. India's manufacturing economy has been growing after state promotion has receded. How, then, does Indian manufacturing develop in this context? Naseemullah argues that Indian firms must create production structures themselves, investing in networks of capital and labor without signals from above. Depending on manufacturers' backgrounds, these relationships are based either on formal rules or on personal ties, creating a patchwork of institutions that crosscut region and sector. As a result, many firms have been able to regain some certainty for investment, but at the cost of national coherence and the possibility of broader transformation. As a mirror case, this book also explores Pakistan's industrial trajectories, in which similar dynamics suggest the broader applicability of this framework.

ADNAN NASEEMULLAH is Lecturer in International Relations and South Asia in King's College London. He received his PhD in political science at the University of California, Berkeley, and has previously taught at the London School of Economics and Johns Hopkins University, where he was Scharf Fellow in Political Economy. His research interests are economic development, state capacity, and political order, in relation to the Indian subcontinent, some of which has appeared in *Studies in Comparative International Development* and *Governance*.

SOUTH ASIA IN THE SOCIAL SCIENCES

South Asia has become a laboratory for devising new institutions and practices of modern social life. Forms of capitalist enterprise, providing welfare and social services, the public role of religion, the management of ethnic conflict, popular culture and mass democracy in the countries of the region have shown a marked divergence from known patterns in other parts of the world. South Asia is now being studied for its relevance to the general theoretical understanding of modernity itself.

South Asia in the Social Sciences features books that offer innovative research on contemporary South Asia. The series focuses on the place of the region in the various global disciplines of the social sciences and highlights research that uses unconventional sources of information and novel research methods. While recognizing that most current research is focused on the larger countries, the series will attempt to showcase research on the smaller countries of the region.

Development after Statism

Industrial Firms and the Political Economy of South Asia

ADNAN NASEEMULLAH
King's College London

CAMBRIDGE
UNIVERSITY PRESS

CAMBRIDGE
UNIVERSITY PRESS

University Printing House, Cambridge CB2 8BS, United Kingdom

Cambridge University Press is part of the University of Cambridge.

It furthers the University's mission by disseminating knowledge in the pursuit of education, learning, and research at the highest international levels of excellence.

www.cambridge.org
Information on this title: www.cambridge.org/9781107158634

© Adnan Naseemullah 2017

First published 2017

A catalog record for this publication is available from the British Library.

Library of Congress Cataloging-in-Publication Data
Names: Naseemullah, Adnan, author.
Title: Development after statism : industrial firms and the political economy of South Asia / Adnan Naseemullah.
Description: Cambridge, United Kingdom : Cambridge University Press, 2017. | Series: South Asia in the social sciences | Includes bibliographical references and index.
Identifiers: LCCN 2016022075 | ISBN 9781107158634 (Hardback)
Subjects: LCSH: Industries–South Asia. | Industrial policy–South Asia. | Economic development–South Asia. | South Asia–Economic policy. | South Asia–Politics and government.
Classification: LCC HC430.6 .N37 2016 | DDC 338.954–dc23 LC record available at https://lccn.loc.gov/2016022075

ISBN 978-1-107-15863-4 Hardback

Contents

Figures

Tables

Preface

Growing up in relative comfort in a country of poor people, it was difficult not to wonder what economic and political changes would need to occur for the economically excluded to have access to the level of ease and opportunity I could take for granted. Development, in other words, was an ever-present idiom. The idea of development made us feel hopeful that poverty and inequality were not predetermined. Liberal political elites, professional middle classes, foreign donors, multilateral agencies, nongovernmental organizations, and even political and social activists could be part of a common project to address the causes of inequity and change the lives of the poor and downtrodden.

My undergraduate and postgraduate education taught me the deep and inherent conflict within the development project, however. From the violent nature of state formation and the pervasive influence of colonialism to the nationalist projects of industrialization and the challenge of structural adjustment, the study of development entailed understanding the often-clashing perspectives and preferences of disparate actors, even while assessing the social and political outcomes of different regimes of development policy. It also demanded rigor and facility in a variety of different disciplinary perspectives and methodological tools. Yet what made the study of development so exciting was its relevance to vital, contemporary political debates: from the adjustment responses to financial crises in East and Southeast Asia, to the debt forgiveness policies of the World Bank and the IMF, to the rise of inequalities and populist reactions in developing countries. In the study of South Asia, development seemed to be at the very heart of struggles over national meaning, state legitimacy, and social citizenship from the beginning. For all their differences, Jawaharlal Nehru and Muhammad Ali Jinnah both spoke of development in the same breath as freedom, and its political salience has not diminished since.

From the mid-2000s, however, the political economy of development as an intellectual enterprise and as a research program has narrowed significantly. In the disciplines of political science and economics, at least, the vast majority of work under this label now consists of explanations for the variation in the provision by governments of public and social goods. In recent years, the syllabi of graduate courses, the content of research seminars, and the subjects of articles and monographs have come to understand the political economy of development in these restricted terms.

There are a number of reasons for this convergence. First, it marks a continuation of a trend that sought to rebalance a postwar focus on large-scale capital-intensive projects such as bridges, dams, and steel mills by the World Bank and other donors. Frances Stewart's heralded "basic needs" approach argued that development planning needed to take into account how citizens could have their basic needs in health care and education better met, rather than simply focus on growth. Basic needs, understood as social goods provision, now drive the development agenda. Second, a focus on social goods provision as more straightforwardly measurable outcomes dovetailed with the World Bank's reorientation toward more rigorous program monitoring and assessment. Third, it follows the recent methodological popularity of "clean" causal identification and the use of randomized controlled studies among social scientists. Intervention in the provision of social goods at the local level serves as an ideal target for research involving such experimental design and has significant policy relevance. Finally, variations in these outcomes are deeply implicated in a framework that is often deployed to understand the politics of developing countries: that of clientelism. Political scientists in particular seek to identify the drivers of the nexus among corruption, patronage in electoral politics, and the diversion of resources away from universal programmatic provision of public and social goods at local and regional levels.

It is hard to question a research agenda that seeks to determine how to make poor people healthier and better educated in order, following Amartya Sen, to provide them with the foundations for greater individual freedom and autonomy in their lives. Understanding how and why some governments succeed and others fail in their responsibilities to ensure universal access to such social goods is also deeply important for the study of politics and society. But the present research agenda in the political economy of development, particularly in South Asia, is silent on an important question: once people are healthier and more educated, where will they find decent, sustainable employment?

Such a question has traditionally been implicated in the structural transformation of an economy, away from agriculture and toward industry. After all, most advanced, industrialized countries built a strong and politically assertive middle and working class through such a transformation, and no populous middle-income country has ever left that category without one. Industrialization, and the wealth it created, led to struggles between capital and labor and the establishment of social rights and structures that could defend equality of opportunity. Such a transformation was at the very core of projects of nationalist development through industrialization in countries emerging from colonial and dependent rule. Their politics were committed to redeploying state power to refashion markets and investment in order to create the conditions for mass employment in value-added sectors and industrial self-sufficiency.

The economic crises of the 1980s and early 1990s proved to be a watershed in the state's project of transforming the economy, however. Through liberalizing market reforms in most developing countries, both policy makers and scholars of development have generally ceded the responsibility for the shape and makeup of the economy to market outcomes, which do not generally favor industrialization. While the causes and mechanisms of market reform garnered much scholarly attention, few have considered the implications of liberalization for industrial development.

In order to understand the conditions for industrial development implicated in structural transformation, we need to know the driving forces and internal mechanisms of contemporary manufacturing. But our explanatory tools for industrial development were fashioned during a period when state-directed development was the norm. As a result, we need to update old frameworks and fashion new ones fit for purpose in the political economy of industrial development after the demise of statism. This book seeks to create some space in the political economy of development for discussions of the industrialization that is taking place in a radically different context from that of the era of statism.

Why does this matter, particularly in South Asia? The relatively capital-intensive world of manufacturing, as it is currently constituted, does not have the ability to absorb the tens of millions of new workers seeking to enter the workforce in positions that would provide them with living wages, the accumulation of savings and dignity. But it is the only portion of the economy with the *potential* to do so. Agriculture has stagnated; farmers' suicides and violent conflict among groups over land are regular features of the countryside. And the coveted jobs in technology services are reserved for those solidly in the middle class already, with university degrees, technical proficiency, and English proficiency. The vast majority of aspirants working in the services sector – the petty clerks, street hawkers, auto-rickshaw drivers, domestic servants, mechanics, barbers, cooks and *paan*-wallahs – are unlikely to see their wages rise or their positions become less precarious. Manufacturing can provide better and longer-term skilled employment because the returns to manufactured goods have clear added value, because workers have the capacity for collective bargaining over these returns, and because working in manufacturing itself enables the acquisition of skills and the accumulation of savings.

This ideal seems a very long distance from the realities of manufacturing in South Asia today. But in order for us to think about how manufacturing can acquire the capability to fulfil this rule, we must understand the past trajectories and current constitution of industry in the subcontinent. Further, we need to understand why manufacturing has not actually declined after liberalization, when our current understandings of industrial development necessitate the autonomous and powerful state to direct industrial investment.

To that end, this book offers a theoretical framework, a history, and an argument. Modifying the "varieties of capitalism" microfoundations at the firm level, I locate investment in manufacturing within a coherent network of institutional relationships between the firm and key factors of production. The sources of such institutional networks vary over time, however. During the period of nationalist development in India, the state governed the factor markets necessary for industrial investment. Yet starting from the 1980s, those commitments were withdrawn through the long and intensely political process of liberalizing market reform.

Despite this withdrawal, manufacturing has persisted and developed over the last two and half decades since the state's withdrawal. In order to understand how this could be the case, I spent a year and a half interviewing the actors primarily responsible for manufacturers – the proprietors, directors, and managers of manufacturing firms in the private sector across India. Through hundreds of conversations in gleaming boardrooms and dusty workshops, I found the requisite institutional relationships and industrial governance to be located not in national or regional governments but at the level of the firm. Market reform has relocated institutions and, ultimately, the governance of industrial production from the state to the factory and the shop floor.

These arguments, inductively arising from fourteen months of interview-based field research, were coupled with other research and analysis that sought to test the external validity of my claims. I used a dataset of roughly eight thousand Indian industrial firms to see whether what I saw in my qualitative research would be evident over a wider universe of manufacturing firms in India. In selecting manufacturing firms, my intention was to widen my interview sample of approximately 160 firms but ensure comparability between the two samples. As a result, my large-N analysis is conducted on a dataset that does not represent the full range of manufacturing concerns. In particular, it largely the misses the small workshops and petty fabrication outfits that have been the subject of excellent study by scholars in economic sociology, geography, and anthropology. A comprehensive econometric analysis of causes and mechanisms of production in the full universe of Indian manufacturing is very much necessary, but unfortunately it falls beyond the scope of this book.

To see whether these arguments can travel across national boundaries, I conducted research in Pakistan as well as India. In an effort to extend the explanations of industrial governance after liberalization, I have conducted research and analysis in a neighboring country, partitioned from the same colonial territory and sharing many social characteristics but differing dramatically in the nature of state formation and attendant processes of statist industrialization. Such a design provides at least a suggestion of the potential relevance and utility of this firm-level framework to other cases of countries in the middle-income category with continuing industrialization after market reform.

This book has two key implications for the politics of development in South Asia and beyond. First, it calls for some humility in thinking about the power of the state to affect economic outcomes. If the strategies and tactics of industrial promotion are to be reframed successfully in contemporary South Asia, it must start with recognition of the state's changed role in the industrial economy. Of course, this also suggests some recognition on the part of those who maintain an exclusive focus on social goods provision that what the state might do in providing social goods to fulfill basic needs does not fully encompass the means and ends of development. Second, the book suggests that the industrial bourgeoisie cannot be easily thought of a class or interest group united in policy preference and political alignment. Manufacturers have a variety of experiences and act to instantiate those values on the political economy. This complicates any simple narrative of political and economic reform and can have large implications for the politics of both countries. In general, the book affords what I hope is a new perspective on the politics and economics of manufacturing in South Asia, entailing new frameworks with which we might understand its internally complex nature and its trajectory over time.

Acknowledgments

This book grew out of my graduate work at the University of California, Berkeley, and was written and revised at the London School of Economics, Johns Hopkins University, and, finally, King's College London. I am grateful to each of these institutions for providing me with opportunities through this process. Additional thanks go to multiple institutions that have helped me fund my research and writing, including the National Science Foundation Graduate Research Fellowship, the John Simpson Memorial Fellowship at UC Berkeley, and the U.S. Department of Education's Fulbright-Hays Doctoral Dissertation Research Abroad Fellowship. I have also benefited from presenting this book project at various stages at the University of California, Berkeley, Boston University, the London School of Economics, the University of Toronto, Arizona State University, the Johns Hopkins University, King's College London, the Indira Gandhi Institute for Development Studies, Mumbai University, and at the annual meetings of the Society for the Advancement of Socioeconomics and the American Political Science Association.

Extremely detailed, incisive, and sustained comments and suggestions from three anonymous reviewers have transformed this book and, in so doing, improved it immeasurably. Lucy Rhymer, my editor at Cambridge University Press, has guided the book through out; I thank her for her initial interest in the manuscript and her continuing faith in it. Robert Judkins and Anand Shanmugam have managed the production process impeccably, and Susan Thornton provided excellent copy-editing. I am also deeply grateful to the editorial board of the South Asia in the Social Sciences series at the Press – Partha Chatterjee, Christophe Jaffrelot, Pranab Bardhan, and Stuart Corbridge – for providing invaluable feedback and including my manuscript in the series, and to Qudsiya Ahmed for facilitating my inclusion.

This has been a long road, and one that I could not have walked alone. I would like to thank James Kurth, Kenneth Sharpe, and

Stephen O'Connell at Swarthmore College for their wisdom and their initial encouragement. At Berkeley, I am deeply indebted to the guidance of a number of individuals. Kiren Chaudhry first introduced me to the powerful frameworks and insights of the political economy of development. Peter Katzenstein provided valuable feedback on research design at the Institute for Qualitative Research Methods; David Collier and Laura Stoker provided stellar training in the world of research methodology. Mark Bevir, Kevin O'Brien, and Raka Ray provided key insights and interventions in the nerve-wracking process of framing a dissertation. The participants of the South Asian Politics Colloquium at Berkeley provided an intellectual mother ship and gave me a space to test out my ideas: Nafisa Akbar, Matthew Baxter, Jennifer Bussell, Francesca Jensenius, Manoj Mate, Susan Ostermann, Rahul Verma, Gilles Verniers, Anasuya Sengupta, and Vasundhara Sirnate have been excellent interlocutors. Pradeep Chhibber has been an exceptional mentor throughout, challenging my ideas with purpose and helping me negotiate evidence and concepts in the context of building a larger narrative. He has read and critiqued more drafts of this book than anyone; I am humbled by the faith he has maintained in its promise.

   Fieldwork presented significant challenges, which were overcome with the assistance of a number of key people. Pratap Mehta was kind enough to host me at the Center for Policy Research in New Delhi; I benefited a great deal from his insights in Indian politics and political economy. G. Koteswara Prasad at the University of Madras provided me with assistance and support during my research in Chennai. Staff at the American Institute of Indian Studies and at the United States Educational Foundation in India negotiated research clearance for my project and provided a welcome to India, while Muhammed Razzaq and the staff at the American Institute of Pakistan Studies were gracious hosts in Lahore. In India and Pakistan, I very much appreciated the sanity-preserving company and incisive guidance of Tania Ahmed, Melia Belli, Yuti Bhatt, Beverly Bhaangi, Faisal Chaudhry, Stella Cridge, Adnan Farooqui, Raghu Karnad, Ajay Madiwale, Kate Miller, Leo Mirani, Shruti Ravindran, Anindya Saha, Barton Scott, Sucharita Sengupta, E. Sridharan, Paul Staniland, Ananya Vajpayee, and Anita Weiss. I am also owe a deep debt of gratitude to the many interview respondents who, through our conversations, built the perspectives and insights of this book.

The writing and revision of this book were made possible by the support, insight, and suggestions of colleagues and friends in London and Baltimore. At the London School of Economics, I am grateful to conservations with and encouragement from Sharad Chari, Asher Ghertner, Daphne Halikiopoulu, Steffen Hertog, Jonathan Hopkin, Bill Kissane, Christel Koop, Martin Lodge, Kira Matus, Sue Sharkey, Pon Souvannaseng, and David Woodruff. At Johns Hopkins, I am deeply thankful for the support and company of Margaret Keck, Naveeda Khan, Michael Levien, Mary Otterbein, Lester Spence, Chloe Thurston, and Emily Zackin. And finally through a difficult first year at King's, I have benefited from the support of Hannah Bond, Rudra Chaudhuri, Theo Farrell, Christophe Jaffrelot, Sunil Khilnani, Peter Kingstone, Joanna Pauk, and Srinath Raghvan. At various points during the process of writing and revision, I have greatly benefited from conversations with and comments from Amit Ahuja, Caroline Arnold, Pranab Bardhan, Douglas Fuller, William J. Hurst, Atul Kohli, R. Nagaraj, Darius Ornston, Aseema Sinha, Ashutosh Varshney, and Michael Walton. Finally, this book would not have been finished without guidance and friendship of scattered comrades and fellow travelers. I especially want to thank Sener Akturk, Jennifer Brass, Jonathan Chow, Jennifer Dixon, Tanwen Ellis, Samuel Handlin, Jonathan Hassid, Colin Moore, Raymond Orr, Bhrigupati Singh, Prerna Singh, Suzanne Scoggins, Rachel Stern, and Adam Ziegfeld. Jody LaPorte and Jessica Rich deserve special recognition for going above and beyond the call of duty as sources of inspiration, guidance, and encouragement.

I deeply appreciate how family scattered across the globe have quietly held me in their thoughts throughout this process. My grandmother, mother, sister, and brother-in-law – Mollie Barger, Jennifer Barger, Sophie Naseemullah, and Jesse Alter – have been special fountains of support and love through three transatlantic moves over five years. Last, I wish to thank my father, Muhammad Naseemullah, whose curiosity, intellect, and dedication to improving the lives of the excluded continue to serve as a source of inspiration to me. I am very sorry that he never lived to see this in print, but his passion is present on every page. I am dedicating this work to his memory.

Abbreviations

ACMA	Automotive Component Manufacturers' Association
AIML	All-India Muslim League
ANP	Awami National Party
API	Active Pharmaceutical Ingredients
ASSOCHAM	Associated Chambers of Commerce and Industry
BJP	Bharatiya Janata Party
BRIC	Brazil, Russia, India, China
CBTPA	Caribbean Basin Trade Partnership Act
CEI	Council for Engineering Industry
CII	Confederation of Indian Industry
CITU	Center for Industrial Trade Unions
CKD	Complete Knock-Down [Kits]
CMIE	Center for the Monitoring of the Indian Economy
CPI	Communist Party of India
CPM	Communist Party of India-Marxist
CRAMS	Contract Research and Manufacturing Systems
DFI	Development Finance Institutions
DMK	Dravida Munettra Kazagham
FDI	Foreign Direct Investment
FICCI	Federation of Indian Chambers of Commerce and Industry
GATT	General Agreement on Tariffs and Trade
GDP	Gross Domestic Product
GKU	Girni Kamgar Union
GM	General Motors
GVC	Global Value Chains
HDFC	Housing Development Finance Corporation
HM	Hindustan Motors
HMS	Hind Mazdoor Sangh
HR	Human Resources

ICICI	Industrial Credit and Investment Corporation of India
ICT	Information and Communications Technology
IDBI	Industrial Development Bank of India
IIM	Indian Institutes of Management
IIT	Indian Institutes of Technology
IMF	International Monetary Fund
IMWO	International Metal Workers' Organization
INTUC	Indian National Trade Union Congress
IPO	Initial Public Offering
IT	Information Technology
JV	Joint Venture
LIBOR	London Inter-Bank Offered Rate
LIC	Life Insurance Corporation (of India)
LUMS	Lahore University of Management Sciences
MD	Managing Director
MFA	Multi-Fiber Agreement
MNC	Multinational Corporation
MOSPI	Ministry of Statistics and Programme Implementation, India
MQM	Muttahida Quami Movement
NAFTA	North American Free Trade Agreement
NCR	National Capital Region (New Delhi)
NIC	Newly Industrializing Countries
NIFT	National Institute of Fashion Technology
NPC	National Planning Committee
NREGA	National Rural Employment Guarantee Act
NWP	Nonwage Portion (of total labor costs)
OBC	Other Backward Classes
OECD	Organization for Economic Cooperation and Development
OEM	Original Equipment Manufacturer
OPEC	Organization of Petroleum-Exporting Countries
PAL	Premier Automotive Limited
PICIC	Pakistan Industrial Credit and Investment Corporation
PIDC	Pakistan Industrial Development Corporation
PIFC	Pakistan Industrial Finance Corporation
PIL	Public Interest Litigation

PML-N	Pakistan Muslim League-Nawaz
PML-Q	Pakistan Muslim League-Quaid
PPP	Pakistan People's Party
PWF	Pakistan Workers' Federation
R&D	Research and Development
RBI	Reserve Bank of India
RIM	Reliance Industry Mobile
RMMS	Rashtriya Mill Mazdoor Sangh
SBI	State Bank of India
SEZ	Special Economic Zone
SLR	Statutory Liquidity Ratio
SME	Small or Medium Enterprise
TELCO	Tata Engineering and Locomotive Corporation
TRIPS	Trade-Related Intellectual Property Rights
TUFS	Textile Upgradation Fund Scheme
TVS	TV Sundaram (automotive company)
TWU	Textile Workers Union
UDCT	University Department of Chemical Technology, Mumbai
UP	Uttar Pradesh
USAID	United States Agency for International Development
VoC	Varieties of Capitalism
WDI	World Development Indicators, World Bank
WTO	World Trade Organization

1 | Introduction

India had one of the fastest-growing economies in the world over the last two decades. Economic growth reached double digits, and the country has since been regarded as one of the emergent global economic powers of the twenty-first century. The OECD has projected that India's share of global GDP will more than double by 2060.[1] This economic emergence has been due, at least in part, to manufacturing. The transformation of raw materials and other inputs – from cotton to basic chemicals to iron and steel – into intermediate and finished goods, from shirts to gears to medication for hypertension, is an important part of India's growth story, one often overshadowed by the services sector in general and information technology (IT) services in particular. Growth in manufacturing value added has frequently surpassed overall per capita growth in the economy over the last two decades (fig. 1.1), with output in consumer durables tripling and capital goods more than doubling over less than a decade (fig. 1.2).

What causes and sustains this industrial growth performance? Scholars of comparative political economy have long argued that the

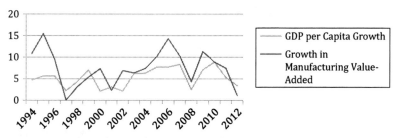

Figure 1.1 GDP and Manufacturing Growth in India, 1994–2013.
Source: World Development Indicators, databank.worldbank.org

[1] Braconier et al. 2014.

1

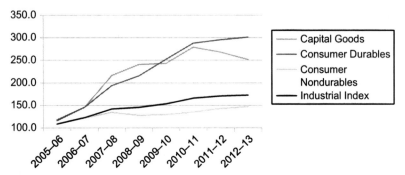

Figure 1.2 Indexed Growth in Manufacturing by Segment, 2005–2013.
Source: Index of Industrial Production, MOSPI (100 = 2004–2005)

state plays a crucial role in facilitating industrial development.[2] This is seen as particularly the case in developing countries, such as those in South Asia. Yet the persistence of growth in manufacturing in contemporary India is taking place in the context of an Indian state with little willingness and less capacity to promote industry effectively.

Most concretely, the contemporary Indian state has not proved willing to execute long-term investments in public goods. Intense electoral competition has led governments to favor short-term clientelistic spending on crucial constituencies over more diffuse, long-term public investments such as infrastructure. In a telling episode in July 2012, the national electricity grid failed twice, affecting up to 600 million people and shuttering tens of thousands of industrial units.[3] Writing on the Delhi satellite city in 2011, Jim Yardley asks, "[Gurgaon] represents a riddle at the heart of India's rapid growth: how can a new city become an international economic engine without basic public services? How can a huge country flirt with double-digit growth despite widespread corruption, inefficiency and governmental dysfunction?"[4] The answer, he argues, "is that growth usually occurs despite the government rather than because of it." These dynamics are more generally reflected in the conditions for investment; the World Bank's 2014 Ease of Doing Business index ranked India 142nd out of 189 countries, below Sierra Leone and Uzbekistan.

---

[2] World Bank 1997; Wade 1990; North 1990; Kohli 2004.   [3] Magnier 2012.
[4] Yardley 2011.

More subtly but no less importantly, the state has substantially less influence over the provision of key factors of industrial production. As state-promoted "development finance" institutions have been dismantled or privatized, manufacturing must compete in a tight and chaotic capital market with an in-built preference for quick returns and an aversion to long-term, concentrated investments such as manufacturing enterprises. Industrial labor is increasingly fragmented and footloose, as state-mediated encompassing arrangements between organized workers and management have broken down. And government institutes for technical and vocational training have chronically undersupplied industry with skilled workers; thus manufacturing enterprises have difficulty recruiting and retaining them in order to meet the demands of production. The provision of land and energy to manufacturing enterprises has similarly fallen from the focus of the state's attentions and abilities.

These particular aspects of relative state incapacity in supporting industry are together a product of a wider phenomenon, that of *economic liberalization*. India, along with many countries in the developing world, went through a complex series of liberalizing economic reforms that drew the government out of the notion that it can, and indeed must, direct industrial development. From the beginning of the 1980s through the middle of the 1990s, the Indian state dramatically changed its role in the economy. State actors have by no means disappeared from the economy, but the state's institutional capabilities in structuring *industrial* investment have become severely circumscribed.

Yet popular and powerful state-institutionalist theories, through which we have come to understand industrial development, were formulated in the era of state-directed development from the 1950s until roughly the late 1980s, and thus in a context before this liberalizing turn. The very foundations of the political economy of later industrialization have from the beginning been predicated on the actions of the state.[5] Dependency theorists argued that the state needed to empower itself in order to execute import-substituting industrialization, through trade restriction and active industrial policy.[6] Scholars of the developmental state tradition located the remarkable economic successes of the previously backward East Asian "tiger" economies in

[5] List 1856; Gerschenkron 1962.
[6] Gunder Frank 1966; Cardoso and Faletto 1979.

powerful, autonomous state institutions that directed capital and disciplined labor; comparativists then explained the economic success and failure of developing countries through the differential capacities of their states to direct development.[7] These state-institutionalist frameworks, though powerful explanations for what drives cross-national variations in growth in the postwar decades, have not fully contended with fundamental changes in the role of the state during liberalization at the end of the twentieth century. The persistence and growth of manufacturing after economic liberalization in India thus pose a challenge to classical institutional theories of "late" industrialization that have privileged the state as the paramount driver of development.

Free market advocates, by contrast, have long argued that this withdrawal of the state may in fact be the *cause* of India's relative successes in manufacturing. In their view, the state's withdrawal has led to the unleashing of "animal spirits" and thus a surge in investment and sustained production, without the smothering impact of government interference.[8] There are some problems with this perspective, however. The first is empirical: Indian manufacturing grew at a steady pace during the Nehruvian era of high statism – averaging 6.9 percent between 1955–1956 and 1965–1966 – and then again from the early 1980s onward.[9] Liberalization cannot by itself be the cause of successful industrial development, if manufacturing grew both in the presence of statism and in its absence. Second, in India, as in most developing countries, market institutions – from developed financial mechanisms to rigorously enforced property rights – are both necessary for the functioning of "free market" capitalism and underdeveloped relative to those in industrialized countries.[10] Further, the development of such market institutions is the outcome of historical political and social struggles in which the national state plays an important role.[11]

---

[7] See Johnson 1982, 1995; Amsden 1989; Woo-Cummings 1991; Evans 1995; Herring 1999; Chibber 2003; Kohli 2004; Doner, Ritchie and Slater 2005; Vu 2010.

[8] For proponents of the free market perspective, see Bhagwati 1993; Das 2000.

[9] Bardhan 1984, 18. McCartney (2009, 2010) makes this argument explicitly.

[10] For more on developed market institutions, see Vogel 1996; Hall and Soskice 2001.

[11] Polanyi 2001 [1944]; Zysman 1994.

Most importantly, successful industrial development requires institutional coordination among disparate actors over time. In India, straightforward market incentives would not suggest this course of action, regardless of the long-term potential, because of the presence of simpler, shorter-term alternatives for investment, from real estate to the consumer retailing of imported goods. Absent institutional structures, such as those provided by state-directed development regimes in the postwar decades, industrialization in developing countries would not – indeed, could not – flourish.

So how might we understand how manufacturing works after economic liberalization, particularly in the Indian context? The first part of formulating an answer to this question lies in the core concept of institutions: interrelated collections of formal rules, mutual understandings, and regulated practices provide the relative certainty and facilitate the coordination necessary for manufacturing. For industrial development to occur, institutions must enable private sector industrial firms – as the key frontline drivers of Indian industry – to invest capital and to recruit, train, and retain workers. Capital and labor are, after all, the most use-intensive and thus the most crucial factors of production in manufacturing.[12]

If capital and labor are the two most important factors of production for industry, everything depends on the predictable supply of these factors to manufacturing firms. I contend that industrial production is only possible if firms are able to overcome coordination challenges relating to labor and capital to enable the provision of trained workers and "patient" finance at a big enough scale and for long enough to arrange and deploy manufacturing processes. In order to do this, there has to be a coherent and durable framework of institutional relationships that link firms to their workers and sources of capital. Collectively, I call this institutional framework *industrial governance.*

---

[12] This book does not focus on land and energy; while certainly important, they constitute fixed and variable costs, respectively, that are largely exogenous to the continuing institutional relationships that preoccupy manufacturers. Securing premises is a prerequisite for investment in manufacturing, but once land is secured and a factory is built or bought, land figures little in the ongoing daily business of production. Beyond protest, manufacturers can do little about the high cost and uneven supply of electricity in India because there are no ready substitutes to government provision. For more on the political economy of land and power in India, see Levien 2013 and Chatterjee 2015.

In most of the extant literature on the political economy of industrial development, the state is thought to provide this industrial governance and thus direct the provision of capital and labor, by creating rules and channeling resources for industrial promotion. And in fact, during the era of statist development from independence until the 1980s, the Indian government, directly and through allied agencies and organizations, expended significant amounts of resources and political capital to this end. This book explores the nature and institutional sources of contemporary industrial governance after the state withdraws from governing the industrial economy.

Industrial Governance after Statism

There are several potential candidates for new forms of industrial governance that could explain how industrial production might be structured after statism. One possibility focuses on subnational governments. This perspective is informed by the remarkable regional variation in economic development in India, as well as other countries in South Asia and beyond. Indian market reforms have, moreover, been accompanied by the devolution of resources and political authority to state governments. Certain states have assertively claimed ownership over economic success within their borders. Narendra Modi, India's current prime minister and the former chief minister for Gujarat for more than a decade, campaigned throughout the 2014 elections on spreading "the Gujarat model" of industrial promotion – what Aseema Sinha has called a "subnational developmental state"[13] – to the rest of the country. It seems plausible that state governments in the pursuit of regional development provide industrial governance around sites of industrial growth.

A second possible alternative to statist industrial governance suggests the importance of institutions at the sectoral level. Globalization, the deepening of international trade and investment, has affected different industries in distinctly different ways. It seems equally plausible that globally competitive Indian industries, famously IT services but also pharmaceuticals and automotive components, might benefit significantly from institutional signals from partners, patrons, and clients in global markets, whereas industries facing threats from international competition might instead resort to

[13] Sinha 2005.

defensive protectionism, and thus substantively different forms of organization. Further, the export-promoting agencies of the Indian state and the organizational capacities of business associations – both are organized by sector – might provide new institutional structures after the depletion of the more encompassing industrial promotion regime under statism. In this context, a variety of forces and actors might combine to provide industrial governance at the level of industry or sector.

In locating the institutions that support contemporary industrialization, I take a different explanatory approach. Rather than subnational or sectoral institutions providing industrial governance after the retreat of the central state, I argue that sources of stability for industrial production can be most clearly located at the level of the firm. As I hope to demonstrate throughout this book, in the absence of credible external cues, industrial firms *as institutional actors* structure their ambient environment themselves in order to invest successfully in manufacturing. Indian firms thus proactively make and maintain long-term relationships with financiers and with workers.

By suggesting that firm owners, directors, and managers proactively participate in creating coherent institutional frameworks for production, I depart from the conventional wisdom on the institutions behind industrial development in three ways. First, I place the focus of my analysis on the firm as an institutional actor, and thus a political agent. Firms are not often considered in this way, because of a ubiquitous framing of their motivations as straightforward profit maximization. But Susan Strange argues that the firm can be seen as a political actor if politics are defined by "the human ability not just to act but to act in concert" rather than simply by what governments or politicians do:

From the moment when its originator conceives the enterprise, he or she needs the supporting wills of creditors, employees, managers and salesmen to achieve the dream. Bargaining, persuasion, the offer of inducements, the threat of negative sanctions, the inspiration with a common vision – all these activities are little different from what politicians do when they seek election. If business people in action simply told their financial backers or their employees that the enterprise would reduce transaction costs by internalising them, they would not get very far. The cold logic of economic theory will not get people acting enthusiastically in concert to compete energetically with rival firms.[14]

[14] Strange 1996, 36.

(a)   (b)

Statism   "Governing Firms"

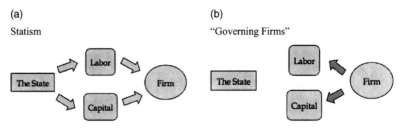

Figure 1.3 Industrial Governance during and after Statism.

Most extant political economy scholarship, by contrast, understands industrial firms and their directors as relatively short-term rational, even mechanistic actors, straightforwardly responding to the incentives and constraints provided by states, or the signals of international markets in such a way as to maximize profits. In other words, they are often understood as *institution-takers*.

This book takes a more ecumenical and empirical approach. The state might indeed influence or even direct a firm's strategies and practices, either with sticks such as regulatory enforcement or with carrots such as incentives. But this is the case only when the state deploys enough resources and political capital to provide such sticks and carrots coherently and credibly. When these signals from the state are weak, confused or absent, however, manufacturers must pro-actively form relationships with capital and labor and thus structure the institutions necessary for production absent direction from the state. In these instances, manufacturers are *institution-makers*.

Second, the interests and capacity of the state to promote industry through directing factor markets can change significantly over time; thus, the model of firms as institution-takers might have been appropriate during the statist era, but it may be less so after its conclusion. I outline histories of national development and of the international economy that inform the broader politics behind the rise and fall of statism in industrial governance, linking macro-historical processes to the dynamics at the firm level. The early postwar period saw the Indian government, among those in many developing countries, build up an autonomous state apparatus to direct the factor markets crucial to industrial development. Manufacturing firms operating in this context saw their activities both supported and disciplined by the powerful institutions of industrial governance emanating from the state. The results of this project were mixed both within and across country cases: South Korea was more successful than Nigeria, and within India, pharmaceuticals were more successful than heavy engineering. Yet starting from the late 1970s and then building in the 1980s, international forces and changes in domestic political economies combined to induce a fundamental shift in the broad relationship between the state and the industrial economy, from statism to liberalizing economic reform.

I contend that the level of institutional agency and autonomy on the part of firms is an outcome of economic liberalization: state actors – at national, regional or sectoral levels – are less interested in and capable of expending resources and political capital to define a single set of rules for industrial production through the control of factor markets. The signals from these agencies are weak and cannot be relied upon to structure industrial production. This is in stark contrast to the statist era, in which the state provided the rules of engagement for capital and labor, and used its disciplinary authority and abilities to concentrate and allocate resources to enforce a coherent regime of industrial governance. In other words, I contend that there has been fundamental change in the structures of industrial production over time, which has been neglected in favor of variation in the state's institutional capacity to promote industry across different countries.

Third, through my research, I uncovered significant variation in the ways that firms overcome these institutional challenges. This variation is in part a consequence of the retreat of the state from industrial governance; the lack of clear external signals leave firms to their own devices in terms of creating and maintaining institutional structures. But firm-level variation is a distinctive feature of Indian industrial economy, one that has been largely unnoticed due to our emphasis on national (or regional) models of capitalism in political economy. A focus on variation in structures and practices at the firm level can provide us with insights into the nature and social consequences of industrial capitalism in contemporary India that might otherwise have been overlooked. But how might we characterize and account for such variation?

Industrial Variation after Statism

Over interviews with more than 160 firms across several sectors and states, I found that firms in India broadly tend to structure their key institutional relationships in one of two ways. Some firms build their relationships through formal, explicit, contractual rules – in a way, replicating, at the level of the firm, frameworks of industrial production that exist in more highly institutionalized institutional macro-environments, such as in Aichi prefecture or in Baden-Wurttemberg. Other firms govern themselves through dense networks of personal ties and more informal understandings, submerged in social norms and maintained through larger kinship and community structures.

The character of firm-level institutional practices can diverge quite markedly, even for notionally quite similar enterprises. Consider two examples. In the Delhi National Capital Region (NCR), a textile trader turned industrialist, with a yarn empire of $500 million in annual sales accumulated over less than a decade, operates out of a small and rundown office in the Okhla Industrial Estate. He buys "sick" spinning mills and transforms them into productive units through the renegotiation of longstanding labor contracts. Labor relations for this firm, even given its size, are closely tied to personal relationships. Recruitment occurs mostly from rural areas, and relationships with *mukadams* or labor brokers, are important in this process: "to get labor, you need to talk to people." (2007-del2).

By contrast, just across the Yamuna River in the North Okhla Industrial Development Area, a glass office tower houses the textile operations of a venerable Marwari family, also worth $500 million in annual turnover, which has diversified and technologically upgraded their traditional spinning operations, as well as moved production downstream to fabric production and apparel manufacturing. Labor relations here are focused on formal, institutionalized training, or the development of human capital: "We have formal training systems – we give formal classroom and on-the-job training to all workers. We pick up youngsters with primary schooling and we train them for four months or six months." My respondent, the managing director, also placed a premium on human relations policies that institutionalize incentives for performance: "A worker is a human being and you need to treat him as such: [provide] a good environment, treat him well, and pay enough to cover cost of living. Why can't he be a partner? He should be as responsible as you are, he just needs to be motivated enough" (2007-del20).

These two institutional responses resonate in every state and region, in every sector and industry, with exporters as well as domestic firms, and with small firms and large ones. Presence of this variation in all these contexts constitutes *prima facie* evidence that subnational states or sectoral agencies or associations have not replaced the national state in leading to local convergences through the governing the factor markets. Additionally, both institutional forms can successfully structure industrial production. In other words, there is no one clear national path to success for Indian industry, onto which surviving and successful enterprises converge. By forming and maintaining relationships through either of these modes, firms are able to induce predictable long-term behavior from workers and sources of finance.[15] In addition, they may structure the ways that different export-oriented firms engage with the international economy.

What are the origins of such institutions? In my view, differences in firm institutional structures can be traced to features and characteristics particular to that firm, and in particular to the perspectives of the individuals and families that own most or all of the enterprise. Corporate governance in South Asia is characterized less by routinized principal-agent interaction and bureaucratic stockholder oversight than by the very personal engagement of a firm's owners and directors, who manage most aspects of a firm's strategy and even many of its day-to-day activities. The nature of this management, and thus the firm's institutional structures, depends at least in part on the social contexts and socializing experiences of those who invest or reinvest in manufacturing. To paraphrase C.S. Lewis, what you see and what you hear depends a great deal on where you come from.

For those Indian manufacturers who invest in manufacturing enterprise after long years trading yarn, fabric or automotive components, or those farmers who invest amassed agrarian capital and invested it in manufacturing, or foremen saving up capital to buy powerlooms and set up workshops and thus become bosses in their own right, the Indian economy is constituted by a dense network of personal ties, through which business gets done and production is arranged. For the young scions of venerable business houses returning after management degrees from foreign universities, by contrast, doing business in India

---

[15] These two forms are best thought of as empirical tendencies rather than ironclad laws; hybrid forms that do not conform to this argument of institutional bifurcation certainly exist. I argue that structuring production through formal institutions or personal networks based on the backgrounds and perspectives of manufacturers constitutes a more successful characterization for the variation in firm strategies than the regional and sectoral alternatives.

as elsewhere means the application of "best practices" and the execution of formal rules and policies.[16] I argue that while differences in these perspectives were certainly present (though perhaps in less stark terms) during the height of statism, they did not drive the ways in which industrial production was structured, because the state deployed a set of institutional frameworks to which firms had to adhere in order to take advantage of the state's largesse and to avoid its sanction.

Other factors at the firm level also impact firm governance, but in ways broadly complementary to the backgrounds and perspectives of manufacturers. Small firms are less likely to be successful at getting bank loans, but owners of smaller enterprises are also more likely to prefer investing family or community capital than loans from anonymous institutions. Firms firmly integrated into global value chains (GVC) are more likely to mirror the formal practices of the multinational corporations with whom they are deeply engaged than exporters who diversified between domestic markets and sales in markets in the Middle East and Central and Southeast Asia.

As I will elaborate upon in later chapters, a combination of manufacturers' backgrounds and experiences and complementary firm-level factors such as size and export orientation serve as a better explanation for the contemporary variation in institutional frameworks than either a firm's geographic location or the industry in which it produces. This comparative claim strongly implies that subnational or sectoral models of industrial governance are at best incomplete explanations for the nature of industrial production after statism; firms do not seem to converge around the signals emanating from state governments or sectoral agencies and arrange their production accordingly, but rather rely on their own experiences and perspectives as more reliable guides for creating and maintaining productive institutions. The outcome of these varied production structures at the firm level is a regime of industrial development, but one that is not particularly legible through the lens of the state. This illegibility has significant consequences for understanding the role and meaning of the state after liberalization, and its future as an actor in industrial development.

[16] These differences map roughly onto the "office to factory" and "field to factory" trajectories of nonmercantile caste groups into business outlined by Damodaran (2008). Here, however, the emphasis is on context and experience rather than ascriptive identity.

The State after Statism

Much has been written on the politics of economic liberalization. There has been a vigorous debate on the causes of economic reform: precisely how and why economic actors, including those with much to lose from change, would acquiesce to these policy transformations.[17] But relatively little research has focused on a core question of political economy: after liberalization, what is the place of the state in the industrial economy, particularly in developing countries?[18] This book adds to this research by examining the institutional micro-foundations of manufacturing before and after liberalization, and by placing industrial variation in the wider social context of social responses to the state. As such, it offers additional insights to the identity and place of the state after statism. It also represents a slight departure from careful accounts in Indian political economy that emphasize broad continuities in the *formal* institutional capacities of the state, while locating them in the dynamic engagement between the central and state governments.[19] I discuss the broader history of the rise and fall of statism in Chapter 3. Here, I will just introduce the proximate causes, rooted in political economy, of the state's transformation in roles and capabilities in conjunction with liberalization.

The most prominent questions on the consequences of liberalization are essentially Lasswellian: the politics of who gets what, when and how? The winners, as many scholars have argued, rewrite the rules of political economy such that their gains are institutionalized. Nowhere was this process more evident than the creation of economic oligarchies in the former Soviet Union, but it is almost axiomatic that economic reforms have increased structural economic inequality in most developing countries. Closely related is the notion of state capture, in which elites gain control of the policymaking process, by implicit influence or explicit corruption, in order to consolidate or defend their economic interests.[20] State capture is often characterized as a national phenomenon, but it can have regional and local

---

[17] Kingstone 1999; Jenkins 2000; Etchemendy 2011; Mukherji 2014.
[18] The most sustained meditations on the place of the state in the era of neoliberalism have related to neoliberal reform in advanced industrial countries. See Streeck and Thelen 2005; Schmidt 2009.
[19] For an excellent conceptual account of these dynamics, see Sinha 2010.
[20] Hellman, Jones and Kaufman 2000.

variants. Regionally powerful economic groups might ally with rising political leadership in state governments or even sites of local authority in order to pursue mutually beneficial but typically exclusionary activities.[21] Fiscal decentralization, the rise of previously excluded regional groups, competitive clientelism and the increasing cost of electoral finance certainly reflect some of these dynamics in the Indian context.

The politics of liberalization and capture have profound consequences on the interests, roles and capacities of the state. Jonah Levy, writing on the advanced industrial world, has framed the change in the state's role as from a market-steering orientation to a market-supporting orientation.[22] Schamis has persuasively argued that market reforms in developing countries have led the state to withdraw from key factor markets, while increasing its capacities in the (selective) enforcement of property rights and through increased fiscal space.[23] These new capacities inform a new dominant role for the state, as a key actor in the allocation and redistribution of rents. Thus Atul Kohli's influential characterization of the consequences of economic reform in India is correct, but also incomplete: rather than India adopting a broadly "pro-business strategy," it is a regime that privileges *some* businesses – those implicated in a political economy of rent allocation and clientelism – over others.[24]

To understand the state's role in rent allocation in the contemporary economy, it can be useful to differentiate between types of economic activity. Gandhi and Walton, in their analysis of high net-worth economic actors, posit a useful distinction between types of business writ large: "sectors such as real estate, infrastructure, construction, mining, telecom, cement and media have been classified as 'rent-thick', because of the pervasive role of the state in giving licences, reputations of illegality, or information on monopolistic practices."[25] They calculate that sixty percent of the wealth of dollar billionaires in India is derived from activity in rent-thick sectors. I contend that the state's current capacities and the interests of politicians and policymakers converge on supporting economic actors engaged in rent-thick activities, from state governments ceding previously protected forests for mineral

---

[21] For a model of these dynamics, see Bardhan and Mookherjee 2000.
[22] Levy 2006, 3.   [23] Schamis 2002, 6.   [24] Kohli 2006a, 2006b, 2011.
[25] Gandhi and Walton 2012, 12.

extraction to the reserving of telecoms licenses for favored clients to maintaining local transportation monopolies by government fiat. Such "favors" are repaid, in the form of campaign donations, more diffusely reciprocal benefits or even simply cash in suitcases. In other words, the balance of state intervention in the economy has moved from governing crucial factor markets for a universe of industrial firms to distributing rents to a much smaller number of favored clients.[26]

For all this rent-pervasiveness, however, there are large swathes of the Indian economy that are not primarily driven by rent-seeking: Mody, Nath and Walton find that, on average, the activities of listed corporations are more typical of competitive behavior than of the exercise of market power, while Sen and Kar ascribe Indian growth until 2002 largely to the performance of competitive sectors in domestic and export markets, which they term "workhorses" and "magicians," respectively.[27] Manufacturing – and particularly the manufacturing industries on which this book focuses: textiles, pharmaceuticals and automotive components – falls squarely within these competitive, and not particularly rent-implicated, portions of the economy. This is for the simple reason that for these firms to be profitable, their products must be competitive in international markets or compete with imports in domestic markets.

In practice, the Indian government can do relatively little to promote these industries, particularly when economic reforms removed many of the state's key instruments for governing industrial factor markets, particularly in capital and labor. Further, state governments are not particularly more successful than the old national regime in providing a deeply favorable context for manufacturing. My argument here is that structural factors have shifted the balance of power, interests and resources away from broad-based industrial promotion and towards much more targeted incentives to particular firms.[28]

---

[26] Many, particularly Krueger (1974), have argued that inclusion in the industrial promotion regime during the statist era constituted a kind of rent, yet it broadly enabled industrial activity for a large range of firms, rather than narrow rents to selected actors.

[27] Mody, Nath and Walton 2011; Sen and Kar 2014.

[28] The Textile Upgradation Fund Scheme (TUFS) is an exception, but because of the rarity of such schemes, one that proves the rule. TUFS is discussed at greater length in Chapter 4.

This is not to say that there are no politicians or bureaucrats with sincere intentions to help Indian manufacturing, or that policies or practices that promote industrial investment are completely absent. There are certain areas in which the Indian state has substantially increased its capacity and plays a coordinating role for firms. Aseema Sinha has recently argued that particular specialist agencies of the Indian state and international institutions have converged to transform India's relationship to international economy from one of marginality to one of deep and active integration into the multilateral trade regime.[29] A focus on these capacities and interests on the part of state actors might suggest more optimism for the state's encouragement of industry.

Nevertheless, I contend that the political compulsions and infrastructural capabilities of state actors at any level draw them away from encompassing industrial promotion through the management of those factor markets that lie at the very heart of industrialization. In other words, much of the state's interests, efforts and energies in economic intervention have turned from a director of industrial governance to a lead actor in the political economy of rents. This shift explains the retreat of the state from its traditional role in providing industrial governance and animates the search for models of industrial governance after statism.

Studying Politics and Political Economy after Statism

What might this book's focus on industrial structures at the level of the firm, including variation in these structures, mean for Indian politics, the state and political economy? I believe it has two potential implications. The first is heuristic, and relates to how the political economy of industrial development is studied. I caution political economists against the pervasive tendency to use "national models" to understand the dynamics of industrial capitalism. This implicitly assumes that the state, or state-implicated national institutions, continues to play a defining role in industrial governance. The ability of state agencies and institutions to induce particular economic outcomes is after all an empirical matter: it should be subjected to research and not just

---

[29] Sinha 2016. I will discuss firm-level dynamics with regard to the international economy in Chapter 6.

maintained as part of the intellectual scaffolding for political economy. In particular, as the structure of national economies and the world economy changes, it is worth thinking how we can update frameworks that were created to understand political and economic dynamics belonging to an earlier era.

The research described here and presented below introduces a more complex industrial landscape in India, one that is populated by a wide array of actors reacting to the changes brought about by liberalization. In the end, I argue that the best viewpoint from which to comprehend industrial production in this context is at the firm level. I would also argue that institutional research at the firm level might serve as a more promising basis for comparative enquiry into the nature of industrial production after liberalization in other developing countries.[30] While this approach contravenes a favored entreaty within social science to "explain a lot with a little," it enables us to be far more open when assessing the sources of industrial development in a post-statist era.

The second implication more explicitly relates to Indian politics. For a decade now, there has been increasing political mobilization over revitalizing the efficacy and autonomy of the state. Bespectacled, charismatic anti-corruption activist Anna Hazare fasted indefinitely and drew tens of thousands to rallies, Arvind Kejriwal's Aam Admi Party has campaigned for and won office in Delhi state on an anti-corruption platform, and Narendra Modi's BJP swept into power at the center at the crest of popular expectations of a new, more functional and efficient politics after a decade of Congress-led coalitions at the center. Some have suggested that the rise in crony capitalism and regulatory dysfunction is a sign that India is entering its own Gilded Age, foreshadowing a crisis of political and economic legitimacy.[31] Others have advocated for a broad-based movement for progressive regulatory and political reform that will enable the country to create sustainable development trajectories and address persistent issues of poverty and inequality. Given the salience of these issues in contemporary politics, is such a progressive reforming and strengthening of the state likely, or even possible?

[30] For an excellent example of firm-level comparative political economy in developing Asia, see Doner 2009.
[31] Habermas 1975; Walton 2015.

This book suggests a fundamental ambivalence among bourgeois Indian society – reflected among the beliefs and behaviors of the manufacturers I interviewed – over the reform of the state, more than two decades after market reforms. The retreat of government actors from industrial governance is at the root of variation in the institutional responses, but this variation in turn is likely to limit the capacities of reformers to achieve consensus over the re-empowerment of the autonomous state.[32] I suggest that this is because the two institutional forms presented here, and the types of backgrounds and experiences that stand behind them, represent two much broader social reactions to the disruptions and uncertainties facing the Indian bourgeoisie after liberalization. The first is the individual and collective strategy of extending the private sphere beyond the household and ever outward through the use of personal ties. Many "public" interactions are indeed actually constituted by and operate through dense clientelistic networks and personal connections, and represent what Kanchan Chandra has argued characterizes India's "patronage democracy" and what Pradeep Chhibber and Irfan Nooruddin have called the "known-to democracy," where success in any endeavor requires being acquainted with those of prominence, including elected officials.[33] For many, the goods of the state, previously dominated by an elite few, need to be more liberally distributed to communities hitherto excluded from political and economic power. While this expansion is arguably consonant with greater justice for the marginalized, it is also fundamentally inconsistent with strengthening the autonomy of the state.

The second is to throw support behind public institutions that approximate ideals of efficiency and autonomy, such as the Supreme Court and the Election Commission, and demand that such autonomous technocratic governance be expanded to ever-increasing spheres of public life.[34] Thus tens of thousands of urban, middle class Indians joined anti-corruption protests and gotten involved in politics, in

---

[32] This relates to an influential argument within social science that a powerful, united, and purposive bourgeoisie is important in allowing substantive institutional change to occur, in areas as far afield as democratization and welfare capitalism. See Rostow 1970; Easterly 2000; Swenson 2002; Mares 2003; Ansell and Samuels 2010; Mizruchi 2013.

[33] Chandra 2004; Chhibber and Nooruddin 2010.

[34] Mehta and Kapur 2007; Mate 2010.

defense of these ideals and in support of institutions like the Jana Lokpal, a committee of (unelected) civil society grandees that could prosecute sitting members of parliament for corruption.[35] This instinct towards political discipline and economic modernization is compatible with the polarization and majoritarian politics behind Modi's victory in the 2014 elections.[36] Ultimately, these two clashing responses to the state's stagnation represent two possible visions for the future of Indian politics and society. And crucially, it represents a stark choice for the future of the state as the primary actor in influencing Indian life and politics.

This book is then also about the bifurcation in the ways that individuals, organizations, and firms think about governance in India, its causes and its consequences. I focus on the variant ways in which manufacturers facing a brave new world after liberalization managed to replace the national-level institutions that provided capital and managed labor with more local industrial structures, and thereby maintained production. The different backgrounds within the contemporary Indian bourgeoisie lead to two very different ways of making and maintaining industrial investment, producing two different flavors of industrial capitalism that crosscut region and industry. Such divisions in background and outlook within the manufacturing community reflect broader divisions among the Indian middle classes in its views of the state, and particularly whether powerful and autonomous state institutions are rules-enforcing ideals of getting things done or foreign and alien entities, hostile to society and the economy. This perspective of the conflicting spirits behind Indian industrial capitalism, in other words, complicates any account of institutional reform that is suggested by more state-centric accounts of industrial development.

The Empirical Approach: Cases, Patterns and Mechanisms

This book deploys two types of evidence in support of its claims. First, it uses quantitative analysis of over 8,000 firms to analyze broad *patterns* of firm strategy and the relative influences of different governance forms on firm behavior in the aggregate. Quantitative analysis can adjudicate between these rival (and complementary) influences with regard to explaining the variation in measures that serve as proxies for

---

[35] Varshney 2011; Bardhan 2011.   [36] Jaffrelot 2015.

the broad strategies and practices of firm. To this end, I employ the manufacturing superset of firms in the Prowess dataset compiled by the Center for the Monitoring of the Indian Economy to assess the influence of region, industry, and firm-level characteristics such as age (a rough proxy for background), size and foreign exchange earnings on the strategic behavior of manufacturing enterprises with regard to acquiring capital and managing labor.[37]

Yet to understand the concrete mechanisms and strategies by which firms across different regions and industries solve the coordination challenges of capital and labor, I turn to over two hundred qualitative in-depth interviews with manufacturers and other industrial actors in four industries across seven states in India. This much smaller sample involves the roughly 160 enterprises I visited during fieldwork in 2007–2008, and whose owners, directors and managers I interviewed. While I took care to maximize variation in a number of relevant indicators – I visited firms in different states, producing in different sectors, with different ages, sizes and levels of international engagement – I cannot describe the sample as random. I use my interview-based evidence to explicate the more specific *mechanisms* of acquiring capital and managing labor; what are the concrete strategies and practices deployed by manufacturers to solve these coordination issues? How did they come to adopt these strategies? What is the character of the relationships they form with workers, financiers and international firms, and are they influenced more by the internal orientation of the firm or the policies, incentives and rules of state governments or sectoral regimes? Thus, the use of dual research methods, separately and pragmatically, allows us some insight into the patterns and mechanisms of industrial governance after statism.

These two universes of cases constitute distinct but overlapping notions of what is an industrial enterprise in India. My interview sample was largely drawn from the directories of industry associations and regional chambers of commerce. This includes firms large enough to require the recognition of the association and thus willing to pay for associational membership; yet associations and chambers contain a

---

[37] Economists and fellow travelers have long used CMIE Prowess data to draw broad conclusions about the nature and prospects of the Indian economy. See Chhibber and Majumdar 1998, 1999; Majumdar and Chhibber 1999; Topalova 2004; Goldberg et al. 2010. But this book is, to my knowledge, the first time that these data have been used to adjudicate institutionalist arguments on Indian development.

large proportion of private firms, and can constitute medium-sized enterprises as well as large firms. Just above a quarter of the firms at which I interviewed (and in which respondents were willing to divulge financial data) had annual sales of less than Rs. 100 million, or $2.5 million in 2008. The Prowess dataset contains many more cases, but is biased towards larger firms due to its reliance on the public availability of annual reports and thus on publically listed firms: private firms comprise only 12 percent of the sample. There is some diversity in size, however; the median annual sales turnover is Rs. 369 million, but twenty percent of cases in the dataset have annual sales of Rs. 100 million or less.

The firms that constitute these two samples form a group that is internally quite diverse, but nonetheless mostly share some internal characteristics. First, they operate factories and not workshops, to follow Mark Holmstrom's distinction.[38] Most of the industrial units I visited were housed in big buildings with capital machinery, security guards, canteens, shift schedules and offices that are a world away from the slum-sheds in urban peripheries which extended families make cheap furniture or mend bicycles, the small state-affiliated handicraft cooperatives, brick kilns that dot the Bihari countryside, the rolling of *bidis* or country cigarettes in village courtyards, or the ubiquitous construction crews that are building up India's large towns into small cities. Much excellent work has appeared recently mapping out these landscapes of deeply informal production and work, but they are not the object of this book.[39]

On the opposite end of the scale, most of these firms are relatively far removed from the megaliths of Indian business; only 28 percent of the Prowess sample is categorized as belonging to a larger industrial group, and many of these groups contain only two or three companies. Indian manufacturing is, at least by numbers, fairly disaggregated, particularly in relation to other developing countries like Korea and Mexico. Further, the big Indian industrial conglomerates – the Tatas, the Birlas, Mahindra and Mahindra, Reliance Industries – have been steadily shifting their activities from their core manufacturing business into other higher-margin or more consumer-facing arenas, including

---

[38] Holmstrom 1984.
[39] Examples include Breman 1996; Harriss-White 2003; Agarwala 2013; Harriss-White et al. 2015; Ostermann 2015.

oil refining, retailing, finance, technology services, retail groceries and real estate. As a result, the firms from two comparable samples under focus for this book represent a particular subsection of what it means to be an industrial entrepreneur in India, between the tycoon and the tinkerer. While this is a necessarily constrained perspective that does not do full justice to the diversity of manufacturing activity in India, the dynamics and variations of firm strategy and their connections to institutional structures that are uncovered by research at the firm level should help us understand the meanings and mechanisms of industrial capitalism in post-liberalization India.

Beyond India: Industrial Governance in Pakistan

India is an important case in the political economy of industrialization, but it is a rather unique one in the universe of developing countries. Exactly how far can an argument about industrial structures after liberalization that was developed through research in India travel beyond India's borders? This is an important question because many countries throughout the developing world have experienced the drawing back of the state in industrial governance through the processes of liberalization. Any extension of the argument based on comparative research should start with cases that have some dimensions of comparability with India, but yet are different enough to constitute added leverage for the argument through external validity.

I thus present a "mirror case" in the changing roles of the state and the nature of industrial governance in Pakistan, as a way of both broadening the argument and testing its propositions in a case that is significantly different on one key dimension: the causes and consequences of state-led industrialization. Pakistan and India are naturally comparative cases; unlike the BRIC countries but in common with many countries in the developing world, Pakistan falls into the same World Bank "lower middle income" category as India by per capita income. Neither country has significant rentier income, and both share administrative and political legacies of British colonialism. But the nature of Pakistani state formation led to a strong, centralized, bureaucratic authoritarian state apparatus, and a state-led industrialization that followed security imperatives rather than ideological interests. Thus the Pakistani state established a strong, even "overdeveloped," state-promoted and -directed industrial development regime in close coordination with a much more narrow and state-implicated bourgeoisie.[40] By contrast, the Indian state during this period has been characterized as "soft," captured by dominant class interests and thus ineffective relative to countries like Pakistan and Korea in managing statist industrialization.[41]

Yet Pakistan also experienced a thoroughgoing series of liberalizing reforms around the same time as India, and thus ended with the same outcomes as India: a state drawn out of governing the factor markets crucial to industrialization. We see the same incapacity of provincial governments or sectoral agencies to take up industrial governance, and patterns of variation in the institutional structures of production that display remarkable similarities to those in India. The 'mirroring' of these dynamics between cases with such different levels of state power during the statist period goes some way to arguing that the trajectory of industrial governance in India is not simply the consequence of state weakness or a product of factors unique to the Indian case.

The Pakistani case also solidifies a preliminary framework for broader comparative study by defining the industrial governance concept as not relevant only for India, but rather key to understanding manufacturing after statism in a broader variety of developing countries. The level of institutional agency among industrial firms may be an outcome unique to South Asia – arguably the product of fragmented markets, corporate governance and investment regimes specific to the region – but the broader question of where industrial governance is located after liberalization is an important and understudied one in the political economy of development. Moreover, research at the level of the firm is more likely to provide insights into the institutional dynamics behind industrial production than at higher levels. This book provides some of the tools important for embarking on this search in other regional contexts.

Chapter Outline

This book is organized thematically. Chapter 2 presents the conceptual framework for the book, and places it within the context of dominant

---

[40] Papanek 1967; Alavi 1972; Jalal 1990; Khan 1999; Naseemullah and Arnold 2015.
[41] Myrdal 1968; Herring 1999; Evans 1995; Chibber 2003; Kohli 2004.

theories and historical narratives of the political economy of development in India. I use the necessary relationships at the firm level borrowed from the "varieties of capitalism" literature in the study of advanced industrial economies to construct a framework for understanding industrial governance. I present alternative arguments for industrial governance extant in the literature, and propose the means by which we can adjudicate such a debate through research design and firm-level analysis.

Chapter 3 surveys the literature on the state in the Indian industrial economy. It then describes the political dynamics behind first the rise and then the fall of statist development in India. Chapters 4 and 5 focus on the key factor markets for industry – capital and labor – in India, and how firms have managed these crucial relationships after the retreat of the state from managing those activities. Chapter 4 focuses on securing finance for industrial investment. It outlines the many ways in which the state guaranteed funding for investments via a variety of industrial development and investment agencies, as well as state-regulated and nationalized banks. Yet since liberalization, industrial firms have had to compete with a variety of other potential investments for scarce finance. The chapter examines the patterns of investment and financing and details how different firms have coped with this challenge, through formal institutions or personal networks. Some firms use a full range of options available in the organized financial sector, from borrowing from government-owned, private and foreign banks to selling debt and equity directly to the public to attracting venture capital and private equity firms in India and abroad. Others forgo debt or equity transactions with organized finance entirely, choosing to finance their development entirely through family or community capital.

Chapter 5 focuses on the recruitment, retention and training of labor. It details how the nationalist state helped management establish and maintain workable, if not completely peaceful, relationships with labor though protective legislation and party-affiliated trade unions such as the Congress-affiliated INTUC. Since the 1980s, wildcat strikes, the decline in the organizational power of trade unions and changes in the industrial landscape have all led to an economy-wide fragmentation of labor; few in the industrial labor force are formally unionized or subject to fully implemented labor regulations. Yet, skilled labor is a scarce and thus valued factor of production in Indian industry. The chapter examines the patterns of worker management across firms in India and details the different strategies and practices firms implement to recruit and retain labor, maintain a skilled workforce and workable labor-capital relations in an environment of pervasive informality. Some firms rely on establishing rules of and departments around human resources, and both hire and retain workers through complex sets of institutional incentives. Other firms, however, deploy labor management through intermediaries such as labor contractors and otherwise recruit and anchor workers through implicit ties of social obligation through family or co-ethnic obligation.

Chapter 6 examines the relationship between firm-level institutional structures and modes of interaction with the international economy. I outline the ways in which firms have been able to fruitfully act within and in relation to foreign markets without necessarily converging on one form of engagement. Some Indian firms have been remarkably successful in integrating themselves into GVC and production networks by emphasizing transactional efficiency and flexibility. Other exporters, however, interact with a wide array of interlocutors in many different emerging and developed country niche markets based on personal connections and specific knowledge of what it means to do business in these diverse contexts.

Chapters 7 and 8 turn from India to its mirror case, Pakistan. Chapter 7 outlines the trajectory of Pakistan's development, in a radically different political context, through its own versions of the rise and fall of statist development. It outlines the ways in which early bureaucratic authoritarian governments, particularly the Ayub Khan regime from the late 1950s to the late 1960s, managed to create an industrial economy and an industrial bourgeoisie out of whole cloth in a largely agrarian society. It then outlines the crises, related politics and international pressures that destroyed the consensus of state-led development.

Chapter 8 outlines how Pakistani industrialists have been able to cope with a deinstitutionalized industrial landscape. It surveys the diverse strategies that manufacturers in Pakistan employ in securing finance and recruiting and retaining workers, including the use of Islamic finance, the reliance on community investment and the gendered employment of workers. The empirical analysis of the Pakistani state suggests a beginning for a framework for a comparative politics of industrialization after statist development, which is continued in the conclusion.

Chapter 9 concludes the book. It reflects on standard operating procedures for the political economy of industrial development, and how our concepts and methods might require reevaluation when looking at relationships at the level of the firm. This is particularly the case if state policy turns out to be a more partial or unreliable guide to understanding outcomes in industrial production. I provide examples of how we might seek to understand industrial governance in other national and regional contexts, in which actors as varied as large conglomerates and political parties can provide the institutional frameworks necessary for investment in manufacturing. I then provide some of the groundwork for applying this research to the future of the Indian state as a cardinal actor in society. I locate the dual modes of firm institutional structure within two opposing reactions of Indian society to the increasing ineffectiveness of the state: to let the state stagnate while focusing on building alternatives through personal networks, or to reinvest in the resources and authority of state institutions. I argue that divergent institutions of representation and contestation in India might lead to differences over the future of the state.

2 | *Theoretical Framework*

This book arises from two intersecting puzzles. First, Indian industry seems to be growing in spite of an ineffectual state. This result might not be surprising to those devoted to the principle of free markets and understanding government as simply a hindrance. However, free market ideology is primarily concerned with distribution and aggregate welfare rather than development, and freer markets and trade should not privilege *manufacturing*, when costs there are high relative to other sectors. Most arguments in the political economy of industrial development, by contrast, suggest that a strong and effective state is necessary to overcome the capital requirements and coordination challenges necessary for industrialization in the developing world. The fact that Indian manufacturing has nearly doubled in the last decade, largely unsupported by their government's rather feeble industrial policies and regulatory frameworks, thus begs for an explanation.

In private sector–dominated economies such as those of India and Pakistan, industrial growth is an aggregate function of the growth in the production of private sector manufacturing enterprises. The second puzzle relates to the mechanisms driving this production: the investment decisions and production strategies of manufacturing firms. What we know about economic institutions suggests that sustained economic activity is (only) possible when the rules of the game are clear, recognized, and followed. A key implication of this is that the strategies of economic actors should exhibit some common characteristics when governed by the same rules and regulations, whether those rules are national, regional, or based on industries or sectors. We should thus see firms within a city or province act upon the institutions set forth by regional governments or municipal associations, or firms within the same industry follow the same sets of incentives put forth by trade associations, sectoral agencies, or multinational buyers. Indeed, the emergence of regional or sectoral political economies to make up for the deficiencies of national governments is a plausible and even widely assumed explanation for the presence of economic growth in weak or declining states.

My field research, however, uncovered unexpected dissonances that challenge these potential explanations. Time and again, I encountered similarly sized firms in the same industries and the same regions and cities that have established and maintained markedly and consistently different practices with regard to the core challenges of industry: acquiring capital and recruiting and retaining workers. That firms facing broadly the same sets of external – national, regional, local, or sectoral – rules would act so differently so often constitutes a challenge for how we understand the institutional foundations of industrial production.

To understand the nature of industrial development, we must reexamine some of the assumptions we have made about what drives the institutional frameworks that enable manufacturing. Regional and sectoral frameworks of industrial governance, just as with statist industrial governance, all assume that firms and those that direct them are *institution-takers*. In other words, regional or sectoral agencies or institutions transmit clear and powerful rules that firms must follow in order to produce effectively; firms are, in these models, simply rules-following profit maximizers, guided by larger institutional structures in their relationships with capital and labor. These frameworks leave little room for agency at the level of the firm and operate under the assumption that national governments or regions or sectors provide all the institutional guidance necessary for solving the coordination problems inherent in industrial production. But if these frameworks do not provide clear guidance and industrial production does occur, what other sources of governance are possible? In the following, I outline my own institutional explanation for industrial production in South Asia, the "governing firms" approach, in which manufacturers themselves are *institution-makers*.

The key contention of this volume is that in India, institutional frameworks supporting production have in fact been reconstituted at the firm level, through the ideas and actions – as well as the structural constraints – of owners and managers in establishing long-term relationships with workers, agents of global markets, and sources of capital. These relationships cluster around two very different structures of industrial production. In the absence of strong, credible, and unitary signals from external institutions such as states or global markets as to how production should be organized, firms must forge their own institutional relationships with other actors in political economy to acquire capital and recruit, train, and retain workers. The resulting clusters cut across region and industry, but are much more coherent if we understand firms as the relevant governance actors.

This chapter frames the puzzles that animate this book, as well as the basis for my explanation, by delving into the institutional underpinnings of industrial production. I begin by discussing the importance of institutions to economic activity and growth. I then contrast these general theoretical assertions with the more specific challenges of industrial production, and the institutional requirements for overcoming these challenges; the latter I call *industrial governance*. I then present the industrial governance frameworks that are thought to support industrial production: first, national, and then, regional and sectoral. I argue that a plausible alternative to these external frameworks is that of firm-level institutional structures animated by the "microconstructivist" perspectives of industrialists. With these structures, the firm creates necessary frameworks through its own relationships with capital and labor, as well as other firms and global markets, without relying on overarching national, regional, and sectoral frameworks with coherent and credible signals to direct firms. Finally, I discuss my research design for adjudicating empirically among these explanations, and how this framework travels to Pakistan and beyond.

The Institutional Foundations of Industrial Development

Institutions are the best intellectual tools we have for understanding how social behavior is patterned and regulated, in the economy as elsewhere. While there is huge debate about the definitions, aims, and scope of the concept, there is a general consensus that institutions, at minimum, reflect "a system of rules, beliefs, norms and organizations that together generate a regularity of (social) behavior."[1] Institutions can be formal and even legal, in which case rules are codified and enforced by explicit threat of sanction. Or they can be informal: broadly social agreements or understandings that carry with them both stable incentives for cooperation and implicit costs for defection. Institutions can also be found in different sizes: some can serve to

---

[1] Greif 2006, 30.

regulate behavior across national populations or even nation-states, while others may serve to impose regularity on a city, a neighborhood, a workplace, or a classroom. The essential elements of any institution – formal or informal, large or small – are that they constitute a shared if sometimes implicit recognition of the rules or norms in question, and that they serve to regulate behavior.

Institutional economics has focused on the part that transaction-based microinstitutions play in economic development. Douglass North has argued that the depth and density of economic interactions that create growth are predicated on the presence of institutions that decrease the costs of transaction among individual actors, which can be prohibitively high when fraud, deceit, and other forms of defection are rampant: for North, institutions "determine ... costs and hence the profitability and feasibility of ... economic activity."[2] North and others in this research program have focused mostly on the formal, legal institutions that secure property rights and enforce contracts; they have regularly looked to the state, and to the overarching constitutional settlements that limit and regulate the state, to provide such institutions.[3]

Other scholars have relaxed the assumptions of the formality and legality of such institutions. In his study of the institutional foundations of the commercial revolution in the late medieval period, Avner Greif has identified informal yet complex institutional arrangements arising among social groups that precede or operate apart from the modern nation-state, such as Maghribi traders or the merchant–oligarchs of Italian city–states, to provide the security and stability necessary to conduct long-distance trade without force-wielding bureaucracies.[4] Elinor Ostrom has argued that collective social norms can substitute for external enforcement of property in the "tragedy of the commons," where individual incentives are misaligned with the social good in maintaining common pool resources, thus maintaining long-run activity.[5] Maurer, Razo, and Haber argued that economic exchange can happen in contexts of political instability, such as in early twentieth-century Mexico, when private actors themselves expend resources to enforce property rights.[6] And Acemoglu and Robinson

---

[2] North 1990, 1991; Williamson 1985.
[3] North and Weingast 1989; Olson 1993.   [4] Greif 2006.   [5] Ostrom 1990.
[6] Maurer, Razo and Haber 2003.

have contended that economic growth is predicated on more inclusive institutions that can more capably defend individual exchange.[7]

Transactions-enabling institutions such as property rights and contract enforcement are insufficient, however, for explaining *industrial* development. Institutional economics has generally focused on trade, commerce, and economic exchange among dyads of comparable economic agents. It has thus focused on the role of institutions in the general logic of capitalism rather than industrialization specifically. Industrial development produces particular challenges, however, and these challenges must be met with very particular sets of institutions for such development to occur.

Firms and the Coordination Challenges of Industrial Investment

To describe the specific set of institutional arrangements behind industrial development, it is helpful to distinguish between commerce and industry. Very simply put, commerce under capitalism occurs when two agents trade goods, services, and/or monetary instruments on the basis of a rate of exchange determined by the market. There are all sorts of institutions that stand behind this exchange: property rights to make sure of the ownership of the goods, services, and money in question; contract enforcement that prevents one of the parties from taking without exchanging; a price mechanism that reduces uncertainty of the worth of one asset against another. Yet economic development through commerce simply constitutes aggregate increases in the number and scope of these dyadic interactions supported by these transaction-enabling institutions.

Industry, however, requires the simultaneous undertaking of many different interactions in close coordination – workers with their supervisors, suppliers of raw materials with purchasers, entrepreneurs with investors, designers and innovators with the production line – all of which need to occur in tandem for production to be successful. The difference in the complexity of the two can be thought of as the difference between a salad and a soufflé: both can provide nourishment, but the former requires only a simple mixing of items and is finished immediately. The latter, meanwhile, requires the complicated

---

[7] Acemoglu and Robinson 2012.

preparation and precise mixture of ingredients and is only ready after being in the oven at a particular temperature for a precise amount of time. Likewise, while both commerce and industry produce economic growth, the latter requires more complex coordination among different agents that must work together in order to function, and achieving returns on the investment requires some time.

Firms have long been recognized as the key organizations in which these actors are coordinated in the service of industrial production.[8] The most cogent conceptual framework for understanding the relationships between firms and outside actors is the varieties of capitalism (VoC) project, led by Peter Hall and David Soskice. Hall and Soskice's theoretical framework defines firms as the drivers of production. Yet in order to produce effectively, they must make and maintain relationships with their own employees, and with a number of outside actors, in order to solve coordination problems relating to individual workers, industrial relations and wage setting, financing and corporate governance, interfirm relations, and training/skills accumulation.[9]

Distilling and abstracting from the firm-level microfoundations of the VoC model, firms ultimately face serious challenges in the coordination of capital (*corporate governance*) and different aspects of labor (*industrial relations, vocational training and education, and employee relations*).[10] The financing of industry, just as with any capitalist investment, concerns the management and distribution of risk. Yet the distinctive challenges of industrial investment involve the time lags inherent in these projects; it is not uncommon to see gaps of several years between initial investment and the establishment of successful production, as capital machinery must be bought and modified, workers are trained, and supplier and purchaser networks are established. Risk must therefore be carried longer. Industrial projects also

[8] Ronald Coase (1937) famously argued that firms arise when the market does not efficiently provide for inputs necessary for production, and thus the establishment of hierarchical relationships – say, between management and labor – is necessary. Yet the existence of the firm does not determine how it actually manages market or hierarchical relationships over the long term.

[9] Hall and Soskice 2001, 6–7.

[10] A fifth sphere of coordination mentioned in VoC, *interfirm relations*, is also crucial to industrial development; firms play input roles for one another as vendors of components or purchasers of manufactured intermediate or wholesale goods. Chapter 6 pays special attention to these dynamics in the context of global value chains and industry networks.

require a much greater concentration of capital; industrial machinery is more expensive than the capital goods required for restaurants, for example. Financial institutions face more limited capacity for asset diversification and risk spreading when lending to manufacturing as each individual loan is on average larger than those to consumers, traders, or service businesses, and thus more investable funds are tied up with fewer individual investments.

For the industrial workforce, the main challenges involve, as the VoC framework explicitly argues, recruitment, training, retention, and management in the face of shop floor defection, principal–agent concerns, and collective action. Workers who acquire skills from either the provision of formal training or learning by doing at the firm level can move to another firm along with those skills for higher wages, either within the same sector or in adjacent industries. Unlike in services or commerce, skilled workers are not readily replaceable, as skills tend to be specific, learned over time, and increasingly technology-intensive. Thus retention – the successful prevention of defection – is important for any industrial firm. Second, given the challenges of acquiring skilled workers, shirking and absenteeism can constitute a problem in workplaces in which the incentives against such behavior are not clear and powerful. The effective productivity of labor entails the creation of a hospitable working environment, the provision of formal or informal incentives for individual workers to exert adequate effort and attention to their work, and implicit sanctions for deliberate shirking or excessive absenteeism. Third, the presence of working relationships with those who represent workers on the shop floor is key to industrial peace, fostering a productive environment and collaborative innovation and problem solving. All of these are challenges of labor management more broadly, but in industrial production, in which many pieces of work must fit together to make a whole, a small decrease in the productivity of the workforce or the absence of a portion of workers at any given time might seriously decrease or preclude production altogether.

A third, more diffuse and recent but increasingly important area of coordination for domestic manufacturing firms is with agents of the international economy. As innovation and production have become increasingly integrated, technology, innovation, and access to markets for intermediate and finished goods have become vital for many industrial enterprises. Thus industrialists must often create durable, institutional relationships with international buyers, brokers, and multinational corporations domestically and abroad in order to be able to import inputs, export products, and collaborate actively to produce goods. This is also the area where interfirm relations take on the greatest salience, along with the greatest challenges to effective coordination across national borders.[11]

Industrial Governance

Taken together, the relationships firms must establish in order to acquire capital patient enough to overcome time lags and concentration and to recruit, train, and retain labor are the necessary elements of the institutional framework that supports industrial production. Capital and labor, after all, have long been considered the most crucial factors of production for manufacturing. Collectively, I call this set of institutionalized relationships *industrial governance*. The presence of industrial governance is functionally necessary for industrial production to occur; its absence necessarily means the absence of effective production.

Yet individual firms do not often arrange the coordination of these factors in a vacuum. Hall and Soskice, in common with a long tradition of "comparative capitalism" research in advanced industrial economies, assume the existence and dominance of historically shaped constellations of national level institutions in industrial political economy.[12] These institutions collectively determine the relationships that firms have with other economic actors, creating economywide varieties of capitalism that maintain national distinctiveness even in the face of institutional and economic change. The Hall and Soskice framework thus explicitly assumes that firms are "institution-takers," and that the relationships they have with labor, capital, and other firms are fully determined by causally prior, higher-order institutions at the national level. This may indeed be a good characterization of the relationship among national institutions, firms, and economic actors in advanced, capitalist countries,

---

[11] Because firms do not have to export to produce, I exclude engagement from the international economy from the core of the industrial governance concept. These interactions will, however, be analyzed in Chapter 6.

[12] Hall and Soskice 2001, 16. See also Schonfield 1965; Hall 1986; Albert 1991; Zysman 1994; Amable 2003; Streeck and Thelen 2005.

but it is limited in its relevance to developing countries with wholly different experiences with industrialization.[13]

The crucial difference between the developed and the developing countries is that for the former, these national institutions were developed roughly at the same time as the process of industrialization itself, in the late eighteenth and nineteenth centuries. For developing countries, however, real efforts toward coherent industrial development only started in the twentieth century. The lateness of industrialization and the underdevelopment of industrial institutions were further compounded in countries under de jure and de facto imperial rule; dependent relationships between current or former colonies and imperial metropoles retarded and distorted industrialization in the periphery.[14] For scholars and policymakers in developing countries alike, the actions of a powerful and autonomous state to structure production and enable investment were considered both necessary and sufficient for postcolonial industrialization.

Statist Industrial Governance

Statist forms of industrial governance – in which state actors intervene to structure the relationships between workers, financiers and manufacturers – represent the developing world's modal response to the more gradual development of national institutions among advanced economies. Statist industrialization has a long tradition in both scholarship and policy making, from Friedrich List in the middle of the nineteenth century onward.[15] Alexander Gerschenkron has famously argued that late industrialization required a much larger concentration of capital to catch up to earlier developers; the only institution ultimately powerful enough to execute this concentration for these countries, in his formulation, was the state.[16] Kiren Chaudhry viewed statist policies as the outcome of a failed attempt on the part of newly

---

[13] There have been successful attempts to apply the core insight of institutional complementarity in the VOC framework beyond the advanced industrial democracies, particularly in terms of Latin America and Eastern Europe; see Lane 2005, Hancké et al. 2007, Nölke and Vliegenthart 2009, Schneider 2009, Carney et al. 2009. Other scholars incorporate the VoC framework of national institutions determining firm outcomes in developing country contexts. See Saez and Chang 2009.

[14] Gunder Frank 1966.   [15] List 1856.   [16] Gerschenkron 1962.

independent countries to construct self-governing, national market institutions like those of earlier developers.[17] Statist industrial governance posits a universe in which the state invests material resources, coercive capacity, and political capital to structure financing and capital–labor relations, as well as relations with the international economy, thus presenting initially hesitant industrial firms with institutional faits accomplis.

Indeed, the strength of state institutions seems to explain successful economic and industrial development. Chalmers Johnson inaugurated "the developmental state" research agenda by arguing that remarkable postwar economic growth in Japan was the result of the policies, strategies, and practices of elite autonomous bureaucrats of the Ministry of International Trade and Industry in guiding the activities of firms, banking institutions, and organized labor.[18] A powerful state can create macrolevel relationships, as between local capital and multinational corporations, and "manage" labor contention in the service of the industrial production of capital and consumer durable goods.[19] The most important cases of state-led development, Korea and Taiwan, were East Asian countries that entered the postwar period at the very periphery of the world economy and became fully industrialized economies just four decades later. Many commentators have argued that such extraordinary development would not have been possible without a strong and autonomous state apparatus capable of disciplining the bourgeoisie, guiding firms' investment decisions toward higher value-added activities, extracting capital for industry, and maintaining industrial peace.[20] The experience of the East Asian "tiger"economies thus serves as an exemplar of the intervention of the state in the promotion of industrialization. Further, developmental state explanations of East Asian growth usefully highlight the ways in which state power and authority can determine firm-level institutional arrangements. The East Asian economies, like many in the non-Communist developing world including South Asia, maintained a significant role for the private sector in industrial production. Thus the power of the state was not deployed to produce directly, but rather to create institutions that enabled production by solving coordination problems for firms. This creation and maintenance of state-led

---

[17] Chaudhry 1993.   [18] Johnson 1982.   [19] Evans 1979.
[20] Amsden 1989; Haggard 1990; Woo-Cumings 1991.

institutions that structure the relations of production at the firm level is what I call *statist industrial governance*.

Arguably the clearest articulation of the relationship among the state, institutions, and industrialization is presented in Robert Wade's influential text on East Asian industrialization, *Governing the Market*.[21] Wade's analysis just predates the institutional turn in comparative political economy and is thus aimed at debunking free market explanations of East Asian successes. Yet his "governed market" (GM) theory emphasizes the ways that the state "controled the financial system, making financial capital subordinate to industrial capital, maintaining stability in some of the main economic parameters that affect the viability of long-term capital . . ., modulating the impact of foreign competition in the domestic economy . . . and assisting particular industries."[22] In addition, the state intervened in educational and specifically vocational training systems in order to ensure the supply of skilled workers, while largely excluding organized labor from interest group representation.[23] Thus, according to Wade's GM framework, industrial firms – private conglomerates in Korea, a mixture of state-owned and private small-scale enterprises in Taiwan – were recipients of predetermined state-created and -enforced institutions that guaranteed access to patient capital and produced a productive and nonrestive workforce, as well as moderated domestic firms' threats from foreign competition and facilitated more productive relations with MNCs. In this context, the individual manufacturer was able to invest and augment her production because industrial governance arrangements at the national level have structured the relationships necessary for production at the firm level.

The East Asian tiger economies are clearly special, even exceptional, cases. Few if any industrializing countries were able to become so resoundingly successful in industrial development. Most "newly

---

[21] Wade 1990.

[22] Wade 1990, 27–28. Along with most experts on East Asian industrialization, Wade emphasized the importance of export promotion as a distinct state-led strategy that contributed to Taiwanese and Korean successes. I will discuss export orientation as it applies to South Asia in greater detail in Chapter 6, but for the purposes of the current discussion, I contend that import substitution and export orientation are policy subtypes within an overall statist industrial governance regime *at the firm level*, even though the (very) few states that followed export orientation were more successful.

[23] Wade 1990, 190–191, 327–328.

industrializing economies" (NICs) in the 1960s and 1970s fell victim to the debt crises of the early 1980s; most other developing countries were not even considered contenders for NIC status.[24] Yet I argue that from the point of the view of the institutional arrangements that structured industrial production, most developing countries established statist industrial governance regimes, albeit less effectively than the exemplar cases of Korea and Taiwan. In India from independence to the 1980s, state agencies collectively enforced industrial investment priorities, maintained labor quiescence through either state-driven corporatism or the state-enforced fragmentation of labor representation, and deployed trade policy regimes that protected domestic firms while managing the transfer of technology. As a result, Indian industrial enterprises recognized and licensed by the state faced institutionally predetermined relationships with labor, capital, and the international economy. Such arrangements characterized many other economies embarking on state-led industrialization, from Brazil and Argentina to Turkey and Pakistan.[25]

Yet the era of statism in industrial governance has now passed. Functioning statist industrial governance regimes are just as rare in the twenty-first century as they were ubiquitous in the immediate post-war decades. Even the Korean and Taiwanese industrial economies are not characterized by such intense and sustained intervention in industry by the agencies of the central government; these states have since democratization in the late 1980s increasingly concentrated their energies on welfare provision for the electorate.[26] The decline of statist industrial governance arrangements, broadly in the 1980s, has many intersecting causes, in South Asia as in other regions. First, global recession and inflationary shocks put intense pressure on the balance sheets of national governments from international creditors. Second, democratization and the rise of more inclusionary interest group politics challenged the preferential allocation of policies to industrial promotion. And, third, the neoliberal revolution of ideas challenged Keynesian and development planning paradigms; its influence among economic policy makers would lead to policies that would roll back the size and reach of the state. Together, these factors produced programs

---

[24] For more on the nature and effects of debt crises on NIC countries, see Aggarwal 1987; Felix 1990.
[25] Hirschman 1968; Naseemullah and Arnold 2015.   [26] Wong 1994.

of "market reform" or liberalization in many countries over the 1980s and early 1990s, from the liberalization policies in India and Pakistan to Turkey's new economic policies under Turgut Ozal to the reforms of Fernando Cardoso in Brazil.

In some countries, the decline in statist industrial governance due to neoliberal economic reform has simply meant deindustrialization: in Argentina, for instance, manufacturing value-added as a percentage of GDP declined from 41.2 percent in 1965 to 19.5 percent in 1993 and 19.7 percent in 2012.[27] For countries in which manufacturing is still significantly growing, however, we return to the first puzzle that motivated this chapter and the book as a whole: how can manufacturing develop without a strong state? The literature on the political economy of industrial development, focused as it is on comparing across country cases in the postwar period, has generally not analyzed changes over time, and particularly the nature of industrial development before and after economic liberalization. To understand the nature of industrial development after liberalization and the decline of statism, therefore, we must search for sources of industrial governance apart from the national state that might provide an institutional basis for industrial production, in South Asia as elsewhere.[28] The first, and most widely accepted, candidate for industrial governance after statism is regionalism.

Regional Industrial Governance

Looking to subnational units for understanding political and social outcomes has natural appeal for comparative political economy in the developing world, for two reasons. First, a combination of liberalization and democratic assertion has empowered subnational governments at the expense of national states; the decentralization of resources and authority to regions and cities (and below) has often been included as part of the same broad policy transformation as neoliberal reform.[29] Second, explaining variation in outcomes among subnational units has become a popular research pursuit for scholars

---

[27] World Development Indicators, World Bank. Databank.worldbank.edu, accessed January 14, 2014.

[28] This follows a strain of thinking in the VoC literature that has recognized "varieties of capitalism" at regional or sectoral levels. See Crouch et al. 2009.

[29] Rondinelli et al. 1983; Litvack et al. 1998; Eaton 2001.

of large states with federated polities such as India, Indonesia, South Africa, Nigeria, Mexico, and Brazil.[30] This strategy arises from the fact that much of the variation in which we are interested occurs within states rather than between them, and because studying subnational units increases degrees of freedom and thus analytical leverage. Indeed, many recent books and book projects on Indian politics and political economy have explicitly compared political and socioeconomic outcomes across Indian states using state-level explanatory factors.[31]

Regional analysis is also an important, if underemphasized, tradition that challenged the domination of national-level institutions in comparative political economy. Michael Piore and Charles Sabel argued that the crisis of Fordist mass production in the 1980s facilitated the rise of an alternative "flexible specialization" model rooted in specific regions in some advanced industrial economies.[32] Sabel went on to link these flexible specialization arrangements, relying on clusters of closely coordinated small firms, to strong regional institutions in areas such as Baden-Wurttemberg in Germany and Emilia-Romana in Italy.[33] Sabel and Zeitlin and Gary Herrigel, analyzing the history of industrialization in Europe, have recovered a tradition of craft production as a coherent and plausible alternative to mass production or as a complementary set of provincial production structures without which industrialization in countries such as Germany would not be possible.[34]

To outline a regional alternative to industrial governance arrangements as it relates to manufacturing firms clearly, I turn to an unlikely source. Richard Locke's *Remaking the Italian Economy* argued that Italian industrial growth arises from diverse regional sources and the institutional frameworks around small firms and industrial districts rather than national economic and industrial policy.[35] Italy may be limited in its applicability to the political economy of developing counties more generally, but the strength of regional institutions coupled with a fragmented and ineffective national government in the Italian case can be abstracted in order to provide a firm-relevant model for industrial production that relies on regional institutions.

---

[30] Snyder 2001.
[31] Murali 2010; Kohli 2011; Bussell 2012; Mangla 2013; Agarwala 2013; Singh 2016.
[32] Piore and Sabel 1982.   [33] Sabel 1989.
[34] Sabel and Zeitlin 1985; Herrigel 1996.   [35] Locke 1995.

Locke's model assumed that sets of subnational institutional configurations structure the relationships between firms and other economic
actors. For Locke, cases of industrial success and failure are

situated in different localities characterized by alternative patterns of associationalism, intergroup relations, political representation and economic
governance. In other words, the divergent patterns manifested in the Italian
economy are the product of the very different sociopolitical networks within
which firms and unions are embedded.[36]

He argued that the late and uneven nature of state formation and
economic integration in Italy has precluded the development of
national institutions seen in other European countries and created a
more composite pattern of regional economies, which entail different
forms of intergroup relations, the density and content of associationalism, and links to central policy makers.[37] Following the intention of
the book in identifying the sources of Italian economic dynamism in
industrial districts using "polycentric" networks of relationships, he
argued that

local firms and unions are more likely to remain open and responsive
organizations when they are tied to other like-minded entities through multiple, horizontal ties. Economic actors embedded in these dense but relatively
egalitarian networks will more easily be able to share information, form
alliances, build trust and resolve conflicts through negotiation with other
forms than will other firms and unions situated in more fragmented or
hierarchical networks. As a result, different sociopolitical networks will
shape the understandings, the resources and thus the strategic choices of
local economic actors in very different ways.[38]

Thus economic activity in Italy is not determined by the national state
or by national institutions but rather by much more local or regional
political economies; the relationships among the firm and other economic actors are determined by regional or local rather than national
economic governance frameworks.

Elegant as Locke's theoretical framework is, his emphasis on associationalism and intergroup relationships occluded the role of subnational
state institutions, necessary for a full accounting of the power of regional
governance on economic outcomes. Aseema Sinha, in her award-
winning monograph, posited that "sub-national developmental states"

[36] Locke 1995, 21.   [37] Locke 1995, 22–24.   [38] Locke 1995, 25.

may lie behind industrial successes in federal democracies such as India.[39] Sinha argued that center-state relationships and the political incentives of regional elites either to engage or to resist national political configurations determine whether political actors in subnational states work together with private sector actors to manage the central state's regulatory regimes, fashion institutional incentives, and facilitate the direct provision of services to encourage investment.[40] Abstracting from the specifics of an argument grounded in the federal democratic politics of India, we see provincial politicians and administrators variably expend resources and political capital to establish institutions in order to structure the relationships among firms and economic actors such as labor and capital. Taken together, Locke's and Sinha's frameworks form a model of industrial governance that deploys itself not economywide by central states or evolved national institutions but in particular regions, subnational units, and localities by either associational traditions or subnational state actors.

Regional industrial governance is certainly a plausible explanation for the persistence of industrial production in instances when the central state is ineffectual, for a couple of reasons. First, it accounts for the fact that growth is rarely even across the territory of developing countries: India, in particular, is characterized by intense regional inequality between rich states in the South and West and poorer states in the North and East. It is also plausible that regional and local bureaucrats (not to mention associational entrepreneurs) are better at supporting industry in the former, as a result of the relative proximity of state capitals to regional business hubs. Indeed, the economic growth of Indian states such as Gujarat represents popular explanations for regional economic development in the face of national mismanagement; the BJP's 2014 election rhetoric involved extending Narendra Modi's "miracle" in Gujarat to other parts of the country.[41]

Yet there are several reasons for overall skepticism as well. Importantly, political conflicts over resources, policies, and authority that are present at the national level are likely to be replicated in states and

---

[39] Sinha 2005.   [40] Sinha 2005, 14–18.

[41] There are many reasons to be skeptical about Gujarat's success story and the role of the BJP state government in driving it. Crucially, Gujarat has since before independence been an urbanized and economically vibrant region, casting doubt on the importance of recent state governments' interventions. See Sachs et al. 2002; Jaffrelot 2014.

provinces. Exactly those political forces most interested in channeling political resources away from the promotion of industry, such as rich farmers, are often the most politically powerful in regions and localities. Second, increasingly interregional markets for capital and labor might also circumscribe the capacities of state governments to promote industry; it is not uncommon in India for an industrial enterprise to maintain units in Delhi, Punjab, and Himachal Pradesh, or for workers from Bihar and Orissa to migrate to manufacturing jobs in Mumbai, Surat, and Ahmedabad.

Third, the power of associationalism as an organizing principle for regional industrial production is questionable, at least with regard to South Asia. The potential strength of associational life and the influence of associations on directing certain political and economic outcomes have been well documented in the region.[42] And yet there is a weakness to formal associations in India, both more generally and with regard to economic organization and collective action.[43] This seeming contradiction becomes more clearly explicable when scale is introduced; South Asian society is composed of deep and intense links among a close circle of family and associates and an equally deep mistrust and suspicion outside that circle. Industry, unlike some other economic activities, requires relationships with those that are normally far beyond regular circles of association, across cities and states. The relationship between peer firms, in particular, is often characterized by suspicion if not downright hostility. Such affective negativity is unlikely to translate into the cooperative sharing of information and diffusion of innovation between separate organizations that characterize Locke's industrial districts under flexible specialization.

Finally, the politics of the states and regions in India that exhibit the most sustained industrial investment and growth differ from one another quite significantly. To many, Gujarat represents an idealized autonomous, powerful state apparatus with economic growth "propelled by a close working alliance between the region's political and economic elite," with characteristics of developmental state institutions at the regional level.[44] But Maharashtra, Andhra Pradesh, and especially Tamil Nadu have protoypically populist politics, with parties at the state level competing with one another for the distribution of

---

[42] Rudolph and Rudolph 1967; Varshney 2002.
[43] Kochanek 1974; Chhibber 1999.   [44] Kohli 2011, 179; Sinha 2005, 92–98.

clientelistic goods and services to key electoral communities, bureaucrats deeply constrained by the political compulsions of politicians, and strained relationships between governments and business. And yet they are states with manufacturing growth rates that rival Gujarat's. The subnational developmental state framework of Sinha and Kohli, in short, explains what distinguishes rich states from poor states much more successfully than it defines an internal political structure common to states that enjoy industrial success.

Ultimately, the presence and influence of regional actors and associations in providing industrial governance are an empirical matter, to be adjudicated alongside other candidates for the sources of industrial governance. The next section provides an alternative framework, based not on geography but on product category.

Sectoral Industrial Governance

A second plausible alternative to statist industrial governance is institutional frameworks based on industries or sectors. Less prominent in comparative political economy, cross-sectoral analysis is an important tool of explanation for international political economy and industrial economics, where industries cross national boundaries, international norms impact global production and trade, and changing trends in the international economy differentially impact domestic industry.[45] Industries differ by unit size, concentration, capital and technology intensity, and forward and backward linkages with other domestic and international firms. This provides a rich array of variation, from which to draw out inferences on the nature of production by sector. The variation in the organization of production may be driven by sector-specific institutional frameworks, and thus can provide a sectoral industrial governance framework with which to explain development after statism among strong and well-institutionalized sectors within which firms can produce.

Sectoral industrial governance works under the principle that firms in the same industry face the same institutional rules, and thus convergence in practices within industries and differences between them. There are three potential sources for sectoral industrial governance. First and most cogently, the integration of global manufacturing, as

[45] Gilpin 1975; Kurth 1979; Aggarwal 1985; Keohane and Milner 1996.

well as the disaggregation of production, has meant that there are global as well as domestic sources of sectoral governance. The literature has developed from simple models of the ways that comparative advantage under globalization might determine industrial survival and protectionist response to more complicated insights on the ways that multinational buyers and end producers might determine the ways that subcontracted firms establish practices and strategies through GVC.[46] The mechanisms of GVC governance can be as abstract as certifications or regulations, but are most often in industries driven by oligopsonistic retailers or end-stage manufacturers that actively structure the relationships with client manufacturing firms, in some cases even participating in equity joint ventures (JVs) with local firms.

The second is that of industry-specific central government agencies: the Ministry of Textiles and Offices of the Textile Commissioner, the Ministry of Heavy Industry, the Ministry of Health, as well as industry-specific regulatory and promotional agencies within broader ministries such as Commerce and Industry. The argument for sectoral industrial governance based on government agencies would follow the same broad lines of regional governance: some sectoral agencies, for either explicitly political or more broadly organizational reasons, may be more effective at creating and enforcing the rules that enable firms' coordination challenges than others, creating sectoral variation in growth.[47]

A third source of sectoral governance is associationalism: the capacity of industry-specific manufacturing associations, such as the Automotive Components Manufacturers' Association or the Indian Drug Manufacturers' Association, to create rules or norms to solve coordination challenges for member firms. Such employers' associations have far greater loyalty, self-identification, and active participation than either regional or municipal chambers of commerce or federated peak associations such as the Confederation of Indian Industry (CII) or the Federation of Indian Chambers of Commerce and Industry (FICCI). There are good reasons for this; firms within the same industry are more likely to be faced with common core challenges – from the shortage of particular raw materials to specific regulatory changes – than businesses in the same geographic region. These three sources of sectoral power arise out of different politics, yet they together portray institutional

---

[46] Frieden and Rogowski 1996; Gereffi et al. 2005. [47] Pingle 1999.

regimes of industrial production after statism being organized along sectoral rather than geographic lines. Together, these three factors constitute sectoral regimes of industrial governance.

I have argued previously that interconnected institutional frameworks are necessary for industrial production, either in statist, regional, or sectoral firms, or at the firm level. If we relax this assumption and assume that market competition by itself provides the institutions, incentives, and resources necessary for investment, we still need to account for the differences in the way that production is organized. In institutional analysis, such variation can serve as a bellwether for the rules that shape the organization of production. In what follows, I will present the foundations for my own argument regarding industrial governance at the level of the firm.

Governing Firms

I argue that to understand the institutional structures behind contemporary industrial production, it is profitable to situate our analysis at the level of the firm. For political economists, the firm level is a rather uncomfortable location; we are much more accustomed to studying explicitly political, bureaucratic, and social actors, from government officials to civil society activists. Firm-level analysis is usually the domain of management studies.[48] Yet, this book departs fairly radically from the focus in management studies on the aggregate indicators of firm performance or the case-study analysis of particular well-known firms. Rather, I frame the firm as a site of institutional dynamics and its directors as social agents driving these dynamics. I argue that firm-level production structures are alternative institutions capable of enabling industrialization when the other forms of industrial governance are unable to provide the clear and credible signals necessary for directing firms. But to understand where these structures originate, we must explore how manufacturers might play a dynamic role normally reserved for the state. But, first, we need to address the deep structuralism that normally attends the political economy of development.

---

[48] The management literature on firm strategy and practice in South Asia is vast. For a sample, see Gaur and Kumar 2009; Ramamurti 2009; Govindarajan and Ramamurti 2011; K. Ramaswamy 2012; Narain et al. 2013.

Agency at the Firm Level

Political science, sociology, as well as some variants of economics, have long struggled with the relative questions of structure and agency in institutional analysis and in explaining sociopolitical and economic outcomes. Scholars have traditionally emphasized the former to the exclusion of the latter. More recently, the role of ideas and identities has emerged as a means of understanding the origins of institutions and the drivers of institutional change.[49] Welcome as this ideational turn is in broadening the scope and content of institutions, it has largely remained limited to the ideas and actions of politicians and their followings in explaining the content and scope of institutions. Such elite explanations are more consistent with statist, regional, or sectoral models of industrial governance, where firms follow the rules set by lawmakers and bureaucrats. They are less relevant to contexts where these signals from above are weak and inconsistent, and those actors arranging production on the ground must make and maintain an internally coherent and consistent institutional framework without recourse to such signals. I argue that this coherence and consistency – what the VOC calls "institutional complementarities" – is a product of more quotidian ideas and perspectives that, I argue, drive the Indian political economy after liberalization.

There are traditions in institutional analysis and political economy that locate institutional legitimacy in ideas and cultural norms. "Sociological institutionalism" has been focused on the shared *social* understandings that drive regulated behavior in socioeconomic settings. Organizational sociologists sought to understand the common cognitive maps and cultural practices that provided coherence and functionality to the organizations of advanced capitalism beyond simple means–ends rationality and profit maximization.[50] Such a focus on legitimated cultural practice echoes the importance of ideas and their relationship to collective action in Weber's famous study of the religious beliefs behind the development of early industrial capitalism.[51] In particular, the notion of legitimacy – what Campbell calls "a logic of social appropriateness" – is a central principle for understanding

---

[49] Blyth 2002; Berman 2006; Abdelal et al. 2006; Hanson 2010.
[50] For an overview, see March and Olson 1984; DiMaggio and Powell 1991.
[51] Weber 2002 [1905].

the normative basis of institutions.[52] This research tradition was developed to explain the similarities among big, slow-moving organizations that are seen to dominate capitalism in advanced, industrialized countries, however. As such, the emphasis has been explaining the remarkable convergence of capitalist practices across firms and countries, rather than explaining fine-grained differences within national cases.[53]

To address this tendency to explain similarity across cases rather than differences within them, I turn to another research tradition in political science and especially international relations: that of constructivism.[54] The constructivist research tradition is committed to the role of ideas as "shared inter-subjective understandings" in constructing interests and identities and thus explaining the basis for outcomes. A constructivist understanding of institutions would thus seek to identify the specific ideational sources – rather than broad cultures of rationality – behind the norms and rules that might inform differences in social behavior.

Constructivism has been quite influential in explaining outcomes in political economy. Yoshiko Herrera explicitly invoked the constructivist tradition in her research on whether regional elites in subnational units across the Russian Federation sought greater fiscal autonomy vis-a-vis the central state, explaining their political actions as a function of their subjective perceptions of regional economic conditions.[55] Keith Darden, studying the variable participation of post-Soviet states in regional and international economic institutions, arrives at a similar intellectual framework, in which where different countries of the former Soviet Union pursued integration or autarky not based on realist structures or neoliberal self-interest but rather on four different ways that nationalist leaders understood the economy: organicist, liberal, extractionist, or mercantilist.[56] Constructivist political economy can thus delineate a causal chain between the ideational or cognitive frames of political leaders to economic policies and institutions; such linkages are especially useful in developing country contexts.

---

[52] Campbell 1998.
[53] For more on isomorphism across cases, see DiMaggio and Powell 1983; Fligstein 2001.
[54] For a broad overview on constructivism, see Adler 1997; Finnemore and Sikkink 2001.
[55] Hererra 2005.   [56] Darden 2009.

The frameworks proposed by Herrera and Darden focus on the construction of identities and interests among *political* elites; they still implicitly assume that economic actors are guided by the incentives and constraints set forth in an "institution-taking" manner. In the "governing firms" framework, I contend that the ideas and interests of manufacturers are just as constructed. Further, their ideas and interests lead substantively to the formation of institutionalized relationships at the firm level, at least in the absence of powerful external institutions that can drive the formation of these relationships. To distinguish my approach from the ones mentioned previously, I term this *microconstructivism*, as it applies to the transactional building blocks of the industrial economy rather than higher-order formation of national economic policies or even regional or sectoral governance. This focus on everyday "cognitive frameworks" is central to understanding the ways that manufacturers might go about structuring the institutionalized relationships that constitute industrial production.

Microconstructivism and Firm-Level Institutional Structures

Industrialists – those who own, direct, and manage industrial manufacturing – are the actors that must in the end create and maintain the firms' relationships with capital, with labor, and with the international economy in order to succeed in production.[57] The establishment of such relationships becomes a straightforward matter if statist, regional, or sectoral industrial governance arrangements dictate the form of these relationships: whether firms were locked into corporate governance regulated by explicit fiduciary responsibilities to shareholders or relationships with labor were completely determined by peak-level tripartite bargaining and rigorous labor laws. The formation of these relationships becomes a different matter entirely if external institutional frameworks are weak or absent. In this context, industrialists must form these relationships without reference to an established script

---

[57] In some contexts, corporate governance through either shareholders or stakeholders drives isomorphism across firms, facilitated by the employment of technocratic and professional corporate executives from a common pool of managerial talent. In South Asia, however, the interests and strategies of "firm promoters" have a disproportionate, even autocratic, role in the management of the firm. For more on the conformity and coherence in corporate governance in the industrial economies, see Teece et al. 1994; Vitols 2001.

handed down from above. In order to do this, I argue, they must rely on their own perspectives, instincts, and values.

The sources of such internal perspectives are varied and complex: they are the products of complicated interactions among background, experience, inspiration, prejudice, and circumstance. And yet, the inductive study of the ways in which firms in India organize their production, arising from more than 160 interviews with manufacturers, suggests clustering around two distinctive visions of the nature of industrial production. These two broad perspectives lead industrialists to form and maintain relationships with capital and labor in distinctively different ways. These perspectives do not correlate with particular regions or industries.

Understanding how to structure industrial production through these internal compasses has two key advantages. First, it provides industrialists with a coherent but flexible heuristic when faced with the many disparate challenges, from demand and supply shocks to labor agitations to fluctuations in operating costs. Second, it provides firms with shortcuts in forming relationships with those with similar perspectives, thus establishing sorting mechanisms that reinforce the coherence of institutional frameworks at the firm level: in other words, enabling trust and collaboration through elective affinities with actors with similar perspectives.

Cognitive Globalization: Production through Formal Rules

The first such cluster of perspectives arises from the ideational or cognitive impact of globalization, as distinct from the material fact of increases in the flows of goods and services across borders. Cognitive globalization affirms the presence of a common ever-expanding set of "best practices" that can serve as a model for solving coordination difficulties. This is an extension of the (contested) principle that the laws of capitalism – just like those of Newtonian physics – are universal. Yet the ideas and perspectives that are held in practice by manufacturers arise from the spread of managerial science and business administration, the common practice of formulating strategies by seeking to emulate the successes of exemplar enterprises both in the same countries and across the world. Culturally, the cognitive globalization perspective puts emphasis on technocratic commitments, and on speaking a common language of business and industry, even for manufacturers with little or nothing to do with the business of imports and exports.

Those industrialists who are informed and inspired by cognitive globalization perspectives are more likely to solve the coordination challenges through establishing and maintaining formal and explicit relationships with other actors, thus creating a formal industrial governance framework supporting industrial production for the firm. The institutional applications of formal rules-based governance with regard to labor can include explicit "human resources" guidelines and incentives, formal training programs, personnel departments, and, in some cases, active engagement with formal labor representation. In industrial financing, such manufacturers tend toward contractual relationships with formal institutions such as banks and formal mediation of investment from the public through debt and equity exchanges, even while seeking to use market institutions to arbitrage between competing financial institutions. Relationships with the international economy often involve integration into structured GVCs, as well as tactics of acquisition and coownership to anchor relationships with multinationals.

Moral Economy: Production through Personal Networks

Moral economy perspectives, by contrast, share a commitment to the local, the particular, and the organic embedded in the notion of economic exchange. The moral economy is normally understood as referring to precapitalist social arrangements that were challenged by the market and its attendant processes of commodification; it is thus often considered a relic of a dead economic order, or at least one under threat in the rural peripheries and hinterlands of developing countries.[58] Here, I am arguing that even though the moral economy does not characterize entire economies, it can still persist at the level of individual motivations and relationships. For those who see their economic lives as inseparable from a larger normative order, trust built up over time among particular individuals is crucial for economic interactions, while rejecting a more generalized faith in the rationality of institutions. Thus, normative

---

[58] The "moral economy" is understood as a set of economic relationships governed by moral principles or social values rather than the market. For more on the concept, see Booth 1994; Scott 1977; Thompson 1971; Polanyi 2001 [1944].

commitments can lead to an avoidance of interacting with formal, alien institutions and an attraction to informal institutional frameworks made up of organic personal networks.[59]

Those more oriented toward a moral economy conception of the meaning of economic production are more likely to solve coordination failures with reference to personal networks and particular relationships with economic actors built up over time, thus creating an informal governance framework at the firm level. Industrialists with this orientation tend to acquire capital through reinvestment or investment from a family or a small community intimately connected to the firm's operations. In labor relations, manufacturers rely on affective relationships and familial idioms with workers, either directly or through intermediaries that maintain kinship ties to small groups of workers. And interactions with global markets often involve relationships built over time with smaller actors and in less regulated markets in the developing world, where personal networks rather than contractual obligations guarantee commitment.

Identification and Measurement

These perspectives and their relationships to institutional strategies arose through long conversations with respondents on the nature of production and industrial strategy. Yet there are certain key identifiers that have proved useful explanatory characteristics independent of the firm's strategies. These include the education, family background, and work experiences of manufacturers, and ultimately the age of the firm.

The first, and most clear, indicator was of educational background. There are several reasons for its primacy. First, it is a fairly objective indicator and one that respondents most often mentioned – which degrees they received and from which institutions – in interviews. Education is a highly valued asset in South Asian society, making schooling important for socialization and educational choice an

---

[59] This view of informal practices as a viable and discrete choice among a larger repertoire that includes formal practices stands in stark contrast to the dominant view of the role of informal institutions either as complementary to functioning formal institutions or as a functional substitute for their absence. I argue that such choice stems from the notion that there is no agreement over which institutions are the "correct" ones. See Helmke and Levitsky 2004.

important indicator of individual and family priorities. Second and relatedly, education and professional training are often cited as a core determination of different outlooks, practices, and professional strategies.[60] Third, there is wide variety in educational experiences among manufacturers in my interview sample, so my explanatory variable is not particularly truncated.

In India, the educational backgrounds of industrial capitalists demonstrated a stark dichotomy. Manufacturers with moral economy perspectives were educated in mainstream local universities and polytechnics. Most received diploma or undergraduate degrees, often in commerce or substantive fields such as pharmacy or engineering. A few did not attend a university. By contrast, manufacturers with cognitive globalization perspectives tended to be educated in universities abroad, mostly in the United States or Europe, or in elite technical institutions in India, such as the autonomous University Department of Chemical Technology (UDCT) in Mumbai or the Indian Institutes of Technology (IITs) or of Management (IIMs). The two types of educational backgrounds relate to two different types of socialization and the establishment of different social networks through which capital and connections are generated. Educational background was thus a crucial first indicator for categorizing perspectives.

Work experience was another important indicator. Most first-generation entrepreneurs in my sample pursued careers before they invested in their own enterprise. Such work experience is important, and follows the same lines as education. Thus, significant work experience abroad or with multinational corporations in India tends to shape cognitive globalization perspectives even in the absence of foreign education, whereas experience in trading in domestic markets or as a supervisor in domestic firms lends an experience of relationality that characterizes moral economy perspectives. In general, educational background and work experience tend to correlate with one another, as someone with a foreign or elite domestic education is likely to work in more technocratic spaces, but work experience can serve to provide cognitive globalization perspectives to those who would otherwise be categorized differentially.

In India, the age – or age cohort – of a firm can provide an alternative indicator that constitutes a rough proxy for the perspectives of

---

[60] See, for example, Fourcade 2009.

industrialists. For older firms, established before independence or during the period of Nehruvian high statism, investment in manufacturing entailed deep engagement with the formal institutions of the state: the industrial licensing regime, development finance institutions, tripartite bargaining with workers. This trend toward formalism is rather sticky, and later generations, while modernizing enterprises on the basis of a new technocratic outlook, would tend to replace older institutions with newer ones while maintaining a commitment to formalism. In newer firms, however, industrial investment has usually occurred when traders, farmers, or foremen amassed capital throughout the post-Nehru decades and, as such, generally with a more organic understanding of finance and labor management. In addition, firms established after 1991 wholly developed in a context of state withdrawal, and thus without the expectation of the formal institutions of the state organizing production. In other words, firms established in distinct eras of India's political economy are likely to be shaped by that context, in a manner broadly consistent with manufacturers' educations and experiences. This indicator is particularly useful when the biographical details of a manufacturer are unavailable, as with quantitative analysis on the Prowess/CMIE data.

It is important to recognize aspects of a respondent that I did *not* consider when coding for perspectives. In general, I have avoided ascriptive characteristics such as caste or religion, because these have at best a second-order effect in the way that industrialists think of the economy and establish characteristics. Moreover, members of commercially active ethnic and religious communities – Gujarati Jains, Marwaris, Sikhs, Naidus, Chettiars – exhibit a wide internal variation in background and perspective that does not make these characteristics particularly useful indicators for the way they understand their work. The size and dispersion of these communities are unlikely to constitute coethnic networks of trust and governance in contemporary industrial investment.

And by no means do I want to argue for a deterministic relationship between the perspectives of industrialists – exhibited either in education or experience or the age of the firm – and the way the firm is governed. What I have outlined here is a tendency of clustering to two different ways of understanding the economy and then an affinity between these perspectives and two broad categories of firm-level institutional structures. There are certainly hybrid cases, in which strategies of capital and labor stand in contradiction. Yet "governing firms" represents an internally consistent and empirically testable model, the explanatory power of which must be adjudicated in relation to the other industrial governance possibilities I have outlined.

The Structural Characteristics at the Firm Level

Realistically, institutional outcomes are always the result of a combination of the volition of actors and structural factors that shape their preferences and outlook. There are characteristics of a firm that, at least in the short term, constrain the firm's choices with regard to institutions. Some of these constraining structures, however, reflect or amplify the perspectives of manufacturers, and thus could be considered complementary and constituent elements in a broader notion of firm-level industrial governance. Here, I consider two: a firm's size and its level of export business.

The first of these characteristics that might drive differences in the ways that production is organized is firm size. The "markets versus hierarchies" distinction in institutional economics is relevant here; larger firms are able to organize more of their operations on the basis of hierarchical directives within the firm, whereas smaller firms must rely on more transactions within the market or within networks to continue their operations.[61] Moreover, smaller firms can be embedded within industrial clusters in which customary interfirm dynamics hold sway.[62] Differences in size can also mean differences in the firm's ability to attract investment as well as the organization of corporate governance, with smaller firms often existing as proprietorships, partnerships, or private firms with limited liability, while larger corporations are more often able to "go public" and thus are theoretically (though not in practice) more subject to oversight by shareholders.[63] As a result, scholars treat the requirements of small and medium enterprises (SMEs) separately from those of larger corporations; without making judgments about the superiority of one over the other, scholars recognize stable differences in the nature of production and thus capacities for collective action on policy and regulation.[64]

---

[61] Coase 1937. For illustration, think of the differences between an integrated textile mill, in which the weaving unit has guaranteed access to yarn from the spinning unit, and a power loom operator who must rely on the market for yarn.

[62] Schmitz and Nadvi 1999.　　[63] Schneider 2008.

[64] See, for an overview, Nichter and Goldmark 2009.

Yet firm size is, over the longer term, often a product of the perspectives of manufacturers. Those with greater commitment to organic growth may be smaller longer, and some manufacturers grow by establishing multiple small firms and thus could take advantage of the benefits of smallness with regard to familial modes of worker management without suffering smaller returns. Those with more technocratic perspectives, by contrast, might care more about achieving economies of scale and look favorably upon the use of leverage as a means to growth. Certainly, there are firms that would like to grow based on debt or establish professionalized human resources offices but are constrained from doing so by the size of the firm, which over time is a function of the firm's bad luck (or incompetence) in convincing banks of the need for investment. Yet as a general matter over the longer term, firm size can facilitate institutional sorting just as much as it might constrain options.

A second important firm-level characteristic is the level of engagement with the international economy. Plausible differences between successful exporters, on one hand, and domestic firms, on the other, arise from insights from the study of international political economy that identify qualitatively different political and economic conditions facing export-competitive areas of an economy as globalization decreases cross-border transaction costs.[65] It makes intuitive sense that exporters face different production and distribution challenges and are subject to different market pressures than firms that produce entirely for the domestic economy. Further, many countries in the developing world have created particular institutional mechanisms for the promotion of exports, from wholesale export promotion zones with exceptional legal and regulatory frameworks to export promotion agencies. In India, there are a number of industry-specific Export Promotion Councils that function as a hybrid between an industry association and a government agency, which were repurposed from agencies that distributed import and foreign exchange quotas during the statist licensing regime. Thus, we might see patterns of firm behavior that correlate with the level of exposure to the international economy.

Here again, both the level and the nature of international engagement might facilitate rather than constrain the perspectives of manufacturers in determining structures of production. After all, even more

[65] Frieden and Rogowski 1996.

than size, manufacturers choose whether to enter export markets either fully or partially, and the manner of this entrance. A mixture of domestic business and export sales to markets in developing countries is perfectly consistent with moral economy perspectives and governance by (cross-border) personal networks, while any firm choosing a deep level of engagement through production relationships with a multinational corporation might adopt or reflect that corporate outlook. Unfortunately, large-N firm-level data cannot distinguish among these types of international engagement, and, further, distinctions between GVCs are only explicable industry by industry. Thus, while I include measures for the level of exports in total business in the empirical chapters on capital and labor, I explore these issues in greater depth through industry-level accounts of international integration in Chapter 6.

Size and international orientation are firm-level characteristics that should be included, along with the perspectives of manufacturers, in a full accounting of firm-level institutions of industrial production. I have argued earlier, however, that these characteristics are, theoretically, not so much competing as complementary. Thus, manufacturers' perspectives, along with firm characteristics, serve as different facets of the same broad argument for institutions operating at the firm level. This explanation for the patterns and mechanisms of industrial growth in South Asia contrasts with popular regional and sectoral accounts. In what follows, I will sketch the manner by which these competing explanations are assessed through empirical research.

Research Design and Case Selection

Research design, and particularly case selection, is the first step in adjudicating among explanations for the institutions of industrial production after statism. When I started to research the forms of industrial governance in India, my first point of departure was to conduct research at the level of the firm. Many political economists choose to conduct their research at other levels of analysis, but at the outset, I wanted to remain neutral with respect to the potential influences at work in the construction of industrial governance after the state. Firms are surely where the rubber meets the road, where the mechanisms whereby institutional influences and incentives translated into production are most evident. I set about fashioning a research strategy that incorporated as many potential sources for governance as many possible into its design, by varying the contexts in which a firm is situated to adduce influence.

First, following the dictates of sectoral governance theories, I chose different industries within which I would analyze firms: textiles, garments, automotive components, and pharmaceuticals. These industries vary from one another in terms of age, the intensity of individual factors of production and the mix among them, and levels of international and domestic competitiveness. Yet all three are prominent and relatively successful industries in India. Moreover, they contain a variety of product categories within the same industry – yarn and fabric, shirts and *lunghis*, active pharmaceutical ingredients (APIs) and dosage-form formulations, gears and carburetors. They are also represented by specific industry associations, with which members identify and within which any collective action might be organized.

Second, following the dictates of regional governance theories, I chose different regions, states, and cities within which I would analyze firms. I conducted research in northern, western, and southern regions; these regions exhibit marked differences in political traditions, caste and communal relationships, and cultural (even subnational) cohesiveness.[66] Within these regions, I conducted research on firms based in Punjab, New Delhi, Haryana, Uttar Pradesh, Maharashtra, Gujarat, and Tamil Nadu; these states, and state governments, vary in effectiveness even within the same region, with Gujarat being lauded and Maharashtra derided for their respective environments for investment and stability of rule. And, finally, I conducted my research in ten different metropolitan areas, some within the same state, some spanning states: Ludhiana, Chandigarh, the Delhi NCR, Mumbai, Pune, Ahmedabad, Surat, Chennai, Coimbatore, and Tiruppur. Most industrialists self-identify at the metropolitan level and can mobilize through municipal chambers of commerce and industry even while they might lobby or receive guidance from state governments.

Finally, within industries and cities, I contacted a wide variety of firms in different product categories and at different sizes and levels of export business. My case selection strategy was relatively simple: I would contact, via "cold calling," firms listed in industry association directories – principally the Indian Drug Manufacturers' Association,

----

[66] Singh 2016.

the Automotive Components Manufacturers' Association, and the Center on the Indian Textile Industry – in different cities. The selection process was not fully random because of the exigencies and social interactions involved with arranging interviews, but I took some care not to select firms purely on the basis of characteristics such as size. As a result, I believe that my final sample of 160 firms in India represents a characteristic sample across industries and regions.

I based my analysis on two samples: one interview-based and small-N, the other a large-N dataset with more than eight thousand firms. During fieldwork, once firms were contacted and meetings were arranged, I conducted semistructured interviews, ranging from thirty minutes to more than two hours, with respondents who were always part of the management and were most often members of the family or group that owned and directed the firm. I asked my respondent for his or her personal background, the background of the founder of the firm, the firm's history, and its contemporary characteristics: its products, its raw materials, its suppliers and customers. I then focused on the two key dimensions of industrial governance: the firm's strategies for acquiring capital for everyday activities and growth and how it recruited, retained, and trained its workforce. I also asked how they managed relationships with firms in other countries. Finally, I asked about the firm's relationships with and perspectives on the state in different forms, from the national state to particular ministries.[67]

Separately, I used the Prowess "manufacturing superset" dataset of Indian firms from the Center for the Study of the Indian Economy. To ensure broad comparability between the two samples, I excluded foreign- and government-owned firms, as well as those firms coded as "production support," such as insurance and finance companies. I used finance and labor cost data from 2008, to ensure comparability, as well as finance data from before liberalization for time-series comparison. Thus, large-N data were used to support some of the competing hypotheses that arose from interview-based fieldwork.

The data can be used to adjudicate competing hypotheses. If regional industrial governance arrangements were indeed enabling industrial production, we would expect both some mention of the importance of regional institutions and patterns of firm-level outcomes that show

---

[67] For more details on the characteristics of the interview sample, see Naseemullah 2013, 47.

some commonality or convergence among firms in the same geographic jurisdiction. If sectoral industrial governance arrangements were enabling industrial governance, then we should see both recognition of the influence of sectoral institutions and patterns of firm-level outcomes along sectoral lines. If, on the other hand, the "governing firms" model holds sway, we should expect manufacturers' backgrounds and experiences, in the qualitative interviews, and the age-cohort of firms, in the large-N data, to be comparatively better at explaining differences in firm-level organization than region or sector. In addition, size and international orientation might have separate but complementary effects. Further, the mechanisms of governance should see manufacturers oriented toward cognitive globalization tending to establish firm-level institutional frameworks based on formal rules, and manufacturers oriented toward the moral economy tending to establish firm-level frameworks based on informal networks.

Studying India and Pakistan

Alongside my research into firm-level political economy in India, I analyzed the structures of industrial production in the Pakistani economy. Pakistan might seem at first blush to be an odd choice to place beside India in economic terms; India is currently expected to emerge as a global economic power over the next two decades, whereas the headlines on Pakistan are dominated by political instability, terrorism, and state weakness. But Pakistan is a surprisingly good comparative case for India, because remarkable similarities are twinned with differences in variables of interest to the political economy of industrial development. I call this "mirror case design." It first leverages structural similarities between two cases in order to establish comparability of the second case. This is particularly important in cases such as India, which is often considered, because of its size and internal diversity, to be sui generis, or else paired with Brazil or China on the basis of little more than the salience of common membership in the "BRICs" category. Pakistan and India have the same institutional roots in colonial India; the formal structures of government are thus quite similar, and legal traditions derive from the same statutes. And despite the religious and cultural differences between Muslim-dominated Pakistan and Hindu-majority India, cultural and economic practices at the local level display a remarkable amount of cross-border continuity.

Second, it utilizes just-as-remarkable differences between the two cases in a key variable under analysis in this book – the autonomous power of the state – in order to establish a "most different systems design" based on Mill's method of agreement.[68] One of the most significant divergences between India and Pakistan in the decades following independence is the state's strength and autonomy. The bloody circumstances of partition and the creation of Pakistan forced upon the new nation a sense of "systemic vulnerability," which Richard Doner and his colleagues have defined as necessary and sufficient for the formation of developmental state institutions.[69] Further, Pakistan's bureaucratic authoritarian rule in the 1960s and the domination of the state by military officers and civilian bureaucrats, in marked contrast to India's democracy, stem at least in part from statist reactions to strategic threats and systemic vulnerability, as Ayesha Jalal and others have argued.[70] Pakistan thus had to construct its industrial capacity out of whole cloth, as a part of a broader project to achieve self-sufficient development in order that resources could be reserved for defense expenditure. The result is that even today, more than four decades after the fall of the Ayub Khan regime that represented the height of statism, Pakistani politics is still aggressively centralized and strongly influenced by the military's strategic perspectives.

For all the meddling of the army in civilian politics and in the political economy of land and rents, the Pakistani state has, as in India, withdrawn from directing factor markets in order to promote industrialization, even though industrial promotion was seen as vital for the country's security in the heyday of the statist era. That we seem to be seeing the same fall of statist industrial governance and indeed the rise of institutions of industrial production at the firm level in India's quite different western neighbor, then, is at least a preliminary indication that what is occurring may be part of a more generalized trend, rather than a peculiarly Indian phenomenon.

---

[68] Przeworski and Teune 1970; Tarrow 2010.

[69] Doner et al. 2005; see also Waldner 1999. Naseemullah and Arnold (2015) argue that the same conditions of systemic vulnerability evident in the early years of Taiwanese and South Korean industrialization were also present in Pakistan and Turkey after state formation.

[70] Alavi 1972; Jalal 1990; Khan 1999; Stern 2001; Yong 2005. For a contrasting view that focuses on the dominance of landed elites in the Muslim League, see Tudor 2013.

Further, the addition of the Pakistani case specifically can thus start building a conceptual bridge to other cases, because Pakistan is arguably much more representative of the experience of most developing countries than India. Most do not have uniquely Indian characteristics of size and prominence, and thus have to compete for investment internationally and even within their own regions. Most developing countries, moreover, have to grapple with legacies of authoritarian rule, if not continuing autocratic governance. Thus, the particular dynamics between the state and the economy in Pakistan presented here might allow us to reflect on and thus sharpen our research lenses in conducting analysis of other cases.

Chapters 7 and 8 present Pakistan as a mirror case to India. Chapter 7 describes the politics behind the rise of statist industrial governance in Pakistan as part of a general process of violent state formation and the construction of developmental state institutions, comparable to those of Korea, in the context of "systemic vulnerability." The chapter then describes the end of statism in industrial governance as an outcome of provincial resistance to the distributional consequences of industrialization, the rise of an alternative provincial bourgeoisie, and changes in the world economy that challenged dirigiste economic policy. Chapter 8 then locates the institutional structures of industrial production not at the national level, nor that of provinces and sectors, but rather at the firm level. This research is based on more than seventy interviews with respondents in the textiles, garments, automotive components, and pharmaceuticals sectors, which took place in Lahore, Faisalabad, Sialkot, and Gujranwala in Punjab and Karachi in Sindh. Some of the institutional strategies in Pakistan exhibit similarities to those in India, while others – such as Islamic banking – are quite different. Yet I find that Pakistani manufacturers, like those in India, form their own institutional relationships to labor and capital, based on their backgrounds and experiences, in the absence of clear and credible signals from the state.

Conclusion

This chapter has provided the major theoretical and conceptual building blocks for this book. I have grounded our understanding of industrial development in the institutional frameworks and attendant relationships necessary to acquire finance; recruit, train, and retain workers; and engage with other firms at home and abroad. I suggested that during most of the postwar era, the state in India, as elsewhere, invested material resources and political capital to providing these "industrial governance" frameworks. The decline in statism in the era of liberalization and the continuation of industrial production in this context lead us to ask what alternative sources of industrial governance are structuring industrial relationships and thus enabling industrial growth. I presented several plausible alternatives to statist institutional frameworks: industrial governance based on region and on sector. I then presenedt my own argument – "governing firms" – which locates the institutional structures of industrial production at the firm level, with manufacturers forming durable relationships with workers and sources of finance based on cognitive globalization and moral economy perspectives. I concluded the chapter with discussions of research design and what evidence might adjudicate among these alternative explanations in explaining production after the withdrawal of the state from industrial governance.

In the chapters that follow, I will present much more detailed narratives of different aspects of industrial production after liberalization in South Asia, from labor to finance to the international economy. These narratives focus on both the aggregate firm-level outcomes in the organization of production and the mechanisms available to manufacturers as they negotiate challenges of manufacturing in relation to institutionalized relationships. They also tell the story of the rise and fall of statism as the dominant institutional mode of industrial governance in the postwar period. Chapter 3 picks up this narrative with the politics behind the rise and decline of statism in India.

3 | *The Rise and Fall of Statist Governance in India*

The political economy of Indian manufacturing has undergone a profound transformation, from an era in which the state maintained commitments to structuring and enabling industrial production to one in which the state's many activities in the economy do not include any systematic industrial governance. This shift runs through deep, intense, and confusing debates over the nature of India's "neoliberal turn" and the state's changing roles in and relationships to the economy, either as a triumph of economic success or as the harbinger of inequality and social violence. This chapter seeks not to intervene in these debates but rather to clarify the state's changing role in a specific corner of the economy: that of industrial promotion through structuring factor markets.

In my view, the postindependence economic settlement – a product of the politics within the Indian nationalist movement, its relationships with capitalist allies, and the autonomous growth in the state's capabilities – constituted a protected alliance between the government and industrial capitalists, one that provided political capital to institute, maintain, and protect statist industrial governance. The resulting laws, policies, and practices drew a sharp distinction between recognized industries and small-scale craft production – in other words, between factories and workshops – that were each supported by separate institutional frameworks.

Three decades later, several different factors combined to redefine the state's role in governing industry: the rise of hitherto excluded interest groups, declines in industrial efficiency, increases in trade union militancy, disruptions in the international economy, and changes in ideas of economic management. These pressures and the resulting changes in policy, grouped together under the broad rubric of liberalization, challenged statist industrial promotion and governance. Liberalizing policies and the dissipation of state-institutionalist frameworks that hitherto structured the market for factors of industrial production also muddied the distinction between factories and workshops, allowing industrial enterprises with different institutional and ideational foundations to compete effectively. The implications of this change in particular areas, such as finance and capital–labor relations, and how firms have adjusted to this withdrawal in order to enable production are explored in later chapters.

This chapter proceeds as follows. I begin with an exploration of the many debates about the state's role in the economy, before and after liberalization. I then discuss the politics behind and the mechanisms within statist industrial governance, from roughly independence in 1947 until the 1980s, as well as how this framework enforced distinctions between factories and workshops. I then outline the political pressures that rose and combined to challenge the statist industrial development regime in the 1980s, leading to a transformation of the state's willingness and ability to govern the industrial economy. I end by setting up the following chapters as a battle of competing frameworks for industrial governance.

Perspectives on the State in the Indian Economy

Scholarly writing on the relationship between the state and the market in India is both abundant and disjointed, a product of many different intellectual perspectives, research questions, and periods under consideration. A full accounting of the literature lies well beyond the scope of this book. But it is necessary to place the basic historical narrative of the rise and fall of statist industrial governance within debates over the empirical and normative place of the state in the Indian economy and thus describe the consonances and dissonances with major extant theories and frameworks.

State and Society in India's Political Economy

Scholarship contemporaneous with the emergence of India's planned economy of the Nehruvian era focused on the principles and mechanisms of the first three Five Year Plans and their outcomes and implications.[1] The political power of the Planning Commission and its mission to transform the Indian economy through industrial and agricultural

---

[1] Hanson 1966; Singh 1969.

development dominated discussions of political economy during the 1950s and 1960s. Later, political economists analyzed the planning era as a dialectic between state actors and social forces. Stanley Kochanek, deploying pluralist analysis in examining the relationship between the state and the economy in India, argued that the fragmented and underdeveloped nature of interest group representation, particularly with regard to business associations, enabled a state-dominated economy.[2] Indeed, the "overdeveloped" nature of the state vis-a-vis civil society was a theme of both pluralists and Marxists during this period.[3] Francine Frankel, in her magisterial history of India's political economy, framed a more dynamic tension between the state-led social transformation – necessarily involving major disruptions to the status quo – and emergent democratic politics, in which powerful vested interests have the capacity and authority to resist such changes.[4]

By the 1980s, scholars started to bemoan the resurgent power of organized actors within society and their capacities to disrupt the development priorities and administrative capacities of the autonomous state. Lloyd Rudolph and Susanne Rudolph argued that the rise of demand groups, such as the assertive post–Green Revolution commercial peasantry, or "bullock capitalists," increasingly put pressure on the state to expend resources toward their parochial interests, increasingly derailing development priorities.[5] Pranab Bardhan similarly argued that India's economic policies were increasingly subject to the interests of "dominant proprietary classes," rich farmers, industrial capitalists, and bureaucrats, leading to a decline in public investment and sluggish growth.[6] Atul Kohli considered the decade overall as one of a growing crisis of governability, brought on by a decline in the cohesion of the Indian state and the Congress party.[7]

Thus, the dominant perspective in Indian political economy is one of the rise of autonomous state power and state-led economic development, followed by the ascendance of interest groups and the fragmentation of the political system, a decline in state authority, and economic stagnation. There are certainly important qualifications to this broad narrative. Aseema Sinha's work on regional variation in economic growth situates explanations in the interaction and cooperation

---

[2] Kochanek 1974.   [3] Alavi 1972.   [4] Frankel 2005.
[5] Rudolph and Rudolph 1987.   [6] Bardhan 1983   [7] Kohli 1990.

between state governments and the private sector.[8] Irfan Nooruddin has argued that the resulting rise of coalition politics in India over the last two decades has had a *salutary* effect in increasing overall growth and reducing its volatility; coalition governments can provide institutionally credible commitments and thus policy continuity because coalition partners are veto players on behalf of particularistic interests against any radical changes or reversals in government policy.[9] As a whole, though, the ascendance of organized social groups and their articulation in the political process run counter to a vision of economic development driven by the autonomous power of the state.

The dominant narrative of shifts in the balance between state and society is broadly compelling; the fragmentation of political power has meant that no one group has been able to command the lion's share of resources for development, as public- and private-sector manufacturing was able to do during the period of statism. Yet certain modifications to the narrative need to be made when discussing manufacturing. For a start, the industrial capitalists are usually included among the rising interest groups demanding more resources. But part of the process of liberalization has meant the decline of most of the giant industrial houses and the concomitant fragmentation of organization and representation, even while monopolistic and oligarchic players have emerged in other areas of the economy.

The shift in the balance of power between state and society is also coincident in a complicated fashion with economic reform, even though analysts tend to see the latter as a product of autonomous policy decisions by insulated political players. Part of the political impetus for liberalization was minimizing the resources expended on regulating and promoting the industrial economy – in areas as diverse as subsidizing credit to maintaining overvalued exchange rates – as the country faced a series of macroeconomic crises. But the withdrawal of the state from expenditure on industrial governance freed up state

---

[8] Sinha 2005.

[9] Nooruddin 2011. A difficulty with Nooruddin's overall argument vis-à-vis the Indian case is that he relies on foreign direct investment as a mechanism that links perceptions of policy consistency and economic growth. India, however, has very low levels of net inward FDI: an average of 1.57 percent as a percentage of GDP between 2000 and 2013, which is two-thirds that of Brazil and one-half that of China. Further, 42 percent of FDI between 2000 and 2011 was from Mauritius, suggesting that much "FDI" is in reality round-trip Indian capital taking advantage of incentives provided for foreign investment.

resources for discretionary distribution to client constituencies, from electricity for farmers in Maharashtra to television sets and laptops to voting households in Tamil Nadu. These linkages are complex and circumstantial, but it is clear that state actors are focusing their resources and political capital in directions other than creating an institutional environment for manufacturing.

Indian Development in Comparative Context

Comparative political economy, meanwhile, sought the determinants of economic success and failure across developing countries; state capacity emerged as the critical factor in determining late industrialization, with authoritarian "developmental states" such as Taiwan and Korea as exemplars. Peter Evans argued, on the basis of a cross-country comparison of the emergent IT industry, that South Korea's successes in new globalized economic production arose from a developmental state that was able to balance policy autonomy effectively with close, "embedded" relationships with social actors, particularly industrial capital.[10] In his view, Brazil and India represented intermediate cases; India's main constraint was a set of governmental institutions that was *too* autonomous – a consequence of colonial administrative institutions and lack of connection between the class and cultural backgrounds of bureaucrats and those in manufacturing – and thus unable to develop deep relationships with the private sector.[11] Atul Kohli studied a similar set of countries to Evans's and made a slightly different argument about the reasons for effective "state-directed development" in some countries and not others.[12] He argued that state institutions that enable the profits of investors are the foundation for successful development; these salutary institutional constellations, in turn, are dependent on patterns of state authority, which are formed from different colonial experiences.[13] Kohli argued that India can be characterized not as a "cohesive-capitalist" state like Korea or as a neopatrimonial state like Nigeria but at an intermediate point between the two: a "fragmented, multi-class" state like Brazil, in which the state's legitimacy lies in a multiclass alliance that precludes a targeted focus on capitalist development.[14] Thus, the

[10] Evans 1995.　　[11] Evans 1995, 69.　　[12] Kohli 2004.
[13] Kohli 2004, 7–8.　　[14] Kohli 2004, 11.

Indian state is too beholden to various competing social interests to commit wholeheartedly to the support of entrepreneurship and rapid industrialization.

In an explicit comparison of Korea and India, Vivek Chibber has argued that the collective oppositional action of the national bourgeoisie against state intervention in the latter was actually responsible for sabotaging "disciplinary planning." India therefore was unable to establish the industrial policy regimes and leverage of the state over capital that enabled Korea to develop successfully on the basis of a transition to export-led industrialization.[15] This comparative perspective does suggest that the latter, with more autonomous and authoritarian state power, was more successful in coercing private sector capital and forestalling the rent-seeking that some consider inherent in a quasi-planned economy focused on import-substituting domestic production.

Comparative perspectives are useful in identifying critical variables and, as importantly, causal processes, through the examination of different cases. Yet these studies are not directly relevant to this book's argument, for a couple of reasons. First, Korea may not be a relevant comparator, because it has proved to be not just a successful case but a rather exceptional one. Second, even though Korea had more successful outcomes, Brazil and India both established structurally equivalent statist development regimes. Last and most importantly, all of these comparative analyses focused on economic policy regimes after World War II but before liberalization, and thus are silent on institutional changes in industrial development in any of these cases over time and particularly after liberalizing reforms. Nevertheless, I include the mirror case of Pakistan because it shared many of the same characteristics of state power and autonomy with Korea during the early postwar decades.[16]

---

[15] Chibber 2003. Sukhamoy Chakravarty, by contrast, argues that the lack of support for export orientation was due to the state's unwillingness to let a small group of textile mill owners, particularly in Gujarat, consolidate economic power and reap economic rents rather than deepening and diversify their investments. See Chakravarty 1993, 16–17.

[16] We argue that Pakistan diverges from Korea as a result of the rise of an agrarian challenge to the statist development regime; Korea escaped such a challenge because of the disruptions of landed power during the Korean War and its aftermath. See Naseemullah and Arnold 2015.

The Neoliberal Critique of State Intervention

Neoclassical economics, rising in the 1970s and resurgent under the Reagan administration and the Thatcher governments, provided an out-of-paradigm critique of statist industrialization, concentrating on the unintended and adverse consequences of state intervention in the economy. Deepak Lal challenged the principles of dirigisme as they had been practiced in third world "development economics," including that of India.[17] Anne Kreuger argued that the complicated system of permits and quotas that defined Indian statist development had over the decades opened up the possibility for rent-seeking, to which efforts and resources were expended instead of investment.[18] And Jagdish Bhagwati has been a constant critic of the Indian government's interventions as welfare reducing, particularly with regard to price manipulation and trade protection.[19]

Neoliberal perspectives of Indian government intervention in the economy, particularly the "license–permit–quota raj," constitute important critiques of the actual operation of statism, even if they are uncomfortable to those on the Left. They are limited, however, by their faith in market mechanisms and general lack of interest in institutions except as deleterious artefacts of populist politics. Relatedly, they make little distinction between industrial development and more general economic growth, trusting in mechanisms such as factor markets and comparative advantage to sort out the most efficient and productive allocation of resources. This book takes as its foundation the idea that manufacturing in late development requires a set of institutions working in concert that are unlikely to be provided by market mechanisms. Moreover, neoliberal critics of statism, even while making universal claims against state intervention, were responding to the much more specific contexts of institutional sclerosis and economic stagnation of the 1970s and early 1980s. Ashutosh Varshney has recently argued that stagnation during this period was a product of Indira Gandhi's arbitrary populist policies rather than development planning under Nehru and Shastri.[20]

---

[17] Lal 1985.   [18] Kreuger 1974.   [19] Jagdish Bhagwati 1989; Bhagwati 1993.
[20] Varshney 2012.

The Politics of Liberalization and Its Discontents

Political economists from the late 1980s were involved in explaining the politics that led to progressively more serious rounds of economic reform, culminating in liberalization under Rao in 1991.[21] Kochanek characterized liberalization under the reform-minded Rajiv Gandhi as constrained by the explicit and covert resistance of organized actors – from the Left within Congress to the bureaucracy to organized labor even to certain interests within the nominally supportive business community.[22] Kohli further specified the broader class interests and social forces that had combined to lend political support to economic reform.[23] Rob Jenkins has argued that the implementation of the 1991 liberalization is best characterized by "reform by stealth," in which major policy changes occurred at elite levels behind closed doors, and thus were not subject to democratic opposition, even as new patronage networks and the adaptability of existing interest groups also contributed to the durability of liberalization.[24] Rahul Mukherji has further explained that profound changes in economic policy arose out of the intersection of exogenous shocks and policy elites passing an ideational tipping point in favor of deregulation and opening up the economy.[25] Even though support had been building among key economic and political actors, 1991 marked an abrupt shift, as an earthquake is the product of pressures and shifts in tectonic plates for months and years.[26] And, the aftershocks of the liberalization program and its implications have been felt and debated ever since, particularly in the practices of state actors at the local level.[27]

More specifically, there have been two broad reactions to liberalization. The first, in keeping with the neoliberal critique of statism, understands economic reform and the retrenchment and rationalization of the state as responsible for India's economic emergence. Specifically, scholars have argued that the withdrawal of the state's regulations for and interventions on the investments and practices of firms – the notorious "license–permit–quota raj" – unleashed the entrepreneurial energies of Indian capitalism, leading to the impressive growth rates of the 1990s

---

[21] For more on cycles of reform, see Denoon 1998.   [22] Kochanek 1986.
[23] Kohli 1989.   [24] Jenkins 2000.   [25] Mukherji 2013a, b.
[26] For more on long-term causal processes such as these, see Pierson 2004, 79–102.
[27] For an overview of these debates, see Gupta and Sivaramakrishnan 2010.

and 2000s after decades of tepid growth.[28] For those committed to the notion of the free market, liberalization and the rolling back of the state have been an unalloyed boon for the Indian economy.[29]

Still others have been critical of the social and political consequences of liberalization, particularly with regard to inequality and social protection. Ironically, given Kreuger's characterization of statism as promoting rent-seeking, liberalization seems to have facilitated a greater quantum and density of rent exchange between political actors and (crony) capitalists. Political commentary is replete with discussions of corrupt ties between business and government, portraying India as in the midst of a twenty-first-century Gilded Age.[30] Kohli has argued that close political alliances and the exchange of resources by politicians, bureaucrats, and big business have contributed to the lackluster human development and increasing inequality of postliberalization India.[31] He has noted that features of this emergent state–business alliance are evident in the concentrated power of business in politics, tracing a causal line from electoral financing by corporate groups to probusiness policies, misappropriation, and explicit handouts to favored clients.[32]

Nowhere are these dynamics more clear than in the quintessentially rent-thick activities involving the acquisition of land by state governments, through eminent domain, on behalf of particular figures in the corporate sector, particularly companies involved in real estate and the extraction of rentier resources. Mike Levien has characterized this process as primitive "accumulation by dispossession," though occurring through the explicit deployment of the state's coercion.[33] The intrusion of market forces, often abetted by the gendarme form of the state, has hurt some of the most vulnerable populations in India, from dislocation of tribal groups by coal mining to farmer suicides as a result of debt related to monopoly-priced inputs.[34] Such intense state involvement in the newly liberalized economy has raised the fundamental question of whether the state actually has withdrawn.[35]

---

[28] See Das 2000 for a full articulation of this position.
[29] Others have contested this causal claim, locating India's higher rates of growth in the 1980s, well before sustained macroreforms. Srinivasan 2006; McCartney 2009, 2010.
[30] N. Singh 2010; Mehta 2012; Walton 2015.   [31] Kohli 2011.
[32] Kohli 2011, 50–72; 118–152.   [33] Levien 2012, 2013. See also Sud 2009.
[34] Shah 2010; Sainath 2010.   [35] Nayar 2009.

How can one argue for a narrative of state withdrawal in the context of so much blatant state intervention? In this book, I do not argue that agents of the state – whether central or state governments, whether ministries or quasi-independent agencies, whether at the national or the local level – are not involved in many deep and profound ways in economic intervention; the state both works as a watchman on behalf of capital and expends billions of rupees in public and private services for important client constituencies. Rather, I contend that the state has withdrawn from a particular kind of developmental intervention: that of industrial govern- ance through the control of factor markets, or, in other words, the structuring of relationships of industrial firms and capital and labor. To be sure, agents of the state can and do go to lengths to assist individual firms and, at times, even sectors. But the contemporary Indian state has not the inclination, resources, or capacity to implement the full, integrated framework of industrial governance that had characterized statist indus- trial regulation and promotion before liberalization. I describe this shift, and the political dynamics before and after it, in the rest of this chapter.

The Formation of Statist Governance

The beginning of postindependence India's efforts to promote industri- alization occurred within the politics of the nationalist movement and the growth of the state. Political conflict within the Congress party produced a developmentalist alliance of left-leaning nationalists and capitalists that provided the political impetus and the policy resources for industrialization. Simultaneously, the growth of the state in response to wartime necessity before independence established both capacities and precedents for state intervention in establishing and maintaining institutional frameworks for industrial investment. Together, these two political processes produced statist industrial gov- ernance through the provision of institutional resources to industry not subject to political challenge, while establishing a protected space and alternative institutional framework for handicrafts and other small- scale economic activities as a compromise to Gandhian conservatives.

Nationalism and Development

The earliest and most powerful nationalist critique against colonial rule held that the British were underdeveloping India through active policies; domestic artisans were being routed by open markets for foreign manufacturing goods, while debt increased and resources flowed out of the country to pay for imports and colonial administration.[36] *Swadesh*, or self-sufficiency, and the wearing of *khadi*, or homespun cloth, constituted repertoires of nationalist contention in the emergent Indian National Congress from the turn of the twentieth century. But by the 1930s, two very different visions of nationalist development emerged. Socialist thinkers in Congress such as Jawaharlal Nehru and Subhas Chandra Bose advocated development through rapid industrialization and state-directed economic planning. Following the explicit model of the Soviet Union, India would simultaneously achieve economic self-sufficiency and the abolition of poverty through massive public investments in heavy industry, the centralized allocation of resources, and the rationalization of the inefficient agricultural sector by means of land reform and the application of scientific management to economic activity.[37]

Gandhi and his intellectual followers, on the other hand, advocated a reversion to economic relationships embedded in reimagined traditional cultural values and a rejection of both Western consumerism and industrial agglomeration. In their view, modernization through industrial development, as was evident in the developed economies of the period, sowed the seeds of class animosities that might tear apart Indian society. Gandhi's ideal India would be constituted by autarkic village communities, in which most basic needs would be met by craft production and the rich would keep society's wealth "in trust" for the poor.[38] In the end, Gandhian ideas of development, more idealistic and motivated by a rejection of Western notions of material progress, lost out to Nehru's vision of statist industrialization, in part because the machinery of the colonial state for economic planning and industrial governance was already being established in response to wartime requirements in the late 1930s.[39] Yet the broader political context within the anticolonial movement also compromised Nehru's more explicitly socialistic vision; these politics necessitated the forging of alliances with private sector business in order to shape the institutions of industrial promotion.

[36] Chandra 1966; Habib 1975.
[37] Zachariah 2005, 211–277. See also Chakrabarty 1992.
[38] Zachariah 2005, 156–209. See also Kumarappa 1951; Rudolph and Rudolph 2006.
[39] See Gould 2011.

Divisions within Congress

From the 1920s onward, the actions and policies of the Congress leadership were driven by the potentially irreconcilable goals of agitating against British rule while promoting political order. Both Gandhi and Nehru saw violent political disorder as the largest threat to the integrity of postindependence India and the pursuit of development.[40] Such a threat was already materializing in the form of Muslim separatist demands and widespread communal violence in the lead-up to Partition in 1947; similar demands for ethnic, regional, and linguistic autonomy from the political center had most of the Congress leadership deeply concerned. A more immediate concern was communist infiltration of Congress affiliate organizations on the Left such as the Congress Socialist Party and the All-India Kisan Sabha, as well as the specter of peasant revolt.[41]

The increasing influence of conservatives in the Congress Party led to conflict with the communist-inspired nationalist Left. The political orientations of Congress membership and leadership itself had changed dramatically since its transformation into a mass organization in the 1920s. All-India mass mobilization was mostly accomplished through the absorption of local notables – rich peasants, rural bankers, and merchants – into district and pradesh (provincial) Congress committees. Gandhi's philosophies of class conciliation and gradual uplift through social cooperation rather than conflict had direct appeal for this population, who were, more than anything, afraid of fundamental disruptions to the agrarian order. Vallabbhai Patel, the most powerful conservative within the Congress Party's High Command and Gandhi's most effective proxy in its internal politics, managed the recruitment and organization of regional party committees and thus acquired a sizable and coherent constituency of local notables that remained staunchly opposed to the radical reorganization of society along socialist or communist lines.[42] Congress's role in the transformation of society, following these mobilizations, was for practical purposes thus limited to social reform within existing hierarchies.

Political conflict over Subhas Chandra Bose's reelection to the presidency of the party in 1939, and a subsequent controversial election of

---

[40] Frankel 2005, 65–66.   [41] Frankel 2005, 55–62.
[42] Frankel 2005, 37; see also Weiner 1967, 30–67. For more on the recruitment practices of the independence-era Congress party, see Kochanek 1968.

the conservative Purshottomdas Tandon in 1950, led many of the leaders and cadres of the Left to leave or be expelled from the Congress party altogether and form separate political parties, thus weakening Nehru's autonomous political base.[43] In order to establish and implement rapid state-led and -directed industrialization, Nehru increasingly had to rely instead on autonomous institutions within the Congress Party and later the Indian government that he could shield from direct political challenge, and yet could create the framework under which the party-state's efforts for development would be coordinated. Between 1938 and 1941, Nehru convened and chaired a National Planning Committee (NPC), which comprised technocrats in the service of the British Indian government or princely states, academic economists, and several major industrialists. The NPC was a forerunner of the postindependence Planning Commission and foreshadowed the political power of this subsequent planning apparatus in shaping the Indian economy. As a result of the displacement and fragmentation of the Left within the Congress organization, then, Nehru's key allies in establishing statist industrial development were the elite bureaucrats, and – both significantly and surprisingly – indigenous private sector industrial entrepreneurs.

The alliance of Nehru, economic planners, and industrialization was one born of common commitments to technology and technocracy. While Nehru's ideological convictions might have led him to distrust private capital, his political and personal instincts were to forge alliances with those who shared his modernizing perspective and whose interests were well served by rapid, state-supported industrialization. Important too was the support of *indigenous* industrialists, as agents of industrial self-sufficiency and bulwarks against the domination of the Indian economy by multinational corporations, because unlike MNCs, Indian capitalists would feel no compulsion to repatriate profits back to shareholders in the West.

The Interests of Industrial Capitalism

For India's independence-era industrial capitalists, this alliance provided political protection from socialist and communist pressure – forestalling the threat of nationalization – while allowing them support

[43] Frankel 2005, 72–74; Weiner 1972, 42–64.

for investment activities. Communist involvement in general strikes in 1928 and 1929 particularly worried employers, as did implicit threats of insurrectionary violence in the countryside.[44] Industrialists were concerned that increasingly radical influences in Indian politics and society in the 1930s and 1940s might lead to a violent revolutionary context in which their investments, and even their lives and livelihoods, would be in jeopardy. Moderate nationalists presented the best hope for a stable and secure polity for private investment.

Influence with the Congress party leadership was increasingly essential as the British Indian government abandoned its market orthodoxies in the face of the Great Depression and introduced tariffs and other elements of activist policy.[45] Moreover, changes toward activism in economic policy coincided with the political success of the Congress party in the 1936 elections to provincial legislative assemblies; Congress was able to form governments in eight of eleven provinces. If business interests were to have influence on the increasing power of the government to intervene in the economy by means of fiscal, monetary, and trade policies, they would need to cultivate political relationships with the policy makers within the Congress movement.

Support for planning among the Indian business community was declared at the annual meeting of the FICCI, the apex organization for indigenous businesses, in 1934, with major figures such as G. D. Birla discussing the need to increase the standard of living substantially through government intervention.[46] A full-throated articulation of private sector support of the goal of economic planning was evident in the Bombay Plan of 1944, a document authored by seven leading industrialists. The plan called for doubling the national income by 1960 through both private and public industrial investment and state sponsorship of key "basic" upstream industries, such as power, steel, chemicals, fertilizers, and cement.[47] The Bombay Plan echoed in the private sector the intentions of development planning in the public

---

[44] Chandavarkar 1998, 127–135.
[45] Tomlinson 1982, 135. A crisis in balance of payments between the rupee and sterling in the 1930s arose out of these circumstances, and led to changes in constitutional arrangements including the Government of India Act 1935. See Tomlinson 1979.
[46] Zachariah 2005, 214.   [47] Thakurdas 1945.

sector. In this, it signaled the capacity for cooperation between the state and the industrial private sector toward a common goal, that of increasing industrial investment.[48]

The Growth of the State

The alliance between industrial capitalists and Nehru was facilitated by autonomous growth in the size and capacity of the Indian colonial state's regulatory apparatus, largely in response to mobilization for India's participation in the World War II. Such mobilization led to inflationary financing, which, coupled with the increase of industrial production only for strategic goods, created a shortage of consumer goods. The government's response both during and after the war was to institute a bureaucratic system of rationing and price controls that vastly increased the state's capacity to manage the economy.[49] Additionally, during the war, policymakers started considering the role of the state in postwar reconstruction and development. A reconstruction committee of the Viceroy's Council was set up in 1943, and in 1944, a separate Department of Planning and Development – headed by the Tata director Sir Ardeshir Dalal, one of the authors of the Bombay Plan – was created in order to organize postwar reconstruction of the Indian economy.[50] The Indian colonial government issued the Industrial Policy Statement of 1945, to be echoed by Nehru's policies after independence, which emphasized that the benefits of more active industrial policy should go to domestic capital for reinvestment rather than to expatriate capital.[51] These new government institutions of economic management and planning, formulated as an ad hoc response to the economic impact of India's wartime participation, thus provided continuities of access and involvement of prominent industrialists in the bureaucratic aspects of economic planning that continued beyond the end of colonial rule.

It is important to remember that the politics surrounding the nationalist movement in the 1930s and 1940s created circumstances of constrained

---

[48] Ray 1979. Vivek Chibber disputes this characterization through comparative analysis with South Korea, but in relation to "disciplinary planning" and the capacity of the state to mandate *export-led* industrialization. See Chibber 2003, 94–109.

[49] Tomlinson 1993, 161–162; Rothermund 2002, 123–127.

[50] Tomlinson 1993, 166.   [51] Tomlinson 1993, 166–167.

leverage for Nehru in his quest to establish rapid industrialization as a major goal for the state. Without a powerful political constituency on the Left and facing challenges on the Right, Nehru allied with technocrats and industrialists to establish a protected environment for economic planning and the allocations of resources to industrial development. These alliances were baked in to the ways in which the postindependence state operated its industrial strategies, thereby providing support and guidance to private sector manufacturing.

The Operation of Statist Governance

Public and Private Industrial Development during the Nehru Years

The high-water mark of India's postindependence statist industrial development was during the premiership of Jawaharlal Nehru, a position he held from 1947 until his death in 1964. These seventeen years represented a period in which Nehru, who after the death of Patel was unparalleled in political stature in India, devoted considerable political capital and institutional power to establishing and maintaining development planning as the primary mission of the Indian state. Throughout this period, Nehru served as both the prime minister of India and the chairman of the Planning Commission. As such, he guaranteed that India's three Five Year Plans would serve as a framework for budgeting and expenditure that superseded the cabinet, parliament, and even center-state negotiations, thereby elevating the privileged space of industrial development to the very blueprint of the state's development strategies and practices.

The trajectory of Indian planning during this period followed the very simple notion that, for rapid development to occur, more of the nation's wealth needed be diverted to the high-value "planned" industrial portion of the economy, such as steel and chemicals, from the least productive parts of the economy, such as marginal and smallholder agriculture. This was to be accomplished through forcing increased savings rates in the banking system and other forms of financial intermediation. The indigenous private sector, dominated by textiles and other light consumer goods, occupied an intermediate category – manufacturing firms were uninterested and were considered ill equipped to sink in the levels of capital required for production in the "commanding heights" of the economy, such as steel.[52] Private industrial firms were considered essential in Nehruvian planning, however, as they could satisfy requirements for key consumer goods, from home textiles and tobacco to bicycles and toothpaste, thus freeing the government's hands to pursue the production of capital goods. Thus, the idea behind the Bombay Plan – that of cooperation between the public sector and private sector in fostering industrial development based on complementarity – was preserved in the architecture of the first three Five Year Plans. Between a third and a half of increased manufacturing capacity was in the private sector.[53]

The relationship between the industrial private sector and the Nehruvian state is a subject of much controversy, both then and now, but claims that the government was deliberately discriminating against, or even trying to eliminate, private enterprise are rather unfounded. The documents of all three plans as well as the key Industrial Policy Resolutions of 1948 and 1956 affirmed the importance of the private sector in industrial development. The second Five Year Plan, from 1956 to 1961, projected that the private sector would provide 48.9 percent of the investment in large-scale industries, while total public and private industrial investment as a proportion of the plan expenditure was 22.7 percent.[54] The second plan period saw private sector investment exceed expectations by 28 percent to a total of Rs. 8.5 billion; this investment was funded by Rs. 1 billion in loans from institutional agencies and from central governments, Rs. 2 billion from foreign capital including suppliers' credit, Rs. 1.5 billion from new issues of equity, and the remainder from internal sources.[55] The third Five Year Plan projected that out of Rs. 29.9 billion in industrial investment, or 39.9 percent of total plan expenditure, 45.6 percent would be invested in the private sector.[56] Thus, even at the high-water mark of statism, the private sector contributed just less than half of industrial investment, and the state was involved in arranging the financing of private sector industrial investment, from its own resources,

---

[52] A major exception to this is Tata Iron and Steel Corporation (TISCO), in the company town of Jamshedpur in modern-day Jharkhand. TISCO was established in 1912 to produce domestic iron and steel for the railways. For more, see Lala 1993, 238–242.

[53] Frankel 2005, 94–95, 130–133, 185–188.

[54] Government of India 1956, 51–52, 416.   [55] Government of India 1961, 456.

[56] Government of India 1961, 58, 459.

through development finance agencies or from foreign inflows in the form of development aid and import credits.

Other aspects of the statist regime were certainly less appealing from the point of view of private sector manufacturers. The Industries (Development & Regulation) Act of 1951 established a central system of licenses and permits in which firms needed permission to start production and to expand capacity. In addition, the government forbade private sector involvement in a number of industrial categories, including defense, and restricted private sector involvement in others.[57] Systems of personal and corporate taxation, moreover, prevented investors from taking home windfall profits, with taxation rates exceeding 90 percent in some categories. This system encouraged industrialists to reinvest their profits and diversify their industrial production in an ever-expanding number of product categories.

Many commentators, then and now, have blamed Nehruvian era restrictions on the private sector for suppressing the creativity, innovation, and efficiency of the market, leading to a stagnant economy and the domination of a bureaucratized and sclerotic public sector.[58] Others have noted that the license–permit–quota raj actually reflected the interests of the bourgeoisie, allowing for product diversification, while successfully avoiding policies that were explicitly opposed to their interest, such as export orientation.[59] The reality on the ground was probably somewhere in the middle of these two points, reflecting an alliance built on substantive compromise between the developmental planners of the state and industrial capitalists.

Yet, a potentially more enlightening picture of the nature of state support for private industry is revealed by looking at the firm level. The individual manufacturing firms that received industrial licenses had privileges in receiving scarce capital as the government prioritized institutional credit for industrial purposes. A foreign trade regime of high tariffs and import quotas, started under the last decades of British rule but developed under the Nehruvian state, protected domestic industry from foreign competition under the explicit goal of self-sufficiency. Firms also received import quotas and prioritized access to scarce foreign exchange for capital goods and raw materials that

[57] Government of India 1961, 94.
[58] For a full articulation of this argument, see Das 2000, 103–212.
[59] Chibber 2003, 127–158.

could only be purchased abroad; an overvalued exchange rate made these purchases more affordable. Less explicit but still crucial to industrial production were the ways in which party-affiliated unions were able to create and maintain industrial peace in the 1950s through both coercive and representative means.[60]

Small-Scale Exceptionalism

Part of the political and economic settlement that facilitated statist development also maintained a separate institutional space for handicrafts and village and cottage industries, as a compromise with Gandhians suspicious of the disruptive social consequences of industrialization. For the Planning Commission, too, the protection of cottage industry along with larger-scale recognized manufacturing served a useful purpose: the sector had a greater ability to provide mass employment while stimulating demand for manufactured goods.[61] Mark Holmstrom usefully refers to such a distinction as the difference between factories and workshops, each served by a separate institutional framework.[62]

This reserved space for craft production was embedded in institutions, policies, and legal exceptionalism. The Factories Act of 1948 (amended in 1987), which regulates health, safety, welfare, and the work, does not apply to premises with fewer than ten workers, or twenty workers for those without power.[63] In textiles, integrated mills were restricted from expanding their capacities in weaving, so that handloom (and later power loom) operators, particularly in rural areas, could benefit from expanded spinning production without competition from factory-made cloth.[64] And the Planning Commission arranged institutional support for village industry, from credit to the creation of supply and marketing cooperatives, and allocated resources in planning expenditure for these purposes: Rs. 20 billion in the second and Rs. 26.4 billion in the third Five Year Plans, mostly from state

---

[60] For more on these firm-level dynamics, see Chapters 4–6.
[61] Chakravarty 1993, 14–15.   [62] Holmstrom 1984, 110–181.
[63] The Factories Act, 1948 (Act No. 63 of 1948), as amended by the Factories (Amendment) Act, 1987 (Act 20 of 1987). Government of India. www.ilo.org/dyn/natlex/docs/WEBTEXT/32063/64873/E87IND01.htm, accessed March 1, 2014.
[64] Leadbeater 1993, 170–176.

governments.[65] The institutional protections of cottage industry and craft production thus created and maintained a space apart from large-scale manufacturing, while providing some coherence to the latter through legal and policy distinctions. In other words, the statist regime of industrial governance was defined by its support for recognized industrial enterprises defined by size, scale, and intensity, whereas institutionally distinct craft production was supported and regulated separately. Contemporary firm production structures through personal networks can trace their roots back to the persistence, growth, and transformation of this alternative institutional tradition.[66]

Political Conflict after Nehru

Jawaharlal Nehru, as prime minister and chairman of the Planning Commission, provided the political capital necessary for statist industrial governance, even though many of his other economic policy initiatives, including the rationalization and cooperativization of agriculture, had ground to a halt, mired in national and provincial politics.[67] After Nehru's death in 1964, and that of his successor, Lal Bahadur Shastri, in 1966, the politics of the Congress Party were locked in struggles among Prime Minister Indira Gandhi, the conservative Morarji Desai, and a group of powerful chief ministers known as "the syndicate." In 1969, Congress split among factions supporting the syndicate and those remaining loyal to Indira Gandhi. Indira Gandhi's populist policies, including the nationalization of sixteen commercial banks, led her to victory in the 1971 elections.[68] But they sowed the seeds for mass mobilization against the state, and in reaction, the imposition of the authoritarian emergency period between 1975 and 1977.

During this period, public sector investments in heavy industrialization were scaled back as a result of military requirements and cuts in foreign aid after the 1962 war with China, the 1965 war with Pakistan, and crippling droughts in the mid-1960s. From Shastri onward, the locus of economic decision making moved from the Planning Commission to the ideologically more neutral and malleable Prime Minister's Secretariat.

[65] Government of India 1956, 429–458; Government of India 1961, 426–451.
[66] For a similar argument in Europe, see Sabel and Zeitlin 1985.
[67] Frankel 2005, 163–174.   [68] Torri 1975.

Yet statist industrial governance was maintained and routinized. There are two reasons for this. First, Indira Gandhi's populist rhetoric ran ahead of her policy making and implementation. Comparatively little changed in terms of extending or deepening licensing or control regimes. The nationalization of key service industries such as banking and insurance gave the state even *more* control over the means by which credit could be allocated, both to the public and to the private sector. Second, macroeconomic management and the prevention of crises in the balance of payments required more foreign exchange revenue. In order to garner this extra revenue, Indira Gandhi's governments increasingly promoted private sector enterprises that could be active in export markets.[69] Industry, even in the private sector, represented a solution more than it did a problem for a government committed to its own preservation while balancing leftist resurgence and rightist opposition. Thus under Indira Gandhi, and the subsequent Janata government between 1977 and 1980, statist industrial governance and the state's promotion of industry persisted. The political changes that ultimately destroyed statism were a function of the politics of the next decade.

Challenges to Statist Governance

By the 1980s, several different pressures were interacting to force the state to withdraw from industrial governance. Some of these pressures were internal, such as the rise of demand groups displeased with the distributional consequences of statist industrialization and declines in industrial productivity. Others were external, from shocks to the world economy and changes in the financial support provided to industrial development by foreign aid. Finally, changes in the ideas behind economic management precluded older frameworks in which the state expended resources to create an environment conducive to industrial governance.

The Rise of Demand Groups

As mentioned, statist industrial governance relied on a political consensus or compromise among the leading factions of the Congress

---

[69] Denoon 1998, 48–49; Joshi 1967.

Party. As early as the late 1960s, the reach and coherence of Congress declined as regional parties rose to power at the state level and the national party split into factions.[70] Lloyd Rudolph and Susanne Hoeber Rudolph have characterized this shift as the rise of "demand groups" in Indian political economy, organized sections of society previously excluded from or absorbed as junior partners into political coalitions, and now demanding greater access to state resources as a prerequisite of political support.[71] The Janata coalition government, gaining power after Indira Gandhi's authoritarian emergency regime, was a clear articulation of this fragmentation, with former Congress and opposition activists representing differing social constituencies collectively forming a government coalition without a single dominant voice.

The most important of these demand groups are new agrarian capitalists primarily from other backward classes (OBCs), who started as middle peasants after independence but steadily increased their landholdings, wealth, and political representation through land reform and the salutary but inequality-generating outcomes of the Green Revolution. Ashutosh Varshney has argued that the rise to social prominence of such cultivators, their political organization, and representation in formal politics are a historical consequence of the development of democratic institutions before industrialization.[72] Varshney situates the transformation of rural political power in the 1970s, when agriculturalists and their political representatives successfully frustrated attempts by Indira Gandhi's populist and emergency governments to nationalize food grains trade. This successful mobilization led to the assertion of rural interests in national economic policy, including output price floors and input price ceilings, in successive governments after the emergency.[73] Thus farmers and other partially organized, assertive, and newly powerful groups such as students and government workers transformed the nature of political representation in opposition to economic priorities with an

---

[70] See Kohli 1990; Candland 1997; Tudor and Ziegfeld 2010. It should be noted that Congress was a catchall coalition with deeply ambivalent politics, accommodating both leftists and agrarian conservatives. Thus the political process of Congress decline was actually the spinning off of these factions into more ideologically distinct groups or centers of personal power.

[71] Rudolph and Rudolph 1987, 247–392.

[72] Varshney 1995; Rudolph and Rudolph 1987, 312–332.

[73] Varshney 1995, 87–112.

in-built industrial, urban bias.[74] The successful articulation of interests fundamentally opposed to industry in the formal political process challenged the preeminence of industrial promotion in policy priorities, thus undermining the consensus behind statist industrial governance.

Declining Productivity and Labor Militancy

The early 1980s represented a period in which industrial productivity and stability stalled. Some of these difficulties might be considered to be an endogenous exhaustion of the import-substitution framework. Indeed, many developing countries during this decade faced heightening macroeconomic stability and popular resistance to industrial deepening. In the Indian context, several different explanations were proposed for the low-growth economy.[75] Policymakers associated with the Planning Commission attributed the increase in incremental capital-output ratios mostly to increasing inefficiencies in agriculture and energy, with industry failing to capture greater returns from scale as a result of declining public investment.[76] Others pointed to the fact that the largest Indian industrial houses had pursued a strategy of diversification rather than deepening, entering ever more diverse product categories rather than reinvesting in core industries and upgrading their technologies. In a signal contribution to the debate, Pranab Bardhan attributed the sluggishness of industrial growth during this period to a decline in public investment, arising out of squandering resources to appease a coalition of "dominant proprietary classes."[77] Francine Frankel located sluggish growth in the stunted size of domestic markets, in turn caused by the persistent and rising inequalities in the agrarian economy.[78] Anne Kreuger argued that the complicated system of permits and quotas had over the decades opened up the possibility for rent-seeking, to which efforts and resources were expended instead of added investment.[79] Separately, these diverse explanations shed light on important aspects of India's political economy by the 1980s. Taken together, they go a long

---

[74] For a classic treatment of urban bias in developing countries, see Bates 1981.
[75] For an excellent overview of the debate, see Weiner 1986. For a contemporaneous discussion by scholars on this issue, see Varshney 1984.
[76] Chakravarty 1993, 56–57.   [77] Bardhan 1983
[78] Frankel 2005, 321, 510–514.   [79] Kreuger 1974, 293–295.

way to explaining the causes of sluggish growth, and the weaknesses of the industrial economy. Yet decreasing productivity challenged the logic of industrial promotion as a paramount interest in national development.

Another important source of challenge to private sector industrial production arrangements was increasing labor militancy. Waves of strikes were initiated by independent trade unionists – some would argue political entrepreneurs – providing new, more militant alternatives to workers increasingly displeased with the sclerotic nature of traditional unions dominated by the Congress party. In the immediate postemergency environment, the charismatic labor leader Dr. Dutta Samant led India's most industrialized state, Maharashtra, into paralysis through strike action aimed at increasing wages in response to increasing inflation.[80] Similar waves of militancy were evident in other industrial centers such as Ahmedabad and Kanpur. Samant went on to lead between 200,000 and 300,000 millworkers on an eighteen-month-long strike in Mumbai in 1982–1983. This strike ended without any agreement; more than a hundred thousand workers were fired, resigned, retired, or otherwise were not rehired.

The 1982 textile strike spelled the end of integrated mill-based textile manufacturing in Mumbai, an industry that, at the beginning of the 1980s, accounted for 15 percent of all organized employment in the country.[81] Labor agitations and work stoppages in different sectors in Mumbai and elsewhere, especially at a time when industrial productivity was stagnant, provided a set of structural challenges to an organized private sector industry already facing rising costs. These pressures together made manufacturing firms at once less reliable and more dependent on the state, at exactly the time in which the political capital available for state-supported investment was diminishing.

Changes in the International Economy

Beyond simple agreements between industry and the state, the statist development regime was predicated on a global context and a series of international institutions, mostly arising from the Bretton Woods Accords, that enabled development directed by the state. This context and these institutions supported industry at a superficial level by

[80] Rudolph and Rudolph 1987, 288.   [81] D'Monte 2002, 80–84.

financing public investments through international aid. But at a more profound level, they established a system of stability in international trade, exchange rates, and insurance mechanisms that enabled and supported long-term public and private investments.[82]

India was able to take advantage of these structures in order to pursue long-term industrialization strategies through international borrowing and thus was able to lend capital to manufacturing under far softer budget constraints than would have been possible if the government had to rely on the internal generation of resources for investment. Five Year Plans partly relied on external financing for development expenditure; by the mid-1960s, the external assistance portion of annual plan financing – consisting of grants, loans, and food aid – was fully two-thirds that of domestic budgetary resources.[83] These financial contributions from international aid were consistent with development theory and practice of the period.[84] Other structures of the Bretton Woods regime also supported statist industrial governance. The dollar-based fixed exchange rate system administered by the International Monetary Fund enabled the relatively inexpensive imports of energy, primary commodities, and capital goods. And India, even though it retained its explicit independence from great power blocs, managed economic relationships with both the United States and the USSR, though of course aid flows were subject to the vicissitudes of cold war politics.[85]

In the 1970s, however, the stability and predictability of the Bretton Woods system started to fall apart. Facing increasing inflation from government spending in the Great Society programs and the Vietnam War, Richard Nixon took the U.S. dollar off the gold standard in 1971, thus ending the dollar standard regime and starting a trend of increasingly punitive speculative bets on the values of currencies. In 1973–1974, OPEC's oil embargo increased oil prices fourfold, with

---

[82] This international regime has been described as "embedded liberalism." See Ruggie 1982.

[83] Frankel 2005, 324.

[84] Development economists argued that low-income countries could be trapped in a "savings gap," where too many people living at subsistence could not generate the savings for capital investment necessary for industrialization; foreign aid could replace these savings. See Rosenstein-Rodan 1961.

[85] For India's trade relationships between the United States and the USSR, and the ways that aid funded statist industrialization in the cold war context, see Roy 2012, 224–237.

predictable and disastrous consequences for resource-poor developing countries such as India, which had up to this point been able to rely on relatively affordable imported inputs. The oil shocks of 1973–1974 and 1979 by themselves constitute systemic exogenous shocks to India's system of statist industrial governance. The outcomes of these shocks in the form of the Latin American debt crisis, along with the policies of the Reagan and Thatcher governments, also fundamentally shifted the paradigm of international development. World Bank policy orientations shifted away from providing capital for investment to incentivizing or coercing countries to reform their economies by dismantling state enterprises and regimes of private sector promotion and control, decreasing subsidies, floating exchange rates, eliminating tariff barriers, and generally allowing market principles to govern the economy.[86]

At first, India was subject to fewer pressures for reform than states experiencing debt crises such as Brazil, Mexico, Argentina, or the Philippines, but recourse to external commercial borrowing in the 1980s led India to quadruple its debt by the end of the decade even as it contributed to greater growth through fiscal stimulus.[87] It was also by now largely unsupported by previous regimes of multilateral aid, trade, and investment that had served as crucial bulwarks to the statist development regime, just at the point in which other pressures were mounting within both the political system and the industrial economy. During Congress governments under Indira Gandhi (1980–1984) and Rajiv Gandhi (1984–1989), the Indian state struggled to maintain and incrementally reform frameworks of industrial promotion with substantially lower support from domestic coalitions and donors, and increased reliance on external loans.

Strategic partnerships with the USSR after American rapprochement with China and the Sino–Soviet split yielded some additional resources to cover the costs of development. Yet by the end of the decade, Soviet support became increasingly unreliable as the Soviet Union itself started losing its coherence. And within the commanding policy-making circles of the Indian state, technocrats were increasingly abandoning the previous generation's ideological commitments to socialist planning in favor of market mechanisms as vital tools for stability and growth. Rajiv Gandhi's own abortive attempts at liberalization were

---

[86] Kapur et al. 1997.   [87] Chandrasekhar and Ghosh 2002.

encouraged by this new generation of market-oriented and techno-cratic economic policymakers.[88]

Together, these changes fundamentally challenged the statist indus-trial governance regime. Neither the state nor its political principals could afford the policies that created an enabling environment for manufacturing in the postIndependence decades: fixed and overvalued exchange rates, trade protection, preferential access to credit through state-owned or -regulated financial institutions, or settlements and shop floor stability through Congress-affiliated trade unionism. The political pressures of the 1980s meant that liberalization in 1991 entailed a much more fundamental withdrawal of the state's regulation and pro-motion of the industrial economy.

State Intervention after Liberalization

My argument thus far hinges on the changing political incentives of state actors, from encompassing industrial governance to much more specific interventions in the economy, for electoral reasons or on behalf of particular client capitalists. At the heart of these incentives is India's increasingly competitive and fragmented political system, where polit-icians and parties at provincial and national levels must compete for support from a voting population that is prone to electoral volatility and antiincumbency.[89] To secure political support from relatively fickle voters, politicians – as both elected officials and candidates – expend resources. Such expenditures are said to lie at the heart of India's patronage-based politics.[90] Given the weaknesses of policy implementation in India and the rebalancing of power between bureaucrats and elected officials in favor of the latter, such (populist) expenditures are often concrete and are aimed at attracting interest groups with large members: poor families were promised a laptop for high school students, twenty kilograms of rice, appliances, and gold jewelry for weddings as part of a recent Tamil Nadu state election.[91] Some of these programs have an undoubtedly beneficial effect on human development, such as the Mahatma Gandhi National Rural Employment Guarantee Act (NREGA), in which landless laborers are

---

[88] Denoon 1998, 51–52; Kapur 2004; Mukherji 2013.
[89] Chhibber and Nooruddin 2008. See also Uppal 2009; Ziegfeld 2012.
[90] Chandra 2006; Wilkinson 2006.   [91] NDTV 2011.

guaranteed a hundred days of work on infrastructure, even while still targeted to gather political support.[92]

Industrialists are not a coherent interest group with large numbers, and given that they cannot effectively coerce even their increasingly informal and footloose workforces to vote in a particular direction, are unlikely to receive largesse from the state as a vital voting bloc. This is particularly the case in Indian states with constrained or declining fiscal space.[93] Whether these massive expenditures of resources are on balance good or bad for overall human and economic development is beyond the purview of this book. Yet the politics behind state spending place the majority of industrial firms at the back of a very long queue of coalition partners, core constituencies, and interest groups.

The manufacturing sector is thus unlikely to be privileged in the resources expended in the competition for votes, and thus expenditure or resources or political capital on reestablishing a framework for industrial government cannot be considered a good electoral investment. But could firms not provide resources *to* politicians in exchange for policy preference or out-and-out favors? It is undoubtedly true that certain sections of corporate India have been a major recipient of the state's policy largesse and practical wheel greasing, in return for campaign contributions and other forms of financial support.

There are two conceptual problems with this model of political–corporate exchange as it relates to industrial promotion. The first is that such exchange, when it occurs, happens between individual political actors and particular corporate groups in rent-thick sectors, specifically those with the resources and the connections to engage in the high stakes game of influence. A distinctive feature of India's industrial economy is that it is not particularly concentrated. Most industries contain large conglomerates such as Bombay Dyeing in textiles or Dr. Reddy's in pharmaceuticals but also many smaller firms that, while individually significant in production, are not large enough to command market share or have the resources individually to afford state intervention. Concentration has, moreover, decreased over time in many industries as multiindustry groups such as the Tatas and the Mafatlals either collapsed or became more focused.[94]

---

[92] De Neve and Carswell 2011; Thachil 2010.

[93] Chhibber and Nooruddin 2008, 1077–1079.

[94] Athreye and Kapur report an average Herfindal Index across twelve industries between 1970 and 1999 of 14.5 on a scale of 0 to 100, with a maximum of

While a lot has been written about formal interest representation of the corporate sector, particularly by the younger and more vibrant CII, such organizations largely present a forum in which information is disseminated rather than an effective lobby for the many, often conflicting interests of industries and sectors.[95] And, ultimately, policy formulation, even when it is affected by the mechanisms of business lobbying, often runs aground at the level of implementation by understaffed and underfunded bureaucracies and local political dynamics in areas where industry is located. As a result, the resources that the state commits to implementing policy are still crucial and diverted away from industry.

The second major conceptual problem is the limited favors the state can do for manufacturing firms in a liberalized economy, given that it no longer has the instruments to control factor markets. As a general proposition, the exchange of campaign donations for political largesse is most easily understood when the state has rents to disburse: resources or permissions that a firm needs and that the government has the power to provide. As Krueger has argued, such political goods were plentiful in the license–permit–quota raj days, when the government determined whether a firm could produce and what, what a firm could import and how much, and on what terms they could be financed.[96] After liberalization, however, the state has maintained limited capacities that would make a substantial difference to the capacities of an industrial firm, meaning that only certain firms would benefit substantially from deep alliances with the state. These are members of a category that Gandhi and Walton have defined as rent-rich sectors.[97] Licenses for utilities – telecommunications, power, gas – are one category of such goods; the receipt of a wireless telecom license is lucrative but essential for Reliance's RIM, or Tata Indicom, or Vodafone, and it is only the state that has the power to grant such a license. Relatedly, government

---

30.45 for wool textiles and a minimum of 4.3 for pharmaceuticals. See Athreye and Kapur 2006.

[95] For more on institutions of business representation, see Kohli 2011, 66–72; Sinha 2005b. Another reason to be skeptical of the influence of multiindustry confederations is that respondents, when discussing associations, almost always mentioned their own sectoral manufacturers' associations and the regional chamber of commerce; none ever mentioned CII, or the older FICCI or ASSOCHAM.

[96] Kreuger 1974.   [97] Gandhi and Walton 2012.

relationships are essential if the state has a monopsony on a class of product: military procurement, for instance.

A second important category of goods with which discrete state provision is implicated in land. For mining and mineral extraction, for commercial agriculture, or for real estate and construction, land is an important input, and one for which the state is an important agent. First, protected "forest land" is government-owned and -operated through the Union and State Ministries for Forests and thus could be removed from state control for private purposes. Many of the most important social movements over the last decade have fought against liberalizing state governments and their foreign and domestic capitalist clients over the provision of land and rights for mineral extraction in protected areas where communities have built livelihoods on and have use-rights over forest products.[98] These conflicts are particularly intense in areas of central and eastern India, where low population density and a high proportion of *adivasis*, or tribal groups, in the population coincide with concentrations of mineral wealth and the creation of new political entities – such as the states of Chattisgarh and Jharkand – in which political elites are keen on making deals for mineral extraction. These confrontations are increasingly intertwined with Maoist insurgencies and state-funded counterinsurgencies that are particularly intense in these regions.[99] A more mundane way in which the government can be important in the provision of land is that it has the organizational capacity and authority (though often contested) through eminent domain to gather private land together for the use of large-scale projects.[100] Manufacturing firms do rely on the state for land, but most factories are small relative to real estate, mining, oil refining, and other extraction activities.

The third and last category of goods held by the state that directly impacts capitalist enterprise is a set of permissions and incentives given

---

[98] For a trenchant example of such struggles, see the POSCO-India project, where the eponymous Korean conglomerate signed a memorandum of understanding with the Orissan government to build a $12 billion steel plant in Jagatsinghpur district but has been ground to a halt by a grassroots movement and environmental legal challenges, based on the Forest Rights Act of 2006. Government of India 2012.

[99] Corbridge 2002; Sundar 2006. On the politics of creation of new states, see Tillin 2011, 2013.

[100] For more on the dam project and the *Narmada Bachao Andolan* (NBA, or Save Narmada movement), see Dwivedi 1997.

to foreign companies for activity within the borders of India. As will be explained in greater detail in Chapter 6, the government still has much discretion in what activities it allows MNCs to conduct within India. A long and politically charged battle recently occurred over whether multinational retailers should be allowed to establish operations in India.[101] While India does not give as clear a preference to foreign investment as China does, several state governments – particularly Andhra Pradesh under Chandrababu Naidu, Gujarat under Narendra Modi, and Tamil Nadu under both Karunanidhi and Jayalalitha – have pursued growth strategies that involved the attraction of foreign direct investment (FDI). Yet total FDI as a proportion of India's GDP was merely 1.7 percent in 2012–2013, down from a high of 3.4 percent in 2007–2008, and thus not a dominant feature of the investment landscape.

On the whole, then, the contemporary state has few goods with which to transform the structural context of Indian manufacturing. What it can do, it does for particular client firms in industries where the particular levers of government control have a defining influence on success. For broader issues that affect the quotidian operation of the vast majority of manufacturing firms – issues including the cost and availability of key inputs such as credit, power, labor, and raw materials – the state has less general influence, and that is unlikely to change. The electoral cost–benefit calculus simply does not favor manufacturing, a corner of the economy with few voters and consequently no influence on the outcomes of elections. As a result, the Indian political system has been systematically retreating from institutional commitments to support manufacturing.

Conclusion

This chapter has surveyed the landscape of perspectives that connect the state and the industrial economy in India, before and after liberalization. I have attempted to provide a broad narrative of the politics that led to the rise of state-driven industrialization and the political coalitions that supported it. I then discussed the factors, both internal and external, that led to the profound institutional changes of liberalization that have redefined the relationship between the Indian state

[101] BBC 2012. For a critical view, see Patnaik 2012.

and the industrial economy. I ultimately argue that the neoliberal reform of the Indian economy has precluded a broad governance role for the state in regulating, supporting, and broadly promoting the manufacturing sector through controlling key factor markets.

This concrete shift has accompanied a redefinition of the meaning and ends of development away from an older focus on industrialization. But such a withdrawal of the state from driving industrial development has left us with a puzzle. If the state is no longer expending political capital on providing the institutional architecture for industrialization, then where do such necessary institutions originate? Do they originate from different state or social forms, such as state governments, sectoral agencies, or industry associations? Or are firms themselves responsible for creating the institutional environments within which they can produce?

The next three chapters explore these questions in relation to specific facets of the institutional framework necessary for manufacturing, what I call industrial governance. Chapter 4 examines the provision of capital during and after statism and explores contemporary patterns and mechanisms for firm-level financing. Chapter 5 focuses on the management of workers and particularly their recruitment, training, and retention during statism and after liberalization, looking at overall patterns and firm-level mechanisms for labor management and relations in contemporary Indian industry. And Chapter 6 explores the complex world of interactions between domestic firms and international actors.

4 | Industrial Finance after Statism in India

A core dimension – perhaps the defining aspect – of industrial governance is the acquisition and deployment of capital necessary for industrial investment. Relative to other ventures, manufacturing requires more time and accumulated funds for investment: to build a factory, buy machinery, build a workforce with the necessary skills, and coordinate capital and labor for production. For early developers such as Britain and the United States, a pool of capital was built up slowly as industry itself developed, through reinvesting profits and using public equity and debt exchanges to expand existing enterprises and develop new ones. For later developers, however, financial institutions such as industrial banks became important for concentrating the financial resources of the public and channeling these resources selectively to manufacturing enterprises.[1] In developing and postcolonial countries, the state directed this provision of capital to manufacturing through subsidized credit from regulated banks and specialized financial institutions, as a key function of statist development. This chapter examines the sources and institutional mechanisms of providing finance to manufacturing, once the state and its allied financial institutions have stopped directing capital markets and thus withdrawn from their previous roles in channeling long-term credit to industrial firms.

In India, the provision of finance to manufacturing enterprises, both public and private, laid at the very heart of development planning. Under colonial rule, finance was fragmented and most accumulated wealth accrued to expatriate companies, to be repatriated to shareholders abroad. The postcolonial state, in order to facilitate rapid industrialization, established a number of development finance institutions that would direct credit, over long time horizons at low rates of interest, to

---

[1] For a classical formulation of this argument, see Gerschenkron 1962.

industrial firms. This system, though exclusionary and heavily interventionist, provided stable expectations for firm-level investment in the production of goods as diverse as textiles to pharmaceuticals.

The process of liberalization, however, has led to the increasing marketization of finance in India; banks have converged on simple market principles rather than maintaining a commitment to long-term industrialization when allocating and pricing credit. In such an environment, industry is at a relative disadvantage compared to investments that are shorter term, more disaggregated, and perceived as more secure, from services to consumer financing. How can industrial firms arrange credit in such a way as to finance production and expansion in this environment?[2]

I contend that the two most popular extant accounts of industrial governance do not adequately explain how finance for manufacturing is organized. State governments have not taken the place of the central government in providing credit to manufacturing. As I will demonstrate, the states in India widely recognized as promoting industry do not feature firm-level investment patterns that are very different from those of other states. Further, there is not radical variation in the patterns of investment by sector, where we might expect financial institutions, multinationals, and sectoral promotion agencies to be driving sector-specific patterns of investment.

Rather, I argue that individual firms must arrange institutional relationships with sources of finance themselves. Firm-specific characteristics, such as size, international orientation, and especially age cohort, tend to do better at explaining patterns of investment than either regional or sectoral explanations. Moving from aggregate patterns to firm-specific mechanisms of arranging financing, we see some firms seeking relationships with formal financial institutions and using tactics such as diversification and signalling to secure lower costs of borrowing, while other firms avoid formal institutions altogether and instead rely on deep personal networks and an ethic of reinvestment to secure the capital necessary for production and expansion. This variation in strategy is consistent with the argument that the backgrounds and perspectives of manufacturers, in combination with certain

[2] An alternative source of financing common in developing countries is foreign direct investment (FDI). In India, however, FDI has been relatively small; net inflows as a percentage of GDP were 0.04 percent in the 1980s, 0.38 percent in the 1990s, 1.56 percent in the 2000s, and 1.7 percent in 2014.

complementary structural factors such as size, can define how firms secure financing in the absence of statist governance. In this respect, firms no longer simply operate as institution-takers in a settled environment where signals from state policy and market forces are clear, but rather seek to fashion institutional relationships with various external actors in pursuit of stable financing for manufacturing.

This chapter proceeds as follows. First, I survey the rise of statist industrial financing in India and the construction of development finance institutions to provide the credit necessary for industrial development in the postwar era. Then, I examine the policy changes that withdrew the state from directing industrial finance during liberalization in the early 1990s, and how these changes over time were expressed in firm-level data on investment behavior. Third, I explore contemporary patterns of financing through quantitative analysis of a large sample of manufacturing firms. I demonstrate that some firm-level indicators, including the age of a firm, are more consistently successful at explaining debt–capital ratios than either regional or sectoral indicators. Fourth, I use interview-based qualitative evidence to examine the mechanisms of investment in the industrial environment after statism, and describe how different firms' financing is based on institutionalized relationships with either formal financial institutions or personal networks.

The Colonial Context

At the very center of Indian nationalism in the late nineteenth and early twentieth centuries was an argument that the British Empire, as self-appointed stewards of India's great material wealth, had largely stolen or squandered it.[3] For nationalists, self-rule meant that India would regain control over its own resources and could invest those resources in activities that would lead to the development of the Indian population, rather than the further enrichment of commercial interests in Calcutta or the financiers of the City of London. Reorienting the nature of both public and private finance away from extraction and expatriation of rentier resources or primary agricultural products and toward the development of industrial capacity and self-reliance was a primary

---

[3] For more on the "Imperial Drain" thesis, see Chandra 1966.

aim of the planning apparatus, and it was a goal from which industrial capitalists benefited tremendously.

Imperial public finance before the twentieth century had been founded on the notion that for the government of India to serve its structural deficits with investment from the City of London, they would need to maintain confidence by hewing to neoclassical dogma: no barriers to trade, a silver rupee pegged to the pound sterling, and putative nonintervention by the state in the economy.[4] In reality, many of the explicit policies and implicit practices of the Indian government privileged British commercial interests over "native" business in the domestic economy. This is especially the case given India's special position in the British imperial system, as the main supplier of raw materials and nonsterling exchange with which Britain could balance trade deficits with China and the United States. Raw material exports from and imports of manufactures into India steadied sterling's value and thus maintained panimperial balance of payments.[5] As a result, indigenous capitalists seeking to invest in India could expect no trade protection from the colonial state, at least until the Great Depression challenged the balance sheet neoclassicism of its economic policies.[6]

The internationally open and internally fragmented nature of the Indian economy until the World War I meant that private capitalist investment was limited, concentrated in particular regions, and dominated by expatriate enterprises. India developed a central bank and a national currency only in 1921. Before this time, rupees issued by the government-sponsored Presidency Banks in colonial Calcutta, Bombay, and Madras were legal tender only for their respective currency circles.[7] Thus colonial economic policy enabled some forms of private investment, notably that of export-oriented British merchants and plantation owners, and discouraged others, notably indigenous manufacturing for the domestic market.

Until the 1920s, British residents concentrated around Calcutta dominated private investment, through a peculiar managerial institution called the "managing agency house," wherein several different

---

[4] These deficits were largely the result of "home charges" levied by the British for military and civil administration, and the inability of the Indian government to cover these charges solely through taxation. See Ben Zachariah, 2005, 21; Tomlinson 1982, 133–137.

[5] Bagchi 2000, 166.   [6] Zachariah 2005, 175.   [7] Bagchi 2000, 159.

enterprises were managed collectively by an agency partnership, on behalf of a larger pool of investors.[8] Managing agencies succeeded the less institutionalized British mercantile trade with roots in the East India Company and concentrated on resource extraction and the export of commodities: tea and coffee plantations, coal mines, minerals, and forest products.[9] The expatriate mercantile community, government officers, and offshore interests formed the pool of capital for financing most managing agency investments. The Presidency Banks, along with other private banking institutions, arranged only short-term lending, in the form of lines of credit or overdraft facilities. A. K. Bagchi has argued that the domination by British residents of organized banking deposits and the management of banks, together with a revolving door for managing agencies, banks, and the government, provided yet another barrier to Indian involvement in private investment.[10]

Indian private investment thus could thus only develop around the edges of and in the gaps between British capital. The first Indians to invest in manufacturing in the Bombay Presidency in western India were those who had gathered capital acting as brokers and fixers for the East India Company, British merchants, and producers of cotton and opium in the interior.[11] Indians also played subordinate roles in the trans–Indian Ocean mercantile trade and shifted their investments to domestic manufacturing when they were excluded from that trade in the middle of the nineteenth century.[12] Lastly, Gujarati banking and trading communities, called *mahajans*, established production and distribution through their own channels in the urban centers of Ahmedabad and Surat, taking advantage of the quality of raw cotton from Punjab and Sindh and opportunities for export through the Port of Bombay; a similar indigenous framework for investment formed around the Chettiar and Naidu communities in Madras Presidency.[13]

Even though Indian business started to challenge the dominance of British mercantile interests early in the twentieth century, it faced serious barriers, many of them relating to capital. The development

---

[8] Bagchi 2000, 161–165.
[9] Ibid., 164–165. The one exception to this rule was the jute textile industry that established itself in western Bengal. See Morris 1983, 566–568.
[10] Bagchi 2000, 167–169.   [11] Ibid., 181–182.   [12] Ibid., 63–67.
[13] Leadbeater 1993, 30–32.

of British Indian personal law had outlawed traditional forms of joint-family enterprise that had structured investments and managed risk. Ritu Birla has argued that these new legal frameworks both suppressed and channeled the capital of indigenous communities away from traditional structures of enterprise and into organized banking and thus investment in the British-dominated world of joint-stock companies and managing agencies.[14] Even more perniciously, poverty among the Indian population prevented saving and investment for all but the wealthiest in society, many of them British. Thus, the scarcity of indigenous capital severely circumscribed the capacities of indigenous capitalists to establish a parallel organized banking system.

The last two decades of colonial rule did see some profound changes in the economy and finances of the Indian government, which included the development of new national institutions for the management of the economy. The most important of these was the Reserve Bank of India (RBI), established in 1935; the RBI replaced the Imperial Bank of India, which had simply aggregated the Presidency Banks into one institution without gaining the statutory authority of a central bank capable of executing monetary policy. While the RBI was nominally a private institution, the Hilton–Young Commission established to create it, as well as its first governor, was influenced by emergent Keynesian thinking and thus understood its role in broader, more interventionist terms than the previous leadership of the Imperial Bank.[15] Of course, even though the newly established RBI held some promise in reforming a deliberately underdeveloped monetary and financial system, it lay over a complex web of banks and other financial institutions committed to an older vision of the colonial economy.

The decade preceding Indian independence transformed the institutional foundations of the economy. Defense requirements brought on by the World War II greatly increased India's fiscal responsibilities and led to the institution of a comprehensive framework of price and quantitative controls and thus the building up of bureaucracies of economic regulation.[16] Wartime pressures led to inflation, particularly in foodstuffs, which persisted several years after independence. The new state institutions regulating India's economy were thus faced with the challenge of achieving balances in domestic prices and external

[14] Birla 2008. See also Bagchi 1985.   [15] Raj 1948.
[16] Tomlinson 1993, 160–167.

accounts in an atmosphere of great uncertainty. This context simultaneously created solid precedents for state involvement in stabilizing the monetary economy and facilitated investments that could aid in rehabilitating economic activity.

Of course, a central goal of the nationalist movement, particularly the Nehruvian wing, was the creation of a national space, both as a set of ideas and as a set of national institutions, that differed fundamentally from the British notion of India as a multitude of separate entities with no unifying structure.[17] Moving away from the fragmented economy of the colonial period to a unified one focused on the rapid development of the country involved the creation and development of national institutions with this new purpose in mind.

Industrial Finance under Statist Development

Statist development after independence, at its core, involved public institutions that gathered capital together in a regulated fashion for industrial investment. From the perspective of private sector industrial capitalists, state-directed industrial investment and the new financing regime were largely constructive, because the nature and terms of development financing helped their own investments in addition to those of the public sector. State-directed capital was particularly welcome given the withdrawal of the largely expatriate private capital in the managing agency system, as the agents of British finance sold off industrial concerns such as jute mills, mines, and tea plantations to Indian companies and fled the country, thus removing the major sources of capitalist investment in the preindependence era.[18] With the departure of mercantile capital, Indian industry faced chronic shortages of finance, reflecting a poor country with fragmented markets and a preponderance of subsistence agriculture. Given this environment, banks and development finance institutions needed to step in and do the work of aggregating capital from a thousand hidden corners and supplying it in consolidated amounts for industrial projects.

In order to establish this regime, the postindependence Indian state, once solidly free of colonial control, set about establishing deep reforms in the character and roles of the financial economy. One of

[17] M. Goswami 2004.   [18] Tomlinson 1981; O. Goswami 1989.

the first steps undertaken by the government, in 1949, was to nationalize the still nominally private Reserve Bank, taking the RBI away from any influence of shareholders and placing it squarely under the ambit of government policy. This change in ownership oriented the RBI's long-term goals toward the larger common purpose articulated by the Congress party of enabling rapid industrialization. The Banking Companies Act of 1949 (later renamed the Banking Regulation Act) established the statutory framework through which the RBI could regulate and supervise the commercial banking sector. This supervision included placing limitations on nonbanking business activities, establishing reserve requirements, and mandating that a certain proportion of credit be extended for developmental purposes.

Under the RBI framework, the Indian state established new agencies and repurposed others in the service of this new developmentalist agenda. In 1955, the RBI acquired the remaining assets of the Imperial Bank of India, establishing the State Bank of India (SBI). In 1959, the SBI took over the assets of eight banks of former princely states as subsidiaries, thus creating the largest commercial bank in India, and one owned by the state through the Reserve Bank. To facilitate financing for new and expanding industrial development projects, a number of specialist agencies – development finance institutions – were set up under the aegis of the RBI, and drawing on assets held by the central bank through the Statutory Liquidity Ratio (SLR). These included the Industrial Finance Corporation of India (IFCI), set up in 1948; the Industrial Credit and Investment Corporation of India (ICICI), established in 1955; and State Financial Corporations that were amalgamated into the Industrial Development Bank of India (IDBI) in 1964; as well as state industrial development corporations and a number of other more specialized lending organizations.

All of these agencies served the purpose of directing long-term credit or short-term advances at concessional rates to infrastructure and large-scale industrial development projects. These projects included both public and private concerns. A senior official at ICICI during this period considered building up an entrepreneurial base in Indian industry to be "even more important than helping to augment production ... ultimately, the 'release of creativity' of the people can influence significantly the course of economic life of a country."[19] In 1966, during the high

[19] Parekh 1980.

watermark of statism, IDBI estimated that during the third Five Year Plan, development finance institutions would provide Rs. 307.9 crores (roughly $410.5 million in 1966 dollars) for projects, or 25 percent of total private sector investment during this period.[20] These agencies became even more important in regulating financing for industry after the "decontrol" of a range of industries in the mid-1960s, allowing even more private sector investment directed by the state.[21] Moreover, development finance agencies were responsible for disbursing scarce foreign exchange to both public and private sector enterprises, allowing firms to import capital goods, technology, and raw materials. This responsibility placed development finance institutions squarely in the middle of transactions between domestic firms and the international economy.

By the 1960s, development finance agencies received aid denominated in foreign exchange directly from donor agencies. In 1966, three-quarters of ICICI's loan portfolio was from foreign exchange loans, sourced from more than $182 million in aid from the World Bank, the German Kreditanstalt, and USAID.[22] The foreign aid component of development financing was particularly crucial because of increasing deficits in development budgets, caused by limited penetration of formal banking into the rural economy and the inability to tax agricultural land.[23] Other sources of capital for industrial investment included the life insurance industry – nationalized by the Life Insurance Corporation (LIC) Act of 1956 – postal savings, agricultural cooperative banks, and mandatory social insurance programs of organized sector firms, all of which involved capital invested on behalf of the Indian population. Thus, Indian insurance customers, workers, farmers, and traders, along with official aid assistance from donor countries and multilateral agencies, financed India's industrialization. Such "patient" capital would be invested for years and yield low but steady returns, to be reinvested to continue industrialization.

Interestingly, lending by development finance institutions and publicly owned banks such as the SBI dwarfed direct spending on development from the state.[24] The preeminence of bank lending over state

---

[20] *Economic and Political Weekly* 1966.
[21] *Economic and Political Weekly* 1967.
[22] *Economic and Political Weekly* 1968.   [23] Frankel 2005, 552.
[24] In the Second Plan (1956–1961), institutional lending, including foreign credits disbursed through DFIs, amounted to Rs. 130 crores, or $173 million, and direct

spending meant that even though development finance institutions followed government priorities by lending to the public sector, the private sector was never completely shut out or even particularly neglected. The managers of development finance institutions could channel credit to any private sector concern with sufficient viability and potential to increase long-term industrial capacity at the same rate and on the same terms as the public sector. At the high watermark of public sector involvement in the economy before Nehru's death in 1964, the private sector investment portion of the third Five Year Plan was 44 percent of the total planned investment, which would continue to rise as the public sector outlay fell.[25]

Once an industrial license was granted, a textile, chemical, or engineering firm was virtually guaranteed long-term, low-cost financing to build a factory, acquire capital goods and raw materials, and recruit and train personnel. This firm would acquire its raw materials either abroad or from upstream enterprises that were subject to the same certainties, and would sell intermediary goods to firms subject to the same arrangements or final products in sheltered consumer markets.[26] And if companies faced difficulties, as with "sick" companies in the 1970s and 1980s, development finance institutions could exercise large amounts of discretion in assisting firms and even entire industries.[27]

Such a network of protection virtually guaranteed much higher consumer prices, and thus prioritized producer stability over consumer freedom and choice. The Indian state supported industrial producers to the exclusion of the interests of consumers because the long-term goal was the establishment of industrial self-sufficiency. While this structure of investment constricted individual buying power and arguably placed limits on innovation that occurs as the result of competition for markets, it did allow for industrialists to invest in long-term projects without fear of capital taking flight or massive swings in its costs. In other words, the development finance system – and behind it, the

loan participation from central and state governments amounted to only Rs. 20 crores, or $27 million. Government of India 1956, chapter 26.

[25] Frankel 2005, 240.

[26] For seminal work on the consequences of "effective protection" on the financing of industrial projects in India, see Srinivasan and Bhagwati 1978.

[27] Statutory guidelines for this type of intervention were provided in the Sick Industrial Companies Act, 1985. http://business.gov.in/closing_business/sica.php, accessed September 12, 2012.

state – used its resources to guarantee industrial investments, providing the certainty that allowed firms to invest with confidence and over the long term.

The financing regime of statist development evolved over the decades after the initial reforms setting up structures of banking and agencies of development finance. During the 1960s, the RBI further rationalized the banking sector through a policy of consolidation in which more than two hundred banks were liquidated or merged. Depositors were protected from bank failure through the introduction of deposit insurance. And various attempts were made to extend organized finance in the countryside, including the introduction of the Agricultural Refinance Corporation and a policy of extending bank branches to underserved areas. This reflected the feeling on the part of economic planners that the unreformed institutional structures of the agrarian sector were to blame for chronic deficits, shortage of resources, and – by the end of the decade – inflation.[28]

The late 1960s and early 1970s reflected the end of the supremacy and political autonomy of the Planning Commission. Congress governments after Nehru faced increasing difficulties in resisting external pressures while managing greater domestic demands. Because of the government's leverage over the financial sector through the RBI, Indira Gandhi's most populist politics were directed at the structures of private finance. In 1968, with India facing a balance of payments crisis following droughts and foreign aid embargoes, the government imposed a system of controls on banks to ensure that loan practices were in alignment with the "priorities of the country." The RBI and the Indira Gandhi government established the National Credit Council to determine a productive allocation of capital. In 1969, as part of the *gharibi hatao* [eliminate poverty] campaign, Indira Gandhi nationalized fourteen major commercial banks "to serve better the needs of development of the economy in conformity with national policy objectives."[29]

The 1970s were consumed with containing a war with Pakistan, the fallout from the oil crisis, and persistent drought conditions, which caused runaway inflation and forced the government to restrain and

---

[28] Frankel 2005, 321.
[29] www.rbi.org.in/scripts/chro_1968.aspx, accessed August 20, 2012. See also Torri 1975.

rationalize lending.[30] The Twenty Point economic program of Indira Gandhi's Emergency regime included the standing policy of extending credit to underserved populations, but the thrust of the politics of the Emergency aimed at direct provision of services to the poor, and, thus, financial policies took a back seat.[31] The decade came to a close with the Congress party and Indira Gandhi back in power after the Janata coalition government, and thus (largely unsuccessful) attempts at further implementation of policies on rural development and the extension of organized banking to underserved areas and populations.

Measures to liberalize the banking sector began in the mid-1980s, under Rajiv Gandhi's Congress government. The Iranian revolution in 1979 sent world oil prices, and thus domestic inflation, soaring and heralded further world economic contraction. In India, government borrowing increased to cope with energy costs, thus further adding to inflationary pressures. Foreign currency controls and overvalued exchange rates in India were increasingly put under pressure by the abundance of foreign capital flows, particularly in the Middle East, which was increasingly integrated with South Asia through remittances.[32] As a result, large amounts of money, in rupees and foreign currency, left the control of the organized economy and entered the black market for goods and services.

Further, the Bretton Woods institutions and bilateral donors such as the United States were, after the Reagan revolution and the debt crises of the early 1980s, much less willing to provide the low-cost, long-term official development loans that had been key to financing industrial development.[33] The RBI and the government had to address these issues, but increasingly the intellectual trends within public and financial policy pointed toward solutions that involved de facto dismantling of the structures of development finance and the introduction of market mechanisms.[34] Manmohan Singh, the architect of the 1991 reforms, became governor of the central bank in 1982, and under his tenure, the RBI gave banks permission to undertake a wider range of lending activities. In 1985, the Chakravarty Committee was set up to examine the reform of the monetary system; its recommendations included a policy of inflation targeting, credit budgeting, and more

---

[30] For more on the Tandon Committee report that recommended these changes, see Shankar 1982.
[31] Frankel 2005, ch. 13.   [32] Weiner 1982; Roy 2012, 235–237.
[33] Kapur et al. 1997, 23–27   [34] Kapur 2004; Mukherji 2013.

flexible, and more market-influenced, interest rates, even while it attempted to reform rather than dismantle the structures of development financing.[35] By the mid-1980s, reform of the banking and financial sector was inevitable, given the combination of pressures on the current system and the changing attitudes toward market orientation as a solution to these problems.

Any assessment of the economy during the period between the mid-1960s and the mid-1980s has to include the fact that India suffered prolonged periods of inflation, macroeconomic instability, and fiscal crisis. Macroeconomic reform seemed inevitable given the increasing inability of the state to implement its programs and thus effectively manage a partly planned economy under increasingly severe constraints.[36] Throughout this period, however, the state and the banking system prioritized stabilizing finance for private sector manufacturing. Reform of the structure of public and private finance did not necessarily have to mean that the state and the central bank forgo all commitments to direct capital to industrial development, but the nature of liberalization meant that industrial firms have faced an increasingly competitive and unpredictable environment for the acquisition of industrial finance.

The End of Statist Industrial Finance and Current Challenges

Even though policy changes in the 1980s presaged reform, the most profound shifts of the financial system occurred with the wave of liberalization policies in 1991. In April of that year, following the oil shock caused by the Persian Gulf War, India faced a balance of payments crisis. As a condition of the IMF structural adjustment program, the country was obligated first to devalue and then to float the exchange rate, and drastically decrease government borrowing. The Indian government, instead of simply acquiescing to IMF demands while keeping other institutions in place, used this crisis as an opportunity to implement widespread market reforms in the financial economy. These reforms had the objective of both permanently reducing government and central bank obligations and providing greater opportunities to private sector investors, particularly nonresident Indians.

[35] For more on the committee's recommendations, see India International Center 1996.
[36] For a theoretical formulation of the link between macroeconomic instability and market reforms, see Huang 1994.

The 1991 reforms arose out of tensions within the system, including the rise of new interest group claimants on state resources, and opportunities for forging new ties with cosmopolitan financial capital, to the relative exclusion of domestic industrial capital. As Rob Jenkins noted, this was "reform by stealth," in which the most far-reaching reforms were implemented in areas not subject to democratic contestation.[37] The finance ministry and the RBI were together able to transform the institutions and orientation of the financial sector over a relatively short period.

The wholesale reform of the banking sector was implemented on the basis of the recommendations of two expert committees, both chaired by the former RBI governor M. Narasimhan, in 1991 and 1998, as a number of other policy changes made by the Ministry of Finance and the RBI. In 1993, the RBI issued guidelines for the establishment of private sector banks that could explicitly compete with publicly owned banks. In 1994, nationalized banks were permitted to participate in private capital markets to strengthen their liquidity base, and bank-lending rates were deregulated. That same year, a number of development finance institutions, notably ICICI and the Housing Development Finance Corporation (HDFC), established wholly owned commercial banking subsidiaries. The Narasimhan II Committee of 1998 recommended the phasing out of institutional segregation between development finance and commercial banking, and the establishment of "universal banks," which could participate in commercial and investment banking. IDBI was also converted from a development finance institution to a commercial bank through the IDBI Act of 2003, and the SBI has similarly undergone an effective privatization; thus the largest commercial bank in India now operates solely on market principles.[38]

The Narasimhan II Committee recommendations also permitted foreign banks to establish subsidiaries that would be treated on par with domestic public and private institutions. Since 1998, a number of foreign banks, including HSBC and Citibank, have offered a full range

---

[37] Jenkins 1999.

[38] To quote from the SBI Web site: "The two hundred year old Public Sector behemoth is today stirring out of its Public Sector legacy and moving with an agility to give the Private and Foreign Banks a run for their money ... the elephant has indeed started to dance." www.sbi.co.in/user.htm, accessed August 20, 2012.

of banking deposit and lending facilities. The result of all of these reforms has been that over the last decade, both bank lending and the capital and securities market have been governed according to market principles and not by state institutions driven by developmental objectives. Further, the strategies and practices of nominally government-owned banks, such as the SBI or the Bank of Baroda, facing competition have broadly converged on market principles, in line with new private banks such as Axis or Kotak Mahindra and with foreign banks.

One might expect that private sector industrial firms would welcome such an orientation toward the market and away from credit rationing and the planned economy. Indeed, the sheer amount of capital available under the contemporary marketized credit regime dwarfs what was available under the credit-constrained statist period.[39] Political connections required for receiving industrial licenses are no longer necessary for access to institutional capital, and there are multiple routes for financing, from loans from several categories of banks to the stock and bond markets and private equity.

Beyond the largest multiindustry conglomerates such as the Tata Group or Reliance Industries, however, manufacturing is considered risky relative to other types of investment. This perception of risk is not without reason: a McKinsey report in 2012 suggested that, of India's top thousand manufacturing firms, 54 percent had an average cost of capital that exceeded the return on investment.[40] Further, international credit rating agencies only rate corporations big enough to issue bonds on international markets; domestic credit rating agencies have only recently emerged and rely on much the same information as banks do. In a recent interview, the chairman of the SBI stated loan preferences that explicitly shifted away from medium and small enterprises, and toward "low risk, low reward" loans, consistently mentioning loans to Indian Oil as an objective: "The bigger challenges are in the SMEs and mid-corporate segments. That is why our non-performing asset numbers went up substantially. But we think we are over the hump. Home and car loans have seen a

---

[39] Bank deposits alone stand at Rs. 3,830,922 crore (US$693.4 billion) in 2008–09, as opposed to Rs. 5,910 crore (US$1.07 billion) in 1970–71.
[40] Dhawan et al. 2012.

good growth trajectory."[41] There are two major reasons for this. First, demand for manufactured goods in domestic and export markets tends to be more volatile and goods themselves more substitutable than, say, utilities or foodstuffs. Second, industrial enterprises, being more complex, are at higher risk from problems in the supply of inputs, from power to labor shortages and industrial action. In fact, a FICCI survey of industries reported that for manufacturers, the highest reported risk was that of "strikes, closures and unrest."[42] As I will argue in Chapter 5, the state and its allied institutions have withdrawn from arranging some certainty for labor, through tripartite consultation with business associations and trade unions.

All but the largest industrial firms face higher interest rates because of this perception of risk. Such risk premiums are completely rational for banks and financial institutions, even though they lead to under-investment in economic activities with a long-term potential for increased employment and stimulation for upstream and downstream industries. Higher costs of borrowing can lead to a catch-22, in which firms struggling with higher interest rates are even more vulnerable to the demand and supply shocks that created risk in the first place. The competition for capital and the perception of higher risk for manu-facturing present manufacturers with a challenge. Some, certainly, might follow these market signals and leave industry altogether. Given that manufacturing has grown at a healthy rate over the last two decades, however, we need to understand how firms that remain in production have been able to secure finance.

There are, in practice, two types of sources for capital. The first is the formal financial sector, in the form of government-owned, private, or foreign banks and emergent markets for bonds and equity. These have the advantage of being fairly transparent, but manufacturing firms face the disadvantages indicated in terms of discrimination against long-term investments and thus higher cost. The second is family and community investment, as well as the reinvestment of returns. These financial strategies enable enterprises to avoid the formal sphere of debt and interest, but might present real constraints on the ability to grow quickly to take advantage of market opportunities.

---

[41] Kumar and Vageesh 2003.
[42] Federation of Indian Chambers of Commerce and Industry 2013, 9.

Interestingly, the stock market does not seem to be a major source of industrial investment. It is true that securities exchanges have developed rapidly over the last two decades and have been subject to effective regulation, especially in comparison to other emerging economies.[43] Yet companies publicly listed in the various stock exchanges that derive capital from the sale of equity are either well-established conglomerates that might use capital injection to move into new sectors, such as Reliance Industries and the consumer grocery business, or banks, utilities, and the domestic offshoots of multinationals. There are two separate reasons for this. First, the actively investing portion of the public tends to look upon manufacturing in the same way as the banks do, as a more uncertain enterprise than financial corporations or utilities. Lower sale prices of equity in manufacturing through public offerings, analogous to risk premiums on bank loans to industry, reflect this preference. Second, manufacturers themselves tend to be committed to keeping managerial control of their firms through equity ownership; some even seek to avoid the reporting requirements involved with being listed. Companies are also averse to giving out returns as dividends, when they can be reinvested. Thus, financing industrial growth through the sale of equity is not a guaranteed possibility for any but the most established conglomerates, even though, as I detail later, many firms do choose to conduct public offerings.

Debt-Capital Ratios as an Indicator

An important and well-recognized indicator of firm behavior with regard to sources of capital is the extent to which a firm is able to use debt effectively to finance their production and expansion. A high ratio of debt to (equity) capital indicates a willingness and ability to secure loans in the service of production and growth. A low ratio, by contrast, would indicate that capital was derived from other sources, including reinvestment and family and community investment. Many firms, in fact, do not borrow at all as a matter of principle or policy, and thus have a ratio of zero.

This measure also has a great deal of political salience. The provision of credit is the primary means by which the state, in the form of either state-directed banks or specialized agencies at the national or regional

[43] Rudolph 2002.

levels, conducts industrial promotion.[44] Higher average ratios and a closer dispersion around these averages might plausibly indicate state involvement in credibly directing or facilitating credit to manufacturing. Similarly, higher averages and less dispersion in any Indian state, such as Gujarat, or any manufacturing sector, such as pharmaceuticals, might indicate that a state or sector is credibly providing access to credit for firms under its jurisdiction. By contrast, patterns of investment based on firm-level characteristics suggest that the governance of finance is driven not by regional or sectoral pressures but by decisions by manufacturers in combination with structural factors such as size.

In the next section, I will examine the broad patterns of firm-level investment. By looking at debt–capital ratios over the approximately eight thousand firms in the CMIE Prowess dataset in 2008, and a shadow set of approximately two thousand firms just before liberalization, we can see whether there has indeed been any aggregate shift in firm behavior with regard to investment. Examining the 2008 dataset by state, region, and a series of firm-level indicators will enable us to compare the relative influence of state governments, sectoral dynamics, and firm level indicators in explaining firms' debt–capital ratios. Because of the preponderance of both high values and zeroes in the data, in what follows I have employed a modification of the base-10 logarithm to present the ratios: I add 1 to the ratio, and then take the log. In this new scale, a ratio of 0 is 0, a ratio of 0.5 is 0.176, a ratio of 1:1 (parity between equity and debt) is 0.3, a ratio of 2:1 is 0.47, a ratio of 3:1 is 0.60, and so on. I present multivariate models of these results in Appendix A.

Patterns of Finance: Changes over Time

In this section, I compare aggregate debt–capital ratios in 2008 with those in the years preceding liberalization. If my argument is correct, we should see both a lower average and a wider dispersion during the second period, as the state steadily withdraws from guaranteeing credit for manufacturing firms across India.

---

[44] Other activities, such as providing land, upgrading capital machinery, or providing duty drawback to exporters, may be important in special cases, but these are less common or meaningful to a broad range of manufacturing than subsidizing and guaranteeing credit. For more, see discussion in the Introduction.

Table 4.1 *Comparison of Log Debt–Capital Ratios, Preliberalization and 2008*

	Mean	Standard error	95% C.I.	T-statistic	p-value
1988–1991	.751	.006	.736–.765	18.6	>.0001
2008	.575	.007	.548–.563		

Note: Satterthwaite's degrees of freedom for unequal variances: 5001

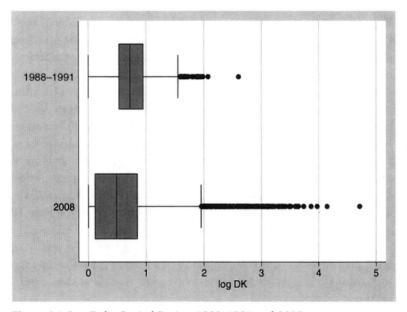

Figure 4.1 Log Debt-Capital Ratios, 1988–1991 and 2008.

Figure 4.1 clearly shows that ratios were both higher on average and less dispersed in 1988–1991 than in 2008. Table 4.1 represents a comparative analysis of group means.

Table 4.1 shows that the means of the log ratios, corresponding to normal debt–capital ratios of just less than 4.6 and 2.8, respectively, represent statistically significant differences. The direction of the difference and the differences in the standard deviations are consistent with our expectations: before liberalization, the state credibly directed long-term credit to manufacturing, and so we would expect both higher debt relative to capital and greater convergence around that ratio. After liberalization and the withdrawal of the state from directing credit to manufacturing, we see a decline in the average ratio but also a much greater variation in these ratios, reflecting a greater divergence of financing strategies among manufacturing firms. How can we account for this variation?

Patterns of Finance after Liberalization

State Governments

It is possible that differences in the policy frameworks of state governments are driving the variation in debt–capital ratios, following Aseema Sinha's logic of sub-national developmental states.[45] States with active and influential policies of industrial promotion, such as Gujarat, would contain firms that would have, on average, higher debt–capital ratios and lower dispersion than other less successful states, for two reasons. First, state governments might be explicitly arranging credit for manufacturing firms through specialized lending agencies or regulated banks, analogous to the activities of the preliberalization central state. Second, the state's policy frameworks might create a more diffuse enabling environment that might inspire firms with enough confidence to take on debt in the service of expansion. Figure 4.2 and Table 4.2 represent the variation in log debt–capital ratios by Indian state in 2008.

In Table 4.2, only Maharashtra and Tamil Nadu have means significantly above the "other states" excluded category. Maharashtra, with some of the oldest firms in the country and the sheer number of firms based there (fully a quarter of the sample), may be significant as a result of other factors. Gujarat, in particular, is a surprise; mean log debt–capital ratios are lower than that of the lackluster West Bengal. This, at the very least, calls into question the idea that the Gujarati state is enabling investment through formal mechanisms and suggests that a significant number of Gujarati industrialists are relying on personal networks rather than formal institutions for financing. Further, Figure 4.2 shows that the more industrialized states in India, with the possible exception of Punjab, all exhibit a good deal of variation in their firms' debt–capital ratios. This constitutes suggestive evidence against the notion that state governments are driving convergence through

[45] Sinha 2005.

Table 4.2 *Comparison of Log Debt-Capital Ratios, by State*

	Mean	Standard error	95% C.I.	$F_{1,8411}$	p-value
Delhi and Haryana	.549	.017	.516–.582	0.02	.881
Maharashtra	**.604**	**.013**	**.579–.628**	**10.38**	**.001**
Tamil Nadu	**.641**	**.020**	**.602–.682**	**18.86**	**>.0001**
Gujarat	.518	.018	.483–.553	2.25	.134
West Bengal	.584	.018	.548–.619	2.14	.144
Other states	.552	.010	.533–.571	Excluded	Excluded

Note: One-way ANOVA, root MSE: .547, R^2: .004. Statistically significant results are in bold

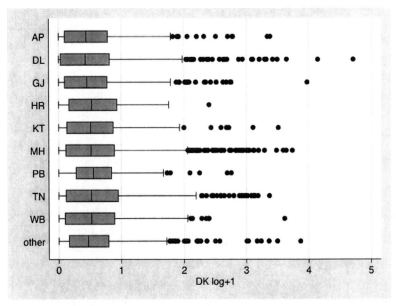

Figure 4.2 Log Debt-Capital Ratios, by State.

either explicit promotion through the allocation of credit or more implicitly through the creation of a conducive environment for investment.

Industries

The political economy of trade and global value chain analysis would argue that different industries face different pressures from globalization

Table 4.3 *Comparison of Log Debt-Capital Ratios, by Industry*

	Mean	Standard error	95% C.I.	$F_{1,8412}$	p-value
Textiles	.706	.017	.673–.739	60.94	>.0001
Garments	.576	.031	.515–.638	.46	.495
Autos and Components	.694	.022	.652–.737	31.96	>.0001
Pharmaceuticals	.572	.025	.523–.620	.72	.397
Other industries	.549	.007	.535–.563	Excluded	Excluded

Note: One-way ANOVA, root MSE: .556, R^2: .01

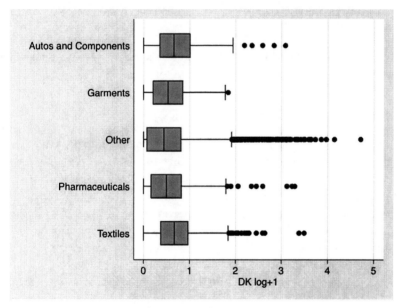

Figure 4.3 Log Debt-Capital Ratios, by Industry.

and may be supported or protected by the state in different ways. Further, sector-specific promotional agencies and associations may be (variably) effective in supporting their client firms. In order to see whether these influences indeed drive outcomes at the firm level, I disaggregate the sample by industry. Figure 4.3 and Table 4.3 represent the variation in log debt–capital ratios by industry in 2008.

Table 4.3 represents significant differences for textiles and vehicles and automotive components in relation to other industries. This is surprising: textile concerns, as India's oldest industry, share little in common with the automotive sector. Capital intensity might explain some differences here, as the manufacture of yarn is more capital-intensive, at least, than apparel manufacture, but the auto and pharma sectors are both technology- and capital-intensive. Further, while the oldest textile concerns were buckling under debt, most of these mills were transferred to the public sector under the auspices of the National Textile Corporation and thus are excluded from the sample. However, the fact that a higher proportion of textile firms had been active before the collapse of statism might indicate a greater sectoral allegiance to formal finance, as a legacy of former practices. Automotive component and vehicle manufacturers are, more than most other sectors, integrated into GVCs, as I will discuss more in Chapter 6. Regardless, Figure 4.3 represents a great deal of variation around the mean for all sectors, and thus suggests little convergence at the sector level.

Firm-Level Characteristics: Age Cohort

Apart from the influence of state governments and sectoral dynamics, there are some firm-level indicators that might drive firm financing strategies. The first is the age cohort of a firm. As I argue in Chapter 2, the age of a firm can be used as a rough proxy for the influences of manufacturers' perspectives and backgrounds. A firm born within a particular era of India's political economy develops initial strategies and practices based on that era; we would expect these strategies and practices to be sticky, absent transformational crisis. Thus, we might expect that the perspectives of the directors of a firm incorporated in 1957, at the height of Nehruvian statism, would be different from those of a firm incorporated in 1994, when the state's retreat and promarket reforms might engender suspicion of formal institutions. Of course, there are undoubtedly many exceptions to this general rule, but the task here is to see whether age cohort, and thus indirectly perspectives and backgrounds, influences a firm's financing strategies. Figure 4.4 and Table 4.4 report log debt–capital ratios by the age cohort of firms. I have established the 1971–1990 cohort as the excluded category because it represents transitional decades between the statist and postliberalization eras.

Both Table 4.4 and Figure 4.4 indicate significant differences in average log debt–capital ratios between firms' age cohorts. Firms

Table 4.4 *Comparison of Log Debt-Capital Ratios, by Age Cohort*

	Mean	Standard error	95% C.I.	$F_{1,8347}$	*p*-value
Before 1950	.785	.025	.735–.834	66.28	>.0001
1951–1970	.719	.022	.677–.762	35.11	>.0001
1971–1990	.577	.009	.560–.593	Excluded	Excluded
Post-1991	.524	.009	.506–.542	16.26	.0001

Note: One-way ANOVA, root MSE: .544, R^2: .02

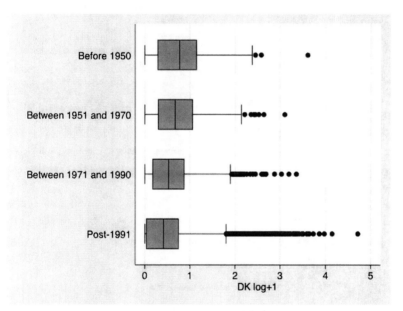

Figure 4.4 Log Debt-Capital Ratios, by Incorporation Age of Firm.

established in or before 1950 and those incorporated during the period of high statism have significantly higher debt-to-capital ratios than those established in the seventies and eighties, as well as those established after liberalization in 1991.

Firm-Level Characteristics: Size

The size of a firm can be understood as a structural constraint, at least in the short term. Small firms are unlikely to receive credit from formal financial institutions, while large firms might need loans, at minimum,

Table 4.5 *Comparison of Log Debt-Capital Ratios, by Size Decile*

	Mean	Standard error	95% C.I.	$F_{1,8400}$	p-value
1st Decile	1.013	.025	.965–1.062	399.57	>.0001
2nd Decile	.862	.016	.831–.894	291.52	>.0001
3rd Decile	.725	.014	.697–.753	127.43	>.0001
4th Decile	.620	.013	.594–.646	43.96	>.0001
5th Decile	.544	.015	.513–.574	10.03	.0015
6th Decile	.469	.018	.434–.503	Excluded	Excluded
7th Decile	.477	.023	.432–.522	.09	.7584
8th Decile	.327	.018	.291–.363	29.94	>.0001
9th Decile	.313	.020	.274–.351	36.17	>.0001
10th Decile	.185	.014	.157–.212	119.09	>.0001

Note: One-way ANOVA, root MSE: .499, R^2: .17

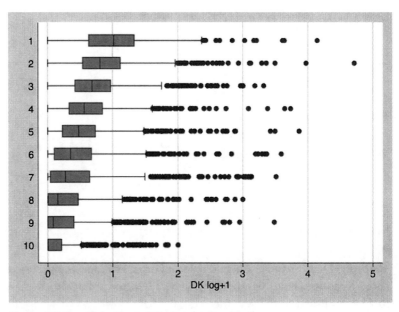

Figure 4.5 Log Debt-Capital Ratios, by Size Decile.

to bridge gaps between production costs and returns. Figure 4.5 and Table 4.5 report debt–capital ratio by CMIE size deciles.

Both the table and the figure demonstrate that firm size has a powerful, significant impact on debt–capital ratios. This suggests that the smaller a firm is, the more likely it is to make use of institutions and practices other than formal finance.

Firm-Level Characteristics: Export Orientation

Export orientation is another firm-level characteristic that, at least over the short and medium terms, might structurally influence a firm's financing. Any government incentives such as duty drawback are channeled through banks, and foreign partners might expect evidence of some commitments to formality. Figure 4.6 and Table 4.6 report log debt–capital ratios for firms at different levels of exports.

Interestingly, while there is a significant difference between firms with at least some exports and those that produce entirely for domestic markets, differences between different levels of export business are less evident. As I will discuss in Chapter 6, this might reflect the different meanings of export orientation for firms.

As I have demonstrated and further elaborate in Appendix A, firm-level characteristics are stronger explanatory factors for the variation in industrial financing strategies (proxied by debt–equity capital ratios)

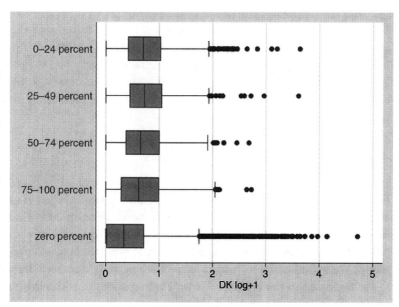

Figure 4.6 Log Debt-Capital Ratios, by Percentage Exports.

Table 4.6 *Comparison of Log Debt-Capital Ratios, by Percentage Exports*

	Mean	Standard error	95% C.I.	$F_{1,8400}$	*p*-value
Zero percent	.481	.008	.466–.496	Excluded	Excluded
Less than 24%	.740	.010	.719–.760	341.80	>.0001
25–49%	.769	.023	.725–.814	125.13	>.0001
50–74%	.723	.029	.667–.779	56.89	>.0001
76–100%	.683	.029	.626–.740	42.71	>.0001

One-way ANOVA, root MSE: .533, R^2: .05

than either states or sectors. In terms of regional governments, only Tamil Nadu seems particularly distinctive with regard to higher debt–capital ratios; firms in Tamil Nadu seem more able and willing to finance growth through debt than other firms. For sectoral regimes, textiles and vehicles and automotive components have higher than average ratios for all sectors. Yet financing strategy differs most dramatically by firm-level characteristics – firm age cohort, size decile, and export cohort – suggesting that variation is most easily explained at the firm level.

Aggregate patterns do not help us understand manufacturers' specific and concrete strategies in the acquisition of capital. These mechanisms are important because they illuminate how industrialists work around the financing challenges of the postliberalization environment. In the following, I present some interview-based accounts of how some arrange financing through engagement with formal institutions, while others rely on personal and community networks and reinvestment for production and growth.

Acquiring Finance through Formal Rules

In India, the modal arrangement for institutional financing required firms to put up between less than a quarter and a third of their own equity for any project, with banks – upon verification of the firm's capabilities – lending two-thirds to more than three-quarters at variable rates of interest. Given the commonness of these funding arrangements, many industrialists with diverse backgrounds discussed their firm's financing in these terms. A textile manufacturer in Mumbai, a commodities trader turned mill owner in 1977, mentioned financing through "long term loans from the SBI, at 80 percent debt, 20 percent equity" (2008-mmb32). An apparel producer in Delhi, from a cloth manufacturing family in Haryana, said he received financing "through banks, and some of your own [capital]. 30 percent [is] ours, 70 percent the banks. The terms are OK" (2007-del39); another private limited company in Mumbai maintained 40 percent own capital, 60 percent through loans from the Bank of Baroda (2008-mmb22). A pharmaceutical manufacturer in Chennai, a former banker who entered manufacturing in 1989, when discussing financing, said that "the promoters bring in 20–33 percent, but mostly banks lend 77–80 percent. The margin is 20–33 percent. Now we are with a new [private] bank – Centurion Bank – from the SBI" (2007-chn7). A Pune based auto components manufacturer said, "To get financing we talk to banks ... we have 70–75 percent debt" (2008-pun6). At the heart of this relationship is the bank's assessment of the firm's ability to repay the loan, which in turn relates to whether the concern is known among the business community. A Ludhiana-based textile concern, started by steel traders and consignment agents for Tata Steel from the 1970s, mentioned that "we get cheapest rate of interest because we are well-rated" (2007-lud2). A Delhi manufacturer, from an old industrial family that started manufacturing by taking over an expatriate concern in the same industry at independence, said of a recent bank loan, "We directly approached them; we are known as business family ... they approved" (2007-del24).

Diversification Strategies

Even firms with a reliance on banks for financing their activities are skeptical of the ways that banks treat industry. One Gurgaon-based and IIT-educated composite textile manufacturer, the head of an old Marwari firm that started textile mills in the area in 1960, was less than sanguine about bankers, from his perspective as a firm to which banks do wish to lend:

To grow, you can't just have your own profits, you must borrow. Banks, they are misbehaving, squeezing us ... but which is mightier, the businessmen or the banker? It depends on the liquidity the market has, what are prevailing rates. People are being practical, given money is easily available. (2007-del20)

For industry facing recently high interest costs during the time of my research, firms pursued a number of different strategies for diversification and the reduction of interest rate uncertainty.

Many manufacturers diversified away from the traditional sources of institutional finance – the nationalized commercial banks – to a range of other financial institutions. One Mumbai-based textile manufacturer, from a Marwari family in manufacturing since 1952, said, "We used to have development financing institutions for long-term lending and commercial banks for short-term. Now, everyone does everything. We borrow in rupees, term loans come from three banks, and two banks for short-term" (2008-mmb10). A director of a pharmaceutical firm that grew from a small drugstore in the 1970s to a multimillion-dollar manufacturing and exporting enterprise, said, "In India, we use foreign, nationalised, and public institutions, like the ICICI, HDFC. We use whichever bank has fund advantage" (2008-mmb39). One Delhi-based mill owner of a firm established before independence explained, "We have had some banks from day one – Allahabad Bank, Punjab National Bank, SBI – we have association with them for long time ... but public issue is used for expansion. Capital markets are cheaper, but textiles are not doing that well, so there is less opportunity" (2007-del12). The director of a Delhi-based textile plant – part of Delhi's oldest industrial group, dating to 1916 – described a cycle of loans and repayment: "We recently bought new capital machines – partly from our own money, 75 percent from Indian banks. We paid off once, but then re-expanded, so again there are loans" (2007-del28).

Some have opted for foreign banks, such as the president of a Delhi-based automotive firm, established in 1971 by an electrical engineer: "Initially, we got finance from SBI and then other banks. Now, Citibank is our banker – we borrow money from them for working capital" (2007-del16). A Mumbai-based pharmaceutical producer went from dealing only with Kanara Bank to doing business with Citibank and Standard Chartered (2007-del18). A Delhi-based mill owner in an independence era industrial family emphasized the coordination among a number of different kinds of banks to spread the risk: "The terms are standard, as per RBI regulation. Interest is based on company's business and risk. We decide on a principal bank, and they spread with other banks, they form a consortium. Credibility [with them] is all about due diligence" (2007-del36). Other firms, with significant international revenues, take out loans in other currencies as a means of reducing uncertainty; several manufacturers used global deposit rates as a foundation for their expansion through debt (2007-chn10, 2008-adb7).

Many firms emphasized building up relationships with banks as a possible source of stability. A synthetic textile manufacturer in Surat, with a management degree from the University of Nottingham, emphasized his relationship with Travancore Bank over seventeen years, borrowing money for upgrading machinery; he mentioned that interest on these loans, at 11 percent, was cheap compared to the prevailing rate (2008-sur1). A former military officer who owns an automotive components firm in Ahmedabad received "finance from the banks, private banking. They have better service, I have known the MD for 15 years. We also receive credit from companies against advance payment" (2008-adb4). This is, in a way, recourse to building relationships, but it remains a relationship formed between two parties committed to formal institutions regulating markets according to more transparent guidelines.

This linkage to formal institutions need not be without other, more political considerations. Meeting with officials of the South Gujarat Chamber of Commerce and Industry, based in Surat, I met a businesswoman who was active in the Bharatiya Janata Party (BJP), in power in Gujarat since 2001, who also ran a textile business with reinvested profits, equity from her relatives, and loans from the Gujarat State Financial Corporation (GSFC) and the Gujarat Industrial Development Corporation, or GIDC (2008-sur2). This respondent's political connections must have not hindered her chances in receiving financing from state government-affiliated funding bodies, but what struck me was her more general take that the Modi-led state government was committed to a more level – and perforce, technocratic – playing field for entrepreneurs like her. It is also worth mentioning that few other respondents operating in the state received funding from Gujarat state financial agencies, beyond allocated land in industrial estates established in the 1960s (2008-adb6).

Private Equity and Newer Forms of Finance

Markets for private equity are new in India and are not without their limitations. The IIT-educated head of the Marwari textile family said:

Financial markets are still far away … the government and the reserve bank are still unable to let go, they got freaked out [because of] the money Indians have stashed elsewhere. So you go one step forward and two steps backward, and send wrong signals in world market. We are giving the indication that these markets are not stable, not based on fundamentals, not worth investing in. (2007-del20)

Yet private equity is alluring as an alternative to more traditional financial sources such as banks, which might be happier with the higher risks inherent in innovation. A Chennai-based pharmaceutical manufacturer who had previously been a banker mentioned, "pharmaceuticals, like IT, is a sunrise industry ... we are actively looking for a private equity partner" (2007-chn7). An industrialist, who was designing innovative clutches for Indian road conditions and who was apparently on the cusp of a major export drive, less than humbly described his firm as "a darling of the capital market" and mentioned that because of this, he was able to insulate himself from "financial investors and big-time players" (2007-del37). These decisions are sometimes made not because of necessity; a Chennai auto components firm run by a Bangalore engineer with experience in the software industry said that they were "toying with the idea of private equity or a public IPO, even though we are in no great need of money" (2007-chn3). Thus seeking alternative, and yet still formal, mechanisms of financing evinces not just a greater appetite for risk but also an interest in broadening the repertoire of options for formal types of financing. Speaking more broadly about foreign private equity, a venerable Chennai-based automotive manufacturer, heading a group that took over from expatriate capital after independence, said, "If you have good programs, they are OK, though the pattern is subjective. Private equity players expect returns" (2007-chn15). A major actor in spinning, who had acquired a number of spinning mills through hostile takeovers, also used a combination of equity, debt, and participation from Citibank Venture Capital Investments (2007-del2). And other larger firms are funded through group diversification into financial services, as with another independence-era automotive components group in Tamil Nadu, thus further internalizing the relationships in the broader economy within the firm's command structures (2007-chn10).

JVs with multinational corporations present another option in this expanded repertoire of financing. An auto components firm focused on high technology in terms of connections with foreign components firms stated that the JVs are less about finance and more about "synergizing," as though in the world of technology, successful synergy is tantamount to physical or financial capital (2007-del40). A director of a composite textile firm that is part of one of India's oldest industrial groups said that the firm divided its financing among equity, bank-based debt, and JVs with foreign buyers (2008-mmb33). One of the first exporters of blended synthetic textiles in Mumbai attracted foreign equity participation for different reasons, such as facilitating market access: "Personally, we promote JVs – we talk to technical experts from the West, [who] want a production base in India" (2008-mmb16).

Some firms, especially in the automotive sector, were established as a joint venture between international Tier I producers and domestic automotive OEMs. One components firm was formed as a JV by Tata Motors and Sungmo, a major Tier I supplier to Hyundai in Korea, as a means of providing components for Hyundai's Indian plant in 1998. Here, the owners of the company exhibit a fairly hands-off managerial approach with oversight by representatives from each company and a customer coordination team (2007-chn9). Thus JVs represent another, more direct, means of attracting international capital and technology transfer.

Firms that govern themselves on formal rules might understand the drawbacks of formal finance in India, in terms of the competition for finance and the distaste for investment in manufacturing relative to other activities. And yet, despite the drawbacks, access to these formal mechanisms represents the most appropriate means of financing production and investment for many firms. Success for such firms requires diversification among a series of opportunities, making use of emergent opportunities for funding and signalling commitments

Acquiring Finance through Personal Networks

Firms that structure their production through personal networks have a very different perspective on formal financial institutions. These firms tend to see these as greedy, capricious, and ignorant of the conditions within the economy. Some talk about how banks are selective in which activities they choose to finance, particularly in garments, where orders are seasonal in nature: "Banks won't finance the small scale, there is no financing if you don't get regular orders" (2008-mmb27). A textile manufacturer that scaled up from power looms and entered value-added activities from the 1950s mentioned that banks do not check companies' credentials carefully, leading to defaults and ultimately higher interest rates: "[We have] 10–20 percent bank financing for working capital and capital goods. There are lots of banks, any bank will lend to you – but they don't do due diligence. We use our own money, so we don't pay interest" (2008-sur5). Mistrust of formal finance is closely connected to the lack of personal knowledge and trust among banks and in capital markets. Firms are understandably hesitant to endure the negative consequences of market outcomes absent these networks.

As a result, both small and large concerns that rely on personal networks tend to avoid the institutions of organized finance, preferring instead to grow organically, through reinvestment of profits, and relying on "promoters" – the owners and private investors, often family or clan members, close friends or trusted associates – for initial and additional capital. Avoiding institutional debt is certainly a rational reaction to an economy in which the cost of capital is high for industry, where these costs can fluctuate widely, and where corruption is prevalent and the mechanisms for adjudication of disputes are quite feeble.[46] Yet the *meaning* of this avoidance is wrapped up with a mistrust of formal institutions and the market in general and the reliance on personal networks, including family and friends, to replace the role of the organized sector in financing production and expansion.

Conservative Financing and Bank Avoidance

Perhaps the easiest way of seeing this is with firms that, far from hewing to institutional requirements of putting in a quarter to a third of one's own equity to receive 60 to 75 percent debt, maintained debt as a half or less of the financing of any investment. A large Ludhiana textile concern maintained 50 percent equity, 50 percent debt (2007-lud1). A knitwear producer in Delhi, a member of an Indian expatriate trading family in Afghanistan who returned to India in 1979 and invested in apparel a decade later, said he borrows only "20–30 percent from the banks … interest rates are up, and so our

---

[46] A recent World Bank study affirmed the importance of alternative finance and informal governance among the SME sector in India, as a reaction against corruption and de facto weak investor protection. See Allen et al. 2006.

profits are eroded" (2008-del31). Another garment manufacturer, who previously worked as an assistant to a Delhi-based designer, made a clear distinction between funding large projects, such as investment in plant and capital goods, and short-term, so-called working capital for raw materials and payroll: "The building and 70 percent of machinery and stock come from me only; the bank is mostly for working capital and some term loans for machinery. Banks mean interest; the more you depend on them, the more profitability decreases" (2007-del33). A Mumbai textile manufacturer who recently had established a garment unit in Bangalore has run his business without any involvement with banks – "We've been self-financed from the beginning. We set up the Bangalore plant with our own capital. We use our own capital for running costs" (2008-mmb7).

Some firms take advantage of bank facilities, but fall short of taking out long-term loans. A manager in a fifty-year-old textile printing firm in Ahmedabad said the firm had an "overdraft facility with bank but otherwise replough [investment] through profits and avoid bank interest" (2008-adb8). A Delhi-based apparel manufacturer with roots and a plant in a village near Lucknow said, "We are not taking credit. We use cash but we have 20–30 days' credit [facility]" (2007-del46). An apparel producer and exporter, a former accountant based in Mumbai, said, "We have our own financing, but we need working capital loans from Bank of India" (2008-mmb9).

This conservative financing is not uncommon even in more technology-intensive sectors, such as pharmaceuticals and automotive components. A partnership-based pharmaceutical firm in Delhi that had recently opened a second plant in Haridwar, as part of a central scheme to increase investment in the hill states of Himachal Pradesh and Uttarkhand, employed bank loans that represented Rs. 2.5 crores ($625,000), or a little more than 10 percent of their total capital (2007-del10). A respondent who coowns a Chennai-based pharmaceutical firm along with several partners from university said, "We get some finance from banks, but most financing from the company – we are not borrowing much. We are cash-rich, so why pay interest?" (2007-chn2). An automotive components manufacturer in Delhi had a policy of paying off loans on capital machinery, and now operates with zero long-term debt: "We go to [the] State Bank of Patiala for working capital; we bought different machines on hire–purchase from them. They are all paid off, after buying one every two to three years"

(2007-del5). Another manufacturer in Mumbai, an engineering graduate rising from humble roots as the son of a grain storekeeper, similarly
transitioned from growth based on debt to growth based on equity:
"Before, we had a twenty-year relationship with Canara Bank, but now,
[finance is] self-generated by operating [the] factory" (2008-mmb42).
And such pride in self-finance is not limited to small firms. A respondent
working for a Maruti ancillary employing two thousand workers over
thirteen units in the Delhi NCR, stated, "We are debt-free, cash-rich and
unlisted [on the stock exchange]" (2008-exp17). One automotive components firm mentioned that they get a small part of their financing from
banks – 10 percent – in order to maintain relationships as insurance
against an emergency (2008-exp5).

For many industrialists, avoiding debt was a matter of principle
before pragmatism, even at the cost of slower expansion. An owner
of a hundred power looms in the Mumbai industrial exurb of
Bhiwandi said, "We stay away from debt; we never take bank loans.
We prefer slow expansion with proper planning" (2008-mmb28).
Another textile manufacturer and trader from the Sindhi community
said, "I won't borrow from the banks. No credit. According to [our]
principles, we never take loans from bankers; we are funded from
profits" (2008-mmb34). One Coimbatore manufacturer, heading a
family-held company with only an overdraft facility, said that he
would only "go to the bank as a last resort, I do not like going for
loans – it's an ethical issue" (2008-coi3). For some Delhi-based garment export-oriented units, too, there was a self-conscious aversion to
debt. One garment manufacturer with an emphasis on design for the
Indian market said, "We are self-financed, no bank loans. Right now,
this is conscious decision – small but sure steps; we don't want to
expand hugely" (2007-del8). Another referred to the policies and
practices established when the firm was founded in the 1990s: "We
are all self-funded; it was a conscious decision by my father at that
time" (2007-del27). An established pharmaceutical manufacturer who
ran an wholesale trading concern in Old Delhi before investing in
manufacturing said categorically, "No bank loans. We are scared of
the consequences ... we only take loans of less than Rs. 1 lakh," or two
thousand dollars (2007-del14).

Manufacturers do tend to be more likely to take advantage of
government policies with subsidized credit, even when such policies
may be arranged through the banking system, because the cost of

credit is appropriately socialized and thus under the control of particular industry-friendly agents of the government rather than financiers. A good example is the Textile Upgradation Fund Scheme (TUFS), a central government policy that allows textile and apparel firms to upgrade their capital at an interest rate subsidy of 5 percent.[47] Firms otherwise uninterested in taking on debt have taken advantage of the TUFS, as a particularistic concern of the Ministry of Textiles for an industry under threat. A Coimbatore knitwear producer expressed support for TUF even while evincing mistrust of financial institutions: "We don't go in for big loans; but we are pursuing modernization from TUF. Margins are low; when we take loans from banks, it erodes our profits" (2008-coi8). A power loom producer in the Mumbai exurb of Bhiwandi said, "I use my own capital, and operate on overdraft facility from the banks. I bought the looms, paid for them. I had twenty-four, and sold twelve to upgrade using TUF" (2008-mmb18). TUFS appeared in a few other interviews with textile and apparel producers – which is significant given that government programs are rarely mentioned – and has by all accounts been a relatively successful program. But TUFS stands out precisely because there are few other government programs that have assisted such a broad swath of industry in such a systematic way. This implies that while the state has *some* remaining capacities to support manufacturing through state-owned banks – and in fact these capacities are bolstered by greater tax revenue – more of its incentives are directed to more explicitly clientelistic policies. Between June and October of 2014, the Chavan government in Maharashtra spent only slightly less on waivers of electricity dues for farmers in the state than the national cost of the entire TUFS program over ten years.[48]

Another area in which the state can be seen to be present, if not especially active, is export promotion. One knitwear producer said, "There are lots of credits from banks, against payment: 30–60 day term loans, Letters of Credit. It's family capital otherwise – it's a partnership. There are special terms with export, but it could be better,

---

[47] Between 1999 and 2010, TUFS assisted 28,180 spinning, processing, garmenting, and weaving units in Gujarat, Tamil Nadu, Punjab, Maharashtra, and Rajasthan, with Rs. 14,247 crores, or roughly $3 billion, in funds allocated for interest subsidies. For more on the politics behind the formulation and implementation of the TUFS policy, see Sinha 2016.

[48] Ashar 2014.

especially compared to China and Bangladesh" (2008-mmb3). It is worth noting that with both TUFS and export promotion, government intervention is composed of particular, bounded schemes rather than the previous regime of directing subsidized credit to manufacturing as a matter of principle.

Other Financing Mechanisms

Apart from financing expansion through reinvestment of profits, there are a number of other strategies deployed by firms as a means of acquiring financing. One pharmaceutical manufacturer in a middle-class family from Chandigarh relied not on institutional finance but rather on loans from his wholesale customers, with whom he has built long-term relationships: "I made my distributors our financial part-ners – [I am] depending on them rather than ... banks. I got finance from stockists and distributors from the beginning. Right now, we run a zero-percent interest company" (2007-del7). Another Delhi-based pharmaceutical manufacturer with an office in a huge and teeming commercial building in Old Delhi talked of the loyalty of his custom-ers – many of whom migrated together from partition – as a source of certainty for finance, enabling his firm to grow organically on the basis of reliable revenue, with only 40–50 days' credit from the retail com-panies to which he supplies his goods (2007-del48).

Ownership Structures

An important sign of a deep reliance on trust and personal networks is to establish and run the firm without recourse to limited liability. In industrialized countries such as the United States, partnerships are a mainstay of small businesses – so-called mom-and-pop stores – and professional groups such as medical or law practices, but industrial manufacturers are rarely unincorporated as either privately held or publicly traded enterprises. Most manufacturing firms in India are "private limited companies," but a significant minority of my sample remained unincorporated. A Mumbai garment manufacturer said that his firm was a three-way family partnership with no plans for incorpor-ation (2008-mmb7).

Part of the issue with ownership and firm organization is one of maintaining control and confidentiality in relation to the rest of the market. An automotive components manufacturer whose firm had made public issues of shares in the past said that they had bought back most extant stock because "once you have higher than 95 percent [ownership], corporate governance reporting requirements are waived, and there's no need to have company secretary. It made sure [that] promoters had complete control" (2007-chn4). The director in a successful firm manufacturing ayurvedic medicine explained the partnership system for financing in greater detail:

> We are a cash rich company – debt-free, loan-free. Partners brought in their own capital, so that's been sitting there for a long time. At the end of the financial year, we decide what to add to capital and the surplus goes to partners. We have eighteen partners – everybody's got their percent of share. Some are working partners; most are sleeping partners. Working partners get salaries. But it stays "within the family" ... there is a trust factor. (2008-mmb2)

Thus, as an alternative to selling equity on an exchange or approaching an impersonal financial institution for a loan, the creation of a limited and trusted community of long-term investors that can agree to provide funds for expansion and production, rather than insisting on routinized dividends or interest, provides the "patient capital" necessary for long-term industrial investment.

"Conservative" forms of financing – whether through organic growth, avoidance of bank debt, or partnership structures – represent a different way of looking at the Indian economy. Firms that rely on personal networks view the structures of formal finance as corrupt, incompetent, or callous to the challenges of industry. Instead, such firms – facing relatively the same objective environment, depending in part on the size of the firm and other such structural considerations – choose to avoid the formal structures entirely and instead to gather capital from personal connections internal to a firm's revenue or from family and community.

Conclusion

The different strategies for avoiding institutional debt, as well as the strategies of diversifying among sources of finance or courting newer forms of capital, are not particularly easy given the competitiveness of India's capital markets. Yet each does provide a way to manage the challenges faced by firms – of fragmented financial markets, and the variable cost and availability of capital. Such strategies are not entirely or even primarily reactive. Those who own, direct, and manage industrial firms tend to have a preconceived notion of the appropriate distance the firm should maintain in relation to the at-times-hostile and uncomprehending institutions of organized finance. What I have been arguing is that Indian political economy after liberalization has not provided alternative credible, common regional or sectoral models around which firms can coalesce. Firms, in order to secure financing to allow for daily production and long-term investment, must form institutionalized structures and relationships to take the place of those that were once imposed by the state and its agents during the era of statist development. The ways in which they do so lead to dualism, ever-greater fragmentation, and a self-enforcing retreat from a coherent Indian model of capitalism.

5 | Labor Management after Statism in India

The formation of a skilled and productive workforce for manufacturing has remained a major challenge for developing countries. In the developed world, early industrialization succeeded social transformations that ended the relationship between peasant and land and thus created the foundation of the industrial laborforce. Economic, social, and political struggles between workers and employers throughout the nineteenth and early twentieth centuries redefined the working class as an active participant in industrial political economy, as either partner or antagonist to capital. In the developing world, by contrast, breaks between preindustrial and industrial work have been a great deal less evident and labor as a political force has been less coherent and powerful. Nevertheless, the question of how workers can be recruited, trained, and retained remains at the heart of industrial development.

The management of labor under statism in India was embedded within a series of state or state-affiliated institutions that sought to arrange the terms of employment in order to balance the nationalist impetus for increasing industrial production, the protection of individual workers, and the demands of trade unions. Two key institutions – legal frameworks for worker protection and tripartite arrangements among unions, employers, and representatives of the state – formally structured the terms of industrial work, at least for organized workplaces. Since liberalization, the state has been steadily withdrawing the resources necessary for the full implementation of the labor regime framed in law. At the same time, the fragmentation of trade union representation has precluded the tripartite arrangements that set the terms of engagement between organized labor and the state. The result of state withdrawal has not been, as might be expected, simply a decrease in labor power and an increase in the power and authority of employers, but rather increasing challenges in the recruitment and retention of skilled workers, with increasing competition among firms for employees and fewer mechanisms available to anchor them.

How do firms manage the recruitment, training, and retention of workers without these statist institutions? It is plausible that state governments and sectoral agencies have stepped in to fill the central state's previous roles. I argue, however, that firms themselves structure relationships with workers, on the basis of the perspectives of manufacturers in combination with structural characteristics. Some firms manage workers through firm-level formal institutions such as human resource departments and both establish in-house vocational training and deploy explicit incentives for productivity. Others, by contrast, rely on personal connections with workers as well as informal networks of recruitment, including labor contracting. This variation in management styles does not follow state boundaries or sectoral jurisdictions but rather is most explicable through manufacturers' perspectives – as defined by the backgrounds and experiences of manufacturers and, as a proxy, the ages of firms – and the structural characteristics of firms.

This chapter proceeds as follows. First, I survey extant research on industrial labor in India, both during and after statist development. Then I use several labor ethnographies to chart the change over time in worker–management interaction at the level of the firm. Third, I use quantitative analysis to examine the patterns of variation in labor management in the sectors and states of India, as well as firm-level indicators. Lastly, I present qualitative evidence of the concrete mechanisms in the ways that different firms recruit, train, retain, and otherwise manage their employees.

The Colonial Context

The initial construction of the industrial labor force was itself the product of the political economy of colonial India. From the start, nascent indigenous industry relied on the migration of workers from the hinterland, individuals whose livelihood required both work in factories in new urban centers and the continuation of peasant cultivation in the countryside.[1] Mill owners and other early industrialists could intervene only partially in the complex politics and social organization that pervaded the neighborhoods beyond the factory gates and

---

[1] Chandavarkar 1998.

even the factory floor.[2] Such complexities were exacerbated by the severe fluctuations in the supply of raw cotton and the demand for cotton yarn in world markets. Mill owners in the nineteenth century were thus compelled to modulate their production sharply on the basis of such fluctuations, periodically shutting down mills and not employing workers in periods of slack. Such variation, coupled with responsibilities in their home villages, meant that workers often resisted long-term commitments to factory work, leading to intense competition for skilled workers and the development of various strategies for recruitment and retention, including 1) the hiring and managing workers through labor intermediaries, called jobbers or *mukadams*; 2) the hiring of *badli*, or alternate, workers on a temporary or daily basis to supplement a quasi-permanent workforce; and 3) the provision of basic social services – workers' housing and health care – to cement loyalty to a particular mill among the core labor force.[3]

Large-scale tensions in industrial relations emerged in the twentieth century. By the 1920s and 1930s, employers' labor rationalization efforts in response to global depression and market collapse led to coordinated and widespread militancy among industrial workers in Bombay and other cities. This militancy resulted in no fewer than eight general strikes and many one-day closures in the Bombay textile industry between 1919 and 1940.[4] Strikes erupted and spread from mill to mill without the aid of "professional" unionists, as trade union organizations were late to develop in India. By the time of the 1928–1929 general strike, official trade unions became more involved and advocated confrontation with employers; some, particularly the Girni Kamgar Union (GKU), became dominated by communist organizers.[5]

The nationalist movement – as the future inheritors of the postindependence state – had a difficult time reconciling these early attempts at working class mobilization with nationalist politics. In the 1920s, Gandhi had declared that industrial laborers lacked the discipline and education to participate in the noncooperation movement.[6] The

---

[2] Rajnaryan Chandavarkar 1981. I use the term "mill owner" freely here because, with a couple of notable exceptions, indigenous industry before independence was dominated by the cotton textiles industry in Bombay Presidency. Jute textiles were manufactured in Bengal, but in mills owned and operated by British manufacturers.

[3] Haan 1999; Arnold 2006, 182.   [4] Chandavarkar 1981, 603.

[5] Chandavarkar 1999.   [6] Cited in Chandavarkar 1999, 213–214.

Congress party's difficulties with domestic trade unionism stemmed from the fact that opposition to British rule meant ignoring or actively suppressing class conflict within Indian society. Most manufacturing enterprises in India, outside the Calcutta jute industry, were owned and operated by Indian capitalists. Those capitalists were, moreover, an important source of funds and political support for Congress and were considered essential political allies. As a result, nationalist leaders affirmed rhetoric of achieving the underlying cooperation or harmony between indigenous capital and labor.

Nowhere was this idea more present than in Gandhi's mediation of a textile labor strike in Ahmedabad in 1917–1918. In achieving an accommodation between laborers and factory owners, he emphasized the paternalistic notion of bonds of familial obligation: "Capital and labor ... should be a great family living in unity and harmony."[7] After the arbitration in which employers were forced to provide higher wages and shorter working hours, in 1920 Gandhi established the Textile Labor Association, which avoided confrontation with employers and emphasized instead arbitration, workers' self-improvement, education, temperance, social reform, and bettering of living conditions.[8]

The relationship among industrial labor, trade unionists, and the Congress party changed profoundly in the 1930s, when attempts were made to formalize and discipline internal Congress organization. The result was a bifurcation between labor leaders choosing to stay in Congress and thus increasingly subject to the orders of the high command and those who pursued independent trade unionism under communist or socialist affiliations.[9] In the 1930s, at the height of the Depression, communist and socialist labor agitations were more overtly political and targeted at the colonial state. During this period, mill owners justified layoffs and rationalizations as a consequence of the government's economic policies. Yet after 1941, when the Communist Party of India (CPI) allied with the colonial state as a result of the Soviet–British alliance, the Congress was the only political organization willing to oppose the government on such issues, allowing for increased workers' support for Congress in key sectoral constituencies

---

[7] M. K. Gandhi, cited in Chandavarkar 1998, 283.

[8] Chandavarkar 1998, 292–296. See also Breman and Shah 2004, 26–30; Patel 1987, ch. 3; Kannappan 1962.

[9] Chandavarkar 1998, 314. For more on the history of the preindependence organized labor movement, see Revri 1972.

and Congress's increasing sponsorship of the trade union movement. As independence approached, the rival party domination of trade union organization – largely between the Congress party and the CPI – structured the ways in which the political organs of the state could intervene in the relationship between capital and labor.[10]

Labor Management under Statist Development

As India became independent and the machinery was put in place for a planned economy, a new labor relations regime was established, one that prioritized the certainty and predictability of labor supply to the public and private sector enterprises key to industrialization. Planners recognized early on the need to create mechanisms for pacifying labor.[11] The Indian state, independently and through the mechanisms of the dominant Congress party played a huge role in relations between capital and labor because of the overriding need to increase industrial production. The two main mechanisms of this intervention were labor regulation and the influence of party-affiliated trade union federations on factory and shop floor relationships.

The enacting of labor legislation in India began in the colonial period, as a result of pressure from progressive social reformers and British competitors in export markets, as well as a response to increased shop floor militancy in the interwar period. Legislation such as the Workmen's Compensation Act (1923), the Trade Unions Act (1926), amendments to the Factory Act (1934), and the Payment of Wages Act (1934) prohibited child labor, established limits on working hours and standards for working conditions and payment of wages, and permitted some union organizing and the principle of union recognition in factories.[12] After independence, however, the government established a more comprehensive labor regulation regime, led by powerful voices within the party: V. V. Giri, the first labor minister, was a former union organizer who would become the president of India. This legislation included the amended Industrial Disputes Act (1947), which institutionalized procedures for collective bargaining,

---

[10] For more on the ways in which party-dominated trade union federations, or "centers," played a crucial rule in electoral and parliamentary politics in postindependence India, see Candland 2001, 70–73. For an alternative view, see Teitelbaum 2006.

[11] Breman 1999a, 30.   [12] Amjad 2001, 32–43.

and the amended Factories Act (1948), which limited working hours to fifty-four per week and ten per day and provided a weekly holiday, periods of rest, and overtime for all factories employing more than ten people permanently or nonpowered factories with twenty or more.[13] The Indian government also passed social security legislation, including the Employees State Insurance Act (1948), and established requirements for allowing layoffs and retrenchment.[14] Together, these regulations provided a formal and stable framework for the conditions of regular employment.

Such stability of employment to permanent factory workers, while available to a small minority of a total workforce, constituted a state-enforced ideal of industrial labor and ultimately the relationship between capital and labor in the leading, industrial sector.[15] The assumption was that this sector would expand and involve an increasing proportion of the industrial workforce. Moreover, as Jan Breman persuasively argued, the rules and requirements of industrial work enforced a certain commonality of experience and identity among labor of vastly different skill levels and statuses.[16] Thus the state's regulatory regimes and the development of a common set of experiences and values among permanent factory labor worked hand in hand for managing quotidian shop floor certainties.

Trade unions, particularly those in the Congress party–dominated Indian National Trade Union Congress (INTUC) federation, constituted a second pillar of the statist industrial relations regime. Relationships between workers and trade unionists in India have always been complicated by the fact that shop floor militancy significantly predated the establishment of the trade union movement. Trade unionists were often middle-class activists rather than representatives that workers elected themselves, and the disparity between unions' and workers' consciousness was reflected in uniformly low formal membership.[17] Individual union bosses could be corrupt and manipulative, uninterested in advocating for their membership but rather

---

[13] Amjad 2001, 151. The exemption of factories with smaller workforces defines the "unorganized sector" as opposed to the "organized sector," an institutional legacy of Gandhian philosophy of the support of artisans and craft workers, on which more below.

[14] Amjad 2001, 98–108, 134–136.

[15] Holmstrom 1976, 139–140; U. Ramaswamy 1983, 145.

[16] Breman 1999a, 28.   [17] Breman 1999a, 32. See also Chhibber 1999.

committed to their own political interests, largely through brokering deals with employers, politicians, and other trade unions.[18] Yet workers during the statist period could easily measure the progress in the conditions of their working lives as a result of union mobilization, with concomitant increases in dignity and self-esteem.[19] As Mark Holmstrom notes, "Once inside the citadel [of the organized sector], with a job to fall back on, improving one's qualifications and getting promotion becomes a gradual process, a matter of more or less, faster or slower process, rather than simply of having a permanent job or not having one."[20] The importance of union representation to individual workers or groups should not be diminished, as it served as a critical channel of institutionalized communication among workers, and between workers and union organizations, management, and politicians.

Moving from the shop floor to the level of entire regions or industries, trade unions – particularly those that were part of INTUC – played a crucial role in negotiations with manufacturers' associations over industrywide issues. Oscar Ornati noted that INTUC, by far the biggest trade union federation after independence, rejected V. V. Giri's initial strategy of free and independent collective bargaining on a case-by-case basis in favor of compulsory arbitration and institutionalized tripartite mechanisms, in other words, a party-aided corporatism.[21] He indicated that the movement away from free collective bargaining was in part due to lack of enthusiasm of trade unions themselves, who did not see gains from free collective bargaining realized, and in part due to the Fabian-technocratic ideology of the Nehruvian Congress party as a whole.[22]

The nature of government intervention in statist development thus balanced the interests of labor in a much wider regime of industrial promotion. In regional and industrial terms, such tripartite structure was replicated. Such official systems were buttressed by the fact that union organizers of the various affiliated unions were also members and activists of the political parties to which they are affiliated, to such an extent that unions were often informally referred to as the "communist union" or the "Congress union." This system of mandatory arbitration and party–union cross-membership contributed to the

---

[18] Breman 1999a, 33.   [19] Breman 1999a, 34; see also Sheth 1968.
[20] Holmstrom 1984, 41.   [21] Ornati 1957, 155–156.   [22] Ornati 1957, 156.

subordination of the needs and demands of workers to the overall strategies of political parties. In areas in which several parties were vying for electoral control, such systems led to vigorous interunion competition, and thus increased militancy.[23] Yet these systems provided a means by which management and labor could communicate under an overall framework built up by the state, and a dominant political party that was deeply embedded in the state. There were certainly many instances of industrial action and frequent grievances in factories and industries throughout the country during the statist period. Yet at least for the permanent factory workers of the organized sector, there were also legal and regulatory protections for labor and institutionalized mechanisms established to mediate and resolve such conflicts.

Such labor assertion and protection might, for manufacturers, have seemed injurious to the overall project of industrialization. Indeed, many industrialists felt that organized labor was a force destructive to traditional authority. One mill owner fulminated, "Your illegal and indisciplinary ways distress me. I am tired and will be compelled to take action ... my advice to you as your elder and wellwisher is work wholeheartedly and maintain discipline ... if you do not follow my humble advice you will compel the company to dismiss all those who have acted illegally."[24] But the industrial relations regime also created a framework of communication for employers in their relations with their workforce. It was clear who needed to be contacted in an instance of shop floor militancy; both employers and workers could rely on mutual expectations of work, wages, conditions, and benefits at least in the short to medium term. Such communication was inherent in the statist industrial promotion regime, with the result that the state was – at least in the decades after independence – deeply implicated in maintaining these structures of industrial relations.

What about work in the informal sector? During the period of high statism, a significant number of workers – perhaps as much as 80 percent of the nonagricultural workforce – were employed in conditions other than that of the organized industrial sector: as temporary, or *badli*, workers in organized sector factories, as workers contracted by *mukadams*. Also included were those working in the "unorganized"

[23] Ornati 1957, 163.   [24] Cited in Breman 1999a, 35.

sector, in workshops rather than factories.[25] Unorganized or informal sector labor is characterized by its casualness, its lack of security, and its formal exclusion from labor legislation.[26] Importantly, the unorganized sector enjoyed tremendous material and political support through the Indian government's promotion of small-scale industries.[27]

But it is also clear that, during this period and indeed recently, a less-than-rigid boundary existed between the "organized" and "unorganized" sectors. The separation was delineated by a shifting series of legal and political mechanisms, particularly the creative manipulation of the regulations of the Factories Act, which lay at the heart of labor legislation. In this sense, perhaps the line between the organized and unorganized sectors is not a boundary at all, but rather gradations away from the ideal–typical relations set out by legislation. Holmstrom thus describes the distinction not as a wall but rather a steep slope with the most protected and privileged workers of the organized factories at the top, but with workers with varying levels of skills and protection at varying points of elevation in smaller firms, and with paths moving up and down.[28]

In the leading industrial sectors of the Indian economy, however, management practices in large factories in both the public and private sectors combined with party-dominated trade unions and regulatory institutions to guarantee stable conditions of employment. At lower altitudes, the state, in its support of small-scale industry, enabled and, by its regulatory exceptionalism, allowed a mode of labor management based on ties of social and economic obligation, as well as the cheek-by-jowl proximity of employers to their workers in small workshops in the hinterlands of the Indian economy. The relationship between the two was certainly unequal, but from the point of view of employers in both locations, and the state that stood behind them, they afford a certain amount of stability.

---

[25] Breman 1999a, 2; Holmstrom 1984, 1–7, 13–18. The 80 percent figure also includes petty services; thus it exaggerates the informal nature of industry.

[26] The Factory Act exempts enterprises with fewer than ten employees from its provisions, constituting the major difference between "organized" and "unorganized."

[27] In fact, many firms sought to be classified as small-scale enterprises in order to gain access to reserved industries and to be eligible for subsidies. See Holmstrom 1984, 110–115.

[28] Holmstrom 1984, 319.

The Breakdown of Statist Labor Management and Current Challenges

By the early 1980s, the structures and practices of statist labor management were falling apart. This disintegration occurred in the context of particularly hard economic times.[29] Cost-push inflation caused a great deal of political instability and discontent, particularly for aspirant urban populations, including factory workers in the organized sector. Internationalization and changing patterns of consumption increased pressures on the Fordist mode of production: of mass production of homogeneous goods based on the assembly line, and a workforce paid well enough to constitute a national market for the goods they produce.[30]

Such manifold pressures took a deep and resounding toll on the organized factory. Many industrial units resisted technological upgrading of aging capital machinery in favor of continuing systems that balanced capital with labor power; as a result, many faced significant decreases in productivity and mounting debt. The textile industry was especially hard hit, with many "sick" integrated mills in traditional centers in Maharashtra, Gujarat, Tamil Nadu, and Uttar Pradesh passing to government control. Such a collapse in the textile industry was precipitated by the increased fragmentation of trade union representation, and the emergence of independent and militant union organizers.

This new generation of aggressive leaders led inadvertently to the destruction of organized employment, as the failure of the Mumbai textile mill strike led by Dutta Samant, involving 200,000 workers and lasting eighteen months, makes clear. Samant called for better wages but also the derecognition of the INTUC-affiliated Rashtriya Mill Mazdoor Sangh (RMMS). The episode seems indicative of the inability of unions to represent workers effectively, even while independent unionists played a part in destroying the system of organized representation.[31] The period of the decline of the integrated mill sector thus coincided with the biggest sustained increases in industrial disputes, measured in worker-days lost, between 1976 and 1986.[32]

[29] Gourevitch 1986.   [30] Piore and Sabel 1982.
[31] Breman 1999a, 36–37; D'Monte 2002.   [32] Teitelbaum 2006, 405f.

At the same time as a significant portion of organized sector employment by private firms was disappearing, the erstwhile unorganized sector was resurgent. Previously small-scale concerns such as those of textiles and automotive components started expanding and scaling up to take advantage of the gaping hole in demand from the ailing organized sector as well as new opportunities, such as supplying to joint-venture automotive manufacturers. The power loom sector is a case in point. These "workshops" started as a reserved sector for small-scale handloom production, but they gradually transitioned into a protocapitalist enterprise capitalizing on niche markets and skills and increasingly locating production in urban settings, to which traditional weaving communities had migrated. The related transition from handlooms to power looms was enabled by the electrification of provincial towns and the availability of secondhand automatic looms from composite mills, with which to adapt traditional weaving processes to mechanization.[33] Haynes argued that part of the success of the power loom sector was the result of alternative means of arranging manufacturing. Workers, predominantly from weaving communities, were linked to owners through caste, family, or cultural ties and thus operated on a paternalistic basis of quasi-family relations. Capital was also not forthcoming from banks, and thus investment was an intracommunity and often self-financed activity between and among artisans and traders.[34] Over the decades from the establishment of the sector, power looms flourished in clusters in regional towns such as Surat, Bhiwandi, Malegaon, and Ichalkarangi in the west, and Tiruppur, Salem, and Erode in the south. The sector has grown markedly, eclipsing the textile production of the composite mills; the share of power looms in total textile production went from 37 percent in 1980 to 68 percent in 1995[35] and represented 88 percent of total textile exports in 1995–1996, either directly or as the raw material for garments.[36]

What have the relative decline of the traditional factory and the transformation of the previously small-scale and informal production meant for labor representation and management–worker relations on

[33] Haynes 2001. Roy argues that this process was much slower outside western India because of relatively low labor costs and relative inaccessibility of capital goods. Roy 1998, 899.

[34] Haynes 2001, 178–180.   [35] Srinivasulu 1996, 3200.

[36] Roy 1998, 898. For more on the social dynamics of disintegrated yet medium-scale production, see Chari 2004.

the shop floor? First, the demise of organized employment effectively meant the end of party-affiliated trade union representation in private sector enterprises; trade union centers have concentrated on protections for public sector unions and resistance to privatization (2006-mmb10).[37] Within the private sector, the retreat of the party-dominated federations has left in its place a multiplicity of different types of trade union activists, some part of international federations and organized industry-wide unions, others lone operators and political entrepreneurs. In the industrial estates that contain much of Indian industrial capacity, labor activism has taken a spontaneous and opportunistic character, with strikes by unit or by industrial estate being fomented by a few activists rather than federated bodies.[38] This might mean more democratic, or at least competitive, trade unionism, but it is unlikely to produce the stable long-term relationships and communication between management and labor that characterized the heart of industrial production during the period of statism.

Second, the state, even while it is unable to change labor legislation substantively, because of the legislative power of parties of the left, has been unable to implement such regulation effectively. In 2010, there were 276,465 factories registered under the Factories Act, but only 68,508 submitted (statutory) information returns.[39] Further, only 12.7 percent of registered factories were inspected in 2007.[40] This lack of inspection (and, perforce, enforcement) is hardly surprising given the total working strength of the labor inspectorate was 417, or 1 member of staff for every 664 registered factories.[41] In 1956, by contrast, 85 percent of registered factories submitted statutory returns, and fully 79.6 percent of registered factories were inspected for compliance at least once.[42] The decreased implementation is likely a consequence of drift, or the inability of institutions to develop their capacities in response to change.[43] As a result, there has been little in

---

[37] Candland 2001, 78–87.
[38] Teitelbaum, following Orati, argues that unions without party-political affiliation are less likely to restrain worker activism at enterprise level because they are not part of encompassing political organizations with higher-order economic goals. Teitelbaum 2010.
[39] Government of India Labour Bureau 2010a, 7t.
[40] Government of India Labour Bureau 2010b, 164 (table).
[41] Government of India Labour Bureau 2010b, 163 (table).
[42] Government of India Labour Bureau, 1956, 21 (table).
[43] For more on institutional drift, see Hacker 2004.

the way of rebuilding or resuscitating institutions.[44] It is therefore much less likely that the regulatory aspects of the state can effectively intervene in the industrial relations of private sector enterprise and maintain traditional regulatory distinctions between the organized and unorganized sectors.

Third, workers themselves, particularly those skilled in industrial processes, have been increasingly in demand and thus are increasingly able to pursue agency in their choices of employment and working conditions. Jan Breman has argued that traditional worker control outside the big bureaucratized factories emanated from long-term debt obligations and the deferral of payments, particularly among farm-workers but also circulatory migrants in the industrial economy.[45] But expansion and structural transformation of the industrial economy have placed serious (and welcome) limits on the extent to which employers can utilize mechanisms of debt bondage to maintain a workforce:

Laborers do not hesitate to leave without notice if the employer or the work itself is found to be too oppressive, and certainly do so to work for a higher wage. Creditors today lack the power to prolong the [employment] contract until the debt has been repaid. They are no longer able to call on the authorities to help, and employers' attempts to exclude "defaulters" from further employment usually fail due to rivalry between employers. In brief, the loss of bonded labor's social legitimacy means that those who pay an advance are no longer assured that the promised labor power will indeed be provided.[46]

Further, even the lowest paid workers in the industrial economy pursue a number of strategies to avoid bonds of obligation by employers: they frequently change workplaces, leave their families as they migrate for industrial work, and, when aggrieved, exhibit – in addition to spon-taneous industrial action – individual acts of resistance including "inertia, pretended lack of understanding, foot-dragging, avoidance, withdrawal, sabotage, obstruction, etc."[47]

Thus, for the workers at the very bottom of the labor market, strategies of exit and voice enable them to shape the nature of their work, particularly when the "craft workshop"–based employment of the previous regime has increased in scale and scope to include medium

---

[44] Jenkins 2004.   [45] Breman 1996, 163.   [46] Breman 1999b, 424.
[47] Breman 1999b, 425.

and even large factories. For those higher up, with more valuable skills and thus greater demand for their services, opportunities to arbitrage employment are ever greater. And in the absence of tripartite mechanisms and fully implemented labor legislation, workers have little incentive to provide their labor power to one employer over the long term. Thus the practical informalization of labor is Janus-faced; while it relieves management of formal statutory obligations, it also gives skilled workers much less incentive to stay in one place and thus more freedom.

The concrete consequence of this shift is a general perception among manufacturers that acquiring and managing Indian labor are sources of significant challenge. The Economist Intelligence Unit has reported that in addition to high absenteeism, "high economic growth and increasing competition among companies mean that labour shortages are now cropping up in both manufacturing and service industries. Turnover rates are increasing as well"; the availability of skilled workers in India was half that of the Asian average in 2014.[48] Indian labor statistics report average annual turnover rates of 20 percent among directly employed workers, and absenteeism – the percentage of days absent to days expected to work – was 8.37 percent in 2007.[49] Absenteeism and turnover are major challenges for industrial firms, when many different sorts of workers need to work together and it takes time for workers to be trained and integrated into production processes.

Change over Time in Labor Management at the Firm Level

The previous sections discussed industry in the aggregate, but it is worth considering how these broad changes have manifested in manufacturing firms. I make use of several ethnographies of industrial labor conducted in South India over two periods to illustrate how aggregate changes affect dynamics on the shop floor, in the union hall (more often, a shack), and in the director's office. These ethnographies specifically focus on labor in factories – in cotton and rayon textiles, engineering, and diamond polishing – and thus stand in distinction

---

[48] Economist Intelligence Unit 2014, 35, 42f.
[49] Government of India Labour Bureau 2010b, 29–33t. Both figures are only for the minority of factories providing returns, and thus might be significant underestimates.

from several excellent works in anthropology and sociology that focus on informal labor in disaggregated neighborhood and cottage industries.[50] Conducting fieldwork in the 1960s and early 1970s, E. A. Ramaswamy and Mark Holmstrom investigated the lives, politics, and labor of cotton textile workers in Coimbatore mills and workers in public and private sector engineering works in Bangalore, respectively.[51] As such, both books afford snapshots of the working of statist industrial governance in factory-based manufacturing during periods just after the peak of high statism.

E. A. Ramaswamy's book focuses on the workers and union organizers of the Socialist Hind Mazdoor Sangh (HMS)–affiliated union in the textile industry in Coimbatore, the TWU, as distinct from the Congress- and Communist-affiliated unions. Interunion rivalry, bound up in both party politics among the Congress, the CPI, and the Praja Socialist Party and individual worker grievances, was at the root of much militancy in the district.[52] Yet he indicated that big issues such as wages, work responsibilities, and bonuses – which had been at the heart of the widespread strikes of the 1930s and 1940s – were by the 1960s resolved through negotiated settlements by a united front of unions, the South Indian Manufacturers' Association, and the regional labor commissioner, covering all textile mills in the Coimbatore district.[53] Ramaswamy's book portrayed unions as both an expression of the heartfelt politics of individual workers and institutions that existed to protect them and promote their interests. This ambiguity between trade unionism as party-political mobilization and trade unionism as a strategy for workplace security and collective action reflected intense interunion rivalry and a conceptual separation between union and party politics. The environment, while contentious and factionalized, did often represent unions as effective representatives of individual workers and thus capable of making agreements and resolving problems at locations as disparate individual shop floors and the entire district.[54]

Holmstrom's work relates more directly to individual workers and their identity and worldview; he conducted his ethnography within newer factories in more recent and capital-intensive sectors than

---

[50] Harriss-White 2003; Agarwala 2013.   [51] Ibid.; Holmstrom 1976.
[52] E. Ramaswamy 1977, 97-117.   [53] Ibid., 70–73.
[54] E. Ramaswamy 1977, 187–89.

textile mills. Holmstrom's general characterization of employment in these engineering firms – once formal "permanent" employment has been achieved – was that it was highly structured and bureaucratized, with stable expectations arising from institutions such as labor legislation and rounds of bargaining with credible unions.[55] He characterized the main struggle as *gaining* permanent employment in the first place, through time in apprenticeship or as a substitute worker and then official job applications facilitated by persons with influence.[56]

Holmstrom portrayed workers' interactions with and activism within trade unions as indivisible from their individual worldviews. He contrasted two groups of union activists, one Jan Sangh–influenced group building ties of subordination with management built on paternalism and the other supporting the Communist Party and its affiliated unions.[57] Yet according to Holmstrom, most workers affirmed the importance of industrial production as a nationalist impulse, and many felt both a sense of achievement in working as well as gratitude for the stability that factory work afforded.[58] Both Holmstrom and Ramaswamy portray factory work in the 1960s and early 1970s as a context full of organization and structures that, while they do not preclude militancy, provide for stable roles, meanings, and – importantly – institutionalized means of communication and negotiation.

The next two ethnographies represent change over time, from the old order of organized-sector manufacturing and industrial relations to the postliberalization context. In the first, this change is explicit: E. A. Ramaswamy conducted a longitudinal study of management–labor relations in a large single rayon fiber and spinning enterprise with three integrated plants in Tamil Nadu from the 1960s through the early 1990s.[59] Two managing directors ran "Rayon Spinners" in the old entrepreneurial–paternalistic style throughout the 1960s. Labor relations – between periods of militancy – were arranged in negotiated settlements among the management (including one of the managing directors); a concatenation of unions affiliated with the Communists, the Congress, and the Socialists; and the regional labor commissioner.[60] By the mid-1970s, three unions had fragmented into seven as factions of Congress, the Tamil nationalist Dravida Munnetra

---

[55] Holmstrom 1976, 52–72.   [56] Ibid., 42–51.   [57] Ibid., 88–98.
[58] Ibid., 108–114   [59] E. Ramaswamy 1994.   [60] Ibid., 31–32.

Kazagham (DMK), and the Communist Parties had split and formed rival trade union federations.[61] After major contention around a wage settlement between 1975 and 1977, during which management enlisted a state INTUC leader to mediate, workers rejected outside intervention and formed a (short-lived) company-level federation that ultimately negotiated a settlement.[62] In the 1980s, the fragmentation of labor representation – with eleven different unions competing for members – led to chaos and precipitated a change in the ownership of the firm.

The installation of a professional chief executive, a former senior bureaucrat, heralded the beginning of a new, bipartite style of negotiation between management and workers, often bypassing the competing political considerations of rival unions and outside organizers. A destructive bonus strike in 1982 substantially weakened the independent power of labor leaders and set the stage for negotiations between workers and management without the facilitation of trade union leadership and the state.[63] Ramaswamy indicated that this new "professional" style of labor relations – involving bilateral negotiation between management and shop floor representation and counterbargaining for bonus agreements – has been largely successful and the company prosperous, but entailed a shift in strategies from relying on state-mediated institutional frameworks to constructing these relationships internal to the firm.

Ramaswamy's Rayon Spinners was a big, old company with an emphasis on formal systems. Jamie Cross, a labor anthropologist, conducted ethnography by participant observation as a trainee in a large diamond-polishing concern, established in 1991 and employing more than a thousand people, in the Vishakhapatnam Special Economic Zones (SEZs) in a city in coastal Andhra Pradesh that grew as a result of public sector investments in steel and chemicals.[64] Recent SEZ investment has been implicated in land appropriation and real estate speculation,[65] but SEZs were initially established as "offshore" manufacturing locations, in which laws and regulations do not apply. In this sense, they make explicit the weak implementation of labor regulations across Indian manufacturing.[66]

---

[61] E. Ramaswamy 1994, 42.   [62] Ibid., 62–70.   [63] Ibid., 95–97.
[64] Cross 2009. See also Cross 2014.   [65] Levien 2011.
[66] For more on the continuities between SEZs and other industrial spaces in contemporary India, see Cross 2010.

Cross indicated that many young men with backward caste, agricultural backgrounds, who sought education in new, private industrial training institutes as investments to allow social advancement, are now employed in the SEZ. Cross argued that managerial surveillance and the workers' self-understanding are filtered through the (paternalistic) idiom of education: regarding discipline, one worker warns, "No! You can't say that kind of thing to a supervisor. You have to treat him with respect, like a teacher," and for another, "It's just like the 10th class, only the head teacher is now the factory manager."[67] Discipline through idioms of education, particularly for younger workers in more recently established enterprises, has replaced the formal structures and outside interventions common in earlier large-scale manufacturing. Further, concerted action was difficult when workers had become more atomized. When some older workers organized a strike for wages, many workers felt some deep ambivalence and chose instead to take leave on the planned strike day.[68] In the outskirts of Vishakhapatnam, there are few employment alternatives other than the SEZs, but in the old industrial estates in the cities and towns of northern and western India, paternalistic idioms are countered by greater mobility and opportunity for skilled workers. Yet disciplinary idioms and atomization seem to be a feature of labor in many firms in India.

These sketches of firm-level change over time suggest the emergence of two broad sets of strategies of managing labor. The first, following the professional management in Rayon Spinners, focuses on building formal rules and internal organization in the firm – usually through the creation of a human resource apparatus – to structure management's relationship to workers. This formal approach might also entail the provision of productivity incentives and fringe benefits as a means to anchoring the workforce, and explicit mechanisms of recruitment and in-house training. The second, as suggested by the diamond-polishing factory in Vishakhapatnam, relies on personal networks and affective ties between management and workers. Also included in these strategies are recruitment through coethnic ties, the provision and management of labor through contractors, and explicit use of educational idioms as a means of acquiring young and pliant workers. The presence of these two sets of strategies might be explained by the variable actions of state governments or the incentives of sectoral regimes. But

[67] Cited in Cross 2009, 363.   [68] Ibid., 372–374.

they might also be explained by the perspectives of manufacturers and especially the context around a firm's founding, in combination with structural factors such as firm size and export levels. These rival explanations are assessed through examining the patterns of labor management in the following sections.

Patterns of Labor Management after Liberalization

Proportion of Nonwage Costs in Total Labor Costs as an Indicator

I use the proportion of total labor costs not spent on wages (the nonwage proportion of labor costs, or NWP) as a very rough proxy for different patterns of labor management. The *Indian Labor Year-book* records the average proportion of wages and salaries to total labor costs at 79.9 percent, with bonuses constituting 4.5 percent, provident fund contributions 8.9 percent, and staff welfare 6.8 percent of total labor costs in 2007–2008.[69] Yet there is substantial variation in NWP across the Prowess/CMIE sample.[70] The nonwage category includes a number of elements: statutory contributions of provident funds, annual bonuses, productivity incentives, in-house training programs, and staff welfare benefits ranging from housing and transportation to medical care and childcare. It stands to reason that firms recording nothing or very little as the nonwage proportion of total labor costs might be using personal networks and affective ties, including payment of workers through lump sums to contractors, as tactics of labor management. It might also record explicit nonimplementation

---

[69] Government of India Labour Bureau 2010b, 74–77t.

[70] As a result of missing data on labor, the size of the Prowess/CMIE dataset is 5,618. Unfortunately, wages and total labor costs in the dataset include managerial and executive compensation and thus do not straightforwardly reflect the wages of workers. However, we are interested in the variations in the relationship between labor costs and wages, as they reflect the extent to which firms use formal incentives and adhere to statutory requirements. CMIE adds managerial and executive costs back in to both wages and total labor costs; as a result, these will affect both sides of the ratio and thus cancel out, leaving the differences of interest to this study. In addition, I will add the proportion of executive compensation to total labor cost as an explanatory variable in the multivariate analysis in Appendix A. I thank R. Nagaraj for drawing attention to these issues in the data.

of labor legislation: employer contributions to provident funds are statutory requirements. Conversely, those who record a relatively higher proportion of nonwage costs in total labor costs are likely to be using formal systems that represent formal institutions in labor management, such as productivity-linked bonuses, and welfare provision as a means of retention. These firms are also more likely to follow statutory requirements as a means to anchor labor, even as monitoring is low. The data presented in the following are for 2008, to ensure comparability with my interview sample.

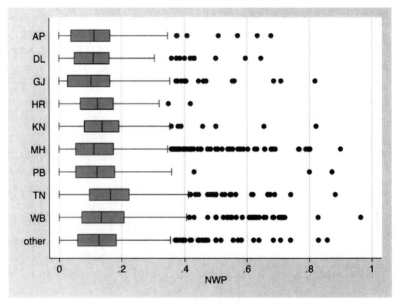

Figure 5.1 Nonwage Proportion of Firm Labor Costs, by State.

State Governments

It is plausible that the policies and practices of state governments might compel or encourage firms to invest more in the welfare and bonuses of their workers. In this reading, states with active and effective labor policies will have more firms with on average higher levels of non-wage labor costs, as bureaucrats and politicians work to encourage training programs, performance incentives, and staff welfare. Figure 5.1 and Table 5.1 record the nonwage proportion of firm-level total labor costs by state.

Table 5.1 *Comparison of Nonwage Proportions of Labor Cost, by State*

	Mean	Standard error	95% C.I.	$F_{1,6672}$	p-value
Delhi and Haryana	.115	.002	.109 –.120	11.35	**0.0008**
Maharashtra	.128	.003	.123–.134	0.15	.6963
Tamil Nadu	.171	.005	.162–.179	73.20	**>.0001**
Gujarat	.110	.004	.102–.119	14.09	**.0002**
West Bengal	.157	.005	.147–.168	31.9	**>.0001**
Other states (Excluded)	.130	.002	.125–.134	(Excluded)	

Note: One-way ANOVA, root MSE: .111, R^2: .02. Figures in bold are statistically significant

Table 5.1 represents significant statewise variation in non-wage labor costs, but in unexpected directions. Tamil Nadu and West Bengal, one of the most successful and one of the least successful states, respectively, record higher nonwage proportions; the West Bengal figure may be due to the power of the Communist Party of India-Marxist (CPM) and its affiliated Center for Industrial Trade Unions (CITU) in the state, which would mean both stronger formal union representation and greater implementation of labor legislation. Tamil Nadu's exceptionalism, mirroring its firms' higher than average debt–capital ratios, as mentioned in Chapter 4, might actually be evidence of state-level industrial governance. Yet firms in the Gujarat and the Delhi region exhibit lower than average non-wage labor costs, which indicate that a preponderance of firms in those regions are explicitly distancing themselves from state intervention, either through statutory requirements or through more discrete incentives. In Gujarat, a policy of explicit nonimplementation of legislation is in keeping with the probusiness orientation of the state government, but Figure 5.1 records quite substantial variation among the labor practices of Gujarati firms, suggesting that firms have not converged on a model of labor management driven by the state government under Modi.

Sectoral Regimes

It is also reasonable to posit that the management of labor differs significantly by sector. Different industries have different skill and

Table 5.2 *Comparison of Nonwage Proportions of Labor Cost, by Industry*

	Mean	Standard error	95% C.I.	$F_{1,6673}$	p-value
Textiles	.140	.004	.132 –.148	5.04	.025
Garments	.131	.008	.114–.147	0.01	.992
Autos and components	**.161**	**.004**	**.153–.169**	**31.00**	**>.0001**
Pharmaceuticals	.122	.005	.113–.131	1.65	.199
Other industries	.130	.002	.127–.133	(Excluded)	(Excluded)

Note: One-way ANOVA, root MSE: .112, R^2: .01. Figures in bold are statistically significant

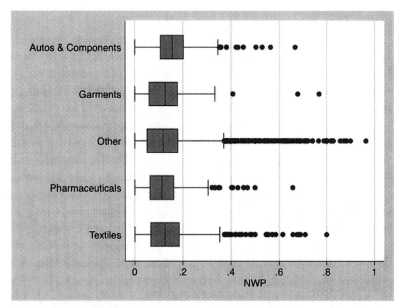

Figure 5.2 Nonwage Proportion of Firm Labor Costs, by Sector.

stability requirements: a worker in a garment cluster is likely to have a significantly different profile from that of a machinist in an automotive ancillary. But broader institutional concerns might also influence the philosophies and practices of human resources: globally linked industries such as garments and automotive components are subject to regulation and inspection by buyers as well as by the state. Figure 5.2 and Table 5.2 report the nonwage proportion of total labor costs by sector.

In a comparison of industry means, only automotive vehicles and components, and to some extent textiles, are significantly higher than the average. This makes sense: as I will further elaborate in Chapter 6, the automotive industry is the most closely linked to GVC through end producer MNCs. Further, worker representation and trade union activism are uncharacteristically powerful in this industry, as a strike at the Maruti Suzuki plant in Haryana leading to a negotiated settlement over welfare and reinstatement of dismissed temporary workers seems to demonstrate.[71] Powerful unions capable of negotiating credibly can lead to higher bonuses and greater welfare. Some of the same dynamics may be driving more modestly higher means in textiles, although Figure 5.2 indicates substantial variation for both textile and garment sectors.

Age Cohort

Moving from regional and sectoral explanations to firm-level explanations, I start with the age cohort of the firm. Like Rayon Spinners, firms that were established and incorporated before independence and during the period of high statism built workforces in an institution-rich environment, in which trade unionism and labor regulation loomed large in the management of workers. Firms established after liberalization, by contrast, faced a context of much more fragmentation and deinstitutionalization. Further, many of those entering industry after 1991 were traders and foremen, and thus accustomed to more personalistic approaches to labor management. Figure 5.3 and Table 5.3 record the nonwage proportion of total labor cost for firms in different age cohorts.

Both Figure 5.3 and Table 5.3 indicate highly significant and powerful differences in the age cohorts of firms with regard to the nonwage labor costs; firms established before 1970 have significantly higher proportions than those later, and especially those established after liberalization in 1991. That firms had on average more substantial commitments to bonuses, welfare, and the like, during statism is not surprising. That firms established in the statist era *still* have, on average, much higher proportions of nonwage costs speaks to the power of context and the stickiness of institutional legacies.

[71] *Times of India* 2011.

Table 5.3 *Comparison of Nonwage Proportions of Labor Cost, by Age Cohort*

	Mean	Standard error	95% C.I.	$F_{1,6622}$	p-value
Before 1950	.207	.007	.194–.221	227.36	>.0001
1951–1970	.193	.006	.183–.204	168.96	>.0001
1971–1990	.128	.002	.124–.131	(Excluded)	(Excluded)
Post-1991	.113	.002	.110–.117	23.5	>.0001

Note: One-way ANOVA, root MSE: .109, R^2: .07

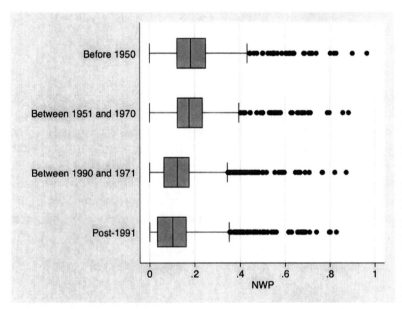

Figure 5.3 Nonwage Proportion of Firm Labor Costs, by Firm Age Cohort.

Firm Size

Firm size can have a powerful structural influence on labor strategies; in smaller firms, relationships between workers and the management are more cheek-by-jowl, whereas for the largest firms, the scale of production by its nature requires that systems be set in place to manage a large workforce. Figure 5.4 and Table 5.4 reports firms' nonwage proportion of labor costs by size decile.

Table 5.4 *Comparison of Nonwage Proportions of Labor Cost, by Size Decile*

	Mean	Standard error	95% C.I.	$F_{1,6664}$	p-value
1st Decile	.154	.004	.146–.161	14.52	.0001
2nd Decile	.147	.003	.141–.152	9.57	.0020
3rd Decile	.142	.003	.136–.148	4.75	.0293
4th Decile	.140	.003	.134–.146	3.60	.0578
5th Decile	.135	.004	.128–.143	0.93	.3360
6th Decile	.130	.005	.121–.139	Excluded	Excluded
7th Decile	.125	.006	.113–.137	0.56	.4561
8th Decile	.099	.007	.086–.119	20.9	>.0001
9th Decile	.070	.008	.055–.085	61.56	>.0001
10th Decile	.067	.014	.040–.095	24.54	>.0001

Note: One-way ANOVA, root MSE: .111, R^2: .01

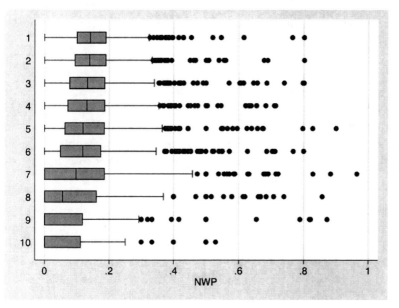

Figure 5.4 Nonwage Proportion of Firm Labor Costs, by Size Decile.

Table 5.4 reports significant differences in proportion of nonwage costs by size. Yet interestingly, Figure 5.4 indicates increasing variation in the strategies of medium and small firms. This suggests that larger firms are more constrained by practical considerations of labor management; it

Table 5.5 *Comparison of Nonwage Proportions of Labor Cost, by Levels of Export*

	Mean	Standard error	95% C.I.	$F_{1,8400}$	p-value
0 percent	.120	.002	.116–.125	(Excluded)	(Excluded)
Less than 24 percent	.151	.002	.146–.155	92.44	>.0001
25–49 percent	.147	.004	.138–.155	22.82	>.0001
50–74 percent	.135	.005	.126–.144	4.34	.0372
76–100 percent	.130	.005	.120–.139	2.04	.1528

Note: One-way ANOVA, root MSE: .111, R^2: .01

is also likely that larger firms are more subject to regulatory regimes and the demands of organized labor for regular bonuses. Small and especially medium-sized firms seem to exhibit a remarkable variation in strategy, suggesting that manufacturers deploy an array of strategies.

Export Orientation

Export orientation may also frame some structural constraints, particularly with regard to regulations and inspections imposed on firms by international buyers and end-stage producers. Workers may also have additional leverage when orders are tight. Table 5.5 and Figure 5.5 report firms' nonwage proportion of labor costs by cohorts of export orientation.

Figure 5.5 suggests significant differences between those firms that produce wholly for the domestic economy and firms with at least some exports. Yet Table 5.4 presents an odd result: firms with less than 50 percent exports have more significant differences in labor management in relation to domestic firms than those with more than 50 percent. As I will explore further in Chapter 6, the meanings and mechanisms of export orientation can differ dramatically, depending on whether exporting firms are engaged with disaggregated sales and linkages between small firms across borders or are integrated in higher-technology GVCs.

As I have demonstrated here and will further elaborate in Appendix A, firm-level characteristics are clearer explanations for the variation in labor management strategies –proxied by nonwage labor costs – than

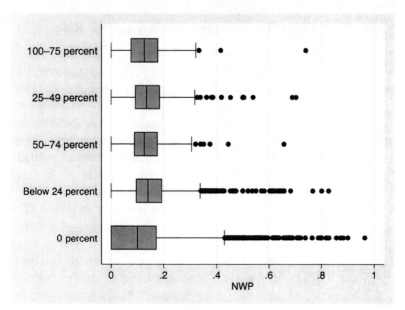

Figure 5.5 Nonwage Proportion of Firm Labor Costs, by Levels of Export Orientation.

either states or sectors. In terms of regional governments, as with financing, Tamil Nadu and West Bengal seem particularly distinctive with regard to higher proportion of nonwage costs, with Gujarat and the Delhi region presenting significantly lower proportions than the average. For sectoral regimes, as in financing arrangements, textiles and vehicles and automotive components have higher than the average for all sectors. Yet labor management differs most dramatically by firm-level indicators – firm age cohort, size decile, and export cohort – suggesting that variation is most readily explained at the firm level.

Aggregate patterns do not help us understand the specific and concrete strategies manufacturers use to manage labor. These mechanisms are important because they illuminate how industrialists work around the challenges faced by recruiting, training, and retaining workers after the fragmentation of the workforce and the weakness of state-driven institutions outlined previously. In the following, I present interview-based accounts of how some firms manage labor through the creation of formal rules, incentives, and institutions, while others rely on personal ties, affective relations, and mechanisms such as labor contracting to accomplish the same aims through different means.

Labor Recruitment and Retention through Formal Rules

For many manufacturers, the key to recruitment and retention of labor is the establishment of clear rules for hiring, promoting, and managing line workers, as well as their supervisors. On the most quotidian level, this often means the establishment of a separate human resources department as an institution within the firm that takes specific professional responsibility for labor issues and signals, to outside investors among others, that they are serious about managing workers professionally. A vice president in one of the large Tier-I automotive firms in Delhi said, "Finding good people is difficult as demand outstrips supply ... [our] retention strategies [are] based the HR department: they are communicative, performance-driven" (2007-del40). A Chennai-based director of another large Tier-I automotive firm emphasized the use of experts to maximize the productivity of line workers, emphasizing both Taylorist efficiency gains and Fordist living wages: "On the shop floor, we have the usual battery of consultants. Attrition is 12% at management level, for blue collar it's less; it's an old company, so we pay high wages" (2007-chn10). Thus the very institutionalization of personnel policy signals a more systemic approach to overall labor management.

A visit to an otherwise nondescript components factory in Gurgaon, an industrial satellite city to Delhi, revealed, on the shop floor, the one-word slogans of the Toyota-originated "lean production" and incremental innovation – *seiketsu, shitsuke* – in Japanese characters with English transliterations (2007-del26). These reminders could not have meant much to the line workers, who were unlikely to have reading fluency in either Japanese or English, but such ideas serve to broadcast particular firm orientations both outward and inward. And the importance of language was explicitly mentioned by a director in a pharmaceutical enterprise from a family with its roots in Mumbai mill ownership in the 1950s: "We've been lucky because we have good management practices ... we have good meritorious systems for promotions – a third of our scientists are women. Right from language we use [we] make it a fun place to work" (2008-mmb6). This language might have been deployed for my benefit, but it still reflects an emphasis on formality, merit, and modern office-speak.

Incentives and Productivity

An integral part of the institutionalization of human resources is remuneration that is based on incentives and productivity. An apparel manufacturer educated in textile design at Manchester University – with a workforce of five hundred, 70 percent of them permanent labor, in a cluster of other garment factories in a Delhi industrial estate – said, "Finding but especially retaining [workers] is hard; the challenge is to keep them motivated, because they can find a job anywhere. We provide a good [working] environment, and incentive schemes" (2007-del27). A Mumbai-based apparel exporter with production facilities in Andhra Pradesh and Gujarat emphasized not just incentives but also buyers' guidelines and the provision of services to women that would enable their labor:

[We have] workers on fixed salaries with production incentives, and total social compliance with retailers. [There is no] child labour, no continuous hours – some overtime once in a while, just a couple of hours. We hire lots of women workers (60 percent in Hyderabad, 30–40 percent in Vapi) … finding skilled labour is difficult [but] we give them a crèche [day care], and we pay for their transportation. We provide continuous production incentives. (2008-mmb3)

A fledgling rubber components manufacturer in the Delhi NCR was adopting global language in his discussion of production incentives: "It depends on the kind of environment and wage levels... [We have] some programs at different levels, quality circles, involving them, motivating and rewarding them" (2007-del17). My respondent mentioned that the Automotive Component Manufacturers' Association (ACMA) was particularly helpful because they sponsored trips that allowed smaller companies to visit companies such as Toyota and Suzuki and to learn their techniques of productivity and worker involvement.

The chairman of a venerable Mumbai-based pharmaceutical manu-facturing firm established just after independence mentioned a frame-work for self-bidding on wages that is designed to decrease resentment and increase participation: "We have a system whereby everyone fixes their own salaries. You apply for a higher salary if you think you deserve it and eight times out of ten, we accept. Other cases, we've said sorry, you're very good but we can't afford you, look for a job elsewhere" (2008-mmb4). A director of a fifty-year-old textile mill in

Coimbatore employing between forty five hundred and five thousand workers discussed how projects by initiated by the Tamil Nadu state government, including infrastructure and populist spending and the NREGA, were implicitly creating a social wage floor and maintaining a tight labor market. He has established a strategy for attracting labor that, apart from wages and benefits, emphasizes flexibility: "We provide monthly wages, provident fund, and medical insurance. But there are six different 'products' – you can choose whatever wage structure, work pattern" (2008-coi5).

Training

A much more concrete aspect of labor management through formal rules and institutions is that of training, in effect building up custom-made human capital to fit the firm's purpose, rather than relying on competing in the tight market for already skilled workers. The director of a textile manufacturing firm in Delhi that is owned by one of the largest steel groups in the country, employing nine hundred workers, who are mostly housed in dormitories by the factory, has high attrition but compensates through training: "Our attrition is 15–20 percent, but it's not a problem because we keep on training freshers, even at engineering level. There is no unrest, no shortage [because] we have a proper scientific system" (2007-del15). An established textile mill in Karnataka, with roots in the British Managing Agency system and employing six thousand permanent workers in two locations, has established an explicit training regime, with inputs from the state government: "We have own training program: it lasts eighteen months, [it is] paid, with an external examination at the end" (2008-mmb13).

Some firms have formed explicit partnerships with universities or even formed their own educational institutions. A decades-old Chennai-based automotive component firm cited earlier has partnered with engineering institutes to provide recent graduates with requisite skills, while acknowledging the difficulties of attracting top-tier engineering talent, from the IIT, to manufacturing. The respondent, himself an IIT graduate, said:

We have a new management program; it's becoming a new management institute. We have a Technology Appreciation Program with IIT Madras that is focused on knowledge renewal ... there are more engineering grads [in Tamil Nadu], but it's hard to find selective candidates. Delhi College of Engineering is good. IITans don't go to industry, they go to MNCs, MNC banks, IIMs. It is second-stringers that come to manufacturing. (2007-chn10)

Another Chennai-based manufacturer, heading a firm that is part of a group founded in 1911, mentioned sponsoring promising candidates for overseas education: "We have training for new workers, exposing them to other workers, classifying them into categories, matching the skill levels. [The firm] is a sponsor for higher education – we send 1–2 candidates for higher training in abroad: Cranfield University, Warwick. The compensation structure is competitive; management is proactive" (2007-chn8).

Others speak of training in a more holistic sense that resembles the strategies of firms that are governed by personal networks. One Coimbatore textile manufacturer employing six hundred workers talks of his recruitment and retention in this way:

They all get paid by the month; there are lots of incentives for work ... in training, we mold them, we give them holistic, spiritual education. It's a year-long process. In Tamil Nadu, there is good, disciplined labor: we give them a lot of freedom along with responsibility, to take these things in the right spirit. Elsewhere, there is work for work's sake – [the workers'] thoughts are on that. (2008-coi2)

Of course, the transcendental content of their training may be simply rhetoric, but such rhetoric can be useful for understanding how managers think about workers' training. Another automotive component manufacturer in Delhi includes in his training and incentives regime a family approach: "For labor retention, [we are] providing courses. We are sponsoring people: Total Employed Family Involvement. There's an annual day, lots of training/retraining" (2007-del21).

Whether training is draped in technocratic or more socially embedded language, it still signifies a way of thinking about labor recruitment that relies less on competition in the market or on socially embedded networks that might provide skilled workers, as we shall see, and more on having greater control of this crucial input in production. This is inevitably a risky strategy – trained workers can leave and find jobs at higher wages – but one that might be considered essential given the requirements of production in niche markets and the difficulty in hiring already trained workers.

Welfare Provision

Beyond competition on wages and training, firms that manage labor by formal rules also emphasize the provision of welfare and services. This is one of the oldest practices in Indian industry; industrialists in late colonial India had to provide services such as housing and medication to recruit workers in the tight and fluid labor markets of the period. In today's tight labor markets, provision of services is a way of supplementing wages and signaling commitments to workers, and thus aiding retention. But the provision of social services in the contemporary context of disaggregated production and migrant labor presents difficulties. One textile manufacturer with production in northern and western India explained seasonal labor migration in terms of training and services:

[some] workers come from local areas, but lots are migrating from Bihar, Orissa, Uttar Pradesh to Gujarat, and even Bihari and Orissan labour to Uttar Pradesh. They settle down and work for a time, then go back. So we get labor, but then you have to train them to get the proficiency. You look after them, engage them in terms of giving them housing, looking after their needs ... we take social responsibility. They go back in cultivation season, and this creates shortages. (2007-del24)

Another textile manufacturer in an old family business with production facilities in Rajasthan mentioned strategies for retaining labor migrating from surrounding states, including "giving [competitive] wages, dorm housing, lots of welfare activities to keep them entertained and focused on the work" (2007-del36). Other factories recruit their workers from the surrounding areas, and thus target their social services provision to a much wider community of which the line workers are a part. A Mumbai-based viscose manufacturing firm frames its work in the language of corporate social responsibility, with direct employment of workers benefiting a much larger population: "[We have] four thousand employees in direct employment and a hundred thousand in indirect. Our technicians are trained, with workers recruited from areas around – we provide housing, a school, a hospital, a bank, a canteen, a green area, a [housing] colony. And we do CSR work with 50–100 villages around our 92 factories" (2008-mmb19).

A rural location for production can have both benefits and costs, but usually requires larger outlay on social services. One components

manufacturer outside Chennai chose a location for production such
that he did not have to compete on wages as much, but provides
more services:

We located our factories in such a way that the local wages are lower, so
we're bigger players and so pay comparatively better; workers would
migrate into Chennai from peri-urban areas. We provided a shuttle bus from
the main road to factory, as [the factory's location] has a railway station and
a bus terminal. We provide workingmen with production incentives in
addition to salary. Also, complete social security – health, etc. for them
and families. And canteen facilities: one good meal a day. We don't have
dormitory housing because it creates disparities. (2007-chn3)

The services that some of these manufacturers provide could be seen as
either a supplement to incomes or an enabling mechanism for commitment and thus higher productivity.

Organized Labor

Although virtually all of my respondents referred to unions as a
nuisance – the product of local and mafia-related politics – a couple
of firms in Tamil Nadu sought to establish relationships with
cooperative unions. A textile and apparel manufacturer in Tiruppur
employing five hundred permanent staff mentioned good relationships with their union: "We have a trade union, but they're very
cooperative. We have bargaining once a year" (2008-trp5). An automotive component manufacturer mentioned the importance of voice
and representation:

We have 805 staff and associates that all come under our internal union. We
need to provide some sort of representation … allow people to voice,
organize an internal election, people get to choose the committee and they
hold monthly meetings with management. Through the internal union, we
settle on long-term contracts: 3–4 years at a time that are periodically
renewed. (2007-chn4)

In large part, cooperation with these essentially in-house company
unions is a way of creating at a much smaller scale the kind of certainty
that sectoral and regional corporatism provided in earlier decades. The
elderly chairman of one of the largest and oldest automotive groups
in the country, based in Chennai, talked of his long and cordial
relationship with his company's union, affiliated with the International

Metal Workers' Organization and not a political party, and of the changes to organized labor over five decades:

> In the 1970s, there was militancy and violence, motivated by competition between Congress and the DMK. Now, the reliance of political parties on organized labor has declined; this realization has come as technology has become more sophisticated, and blue collar has become more white collar. There is no need to be militant. President of our union is [name redacted]. There is one union for the Group. It's IMWO-affiliated and well organized. I wouldn't want it any other way; I don't want a well-fed, vegetarian union. (2008-chn15)

It is also unsurprising, given the quantitative evidence, that the companies with cooperative relationships with labor are almost exclusively in the south of the country, where contemporary political contestation between regional nationalist parties has largely excluded labor activism as a mechanism for electoral mobilization.

Automation

Lastly, automation is a strategy for those with enough capital who are interested in dramatically decreasing the costs associated with worker management entirely. A textile manufacturer in Ludhiana mentioned automation as an answer to the dearth of skilled labor: "we hire 450–500 people from various places in Punjab, UP and Bihar. They are permanent workers but as industry grows, there's a shortage. The solution is automation" (2007-lud1). Another textile manufacturer operating in the very tight labor market of Punjab, with union activism in big spinning mills, mentioned that his strategy of coping with costs is to reduce workers (2007-cdg3). Others pursue automation as a means of changing the nature of the workforce structurally from a large pool of less skilled workers to a small group of technicians. As one Chennai-based auto parts manufacturer put it: "We always need a lot of moderately skilled labor, but we have made a huge investment to push skills higher and higher through automation, so that instead of maintaining a hundred people, you care about ten who are much more skilled" (2007-chn3). Automation is one of the oldest strategies in industry and has been the subject of workers' contestation throughout the nineteenth and early twentieth centuries. Yet in India, where labor is considered not only a crucial input but also the source of national competitiveness, automation strategies highlight both the difficulties in recruiting and retaining skilled workers and the willingness to pursue the "exit" option by substituting a potentially much more expensive input. Those reaching for such strategies are more likely to be the ones who see the economy as less of an organic enterprise in which workers form an indelible part and more a set of substitutable components within a rational institutional structure. But the potential effectiveness of this strategy also does not bode well for India's development in the longer term.

Labor Recruitment and Retention through Personal Networks

Personal and relational strategies of labor management arise from a fundamentally different understanding of what constitutes economic activity: as dense networks of personal ties of reciprocity, obligation, and loyalty rather than systems of rules and incentives. This often self-consciously *affective* relationship between the firm's owners (respondents in northern India often use the Hindi word *saith*, or boss) and workers tends to use idioms of family and obligation in discussing how management relates to labor. One pharmaceutical manufacturer in Delhi used exactly this metaphor in our discussion: "They are like family members, they love me and I love them. Some workers have been with me since 1955, 1960 – now, their children are with me" (2007-del48). A Delhi-based garment exporter expressed a similar sentiment: "We are attached with labor since the start, we are personally training them how to do this or that. . . I know most of them. There is a guy working for us, his grandfather was working here before" (2007-del38).

The point is not to take this language at face value but to understand the assumptions and perspectives that lie behind it. The use of this language and these assumptions was particularly prevalent among those manufacturers who invested in manufacturing after years of experience as workers and supervisors; such experience recalls the idiom of "toil" that Sharad Chari identified as central to the capital–labor dynamics of the Tiruppur knitwear cluster.[72] One pharmaceutical manufacturer talked of how such experience as a sales representative helped him handle relationships with workers:

[72] Chari 2000.

"My advantage is that I worked as a medical representative, so you have the feel, you can handle all the situations. It's not that that difficult" (2007-del32).

Formative experiences trading in and otherwise interacting with local market conditions in India are thus more likely to inspire the building of specific relationships and the use of the small scale and the personal as means of solving labor recruitment and retention problems. One manufacturer mentioned the importance of recommendations from communities of existing workers in recruiting additional labor: "There must be an opening, we go to people already employed. They spread the word in their community, they provide references... Muslims are good, and they bring others" (2007-del5). The community references for new workers have added advantages in giving existing workers a stake in the performance of new recruits and may even lead to greater peer monitoring and skill transfer.

Firms that structure production through personal networks often evince a certain skepticism as to the ability to motivate work and productivity through incentives-based human resources management. One respondent, a Mumbai-based textiles manufacturer, discussed this at length:

Absenteeism is more than you'd like, the workers are coming from villages, they return for their marriages, festivals, and the agricultural season. They also have a sense of satisfaction, fulfillment of their need. They don't mind working less. We pay monthly wages – a twenty-five day month, but fifty percent of people work twenty days a month. Twenty percent absenteeism means twenty more people. On the odd days with more absenteeism, it becomes difficult. Contract labor needs to be regular, only known and planned and not spontaneous. We are running lower than capacity, and sometimes there's no work – but they still need to be paid. This is law – we can only do certain things against it, so we are paying for no work. We provide incentives for those who come regularly – but it's the same group that is regularly attending. (2008-mmb10)

Certainly there are shades of paternalism and some problematic projections into workers' inner lives displayed here, but also a recognition that contemporary workers are pulled in different directions by contradictory commitments. Most North Indian industrial labor migrate to cities such as Mumbai, Pune, Delhi, and Ahmedabad because for most of the year, they are not needed in the agricultural work of their "native places," but they have obligations to return for labor-intensive activities like harvesting; Lewis identified this "disguised unemployment" in the agrarian sectors of developing countries several decades ago.[73]

The textile strikes and industrial transformations of the 1970s and 1980s also put paid to the notion that a permanent urban working class could be created and maintained by formal structures of regulation and representation, leading workers to diversify their own means of generating income. Recognizing that workers are only partially committed to industrial labor is at the heart of the need to form extracontractual ties with the workforce, so that skilled workers return from the harvest and continue to work together. This often means coethnic solidarity. A fabric manufacturer in the periurban power loom cluster of Bhiwandi, roughly forty-five minutes by train from central Mumbai, explained the ethnic breakdown of the city and how workers interacted with their employees:

Workers are mostly from UP/Bihar... my own native place. Local people come – these farmers. All this area is power looms – they come to us directly; when we need them, we hire. Generally, they are experienced – if someone is new, they come with friends and get training with them. They regularly come from [their] native place and go back in May – for marriage, family, crops, and [festivals]. They go in May for two–three months, and we pay daily wages during the period. Workers from UP and Bihar make shirting and sari material, blouse pieces. The workers from Andhra and Tamil Nadu, they do suiting, panting ... other people [firms] do that. In Bhiwandi, different *mohalla* (neighborhood), they make different materials. (2008-mmb27)

In a fairly detailed account of wages and costs for workers in his factory, my respondent indicated that power loom operators could expect to receive Rs. 6,000–9,000 ($150–225) a month, from which they pay Rs. 100 for housing for a room in which ten to twenty workers might stay, Rs. 700 for meals in communal kitchens, leaving just above Rs. 5,000–Rs. 8000 in savings, 40–60 percent of which they remit internally back to their families in northern India. The workers are thus investing in their homes, villages, and families mostly in UP and Bihar, and thus not in the nature and status of their industrial work in Bhiwandi and elsewhere in industrial northern and western India. Such relative lack of concern is a challenge for industrialists. As we have seen, some manufacturers try to shape the structure of incentives. Others, committed to production by personal networks, use

[73] Lewis 1954.

mechanisms such as coethnic recruitment and labor contracting to maintain solidarity and surveillance.

Contract Labor

A major strategy for those firms managing labor through personal networks is the employment of labor contractors or "jobbers," who not only provide groups of workers but also remain responsible for them as foremen; this system subcontracts the crucial responsibilities of labor recruitment, retention, and monitoring. Firms in all industries and regions use contracted labor, and many see it as a solution to finding skilled labor, as a Delhi-based textile manufacturer indicated: "In the last two years, it was hard to find labor. We needed to put in extra efforts to find good people – now, we have jobbers, they bring labor from villages" (2007-del28). Auto component manufacturers in western India also use a mix of permanent direct employees and contract workers: one from Pune mentioned that he goes to contractors for 60 percent of his workforce, while another based in Mumbai goes to contractors to fill 40 percent of his labor requirements, workers who rotate every six months (2008-pun6; 2008-mmb40). A garment manufacturer in Mumbai has formed a workforce out of a mix of permanent and contract labor, with the former mostly working in weaving and the latter in stitching and finishing garments (2008-mmb31).

These practices contravene the spirit of Indian labor legislation and regulation, but the broad nonenforcement of such rules – particularly in the state of Gujarat, as suggested by the quantitative evidence – enables this strategy to be widely deployed. One textile manufacturer in Surat went into some detail on how the labor contracting system works in practice:

In textiles, 90 percent are migrants, from UP, Bihar, Orissa, Andhra Pradesh. The contract system has thrived because of no strict labor laws, and progressed because of demand. The workers are paid handsomely, paid part of gratuity. Contractors are settled in Surat, when someone comes here looking for a job, they must go through them. The contractor is responsible for output: they get paid one rupee per meter. 70 percent [of firms in Surat] have one contractor for one company. Workers stay in one locality. The contractor sets up the workers in a slum area – they live 5–6 to one house, and [the contractor] provides food and security. (2008-sur5)

Another Surat-based manufacturer, employing between fifteen hundred and two thousand migrant workers from Uttar Pradesh, Bihar, Orissa, and Assam, also indicated the universal use of contract labor, for flexibility but also for disciplining workers and dissuading them from trade unionism and militancy: "Labor all comes from contractors. These are relatives, with 5–6 people per group ... there are no problems with labor here, because we get contractors to [take] care of it" (2008-sur4). Further, this respondent muddied the distinction between permanent and temporary or contract labor by indicating that while 60 percent of his workforce was "permanent," they were still managed by contractors as foremen and supervisors.

In neighboring Maharashtra and in other states, much the same system applies, but the politics of the state requires labor contracting to be a more discreet practice. One garment manufacturer based in Mumbai discussed the benefits and the costs:

We have fewer workers on our own rolls – contractors provide whatever we require. They come every day for 8 hours, for two years or more. They are a regular workforce; you pay the contractor, they supply the labor. Once a team is built, they start running. Jobbers work for you ... [but] government rules are such [that] sometimes you can't work in some conditions. (2008-mmb9)

Contracting is ubiquitous in India; even the most rule-bound firms might hire labor contractors to provide bearers and cleaning staff, just as a company in the United States might contract out janitorial services. What distinguishes labor management through personal effort is a conscious effort to replace a permanent unitary workforce with a jigsaw of homogeneous component elements that can be internally disciplined by those who have the capacity to know their workers personally.

Scheme Work

The idiom of education has also been used to govern labor relations through personal networks. In Tamil Nadu, a large number of factories have adopted "scheme work," wherein young women were given three- to four-year training contracts at below market wages, and a lump-sum payment at the end of the "course," implicitly for dowries for marriage. One of my respondents, the scion of an established multiindustry group of companies in western Tamil Nadu, explained the system:

You take a girl from rural areas, apprentice her for three years, make her live in the hostel, eat meals there. They receive Rs. 95–100 per day, and Rs. 30,000 in the end for dowry. Scheme work was set up by [the respondent's father-in-law as the head of a mill in the 1990s]. If you follow the concept dutifully, you get useful skills. Now, there are bad examples, bad politics: issues of bonded labor. Once [the female workers are] inside, they're not allowed to go out. There have been cases of child labor, using underage workers. (2008-coi7)

Most scheme work is ultimately an arrangement between the young female worker's father or other male relative and the firm's recruiter or jobber, and thus there is significant opportunity for coercion embedded in the arrangement. While viscerally distasteful, there is some moral ambiguity in the practice: craft training and the capacity to earn a livelihood ultimately empower women even in the conservative rural communities of southern Tamil Nadu, and the dowry amount provides a little more choice in selecting a "suitable boy" for an arranged marriage.

Another industrialist pointed to the ubiquity of the scheme, and its integration with other forms of labor contracting:

We have 7000 workers per day – 50 percent are permanent. The other 50 percent are under a three-year labor contract with training, they leave after three years. Policy is four–five years old, before than, 80–90 percent were permanent. In the new mills, there are only scheme workers. Out of 1800 units in Tamil Nadu, 1700 units use scheme workers. They come only from the rural areas to get technical training. Agents, to find contractors, canvass people in the villages. (2008-coi4)

Even firms that have been established for a century have pivoted to scheme work for new workers as a way to handle the difficulties of a costly organized sector workforce (2008-coi8).

And the principles behind scheme work are also evident in other industries. One auto manufacturer, otherwise committed to union representation through formal channels for his permanent workforce, mentioned that training programs were being adopted as a new strategy for dealing with the shortage of trained workers, through apprenticeships that do not lead to more permanent work:

We may not be able to guarantee people to stay – the young like change – but we want to predict and control when they are leaving and joining. We provide training packages: it's a two–three year program, and then we give them a big amount and a training certificate at the end. The conditions up front: training (two days a month), and they have to stay during that time. At the end of two years, only 10 percent stick on. (2007-chn4)

Taken at face value, this system does not sound very different from a paid internship or indeed a postdoctoral fellowship; technical apprenticeship is also a deep and enduring feature of the automotive and machine tools industries of southern Germany. But systems like these rely on the Indian understanding of education as one of the only routes to success. The idiom of training, in the extreme case of scheme work or the more measured instances of apprenticeships, provides some certainty for labor retention and the paternalistic control that is implicit in apprenticeship programs such as this. They are also quite different from in-house training programs; for the latter, the goal is a better-trained and more stable workforce, whereas apprenticeship involves a constant cycling and lock-in for several years, rather than retention for a longer period.

Labor management through personal networks does not attempt to transcend the complex social realities facing Indian labor, through structuring incentives for retention and productivity through explicit institutions. Instead, it relies on familiarity, closeness, and community solidarity to achieve the core objectives of labor management: the recruitment and retention of skilled workers, as well as monitoring and discipline, through building affective ties with the workforce, contracting, and apprenticeships to translate the small-scale ethic of the workshop to larger-scale industrial production.

Conclusion

The political economy of Indian labor has undergone profound changes over the past few decades. A structure of representative and regulatory institutions that was created through the twin struggles of nationalism and of labor against capital have largely broken down; the mechanisms of capital–labor negotiations that lay at the heart of statist development have been supplanted by disjointed and competitive labor markets, the selective implementation of labor legislation, and a tremendous shortage of skilled workers. How, in this environment, manufacturers manage to recruit and retain workers, monitor their work, and thus maintain productivity represents a signal challenge to Indian industrial production.

As I have argued, firms address this challenge either by institutionalizing human resources and forming clear and explicit structures of incentives or by personalizing relationships with workers, either through building affective ties among the *saith*, jobber, and workforce or decreasing the scale of productivity and surveillance through labor contracting or apprenticeships. The selection of one set of strategies over another depends on the nature of firm governance more than the formal rules and incentives provided by the state government or sector. As a result, the go-to concepts of comparative political economy used to explain firm–labor relationships – sectoral, regional, or economy-wide labor market institutions – are limited in explaining the landscape of Indian industrial labor. This, I argue, is both a consequence of the state's weakened capacities for governing the industrial economy and the ways in which manufacturing firms must, in effect, structure their own institutions in relating to industrial labor.

6 | Indian Manufacturing and the International Economy

Globalization has transformed the landscape of the manufacturing economy throughout the world. Even in this worldwide phenomenon, however, India stands out: from a deeply inward-looking stance as late as the 1990s, Indian industry has emerged as a globally integrated and dynamic player in the international economy. India is now the world's sixteenth largest exporting country, with exports worth $317.8 billion in 2013. Exports of goods and services as a percentage of GDP grew from 4.4 percent in 1960 and 6.9 percent in 1990 to 12.8 percent in 2000 and 24 percent in 2012. Of India's merchandise exports, 64 percent were of manufactured goods, and this figure reached as high as 75 percent in 2002.[1] Some Indian companies have even become multinationals: Tata Motors's purchase of Jaguar and Land Rover representing only one of several corporations with significant productive assets outside India.[2] Given that consumption, technology, and, increasingly, production cross international borders as a matter of course, the capacities of Indian firms to participate in export markets and overseas investments are a big part of India's global economic emergence. Further, even though exports of services – and particularly of IT services – are seen as the core of India's economic vitality, exports of IT services constituted only about 22.5 percent of India's total exports of goods and services between 2005 and 2012, whereas manufactured goods constituted 43.4 percent during the same period. Indian manufacturing is thus an important component of India's integration into world markets and its emergence as a global economic player.

The nature of India's fast and furious integration into world markets constitutes a serious challenge to some of the core arguments of this

---

[1] World Development Indicators 2015.
[2] Net outflows of foreign direct investment reached a high of 1.6 percent of GDP in 2008. World Development Indicators 2015.

book, because this process is one in which the state must be centrally involved. A core function of any state is control over its borders, and we see the capacities of the central government effectively deployed in managing the movement of goods across national frontiers.[3] Indeed, scholars have lauded the recent efforts of agencies of the Indian state, in coordination with business associations, in facilitating India's remarkable global economic integration. Further, Indian firms pursuing foreign markets are aided by structures of global economic governance, from the international trade and finance institutions to increasingly elaborate transnational networks of production and consumption. These structures are likely to be sectorally specific, indicating that export-oriented firms might just cluster by sector in ways that domestic firms might not. Regardless, any Indian manufacturing firm that enters into export markets should be exposed to strong directions and incentives from the export-promoting state as well as from the institutions embedded in global markets.

Because of this, export orientation and integration into world markets constitute the hardest possible case for the relevance of firm-level production structures; firms in the arena should be able to rely on more effective state institutions and associational networks, as well as clearer signals from the international economy to structure their production. Indeed, previous chapters have borne out the distinctiveness of export-oriented firms, which have, on average, higher debt–capital ratios (Figure 4.5) and a higher proportion of nonwage costs in total labor costs (Figure 5.5). Yet even with firms integrated into the international economy, we see variation in firm behavior that is linked to production structures at the firm level. Firms vary on *how* they interact with foreign markets.

I suggest that the meaning and practice of international integration differ dramatically across Indian exporters of manufacturing goods, and the strategies of these firms in accessing global markets diverge on the basis of the level of formality in linkages with foreign firms. Several strategies are employed within the exporting community: diversifying between different export markets and domestic demand, specializing in niche products, attempting to enter into servicing relationships with

---

[3] Indeed, some argued that even the weakest states deploy the balance of their capabilities at their borders and in their representations to other states, as a function of representing and defending Westphalian sovereignty. See Jackson and Rosberg 1982; Herbst 2000.

the largest multinational retail or manufacturing corporations, building up large networks of individual relationships with small importers or manufacturers in developed and developing countries, and finally, for companies with the requisite capital or connections, acquiring companies or establishing offices abroad to facilitate penetration of foreign markets. The many strategies can be clustered into two broad categories: the pursuit of structural integration into GVCs at different levels or the building up of disaggregated networks of personalistic relationships with individual importers, buyers, downstream firms, and partners abroad. The bifurcation of firm-level production structures is evident in strategies of international integration as well, despite the presence and power of state actors and the signaling of global markets.

This chapter proceeds as follows. First, I will survey some of the literature on globalization and the state and argue for a more complicated relationship than a simple trade-off in power, particularly at the level of the firm. Then, I will briefly describe the ways in which the regime of statist development intervened in the relationship between the domestic economy and the international economy, and how these institutional structures transformed themselves in the process of India's economic integration. I will then present evidence on the international activities of firms in three sectors – garments, pharmaceuticals, and automotive components – based on interview data with more than a hundred export-oriented firms. I will outline how some export-based firms use formal institutions to integrate into formal GVCs while others use personal networks to build specific firm–firm relationships to facilitate exports or other types of international engagement. The relative convergence in the automotive components industry presents an important exception to systemic variations in governance, because a limited number of firms create and maintain networks of governance within their production chains, in India and internationally.

Globalization and the State

Globalization first appeared as a catchall concept for the global integration of markets in the 1970s, when world trade for the first time matched pre-1914 levels, but gained common currency after the end of the cold war as a ubiquitous if poorly defined organizing concept for a world order based on the principles of free trade and economic exchange rather than clashing ideologies.[4] For optimists, the efficiency gains from trade and convergence on a single set of (neoliberal) rules for governing economies would lead to greater overall prosperity and peace between nations; as such, globalization was part and parcel of a much-heralded "End of History."[5] For pessimists, globalization threatened a race to the bottom in terms of wages and welfare, the control of domestic economies by transnational capital, and thus a fundamental challenge to democracy, sovereignty, and political order.[6] For all, the rules of political economy that were written in the immediate postwar period needed to be reevaluated in such a way as to take into account systemic change and how domestic politics might be shaped by new international factors, or what Gourevitch has called "the second image reversed."[7]

Many commentators saw globalization as challenging the autonomous capacity of the state. For some, decreasing the discretion of the state in favor of a set of universal rules and global institutions was a largely positive occurrence, as unchecked state spending was seen as the cause of the debt crises of the 1980s.[8] Others were less sanguine about the ways in which international investors seek to constrain the democratic impulses of entire populations, in order to maximize their profits.[9] Susan Strange, in her nuanced treatment of the subject, outlined the manifold ways in which global economic forces fundamentally challenged the authority and the sovereignty of the nation-state.[10] Still others were skeptical about the "retreat of the state" thesis, noting that globalization has actually strengthened the power of many states in the international system, Russia, China, and South Korea, to name just three.[11] David Held and his colleagues have taken an intermediate approach, one that seems to have been followed by subsequent scholarship: globalization, as a transformational shock, has varied and unpredictable consequences that could expand the state's power or contract it.[12] Kiren Chaudhry eloquently traced the expansion and contraction of the Saudi state in response to the rentier shocks of the 1970s and 1980s that transformed the international economy.[13]

[4] Fiss and Hirsch 2005.   [5] Friedman 1999; Fukayama 1992.
[6] Barber 1995; Chua 2003.   [7] Gourevitch 1978; Kurth 1979.
[8] For the clearest articulation of this position, see Lal 1985.   [9] Rodrik 2011.
[10] Strange 1996.   [11] Wade 1996.   [12] Held et al. 1999.
[13] Chaudhry 1997.

Moving from national effects to variation within countries, commentators have noted that globalization would have differential effects on different industries in relation to the state, based on comparative advantage and factor scarcity. Frieden and Rogowski, in a seminal essay, argued that with the declines in the transactions costs associated with international exchange, internationally competitive sectors will have a qualitatively different response to protectionism and state policy from those industries that will lose out in international competition.[14] Shafer relates the comparative advantage point to state capacity; he has argued that the differential success in developing countries' capacities to respond to globalization, and thus their developmental trajectories, is explained by intersectoral differences, and specifically the ways that the nature and performance of their leading export sector shapes state autonomy and the ability to respond to market signals.[15] He thus suggests linkages to both sectoral governance and the state, which could be an important framework for understanding firm strategies. The challenge to this approach in this context is that India, being a large and internally diverse country, exports a great variety of different goods; no one sector drives the export economy in a way that mining might do in Zambia or cash crops in Costa Rica. Nevertheless, analysis of international integration at the level of the sector is a useful approach, and one that will be employed in the rest of the chapter.

What of India in the era of globalization? The Indian case presents something of a paradox. As late as the end of the 1980s, when countries from China to Chile had committed to greater openness and international integration, India was very much a closed economy, with a substantial apparatus of controls that severely restricted interaction with international markets.[16] By the middle of the current decade, however, India's integration into world markets was deep, wide-ranging, and significant, and India became a global economic player not just because of domestic production but also as a powerful exporter. How did this happen?

Aseema Sinha, in an excellent recent monograph on the subject, takes many strands of the literature in comparative political economy and international relations and weaves together a holistic understanding of the relationship between the state and the institutions that

---

[14] Frieden and Rogowski 1996. See also Lake 2009.   [15] Shafer 1994.
[16] Grieco 1984; Nayar and Paul 2003; Roy 2012.

structure global trade.[17] Sinha argues that the transformation of India's relationship with the international economy was the result of close interactions among empowered agents of the domestic state and representatives of international trade institutions. She constructs a "Global Design-in-Motion" framework to capture these dynamic relationships, in which "woodwork reformers" in the domestic economy empowered state agencies to facilitate India's integration into world markets, while also actively shaping the rules of the game in international trade in India's favor: "Global markets (cross border economic activity) and the global trade regime (international organizations, laws, rules as well as processes) catalyzed a change in domestic interests, and preferences as well as a change in domestic policies and strategies for global integration."[18] Sinha's framework and her empirical findings present a nuanced and coherent picture of the ways in which an "autonomous enough" state has structured India's integration into global markets. As such, it stands as a challenge to my general contention that the state has withdrawn from industrial governance, at least in terms of interactions with the international economy.

Although I generally agree with the outlines of Sinha's framing, I would argue that there are some reasons to be cautious about the capacity of the state in industrial promotion, even in this area. First, unlike other export-promoting economies, the Indian government keeps its exporters at relative arm's length. This is in stark contrast to China, in which export promotion has been hand in glove with the promotion of "national champions."[19] In South Korea and Japan, the highly concentrated structure of industry had similar functional consequences: trade policy has meant both the support and the disciplining of chaebols and keiretsu.[20] India has much less concentrated industries and, to their credit, a bureaucracy with a commitment to establishing broad principles of fairness in international markets, such as antidumping policy, rather than policies that link trade and industry in the support of particular firms. Further, services are a large and dynamic part of India's export profile, and thus it is unlikely that

---

[17] Sinha 2016. See also Sinha 2007.   [18] Sinha 2016, 26.

[19] Fuller 2016; MacGregor 2012. Both Fuller and MacGregor evince skepticism as to the long-run success of this strategy, but that does not take away from the fact that the Chinese state does a great deal for favored firms in the export economy.

[20] Johnson 1982, 1995; Woo-Cummings 1991.

export promotion would be as directly linked to *industrial* policy, with some exceptions such as TUFS.

Second, the resources behind export promotion policies in India, significant as these are, pale in comparison to those in the political economy of rents discussed in Chapter 1. This divergence is particularly biting when it comes to the infrastructure necessary for international integration. Governments at the state and federal level have spent billions of rupees on highways, overpasses, and other physical infrastructure, but these have been geared to the needs of urban motorists as consumers and voters, while leaving interstate highways and ports in a relative state of decay: the port of Singapore can turn container ships around in less than 12 hours, whereas in Mumbai it can take up to 50, and in Chennai up to 145 hours.[21] Third, Indian exports have over the last decade faced relatively severe shocks in exchange rates and trade balances: exchange rates have fluctuated more than 20 percent, making costs for international buyers and thus orders more uncertain. By contrast, China has expended a great deal of resources and political capital in order to keep its exchange rate stable and indeed even undervalued in order to maintain a stable platform for export-based growth.

Finally, the global trade regime that enabled Indian integration has itself stagnated. The failure of the Doha Development Round of GATT to reach an agreement, and the resulting weakness of the WTO, have led many developing countries to secure alternative bilateral treaties with dominant trading powers such as the United States and the European Union. Even though Shadlen has argued that multilateralism still has greater promise as a strategy for industrial development relative to bilateral alternatives, India has suffered from relative exclusion in bilateral agreements or emergent frameworks such as the Trans-Pacific Partnership.[22] The capacities that India had built up as an actor in the WTO need to be refashioned and redeployed in the context of rising bilateralism and regionalism; this is certainly a goal of the Modi government, but the transition will likely take some time and the outcomes are deeply uncertain.

An honest assessment of the Indian state's capacity to promote exports and facilitate the interaction between Indian industry and the international economy would thus be fairly ambivalent. Given that, it

---

[21] Jain 2006.   [22] Shadlen 2005; Miles 2014; Aggarwal 2013.

is perhaps not surprising that industrial firms would need to act independently, though in concert with the state, to create their own institutional relationships with global actors. Individual manufacturers, in other words, act to solidify firm-to-firm ties more generally enabled by higher-order efforts toward integration.

Perhaps more surprising, however, is that there is marked variation in the ways that firms seek to establish these links, and with whom. We usually think of export-oriented firms as converging on one model, driven by institutional signals from the state and the structure of world markets. Yet among Indian exporters, we see diversity: some firms act to integrate themselves into global networks of consumption and production driven by established multinationals, whereas others prefer disaggregated cross-border linkages and sales in the less regulated markets in the developing world. Such strategic diversity reflects the importance of and the varieties of firm-level institutional structures in acquiring capital and labor in the contemporary Indian economy and reaffirms the relevance of the firm perspective even in this "hard case."

This reflection is affirmed by the nature of manufacturing firms' engagement with global markets. Among the exporting firms in the Prowess/CMIE sample, 38 percent of the total, the average percentage of income from export sales was 29.64 percent. Thus most firms that derive a portion of their sales from export still maintain solid ties to the dynamics of the domestic economy, including the challenges of acquiring capital and managing labor. The export economy is not a separate enclave from but rather an outgrowth of the Indian manufacturing universe, and thus the diversity of export strategies reflect broader diversities in the ways that manufacturing firms form institutional structures for industrial production.

In what follows, I will explore these diversities in the context of three sectors: garments, pharmaceuticals, and auto components. All are relatively successful sectors in export orientation, and thus are not driven by pressures for protectionism, and yet each represents particular challenges in maintaining competitiveness. In each sector, I will outline the nature of India's integration into world markets, and the strategies firms adopt with regard to that integration. I find that the auto component sector is somewhat distinctive in achieving a degree of convergence, largely as a result of the unique nature of the industry, which can be understood as an oligopsony.

Garments

In the postindependence decades, changes in international trade and, later, consumer preferences domestically led to the establishment of mass production in apparel. In the 1960s, the Ford Foundation and other development agencies encouraged the export of Indian handicrafts to Western markets as a part of development aid (2008-del50). At around the same time, the rising costs in the United States and other Western countries led to the first international sourcing of garment manufacturing, initially from East Asia; apparel imports to the United States went from a negligible amount in 1960 to $21 billion in 1989 to a high of $73 billion in 2008. Yet the mass import of clothing from producers abroad threatened declining but still very influential domestic garments industry in developed countries.

As a result of calls for protection, the Multi-Fiber Arrangement (MFA) was established in 1974 to facilitate the trade adjustment of domestic textile industries in developed countries. The export of apparel to Western markets from 1974 to 2005 was governed tightly by a multilateral quota regime.[23] Quotas determined how much apparel could be sourced from particular countries, thus limiting overall imports to the West, while providing each developing country opportunities to export to Western markets. The quota regime accompanied a steady shift of global apparel production, first from Hong Kong, South Korea, and Taiwan first to Southeast Asia (Thailand, Malaysia) and then to South Asia (India, but also Pakistan, Bangladesh, and Sri Lanka) as the costs of production in newly industrializing countries increased.[24]

The operation of the quota regime at the international level lent a great deal of power to domestic state institutions. Government actors distributed permits to export within individual countries' quota allocation. Such a system necessitated substantive interactions between apparel firms and state agencies. Paramount among these was the Apparel Export Promotion Council in India (2007-del41; 2007-del42), which existed as partly a government agency, partly a trade association. In India, these quota permits established an exclusive if sizable club

---

[23] On the development and political dynamics of textile and apparel quotas, see Aggarwal 1985.

[24] Joshi 2002, 12.

of garment exporters, who had few incentives to innovate as their shares in the country's fixed quota allotments were guaranteed. In the 1990s, however, even before the expiration of the MFA, guarantees of exports from South Asian countries to developed markets were being increasingly threatened by a series of inter- and intraregional trade agreements, such as NAFTA, the EU, and the Caribbean Basin Trade Partnership Act (CBTPA), which established preferential trade relationships exclusive to members.[25] The regionalization of world trade was a foretaste of the challenges faced by garment exporters in the post-MFA environment.

Since the end of the MFA in 2005, international garment supply networks have become more competitive, and success has become defined more by quality, price, and ability to establish and maintain niches in the network than by tariffs, quotas, and the multilateral trade regime. This is simply because the preferences of powerful multi-national buyers such as Walmart, JC Penney, Ralph Lauren, and the Gap increasingly define the prospects of exports and firm orders. These preferences are largely based on considerations of price and quality, as well as the reliability of order completion.

Firms in South Asian countries, even before the quota regime ended, were relegated to the outer fringes of the value-added hierarchy, producing discount and commodity goods in mass quantities for buyer-driven commodity chains.[26] This niche has increasingly been taken up by China, the firms of which have much higher capacity, better infrastructure for delivery, and much lower unit costs. Moreover, a number of garment exporters have mentioned that the incentives that existed in the 1990s to promote garment exporters are no longer present, even though taxes and restrictions especially at the state level remain onerous and added paperwork has meant hiring more people (2007-del31; 2007-del33). The more recent TUFS program, which allowed textile-related concerns to receive preferential loans in order to update their capital machinery, is an exception to this general rule.

Firms that have been able to adapt to this new regime have done so through investments in technology and quality, often in clusterwide coordinated adaptation as with the knitwear manufacturers in Ludhiana and Tiruppur.[27] India has relatively vibrant upstream industries that provide garment manufacturers with a steady supply of good

[25] Joshi 2002, 15.   [26] Joshi 2002, 17.   [27] Cawthorne 1995; Tiwari 1999.

quality, low-cost cloth and yarn. It also has traditional skills and handicraft cultures that hold the potential for higher-value-added clothing with intricate embroidery and beadwork that, when tastes for such garments are established, cannot be easily substituted. Yet, respondents face a deep – and reasonable – fear that more market share would be lost to China and countries in Southeast Asia, nations with better infrastructure and lower unit costs. But export markets do not include only industrialized countries. Consumer demand for lower cost apparel in the Middle East and Southeast Asia, for example, constitutes a growing site of opportunity for garment manufacturers. Producing garments for export is defined by a growing variety of destinations, products, and channels that was less evident at the height of the MFA regime.

The end of the MFA regime has led garments manufacturers to pursue a variety of strategies, and thus structure relationships to the international economy in a variety of different ways. Choices of institutional strategies follow instincts toward the formal structures of integration in GVCs or the more personal networks of exporters, importers, buying agents, and brokers that cross borders and regions.

Garment Exports by Formal Rules and Value Chain Integration

For many garment exporters, successful production has meant attracting international retailers through a series of signals: unit cost, certainly, but also the long-term ability to follow design and production standards, while remaining flexible enough to adjust to rapidly changing orders and fashion trends. At the time of my interviews, the rupee's rapid appreciation against the dollar was making these signals more difficult to send. A garment manufacturer in Delhi whose father, a chartered accountant, started exporting garments in 1975 had concentrated on achieving compliance with major multinational buyers but had more recently shifted greater focus to the European market, focusing on midsize rather than large buyers (2007-del27). Other manufacturers working exclusively for European or American buyers focused on producing garments with higher-value-added components that are more price-inelastic. A fabric manufacturer who was born in Kandahar, Afghanistan, and worked for the family business until 1979 has developed semiintegrated production and export facilities for polo shirts and women's wear with embellishments; he suggested that moving into higher-value-added production in the 1990s had kept his business competitive until the year we talked, in which his turnover had decreased 40 percent as a result of rising costs (2007-del31).

Value addition does not necessarily mean changes in the production process. A successful garment exporter based in Mumbai with production facilities on the Maharashtra–Gujarat border had successfully broken into manufacturing for *haut couture* labels such as Versace and La Forma through careful attention to the fashion cycles, which entailed traveling to Paris several times a year to anticipate trends. This manufacturer also mentioned his intentions to climb higher up "the value chain" through the establishment of his own recognized brand among international buyers and his focus on "business with a social/environmental leaning" (2008-mmb35). Another much smaller export-oriented manufacturer – an ethnic Sindhi who moved to Mumbai after partition – focused on providing embroidery work to overseas fashion designers; subcontracted workshops produce made-to-order embroidery embellishments under the direction of National Institute of Fashion Technology (NIFT)–trained designers and the manufacturer's own interpretation of design requirements (2008-mmb22). Here, skill and connections to the intensely structured world of international design provide stickiness in the world of garments and fabric exports. The linkages among firms integrated into buyer networks and smaller, more local units, through subcontracting arrangements are particularly important for survival given the volatility of orders.[28]

Garment Manufacturing by Personal Networks

For other garment exporters, however, the key to continued success in international markets is predicated on the idea of person-to-person contacts at a much smaller scale than that of those sourcing for multinational retailers. This might mean cultivating links with smaller buyers in emerging economies with growing demand for ready-made clothing, for instance. A fabric manufacturer in the textile city of Bhiwandi, an exurb of Mumbai, produces low-cost shirts and *lungis* for export to workers in the Gulf (2008-mmb28). Another manufacturer in a textile

---

[28] For an excellent take on these dynamics in the Tiruppur cluster, see Arnold 2010.

trading family in Gujarat specialized in the export of children's clothing to Dubai and other parts of the Middle East and expressed an interest in domestic retail through his own brand to the middle class in India (2008-adb3). Another children's wear manufacturer in an old mill compound in Mumbai mentioned that successes in their export-oriented business were due to his father's efforts constantly traveling to develop individual relationships with smaller buyers in Asia, a job now taken over by my respondent's younger brother (2008-mmb8).

A number of garment exporters to developed country markets have ignored the major retail labels and chosen instead to focus on much smaller clothing retailers. The patron of a family business, with a Horatio Algeresque rags-to-riches story, started trading Rajasthani ethnic fabric within India. After his employers – distant relatives – allegedly cheated his family out of their earnings, he went into exporting Rajasthani ethnic accessories, first as a trader and then as a manufacturer. After attracting notice at an international apparel fair in the mid-1990s, he created a network of buyers among small boutiques in Europe (2007-del38). Another garment exporter served as an assistant to a major international designer who had relocated to India and learned the business through experience. This respondent emphasized that with the right in-house design facilities and the capacity to navigate the customs and clearance hurdles, you can access smaller buyers willing to pay higher prices than mass retail:

My way of working is that I have my own designing and sampling: I bring them to buyers in US, Europe – they may adopt, collaborate, modify, etc. They are very interested. You are proactively going to buyers; the overhead is higher, but I don't have to sit idle and wait for orders. Plus, I'm giving them designs, they come to India for value-added... There are big buyers, but there are so many small buyers, relying on domestic production and importers: someone with 25 retail stores. They can buy [only] 300–500 pieces, but they pay better prices... Small people don't know much about duties and freights, they need help; we provide shipments [with] duty paid. Argentina, Spain – they will pay 25 percent more than big buyers. (2007-del33)

Thus smaller international buyers are willing to pay premiums for services that allow them to negotiate international markets directly, through established individual relationships, rather than relying on sourcing from the big GVCs.

Garment manufacturers and exporters can try to integrate into the large, buyer-driven value chains that connect low-cost manufacturing to wealthy consumers in the developed world. This model has been under pressure during the Great Recession and the unravelling of consumer debt in Europe and the United States, as well as the competition from ever-lower-cost contenders in Southeast Asia and in Africa. Or they can bypass the major conduits of apparel export by cultivating individual relationships with the many smaller importers and buyers throughout developed and emerging economies. Both strategies have their benefits and costs, but the formations of the strategies themselves are predicated on broader relationships to the industrial economy, largely resisting the convergence that we might expect from greater international integration.

Pharmaceuticals

In India, the pharmaceutical industry was essentially a postindependence phenomenon. The Indian Planning Commission classified pharmaceuticals as a "basic industry" that was a social imperative and would thus involve both public and private investment. Industrial Policy Resolutions of 1948 and 1956 encouraged the participation of foreign capital in the industry because of the need for foreign technology, given the lack of an indigenous scientific base for domestic drug manufacturing in the 1950s.[29] As a result of relatively hospitable policies encouraging foreign investment, multinational companies (MNCs) dominated the pharmaceutical industry through the 1960s, first importing medicines for direct sales, and then importing Active Pharmaceutical Ingredients (APIs, sometimes called bulk drugs) from the parent company for formulation in India, often at very high internal or "transfer" prices.[30]

According to many involved in the industry in India, the signal event in the development of the indigenous pharmaceutical industry was the passage of the Patent Act of 1970. This legislation, among other provisions, eliminated patent protection for pharmaceutical products while maintaining patent protection for manufacturing processes.[31]

---

[29] Barwal 2000, 13, 30.
[30] Barnwal 2000, 59; see also Gereffi 1982, ch. 6–7 on transfer pricing.
[31] Mehrotra 1987, 1461. The change of the patent regime was largely the result of reports by the Iyenger and Tek Chand expert committees that found misuse of patent protection by multinational companies.

The resulting law enabled commercial production of a drug molecule patented in the West if that molecule was manufactured through different processes. This legislation spurred process-based and drug delivery innovation in India and prevented multinationals from maintaining market monopolies of APIs imported from the parent company.

The revision of the patent laws enabled private industry to establish sustainable and cost-effective indigenous production of APIs successfully, with profound consequences for the structure of the industry. One prominent Mumbai industrialist explained:

In 1971, the multinational companies controlled close to 80 percent of the Indian business. By the year 2004, when the patent laws changed [back to protecting product patents], it was the Indian companies that controlled 80 percent of the market. But this was done primarily [because] after 1972, people like myself embarked on a program, in spite of the difficulties and in spite of the government, of producing bulk drugs and developing our own indigenous technology. Nobody will help you, you have to do it yourself. And I think, by and large, we succeeded. India succeeded. (2008-bom4)

Many observers have argued that the modified Indian patent regime after 1970 was the principal cause of the surge in local control of Indian domestic market share, and the dynamism of Indian companies in both APIs and downstream formulations, at much cheaper prices than the multinationals. It also provided a domestic production base from which Indian firms started to become competitive internationally, with major firms such as Ranbaxy, Sun, Cipla, Dr. Reddy's, and Wockhart carving out niches in international markets for Indian-made imports.

Deepening import-substitution policies normally lead to a standoff between multinationals and the government. In this instance, however, the new regime ultimately helped the country at very low political or economic cost. Even in the late 1980s, commentators felt that "the disadvantages in joining the Paris Convention [the international product patent regime, to be supplanted by TRIPS under the WTO] far outweigh the notional advantages for any given activity, be it [innovation], technological development or industrial self-reliance."[32] Thus, this explicitly nationalist policy was actually seen as wholly beneficial to the development of the industry.

---

[32] Mehrotra 1987, 1464.

The dismantling of the process patent regime began with the trade policy conditionalities of the IMF and World Bank assistance.[33] Later, as a precondition of India's accession to the World Trade Organization on January 1, 1995, the government agreed to revise its patent laws in accord with the Trade-Related Intellectual Property, or TRIPS, provisions of the Marrakesh Agreement by 2005. Transitional provisions included replacing the process patent regime with product patents, establishing a "black box" for patent applications from multinationals, guaranteeing exclusive marketing rights for patented goods, and increasing the duration of patent protection from seven to twenty years.[34]

Even though the political process by which the Indian government pushed these regulations through without parliamentary or public debate has been criticized, economists and policy makers have been arguing over the welfare consequences of this new regime.[35] While multinationals established monopoly prices over patented drugs, most of the Indian population are too poor to have access to the latest technological innovations and thus would not be affected, while Indian firms' participation in the market (mostly in the generic subsector) would probably not decrease, while expenditures on research and development might increase.[36] Yet the long-term future of the Indian pharmaceutical sector is under question as multinational corporations hold exclusive marketing rights on a wide variety of products for decades. Some MNCs employ the tactic of "evergreening" patents by making minor modifications to existing products and thereby unnaturally extending the life of patent protection (2007-chn11; 2007-del1). Mostly, though, the TRIPS regime has restricted the capacity of the Indian pharmaceutical industry to engage in export markets independently of global players. Multinationals now have the capacity to take Indian firms still following the old practices of reverse engineering to dispute settlement. Such legal and regulatory sticks should in theory force convergence in a regime created and controlled by multinationals as the holders of patents on most innovative products.

In reality, however, the TRIPS regime prompted two divergent responses. For some firms, the regime offered opportunities to integrate into the value chain and act as a production and research platform for

---

[33] Chossudovsky 1993, 385.   [34] Dasgupta 1999, 988.
[35] Dasgupta 1999, 989–992. See also Jenkins 1999.
[36] Lanjouw 1998; Goldberg 2010.

pharmaceutical MNCs. For other firms, however, the regime led to exit rather than loyalty, with export-oriented firms looking to markets in the developing world, where the low unit cost of Indian-made drugs presented compelling imports for countries without domestic manufacturing capacities and where regulatory hurdles are best handled by long-term personal relationships. Even though these firms do not have access to the most innovative drugs, off-patent medications often are prescribed for diseases most prevalent in developing countries and are thus not the focus of most pharmaceutical research.

Pharmaceutical Exports by Formal Rules and Value Chain Integration

The main reason why multinationals have not regained huge market share in India is that the domestic drug manufacturing capacities and lower production costs make it much more profitable for MNCs to subcontract manufacturing under their licenses. Such relationships even extend to research, including cost-effective randomized controlled trials on Indian hospitals (2007-del1). This outsourcing framework is referred to by the acronym CRAMS, or Contract Research and Manufacturing Services, which was worth $3.8 billion in 2012, out of a global market of $60 billion in these services.[37] A pharmaceutical manufacturing firm in Chennai, formed by four partners who had amassed capital in medical sales, exported 75 percent of their turnover in manufacturing under contract from MNCs (2007-chn1). Another manufacturer of APIs receives licenses for products and manufactures them for a U.S. firm and has established an FDA-approved plant for this purpose (2007-cdg1). Some of the major pharmaceutical manufacturers in India are also engaged in research, but in greater collaboration with multinational companies that recognize India's comparative advantage in drug delivery innovation (2007-del45).

Firms also use other tactics and strategies for integration into value chains or the use of the TRIPS regime to expand their own autonomy. One strategy among the larger firms is acquiring or merging with firms in Europe and the United States, providing the parent company in India with both a stream of dollar revenue and access to licenses to produce patented drugs for domestic and export markets

[37] Reddy and Gupta 2013.

(2008-mmb6; 2008-mmb39). Other firms are undertaking research in original molecules themselves, to be patented in an Indian system much more in sync with global standards (2008-mmb4; 2008-adb10). This is particularly the case for the biotechnology in serums and vaccines, important for diseases of the Global South such as leishmeniasis that are generally ignored by pharmaceutical research conducted by MNCs (2008-mmb25). The use of global institutions can also be of benefit to export-oriented firms: one API manufacturer successfully used the institutions of the WTO regime to take Chinese manufacturers to dispute settlement over antidumping through the Indian government (2008-mmb7), with active cooperation from bureaucrats consonant with Sinha's accounts of a selectively activist state.

Cipla, a major pharmaceutical manufacturer in Mumbai with roots in the nationalist movement, morally challenged the rules of the international regime by producing the first affordable AIDS management therapies in 2001, thus calling into question the monopoly profits for essential medication in the developing world. While flouting the TRIPS agreement due to be fully implemented in 2005, Cipla gathered powerful allies such as the Clinton Foundation and paved the way for affordable medication for the HIV-positive populations in the developing world.[38] Thus the integration of a trade regime based on intellectual property has allowed Indian firms to take advantage of their manufacturing capacities to produce drugs under license, to establish their own research into original molecules, and to challenge the rules of the system through international civil society interventions.

Pharmaceutical Exports to Unregulated Markets through Personal Networks

For other exporters, however, the integration into value chains implied by the TRIPS regime could be bypassed by selling to the vast markets for pharmaceutical products in developing and transitional economies, where both the costs of manufacturing and the ability to navigate individual regulatory hurdles are key. For these markets, access to the latest drugs is not as important as building brand reputations for off-patent drugs. Thus the activities of these export-oriented

[38] Yi 2001; McNeil 2002, 2006.

manufacturers are involved in establishing and maintaining relationships with regulatory agencies in different countries, as well as import agents and chemists who act as brokers between Indian firms and foreign publics.

A young doctor from Bihar was trained in medicine in Kazakhstan and after working for Indian manufacturers in Almaty had just started a firm that would produce formulations for South Africa and countries in Central Asia, in a joint venture with a Russian American who owned a pharmaceutical trading firm (2007-del11). Another Delhi-based firm that established a niche market for the production of polio vaccine sells either to the World Health Organization or directly to markets in the Middle East and francophone Africa (2007-del49). A small pharmaceutical manufacturer in Mumbai started production under contract for GlaxoSmithKline, Wellcome and Cipla but then switched strategies and invested in establishing export linkages to countries in the Sub-Saharan African and Asia-Pacific regions, including Vietnam, Papua New Guinea, and Tanzania; 80 percent of his export business is with government institutions in these countries, tenders that usually require contacts and a personal reputation as well as competitive costs (2008-mmb37). More than one firm in my sample exported pharmaceutical ingredients to countries in Sub-Saharan Africa and Southeast Asia; demand for such ingredients increases as domestic pharmaceutical industries develop capacities for pharmaceutical formulations (2008-mmb45; 2008-mmb1).

In one of my last interviews in India, I met with a pharmaceutical manufacturer at a Delhi hotel not far from Indira Gandhi International Airport. This manufacturer, who trained as a pharmacist and worked as a director in a different company before starting his own, had started exporting his goods because he had insufficient funds for a domestic sales force. Instead, he hired pharmacy graduates to form a regulatory affairs department to compile dossiers for licensing entry into developing country markets and has established himself as a major producer for the Ukrainian market and the second largest actor in Vietnamese prescription drugs (2008-del51). Our meeting was sandwiched between other client meetings, and my respondent mentioned that he travels internationally two or three weeks a month, managing his agents in the many countries to which he exports. This form of global integration is one not driven by norms or the structures of value chains but rather of person-to-person – or perhaps more accurately market-to-market – contacts that need to be individually negotiated and maintained.

Globalization has meant different things to different manufacturers, depending on how they believe interactions with the global economy should be arranged. For those who generally arrange their relationships with other firms through formal rules, integration into value chains or broader trade regimes provides structures that allow certainty in interacting with economic agents abroad. For those who arrange production and sales through personal networks, however, exporting means dense networks of personal contacts among domestic producers and importing agents, foreign regulatory authorities, and marketers in countries where cost-effective provision of drugs in the market and out of patent mean more than the expensive innovations afforded by the patent regime. Thus, even in an industry as capital- and information-intensive as pharmaceuticals, globalization and the retreat of the state have not led to convergence on sectorwide strategies and practices but rather a diversity of means by which firms can access international markets.

Automotive Components

In my interview research and quantitative analysis, one industry exhibited clear signs of firm-level convergence on a set of sectoral strategies: automotive components. Figure 4.2 outlined this convergence in the manner by which automotive firms organize their financing; automotive firms exhibit the orthodox debt-based financing that one might expect from a globally integrated and technology-intensive industry. Figure 5.2 showed that automotive firms have higher than average nonwage costs, signaling greater use of productivity incentives and more structured management–labor interactions. Figure 6.1, however, indicates that automotive firms are among the least integrated into the international economy, at least in terms of the Prowess/CMIE data subset for exporting firms.

Why might this be the case?

In general terms, the automotive sector – its history in India, and its global structures – represents the exception that might prove the rule in the ways in which relationships with the international economy are governed. The nature of the automotive industry, and specifically the

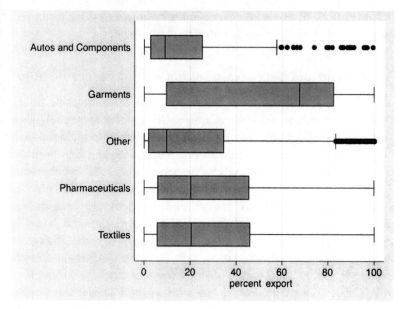

Figure 6.1 Export Percentages of Firms, by Sector.

distinction between a small group of global original equipment manufacturers (OEMs) and the makers of components, has established a globally convergent sector. Several global OEMs have located in India – from Suzuki and Toyota to Ford and General Motors – but much of their production, and thus that of many of their suppliers, is oriented toward the domestic market. As a result, the automotive sector is an example of deep international integration, but through FDI rather than exports. The global governance of automotive markets by a few OEMs structures the market for automotive component firms, particularly those involved in export, providing a true instance of sectoral industrial governance. Convergence around strategies for automotive manufacturers and exporters is thus driven by both the greater integration with the auto majors both in India and abroad, as well as the restriction of alternatives such as the aftermarket. Auto parts last longer and are much more end product–specific than in previous decades and thus depress the demand for generic spare parts. Thus certain industry-specific characteristics can provide sectoral industrial governance, in relating to the international economy or more generally, but such conditions are rare enough to represent the general weakness of industry norms to drive firm practices and strategies in India's industrial hinterland.

The Origins and Development of India's Automotive Industry

In India, independence from British rule, the high dirigisme of the Nehruvian era, and perceptions among MNCs of a desperately poor country brought about a more radical break with auto multinationals than in other regions of the developed world. U.S. and European car makers, when faced with a choice between establishing domestic manufacturing or leaving the country, chose the latter. In the place of the recently departed GM and Ford, three domestic companies – Hindustan Motors (HM), owned by the Birla Group and based in Kolkata; Premier Auto Limited (PAL), owned by the Walchand Group in Mumbai; and Standard Auto Products in Chennai – established production facilities under government licenses. Throughout the 1950s, 1960s, and 1970s, cars such as the Fiat and the Ambassador, by PAL and HM, respectively, were the only cars on Indian roads. The Indian government, in this high-water mark of socialist economic planning, saw personal vehicles as luxury goods. While the government bought Indian-made cars for official use and provided loans for senior civil servants to purchase these cars, car ownership before the 1980s was well beyond the ambit of even the upper middle class. Quite simply, the Indian government did not see automotive products as goods for mass private consumption, and the depletion of foreign exchange required for mass production would be a drain on national resources.

In the 1980s, Indian politics transformed the automotive industry. Sanjay Gandhi, Indira Gandhi's younger son and designated successor until his death in 1980, established a government enterprise for the production of an affordable passenger car – Maruti Udyog – in 1971. The Maruti enterprise's lack of independent success, coupled with Sanjay's death and Indira Gandhi's return to power in 1980, led to a resurrection of the project through a government-sponsored joint venture with Suzuki in 1983.[39] The entrance of Suzuki signaled a major shift in the structure and ethos of the auto industry in South Asia.

---

[39] The Maruti Udyog incident was inextricably bound up with the politics of the emergency period (1975–1977). For more details, see Venkataramani 1990,16.

The choice of Japanese multinationals as partners by state enterprises in both countries was a deliberate one. Toyota, the Japanese auto giant, had in the postwar era established an alternative framework for engineering and industrial manufacturing that was seen as more amenable to localization and domestic production in developing countries than the American model. Japanese systems of "lean production" were better able to capture the gains from technology by decentralizing manufacturing and encouraging subcontracting, collapsing hierarchies and encouraging worker participation, and minimizing inventory through "just-in-time" (JIT) production.[40] The flexibility of production and scale of Japanese cars were attractive for developing countries, particularly in Asia; American-made cars were large vehicles and thus involved high operating and fuel costs.

The Suzuki Motor Corporation was selected from a field of eleven contenders because of the Indian government's preference for Japanese small cars and the family-run and thus unbureaucratic nature of the company vis-a-vis keiretsu-affiliated firms or large corporations such as Toyota. Suzuki was interested because of the crowding of the Japanese domestic market and the government-facilitated necessity for overseas expansion through exports and FDI.[41] Unlike most state-owned enterprises, the Maruti–Suzuki collaboration was a tremendous success: the smaller, lighter (and thus more fuel-efficient), and cheaper Maruti 100 car was able to achieve 75 percent market share in the passenger car segment over the next decade.[42] The success of Maruti and the politically determined entry of the Japanese multinational into the Indian auto market, the first step in a series of liberalizations, unleashed profound changes in the structure and process of auto manufacturing in India. Crucially, the Maruti–Suzuki collaboration led to an exponential increase in and development of domestic components manufacturers.[43]

After the path-clearing entry of Suzuki, a number of other transnational OEMs sought JVs with established Indian companies as a way of entering the Indian market. This phenomenon was first evident in the commercial vehicles and two- and three-wheeler segment and then spread to the passenger car segment through changes in government

---

[40] Womack et al. 1990. [41] Venkataramani 1990, 31, 40–41.
[42] Krishnan 1996, 2t. See also D'Costa 1995.
[43] For more on the adaptations and developments of the Indian auto components industry, see Humphrey 2003; Okada 2004; Sutton 2005.

policy. JVs include Daewoo with CM, Fiat with Premier Auto, Ford with Mahindra, GM with HM Honda with Sriram Industries, Daimler-Benz with Tata Motors in the luxury Mercedes, Mitsubishi with HM, Pugeot with PAL, and Volkswagon with Eicher. Hyundai has set up as a wholly owned subsidiary in Madras.[44] By the mid-1990s, there were upward of ten international OEMs from the United States, Europe, Japan, and South Korea. Most have entered the market through JVs with a wide variety of established concerns. However, while government licensing requirements and restrictions on wholly owned FDI have been lifted, the incentives for local content remain for several reasons.

First, the Indian government has continued to levy relatively high tariffs on importing wholly built cars, CKD assembly, and imported components.[45] Second, because of the lower incomes of Indian consumers, firms must sell their vehicles at a significant markdown from prices in home markets, and domestically produced components drive down costs. As a result, both international and domestic OEMs have strong incentives to build up supplier networks to substitute imports of components, technology, and capital machinery such as machine tools. Third, vehicles and especially components have to be adapted, at minimum cost, from home market specifications to climatic and road conditions in South Asia, a process that requires more substantive collaboration with parts manufacturers. Fourth, transnational vehicle manufacturers and their collaborators, such as Denso and Delphi, have followed recent international trends and identified India as a potential regional manufacturing base from which to export products to smaller developing countries (2008-exp15, 2007-mad9). Indigenous OEMs such as Tata Motors and Mahindra & Mahindra are already envisioning vehicle export as a primary activity, and international companies are becoming more interested in sourcing from Indian component manufacturers (2008-bom43, 2008-bom46). This global placement is partly the result of building up supplier networks since the Suzuki–Maruti collaboration in 1983.

The Automotive Component Manufacturing Association (ACMA) represents the maturation of these relationships, in terms of both

[44] Krishnan 1996, 8t.
[45] The total effective duty for importing new cars into India was more than 100 percent, according to the Foreign Trade Policy, Ministry of Commerce.

indigenization and the success of component firms in other areas, such as exports. ACMA member firms had a collective turnover of $18 billion in 2007–2008, with more than 20 percent, or $3.6 billion, in exports, mostly to international OEMs and Tier-I companies.[46] My respondent at ACMA clearly identified the 1990s as the turning point at which the industry started becoming globally competitive: at liberalization, tariffs and licensing regulations decreased markedly on components while remaining on completed vehicles, and so the industry was under intense competition from imports at the same time as the international automotive industry was facing a crisis of rising costs and was thus actively seeking to source abroad for cheaper components that still met quality standards (2007-del35). As a result, certain Indian component companies that had met the challenge from imported goods were able to integrate themselves into the global automotive supply chain at relatively high levels, while also serving a growing demand for OEMs that were establishing themselves in India. This integration – and the absence of obvious alternatives such as the unregulated markets in the pharmaceutical industry – presents a structure of governance that is generally absent in other sectors, thus enabling convergence of practices among component exporters.

Convergent Strategies among Auto Component Exporters

For most auto component manufacturers interested in participation in global markets, export has meant integration into GVCs. An auto ancillary company in Gurgaon was founded in the mid-1990s as Maruti was looking for component suppliers for a new plant in the Delhi NCR and has consolidated into ten units in the NCR and six in Pune. The firm, with more than three thousand employees, enabled its export activities through the acquisition of companies abroad with long-standing relationships to Tier-I multinationals in Germany, Japan, and Belgium. As my respondent noted, these foreign acquisitions

[are] a front window for us, we export through them, those companies are known in those places, so we get orders for our Indian units. Secondly, we

---

[46] www.acmainfo.com/profile.htm, accessed March 13, 2009. Only 25 percent of exports in the industry go to aftermarket sales, as against 75 percent a decade previously (2007-del35).

supply raw material from India to these units – from our own companies, cheaper than what they can get in the market. (2007-del30)

A venerable manufacturing firm in Chennai – one that was established when an Indian family took over expatriate managing agency investments in bicycle manufacturing as well as tea plantations and liquor distilleries right after independence – established working relationships with Hyundai and Nissan in Chennai, GM in Gujarat, Tata in Pune, and Singhur and Hyundai in Haryana in the manufacture of car-door frames but have recently been utilizing the in-house research involved in their domestic work to press into export markets, now accounting for 40 percent of their turnover through foreign JVs (2007-chn10).

Another much smaller firm in Chennai, established by an engineer who had worked for the "Indianized" multinational Larsen & Tubro before establishing his own cold forging plant for machining components, had, like many other Indian firms interested in export orientation, initially exported through buyers in the United States and Europe, and then established a sales office in the United States. My respondent, the founder's son and a graduate of the Ohio State University in engineering, is director for exports and thus responsible for managing these sales relationships (2007-chn4). A Pune-based firm was started by a family of Gujarati traders in Kenya who had been pushed out by nationalist policies of Africanization in the 1960s. Returning to India, they launched their own survey of economic opportunities and decided on the domestic manufacture of carburetors, with Italian technical collaboration (2008-pun2). They initially supplied components to Bajaj and TVS for the manufacture of indigenous scooters under license from Vespa and Lumbretta, but have more recently entered into export markets, enabled by research and design into systems that manage emissions standards.

Research and design also distinguished a clutch manufacturing firm in Delhi, established by a mechanical engineer from Punjab, that avoided technical collaborations or JVs with multinationals by designing a clutch that had the endurance to withstand Indian road conditions (2007-del37). For years, this company had existed as a domestic player in a market dominated by multinationals, but they were recently approached by a U.S. truck manufacturer to market these specially designed clutches under an American brand and thereby break a U.S. monopoly on clutch manufacturing. Thus, R&D provides a framework within which new supply chains are formed.

Where we might expect distance from such value chains – and where we certainly would have found difference during an earlier period – is with firms producing for foreign aftermarkets: markets for replacement parts for garages and mechanics. Certainly, there are many firms in India that export to aftermarkets. Yet the independence of these markets from the OEM-driven value chains has gradually eroded because aftermarkets themselves have decreased in size. Original parts have increased in longevity and the specificity of parts has forced manufacturers to produce to specification. An electrical engineer trained in Vadodra started manufacturing ignition coils for tractor OEMs in the domestic market, but also maintains 40 percent of sales to Tier-I producers and aftermarkets abroad (2007-del16). He said that the big difference now is that "you have more knowledgeable customers. Work culture has changed – it's now customer-focused. In those days, you could make whatever you want to make."

Small manufacturers also can export to aftermarkets through aggregating and forwarding agents; one manufacturer in Delhi used one that was affiliated with the Engineering Export Promotional Council, an organization with an explicit mandate to maintain standards for Indian products abroad (2007-del21). A Chennai-based exporter to overseas OEMs and the aftermarket was a key figure in the Council for Engineering Industry (CEI), the forerunner of CII, and continues to maintain relationships with other firms in the Chennai auto cluster and firms abroad through innovation and design (2007-chn5). An exporter in Rajkot in Gujarat had been manufacturing engine valves for major domestic Tier-I producers such as TVS but had switched to export orientation with a complete technological upgrading of his capital machinery (2007-exp6). Thus even areas of the export market at further remove from OEM governance are still subject to norms and expectations for customers.

The export-oriented manufacturers in the automotive components sector can clearly be seen as a counterexample to the diversification in engaging with international markets, evident with both garments and pharmaceuticals. And yet the global automotive sector is an industry with unique features capable of establishing broader governance frameworks: a funnellike, oligopolistic industrial organization in which norms and standards converge on particular types, which are increasingly hegemonic at least in the passenger car segments. For less obvious and orthodox corners of the automotive vehicle industry – tractors, rickshaws, or three-wheel transport vans – there is of course more scope for export using particularistic networks. And certainly, manufacturers participating solely in the domestic market would feel less pressure to converge.

For the mainstream export-oriented markets in passenger car components especially, governance frameworks are important for compatibility, quality, and safety standards necessary for the proper function of the end product. Yet, there are very few industries where such precision and compatibility drive the ways in which firms relate to one another, both across and within borders. Thus, the automotive sector can be thought of as the exception that proves the rule that industrial firms generally govern their own interactions with global markets individually and divergently.[47]

Conclusion

Not every industrial firm in India interacts directly with the international economy, even though every single one is impacted by it. The many industrial firms in India exporting at least part of their production do so in the face of intense international competition and significant though limited state support. Nonetheless, much of international political economy is predicated on the assumption that international markets will impose the discipline that sheltered domestic economies do not; export markets are thus where we might expect broad governance frameworks and convergence in firm strategies and practices, particularly by sector. As I have noted, however, Indian firms form different sorts of relationships across borders, through either the rules-based structures of GVCs or dense webs of particularistic ties among importers, agents, brokers, and buyers. The complex topographies of international markets parallel complexity and variation among domestic manufacturing firms, thus providing some coherence and legibility in firm strategies but forestalling any regional, sectoral, or national coherence in the ways that firms relate to the international economy.

---

[47] The auto components sector can here stand in for industries with a certain level of technological sophistication that supply a small number of buyers. Fuller presents similar dynamics of convergence among microchip manufacturers, driven by intellectual property rights protection. See Fuller 2014.

7 | The Rise and Fall of Statist Governance in Pakistan

The nature of statist industrialization in India, its dissolution through market reform, and the subsequent emerging of governance structures at the firm level: were these simply outcomes of Indian exceptionalism? Certainly, India has a number of unique features: its size and heterogeneity and the early coherence of its economic nationalism. The postindependence Indian state maintained other unique characteristics: nonalignment in the cold war, the existence of a powerful catch-all party that structured political representation well into the 1960s, and the preemption of most peripheral challenges to the integrity of India as a sovereign, territorial entity. Such singularity makes India a difficult case to contextualize within the broader experience of industrialization and political economy in the developing world.

India is often compared with Brazil, China, and Russia as fellow BRICs, because of its size and status as an emergent global economic power.[1] Yet these cases share little in common with India: Russia and China industrialized under state socialism from the 1930s and the 1960s, respectively, and Russia has been actively deindustrializing since the collapse of the Soviet Union. Brazil's development trajectory has been dominated by authoritarian rule, FDI, debt crisis, and the rise of a new populism. In 2012, GDP per capita in Brazil was $11,339, in the Russian Federation it was $14,000, and in China it was $6,000, while in India, GDP per capita was $1,500. The BRICS are, in short, a stylized shorthand for large, growing economies outside the developed world, and not a representative or even internally consistent sample of developing countries. If this book's insights on the governance of industrialization after statism are to have any purchase beyond India's borders, as I believe they have, a means of providing a structured comparative analysis to other countries that might be different from India but still would be considered part of the same universe of cases in

---

[1] O'Neill 2011.

the developing world is necessary. Pakistan represents an ideal first case for such a comparison.

At first blush, Pakistan might seem an odd candidate for comparative study. After all, when one discusses successful development, Pakistan is rarely if ever mentioned. If anything, contemporary Pakistan is characterized variously as "a hard country," "a failed state," "the most dangerous place on earth," and even a kind of nonfiction horror story.[2] Pakistan's ambiguous involvement in the U.S. war on terror, the rise of a domestic insurgency in the Northwest, and increasingly violent domestic politics have attracted both academic and popular attention as a paradigmatic case for understanding the dynamics of conflict and political violence.[3]

Yet Pakistan has the advantage of being part, along with India, of several overlapping categories that characterize countries of the developing world. Its 2012 GDP per capita was $1,200, lower than but comparable to India's; both are included in the World Bank's "lower middle income countries" lending group. Neither country is a rentier state: mineral rents were less than 1 percent of GDP in Pakistan, and less than 2 percent in India. And as Pakistan and India were partitioned from the same British imperial dominion, both had common experiences of British colonization, and thus common institutional legacies. In addition, in spite of different dominant religious traditions, Pakistan and (at least North) India continue to share many social structures.

Yet Pakistan and India are also different cases on indicators most relevant to the political economy of industrial development, because of differences in the nature of the state and thus the motivations behind statist industrial development. Pakistan, as an independent country, was born of conflict: first, the social violence of partition and, second, an early war with India over Kashmir. As a result, the builders of the Pakistani state saw political centralization and industrial development as imperatives in order to maintain strategic balance with India, a far larger and initially better equipped power. Such compulsions led eventually to a military-led bureaucratic authoritarian regime and integration into Western alliances in the cold war.[4] These are the conditions of "systemic vulnerability" that Doner and his colleagues have argued were necessary

[2] See, for example, Lieven 2011, Moreau 2007, Granta 2010.
[3] Staniland 2012.   [4] Jalal 1990, McMahon 1994.

and sufficient for the establishment of "developmental states" such as Taiwan and South Korea, in which powerful and autonomous state structures direct the industrial bourgeoisie toward projects of national development.[5] Caroline Arnold and I argue that developmental state institutions much like those in South Korea did develop in Pakistan during the era of statist development; in fact, South Korea's planning framework was explicitly modeled on Pakistan's second Five Year Plan.[6]

India, by contrast, entered statist industrialization for much more purely ideological reasons; Nehru and the Congress Left saw state planning and industrialization as primarily a means to raise living standards, to weaken the grip of traditional structures in the country-side, and to remake Indian society through modernization. This political project was challenged by those on the Right and mediated through what Rajni Kothari famously called "the Congress system."[7] The result was a statist development project that was constrained in terms of resources, and was weakly implemented because of internal political conflict, resulting in what Gunnar Myrdal called "a soft state."[8] These social origins and internal politics made for a weak state apparatus relative to so-called developmental states such as in South Korea, as explicit cross-national analyses have made clear.[9] The Pakistani case of statist development through the 1960s parallels the Korean experience more closely and thus is very different from India's, but it shares enough institutional and social continuities with India to be a more appropriate case for comparison.

Given the differences in the nature of statist development, we might expect that the Indian and Pakistani trajectories of industrialization would continue to diverge. Continued divergence, after all, is in keeping with other studies that have sought to explain the persistence of difference in regime and institutional outcomes between the two countries.[10] For all the state-institutional differences between the two cases, however, the trajectories of industrial development over time in India and Pakistan have been remarkably similar. Despite Pakistan's stronger state, praetorian traditions, and more centralized polity, external pressures and internal political conflicts combined to force the government out of directing factor markets in support of industrialization through

---

[5] Doner et al. 2005.   [6] Naseemullah and Arnold 2015; Adelman 1969.
[7] Kothari 1964.   [8] Myrdal 1968. See also Frankel 2005.
[9] Evans 1995; Chibber 2003; Kohli 2004.
[10] Jalal 1995; Stern 2001; Tudor 2013; Wilkinson 2015.

liberalization. And much as in India, provincial governments and sectoral agencies have not filled the void in industrial governance.

Industrial development in Pakistan after liberalization has not been negligible: Pakistan's average growth in manufacturing value-added between 2000 and 2012 was 6 percent, lower than but still comparable to India's 7.5 percent. The persistence of manufacturing after the fall of statism poses a similar puzzle to that in the Indian case. I argue that in the absence of clear signals from the state, Pakistani manufacturers, like Indian ones, have been compelled to form production structures based on institutional relationships with capital and labor, and they have done so on the basis of parallel – if somewhat more disparate – backgrounds, perspectives, and experiences.

The combination of institutional differences at the outset and similarities in outcomes in these two comparable cases suggests the plausibility of broader application of the themes and frameworks of this book. While it is highly unlikely that other countries will share all or even most of the *particular* dynamics of industrialization after statism in these two South Asian cases, the comparison points to several common themes that can serve as the basis for broader research. First, liberalization is not just a widespread phenomenon but one that affects state-directed development in similar ways. Market reforms have made the state a great deal less likely to direct factor markets to promote industry and more likely to be the lead actor in the political economy of rent allocation.

Second, manufacturers themselves might not always be the key institutional actors; the causal importance of the perspectives and experiences of industrialists may be a function of the exceptional pattern of corporate governance in the subcontinent. Still, I would contend that the search for sources of institutional coherence in postliberalization industrial economies is necessary; manufacturing cannot survive without such coherence. Further, I would argue that analysis at the firm level is more useful than simply assuming that the state, after liberalization, drives the industrial economy. Thus, if specialized state agencies or regional governments or multinational corporations or corporate groups or political parties are providing stable institutional frameworks for industrial investment, then these broader frameworks should be evident at the firm level.

Third, the place of the state after liberalization, in industrial promotion or more generally, is a politically contentious question, around which consensus is unlikely to reemerge. Any hope for a new techno-cratic settlement for the promotion of manufacturing – in India, Paki-stan, or elsewhere – must contend with the political orientations of different segments of the population toward the state. Such viewpoints are both forceful and diverse since the advent of democratic and popular assertions against the older orders on which statism had previously rested. I will return to these themes in the Conclusion by examining the nature of industrial governance in other regions, but the goal now is to describe the processes, frameworks, and arguments in the Pakistani case.

***

This chapter offers an explanation of the political and social factors behind state-led industrialization in postpartition Pakistan. Unlike India, Pakistan faced "systemic vulnerability" from military competi-tion and severe resource constraints.[11] The state structures around the promotion of industrialization arose out of the necessity of directing resources and foreign exchange to national security and defense spend-ing, in addition to the usual normative commitments to raising the living standards of a poor country. As the largely rural territories of British India that became East and West Pakistan did not have any significant industrial endowments, Pakistani industrial planners had to establish a private sector manufacturing base from whole cloth. The Pakistani state, in effect, created the Pakistani industrial bourgeoisie during the period of statist development. Pakistan in the 1950s and 1960s estab-lished a concentrated and successful industrial sector, largely made up of migrant, or *muhajir*, merchants and bankers from the former Bombay Presidency who invested in textiles, engineering, chemicals, and food processing in Karachi.[12] Intense collaboration between the state and the industrial private sector produced phenomenal growth in a diversifying industrial sector. As the country entered the hard decade of the 1970s, however, the Pakistani state and the industrial economy suffered two distinct challenges to its industrial development priorities.

The first arose from Bengali nationalists resisting language chauvin-ism and, as importantly, inequity in the distribution of resources and investment between West and East Pakistan. The victory of the Bengali

---

[11] Doner et al. 2005; Naseemullah and Arnold 2015.   [12] Amjad 1976.

nationalist Awami League in the 1970 elections led to a brutal military crackdown against the civilian population and, after India's intervention, the independence of East Pakistan as Bangladesh. The second arose from resurgent provincial political and interest groups in Punjab and rural Sindh. From the 1970s onward, agrarian interests and powerful regional elites asserted claims to the resources of the state that had been previously reserved for the promotion of the Karachi-based industrial houses. Thus, the liberalization of the 1990s has seen a more sudden retreat of the state from industrial governance, but it continues an early and sharp critique of the statist industrial promotion regime that was implicated in the Ayub Khan regime and the national bourgeoisie dominated by the *muhajir* ethnic minority community in Karachi. Contemporary Pakistani political economy sees state actors, including the military, engaged deeply in the acquisition and allocation of rents, while the factor markets important for industrial production remain undirected.

This chapter proceeds as follows. First, I will describe the economic and political context around the birth of Pakistan, its state-building project, and how these circumstances joined to form the postindependence industrial promotion regime. Then I will describe how statist industrialization operated in the coordination between government agencies and industrial firms. Third, I will delineate the sources of challenge to the industrial development regime, and how these political challenges undermined statist development. Fourth, I will outline the nature of the poststatist industrial economy in Pakistan, and what challenges it poses for manufacturing firms.

The Formation of Pakistan and Statist Industrialization

The movement for political assertion among Muslims in India arose out of the relative decline of the Persian-speaking aristocracy during the first century of British colonial rule. Through serving the colonial authorities as bureaucrats, brokers, and professionals, upper caste Hindus supplanted the erstwhile Mughal elites in positions of political and economic power. By the middle of the nineteenth century, Muslims began agitating against this relative deprivation, perceived discrimination by an entrenched Hindu administrative elite, and the indifference of the British authorities.[13] The All-India Muslim League (AIML),

[13] Ahmed 1991.

formed in 1907 as an elite Muslim counterpoint to the Hindu-dominated Indian National Congress, emerged as a potent – if internally diverse – political force in British India, aided by the British "divide-and-rule" policy of establishing separate constituencies and electorates for Muslims. In 1930, the poet–philosopher Muhammad Iqbal proposed a separate "state" encompassing Muslim-majority regions in British India. In the 1940s, Muhammad Ali Jinnah, the former Congress party activist and leader of the AIML from 1916, participated in negotiations with the British government and the Congress party on constitutional protections for Muslims in postcolonial India. Partition was a consequence of breakdown in these negotiations to balance Muslim autonomy and identity with keeping India united as a federal unit.[14]

State Formation in Pakistan

In 1947, when Pakistan was formed out of the northwestern and northeastern corners of undivided India, bureaucrats and politicians immediately faced the huge problem of maintaining the existential viability of the newly formed state. The independence of Pakistan and India had come about within the bloody context of the mass violence and forced migration that accompanied Partition, in which an estimated half-million were killed and between 10 and 14 million were displaced. The violence of partition, along with conflict over the Indian accession of Kashmir, produced circumstances of deep suspicion between the two postpartition states.[15] A first war between India and Pakistan in 1948 set the stage for long-lasting military contestation between two countries of very different sizes and thus capacities to recruit and retain military personnel, to purchase or manufacture arms, and to extract resources with which an army, a navy, and an air force could be maintained.

Further, the character of the provinces that made up Pakistan presented further challenges. Balochistan and the Northwest Frontier Province (now Khyber Pakhtunkhwa) were sparsely populated regions at the far western periphery of the Indian subcontinent, with largely

---

[14] Jalal 1985.
[15] For an excellent overview of Partition from the perspective of state formation, particularly of national security apparatus, see Zamindar 2007.

tribal populations. The populous provinces of western Punjab and eastern Bengal were largely rural and produced wheat, rice, and the cash crops of cotton and jute to be transported to the manufacturing centers of Bombay Presidency and Calcutta; Partition cut these areas of cultivation away from their natural markets. And Sindh was also a mostly agricultural province, replete with feudal landholdings, but containing the genteel port city of Karachi, which served as Pakistan's capital until 1958. At independence, Pakistan's share of industrial assets was only 10 percent those of India, compared to 23 percent of its landmass and 18 percent of its population.[16] Given the intensity of military competition combined with the absence of access to easy revenue and the need to support the diverse social groups that either supported the Pakistan cause or had acceded to life in a country partitioned from India, Pakistan's pursuit of rapid industrialization was structurally determined by "systemic vulnerability" and the need to preserve resources to limit this vulnerability.[17]

How the Pakistani state reacted to the challenges of state building and of rapid industrialization thus reflected a worldview of compulsion rather than simply one of developmentalist ideology. As Ayesha Jalal has argued, requirements for defense led civilian and military bureaucrats to centralize authority and "depoliticize" the country against provincial assertions of power, which formed the basis for bureaucratic–authoritarian rule under Field Marshal Muhammad Ayub Khan, from 1958 until 1969.[18] This regime had to balance several simultaneous goals. First, it sought to achieve a political accommodation with political elites in the provinces, and in the countryside in particular, to preempt any challenges to its rule. Second, as in India, it embarked on a program of import-substituting industrialization. Unlike in India, however, this program was guided as much by the need to preserve foreign exchange revenue for military spending as the more diffuse project of gaining legitimacy through national development. Third, it had to balance between the two halves of the new country – West Pakistan, consisting of Punjab, Sindh, and the frontier provinces, and East Pakistan, or the partitioned territories of the former eastern Bengal – with radically different interests, economic resources, and political power. The ways in which the Ayub-era

---

[16] Jalal 1990: 64.   [17] Doner et al. 2005; Naseemullah and Arnold 2015.
[18] Khan 1999: 11–12.

political regime attempted to achieve the first two goals allowed for a decade of very successful economic and industrial development, but its failure in distributing the goods of development between Pakistan's two "wings" ultimately led to the undoing of statist development in the 1970s.

The Social Coalition behind the Industrial Promotion Regime

In order to initiate industrial development, Pakistani statists needed political permission and social support from the countryside, essential in a country so dominated by agriculture. This was especially important in Pakistani Punjab, a populous province that had long been an elite stronghold distinct from the politics of the Muslim League. Bureaucrats relied upon long-standing elites of the erstwhile Punjab Unionist Party, a group of agrarian notables with little in the way of ideology or progressive vision, devoted to the maintenance of authority and the status quo.[19]

Robert Stern traced the authoritarian tendencies of Pakistan to the dominance of these landed elites in Punjab by deliberate British policy after 1857, elites whose families were incorporated into the military and civil bureaucracy, thus dominating both institutions in independent Pakistan.[20] Similar inequalities in agrarian relations were evident in Sindh, where much of the land was owned by a small group of quasi-feudal landlords; it was reported in the 1950s that 1.5 million acres of the total cultivated area of 8.6 million in Sindh were in the hands of smallholders, whereas large landowners ("big *zamindars*") held more than 6 million acres, and 124 *jagirdars*, or feudal estate holders, held 1.1 million acres.[21] By contrast, Muslim political groups in East Pakistan, largely composed of smaller *jotedar* peasant-cultivators and tenants under Hindu absentee landowners, had a significantly more radical edge.[22] Mobilized and populist Bengali Muslim League activists, representing an East Bengali population that was larger than any of the provinces in West Pakistan, presented a threat to classically liberal Muslim League politicians from the United Provinces and Bombay Presidency, let alone the feudal landlords of Punjab and their allies in the bureaucracy and the army.

---

[19] Yong 2005, 240–280.   [20] Stern 2001.   [21] Martin 1956, 439 (table).
[22] Stern 2001, 61–71.

As a result of different politics and different agrarian structures, East and West "wings" were differently incorporated in the regime supporting industrialization. In West Pakistan, elite bureaucrats, military officers, and their client capitalists entered into what was, in effect, a marriage of iron and rye with Sindhi and Punjabi *zamindars*, as well as Pakhtun and Balochi tribal leaders.[23] Agrarian elites would maintain social order, suppress popular discontent, and provide political support to the efforts of the central government to promote industrial development, as long as the state would not significantly tax agriculture or intervene in the social domination of the countryside; agricultural tax revenues were less than a third that of either customs or excise in 1964–1965.[24] Of course, this noninvolvement in systems of rural power echoed the inability of the Indian state to reform inequitable and inefficient structures of agricultural production effectively, but in the West Pakistani case, there was a tacit arrangement between the state and elites in the countryside, rather than simply a thwarted implementation of agrarian reform programs.

In East Pakistan, by contrast, the population was de facto excluded from the fruits of development; jute production and export were taxed significantly and provided an important source of foreign exchange, even while investments for industrial development were directed almost exclusively to West Pakistan. Such discrimination meant that East Pakistani income growth was a full 2 percentage points behind West Pakistani in the 1960s, and government spending in the East was 40.5 percent that of the West between 1950 and 1970, despite East Pakistan's larger population.[25] Such uneven economic development was to have serious political consequences just a decade down the road, yet a focus on development in West Pakistan in the 1960s yielded a remarkably successful "development decade" that built up industrial capacity from a remarkably low level to become one of the decade's most serious economic contenders.[26]

The Character of Statist Development in Pakistan

The Ayub Khan regime sought to facilitate rapid industrialization through the promotion of a state-regulated but private sector–dominated

---

[23] Stern 2001, 128.   [24] Papanek 1967, 191t.
[25] Government of Pakistan 1970.   [26] Papanek 1967, 2–10.

manufacturing industry. Unlike in India, however, there was no industry to speak of in the areas that constituted Pakistan at Partition. To the extent that Muslims were able to build up business empires in prepartition India, they were largely in banking and trading. And in Punjab, Sindh, and Bengal, entrepreneurs and petty manufacturers were mostly Hindus, Sikhs, and Parsis, many of whom left for India at Partition.[27]

The Pakistani state in the 1950s created a network of state-owned industrial enterprises through agencies such as the Pakistan Industrial Development Corporation (PIDC), which were rapidly and deliberately privatized in order to create a national industrial bourgeoisie concentrated around Karachi, the center of political and economic power during this period.[28] The recipients of this state "divestment" largesse mostly consisted of Urdu-speaking *mohajir* (migrant) financiers and merchants who had migrated from Gujarat and Bombay in western India to Karachi at partition, particularly from Memon, Khoja, and Adamjee communities.[29] Thus state policy created private sector manufacturing capacity, as well as a Karachi-based *mohajir* industrial oligarchy that dominated that capacity, with forty-two families owning 43 percent of all industrial assets in East and West Pakistan in 1968.[30] In textiles in particular, traders from the former Bombay Presidency set up mills mostly around the industrial hub of Karachi, and to some extent in Punjab, because of Pakistan's advantages in producing superior long-staple raw cotton and trade protections against imported yarn. The established industrial houses involved in textile manufacturing were represented by the All-Pakistan Textile Mills Association, which was formed in 1952 and served to manage relationships between the state and this new industrial elite.[31]

Thus, Pakistan's private-sector industrial economy was enabled, supported, and regulated by a state that was both autonomous, because of its bureaucratic–authoritarian character, and embedded, as a result of

[27] Zamindar 2007, 45–78.   [28] Khan 1999, 18; Papanek 1965, 184–225.
[29] Kochanek 1983, 19–27.
[30] White 1974, 274t. The first, and somewhat more famous, formulation of intense industrial concentration was by the economist Mahbub ul Haq, who declared, on the basis of 1968 Planning Commission data that had never been made public, that the primary beneficiaries of industrial policy were twenty-two families, who together controlled 66 percent of Pakistan's industrial wealth. See Khan 1999, 24.
[31] Kochanek 1983, 155–169.

its role in creating the national industrial bourgeoisie that was then conducting industrial development. These government–business linkages at the heart of an industrial promotion regime were not unlike that of the South Korean chaebols during this period. And, like state–industry linkages in Korea, the state provided substantially many aspects of certainty to the new national bourgeoisie in determining the conditions of their investment through the direction of factor markets.

First, the Pakistani state provided development financing to industrialists through the Pakistan Industrial Credit and Investment Corporation (PICIC) and the Pakistan Industrial Finance Corporation (PIFC), development finance institutions parallel to institutions established in India for the same purposes.[32] Second, even though it was not able to implement the party-dominated repressive corporatism in terms of labor, as in India, the Pakistani state intervened to guarantee industrial peace by brokering agreements with moderate unions and crushing the independence of most radical and militant organized labor groups, including the communists.[33]

The Pakistani state also established a system of tariffs and quotas and industrial and export licenses that simultaneously protected domestic manufacturing and enabled industrial firms to benefit from foreign capital, goods, machinery, and raw materials. Most of all, for the 1950s and into the 1960s, the concentration of industrial power in Karachi and the concentration of political power under authoritarian auspices in Karachi and then in Islamabad enabled a relatively easy coordination of industrial policy, with capitalist oligarchs working together with administrative technocrats in classical "embedded autonomy" fashion.[34] Thus, statist development in Pakistan, as in India but in an even more coordinated fashion, delivered the goods of industrial development through the state's supporting the industrial bourgeoisie.

The government's support for industrialization did not intersect the limited mechanisms of political representation under military rule. The Ayub Khan regime put into place highly circumscribed institutions for representation and elections, notably the "Basic Democracy" system of indirect elections through local bodies, geared toward the implementation of local development initiatives rather than any genuine sense of

---

[32] Alavi 1983, Amjad 1983.   [33] Candland 2001, 71–78.
[34] Papanek 1967, 75–106, Evans 1995.

popular representation or sovereignty.[35] The result of such hierarchical republicanism was to place a gloss of legitimacy on a deeply authoritarian system, and such indirect representative rule "mobilized the bias" away from demand articulation by pressure groups, particularly in provincial politics.

East Pakistan bore the brunt of this exclusion: jute production and export from the region provided resources and foreign exchange to fuel industrial projects, but these were almost universally located around Karachi. And foreign aid and industrial development were disproportionately directed to West Pakistan; foreign inflows directed to West Pakistan as a percentage of provincial GDP were twice that of East Pakistan in 1965, and five times that of East Pakistan in 1960.[36] As Ayub Khan's "development decade" was reaping dividends in economic growth and investment, groups that were marginalized by the regime's single-minded focus on supporting the national industrial bourgeoisie started reasserting themselves, attacking both the industrial oligarchy and the state that supported it.

The Fall of Statist Development in Pakistan

The first articulations against the industrial promotion regime occurred at the end of the 1960s, when excluded interest groups from university students to small farmers and industrial workers started demanding that the economic growth and the massive wealth that accrued from it be spread beyond the state, the army, and the industrial bourgeoisie. A slowdown in growth after 1965, associated with declining foreign investment and the freezing of U.S. aid programs after the 1965 war, contributed to this rising discontent.[37] A wave of protests and demands for greater redistribution were channeled into new political organizations. Zulfiqar Ali Bhutto's Pakistan People's Party (PPP) – an odd coalition of urban students, the industrial working classes, and Sindhi agrarian elites – began attacking the entrenched privilege of the Karachi-based industrial houses under a banner of "Islamic socialism."[38] At the same time, the Bengali nationalist leader Sheikh Mujib ur-Rahman voiced similar concerns about industrial concentration,

---

[35] Sayeed 1961.   [36] Khan 1999, 16.

[37] Although, as Amjad notes, foreign investment contributed less than 6percent to total investment in the 1960s. See Amjad 1982.

[38] *Economic and Political Weekly* 1968b.

but under the Bengali nationalist critique that while East Pakistan provided the lion's share of capital and foreign exchange, virtually all investment occurred in West Pakistan. Further, what little industry existed in East Pakistan was owned by Punjabi (from the *chinioti* community) or *mohajir* capitalists.[39] Both of the PPP and the Awami League coalitions represented ascendant agrarian groups, and importantly, the growing but overshadowed provincial business classes that arose out of capital from the countryside. This rising tide of protest channeled by these new political parties forced Ayub Khan from power in 1969, and the new president, General Yahya Khan, promised fresh elections and a restoration of democratic rule.

Bengali Nationalism, the 1971 War, and the Independence of Bangladesh

The sheer size of India and the myriad crosscutting identities in the country have since the 1950s forestalled any major threat to its integrity. In Pakistan, by contrast, provinces were already largely organized by language, and yet the smaller number of differentially sized and privileged subnational units would inevitably lead to the assertion of excluded and marginalized groups against a core of privileged Punjabi and *mohajir* elites. Such assertions, sometimes violent and often brutally repressed, have continued throughout the last three decades in Pakistan, notably in Khyber Pakhtunkhwa and Balochistan Provinces. But Bengali nationalism was the first and greatest challenge to the integrity of the pre-1971 Pakistani state and, perforce, the regime of industrial development.

Increasingly, regional inequality, the relative neglect of East Pakistan's economic development, and linguistic and cultural chauvinism created an impetus for political assertion on an explicitly Bengali nationalist agenda among the intelligentsia and the political classes. A forceful articulation of this sentiment, Sheikh Mujib's "six principles" called for a much more vigorous federalism and deeply delimited powers for the central government, involved only with defense and foreign affairs. The incompetent management of these demands, first dismissively by

---

[39] Khan notes that by the late 1960s, a Bengali industrial bourgeoisie had started emerging, but mostly consisting of small and medium enterprises. See Khan 1999, 28–30.

Ayub Khan and then desultorily by Yahya Khan ahead of the 1970 elections, only sharpened the mistrust of Bengali political elites of the central state.

When elections were held in December 1970, the Awami League won all but two constituencies in East Pakistan and thus an absolute majority of seats in the National Assembly. On advice from Zulfiqar Ali Bhutto of the West Pakistan–based PPP, Yahya Khan refused to accept an Awami League government and subsequent negotiations among Bhutto, Mujib, and the military junta broke down as the military started deploying arms and personnel to East Pakistan. The military "pacification" campaign began in March 1971 and led to widespread massacres and other atrocities concentrated in Dhaka. The conflict escalated into a war for liberation after independence was declared on March 28; this war between Pakistani military forces and the Bengali liberation force the Mukhti Bahini concluded after Indian intervention in December 1971.

The bloody conflict and mass atrocities inflicted on the civilian population, defeat at the hands of the Indian military, and the independence of Bangladesh – and thus the loss of half of the country – dealt a body blow to the legitimacy of the military regime in what remained of Pakistan. Yahya Khan resigned on December 20 after the end of the war and Zulfiqar Ali Bhutto became president. But the independence of Bangladesh had a number of more serious implications for the new, smaller state of Pakistan. First, it could not claim to represent the interests and aspirations of all Muslims in South Asia. Despite the more than 100 million Muslims who remained in India after partition, there now existed another Muslim state in South Asia with roughly the same population but constituted by a common language rather than just a common faith.

The collapse of such a grand justification for the state opened political opportunities for a slew of more parochial interest groups, some developing into serious and at times violent movements for ethnic or sectarian assertion. What the collapse of the pre-1971 regime also exploded was the notion that national economic and industrial development would, in time, lift all boats. This notion was crucially important for the agents of the state tasked with industrial promotion and the largely *mohajir* industrial bourgeoisie clustered in and around Karachi. After the 1971 war and the liberation of Bangladesh, thus, the consensus around statist development was shattered by political conflict over resources and state commitments among the various assertive actors. The political figure who was most influential in destroying this elite consensus and bringing about such group conflict was Pakistan's president after the 1971 war and prime minister after the 1973 elections, Zulfiqar Ali Bhutto.

The Bhutto Years and the Destruction of Consensus Politics in (West) Pakistan

Zulfiqar Ali Bhutto was, much as Indira Gandhi in India, a figure that both transformed and polarized politics in Pakistan through charisma, economic populism, and divisiveness.[40] From a prominent Sindhi land-owning family and educated abroad, Bhutto took up various government positions in independent Pakistan, including foreign minister from 1962 to 1965. After disagreements with Ayub Khan over the Treaty of Tashkent, Bhutto left office in 1967 and founded an opposition coalition – the PPP – under a banner of Islamic socialism, taking advantage of the popular discontent with the Ayub regime among the urban middle and working classes and rural poor. Bhutto rode a cresting wave of political discontent that forced Ayub Khan from power in 1969 and harnessed this organizational energy to carry the majority of West Pakistani constituencies in the 1971 elections.

Agitation among a wide array of Pakistanis feeling underserved by the Ayub regime, as well as activism among radicals and moderates supporting the principles of Islamic socialism, swept the PPP into power in 1973, but Bhutto's government inevitably had to adjudicate among different demands and interests. The PPP's main slogan "*Roti, Kappre, Aur Makan*" (bread, clothing, shelter), signaled an emphasis on poverty alleviation and the cares of the working Pakistani, much like Indira Gandhi's contemporaneous call of *gharibi hatao*, or "eliminate poverty." Yet crucially, the leadership of the PPP – as opposed to its rank-and-file activists – constituted a spectrum of interests and politics from the Sindhi agrarian elite Makhdum Zaman Talib-ul-Mola, the *pir*, or shrine administrator, of Hala in Sindh, on the right to Rashid Rahim, a communist peasant leader, on the left.[41]

---

[40] See Jalal 1995: 70–85 for a comparison of Bhutto and Indira Gandhi on their populist politics.

[41] Sayeed 1975: 44–45.

The cross-class nature of the coalition meant that Bhutto had to balance between the radical nature of the PPP activists and the support he was receiving from agrarian elites and capitalists disaffected with the Ayub regime. Often, policies were made to benefit the elite rather than party workers at the constituency level.[42]

The Bhutto government's policies transformed the state's relationship to the economy, but in ways that were deeply ambiguous from the point of view of development or social justice. Further, economic nationalist policies under Bhutto ultimately undermined the capacity of the state to govern industry. First, the PPP brought forth a wide-ranging program of nationalization of core industries, including steel, heavy engineering, banking, and insurance. Such policies were explicitly implemented to attack the concentration of wealth produced by statist capitalism of the Ayub regime, particularly *mohajir* bourgeoisie in Karachi; Shahid Burki notes that nationalization led to operative neglect and stagnation of nationalized industries as the government mandated higher wages and lower prices to please key urban constituencies without providing extra investment.[43]

Further, Bhutto's policies for land reform and redistribution actually held constant and in some cases strengthened the positions of those agrarian elites critical to Bhutto's governing coalition.[44] And after gaining power through support from workers, the Bhutto government deployed the state's coercive apparatus against striking workers in Karachi in 1972, killing more than ten and attacking others during the subsequent funerals, as a means of emphasizing the security and stability of the state over the interests of marginal populations while foreclosing the possibility of corporatist settlements by workers and employers in the private industrial sector.[45] The PPP government's coercive capacity was also brutally implemented against ethnic nationalist resurgence in the frontier provinces, most notably a counterinsurgency campaign against the Baluch Peoples' Liberation Front (BPLF) from 1973 until 1977.[46] Bhutto's governing strategy was thus one that was situated among populist legitimacy, elite accommodation, and outright repression of perceived threats.

Bhutto's tenure as the country's leader from 1971 until 1977 and that of the elected PPP government between 1973 and 1977 could be

[42] Sayeed 1975, 49.   [43] Burki 1974, 1135–1136. See also Burki 1980.
[44] Esposito 1974; Herring 1979.   [45] Ali 2005.   [46] Grare 2006, 6–9.

considered quite successful on its own terms of regaining a sense of legitimacy after the system shock of the partition of Bangladesh. But Bhutto's governments did not refashion the elite political settlement that had stood behind Ayub Khan's industrial development regime before the political crisis in 1969. As both a style and a set of strategies for governing, Bhutto instead *politicized* many of the elements of the Pakistani industrial development enterprise. He challenged the Karachi-based industrial capitalists of the Ayub era, attacked the prerogatives and political autonomy of the bureaucracy, and destabilized agrarian relations by calling for socialism in the countryside while also arming favored landed classes with the tools to reproduce their dominance. In other words, Bhutto governed largely by creating and exploiting divisions rather than reestablishing the stable if authoritarian consensus around the country's priorities. He was also forced to rely on politically powerful collaborators that would press upon the government their own demands on the resources of the central state in return for political support. Such demands mark the beginning of a new political economy of rent creation and allocation. Such collaboration inevitably entails excluding other powerful groups, which mobilized against Bhutto and the PPP in 1976 and early 1977, when opposition parties combined to form the Pakistan National Alliance.

Even though the PPP won the 1977 National Assembly elections handily, charges of vote rigging and continued unrest continued. The Bhutto regime effectively ended when Zia ul Haq, the chief of Army Staff, declared martial law and arrested Bhutto and members of his cabinet in July. Bhutto was tried for the murder of the father of a leading opposition figure and was executed in April 1979. The Bhutto regime and its bloody end laid the basis for further contestation among political factions willing and increasingly able to use the resources and power of the state to gain and solidify control and to distribute the financial rewards to themselves and their political allies.

Development after Statism in Pakistan

Zia ul Haq ruled as chief martial law administrator between 1977 and 1980, and as unelected president of the country for an additional eight years. Unlike the Ayub Khan regime, Zia sought legitimacy not through economic development but rather through Islamic conservatism, receiving support from religious leaders and introducing Shari'a-based laws.[47] The regime was also the recipient of international legitimacy and material support, particularly from the United States and the Gulf countries, as the frontline state and staging ground for the mujahideen insurgency after Soviet invasion of Afghanistan in 1979. As a result, the Zia regime's primary goals and sources of legitimacy tended away from Ayub era development or Bhutto era socialism and toward other arenas of political and social life. Pakistan during these years managed impressive growth rates, averaging 6.5 percent between 1980 and 1988. Much of that growth was attributed to sectors other than manufacturing, however. There was an overall decline in industrial productivity during this period, and an increasing capital intensity in industry as a whole at the expense of labor productivity.[48]

Zia's governments did much to change the institutional structure and nature of support in Pakistan's economy. First, some of the Bhutto era nationalizations – particularly in agriculture-dependent sectors – were reversed and private sector investment opened up in industries such as cement and chemicals.[49] Second, the Sixth Five Year Plan from 1983 to 1988 deregulated industrial licenses and export policies and establish a managed float rather than a pegged exchange rate in relation to the dollar. This period also saw significant remittances from labor migrants in the Gulf.[50] Third, and more obviously, the eleven-year period of Zia's rule saw renewed investor confidence due to the end of Bhutto era populism and the policy consistency possible under stable if repressive authoritarian rule, last experienced before the ouster of Ayub Khan in 1969.

The character and interests of a much more divided industrial bourgeoisie in the 1980s were quite different from those under Ayub Khan, however. First, the decade saw the decline of Karachi as an industrial and financial center. After the capital of Pakistan moved northward to Islamabad in the early 1960s, Karachi-based industrialists lost the natural advantages of ready political access to the state. During his

---

[47] Haqqani 2005, 131–159. [48] A. Sayeed 1995; Wazirat 2002.

[49] It is worth noting, however, that Zia's governments did not effect a large-scale reversal of Bhutto's nationalization policies and preferred instead to trust organic private sector investment for rebalancing the sectors. See Zaidi 2005, 111–112.

[50] Zaidi 2005,117–118.

period of political populism, Bhutto had attacked the core of the extant industrial bourgeoisie clustered in the city, causing prominent families to leave industry and even exit the country entirely. And starting in the mid-1980s, after the city experienced increasingly violent ethnic agitations among Pushto , Sindhi, and Urdu speakers in the city,[51] political rivalries among these groups escalated into large-scale violence in the early 1990s, further economically depressing the city and causing capital flight north to Punjab or abroad.

While the industrial monopoly around Karachi declined, an alternative, powerful but resolutely provincial, industrial bourgeoisie emerged in northern Punjab, fueled by capital from the Green Revolution and *chinioti* capital fleeing East Pakistan.[52] The Punjabi bourgeoisie also acquired significant political power during this period. The current prime minister, Mian Muhammad Nawaz Sharif, of the Ittefaq Group, was among the technocratic grandees of Zia's Majlis-e-Shoora (unelected parliament) and served as the chief minister of Punjab.[53] Other business groups in the 1980s and 1990s emerged as a consequence of political connections and savvy manipulation of economic and policy shifts.[54] The political capital of emerging entrepreneurs, particularly those taking advantage of privatization and the opening of the political space in the late 1980s and 1990s, allowed them to concentrate in rent-thick sectors such as telecommunications and utilities, thus further marginalizing industry as a primary activity in the liberalizing economy.

When Zia ul Haq was killed in a plane crash in 1988, a PPP-led democratic government under military tutelage was established under Benazir Bhutto. President Ghulam Ishaq Khan dismissed this government twenty months later, setting the stage for frequent government dismissals and regime instability over the next decade. As a result of balance of payments crises and macroeconomic instability that accompanied the global recessions of the 1980s and the supply shock of the First Gulf War, Pakistan was forced to undertake a series of structural adjustment measures as a condition of stabilization loans by the World Bank and the IMF. Liberalization in Pakistan involved the privatization of public companies, including utilities; the phasing out of tariff- and quota-based protection regimes; the withdrawal of subsidies; a

---

[51] Bennett-Jones 2002, 109–146.   [52] Weiss 1991.   [53] Ahmad 2001.
[54] Asad Sayeed, cited in Zaidi 2005, 126–127.

restriction on government borrowing; and increases in indirect taxation to set the government's fiscal house in order.[55]

These policies, designed to increase private sector confidence and efficiency, nevertheless led to much lower industrial growth rates – an average of 4.8 percent in the 1990s as opposed to 8.2 in the 1980s – and gross fixed capital formation decline of 60 percent over the course of the decade. Akbar Zaidi locates this fall in industrial productivity to marketizing policy reforms that removed any preferential treatment for manufacturing; they doubled the cost of capital and more than doubled the cost of energy inputs between 1990 and 1997.[56] Moreover, political instability deterred concentrated, long-term investments; no fewer than four governments were elected and dismissed between the end of the Zia regime and Musharraf's coup in 1999.

The early and mid-2000s in Pakistan were a time of general prosperity, echoing the speculative boom in the global economy but being spurred by some confidence-building macroeconomic reforms and by massive inflows of capital from aid due to Pakistan's position as a key state in the U.S. war against al-Qaeda and the Taliban.[57] The military rule of Pervez Musharraf led to the expected divisions and pressures among interest groups and regime challengers, however. Musharraf and his political allies, the PML (Q), appointed self-described technocrats to the cabinet. Even though the Musharraf regime and the PML (Q) government presided over a period of prosperity, the capacity of the state and the regime to translate good fortune to industrial governance was hugely circumscribed. At a time of unprecedented inflows of capital and liquidity, in which billions in aid abated Pakistan's chronic balance of payments problems, manufacturers were facing high costs of credit.

The "technocrats" of the Musharraf regime arose from global finance – Shaukat Aziz, the prime minister from 2002 until 2007, was a vice president in Citibank – and thus maintained perspectives on economic policy at variance with that of industry. The government during this period placed great emphasis on the interests of the consumer, lowering the cost of credit for consumer loans and facilitating the mass use of credit cards. But more broadly, the Pakistani state had

[55] Zaidi 2005: 120.   [56] Zaidi 2005: 123–124.
[57] For a sympathetic account, see Rafi Khan 2004; for a more critical one, see Burki 2007.

few tools at its disposal for actually establishing industrial governance arrangements. This absence is the product of past political and economic struggles that attacked regimes of industrial promotion and politically foreclosed the possibility of their reemergence.

The end of the Musharraf regime has ushered in democratic rule, first by a PPP coalition government from 2008 and, after their defeat at the polls in 2013, a PML-N government. Both democratic governments have faced serious economic challenges, stemming from the lack of confidence in investment, endemic violence, and the continued stagnation of the world economy.[58] There is no evidence that the state will be empowered to control the conditions for industrial investment in anything like the manner of the developmental regime of the Ayub era. Further, regime instability and the possibility that governments or ministerial appointments will change before their term ends have predictably decreased the reliability of policy programs, even those that might actually help industry. As a respondent mentioned, in Urdu:

Progress is being halted; we need policies for 20–30 years; unless governments give this much time, progress cannot be made in anything. Because to do the feasibility on a megaproject, two to four years are required. But here, governments do not remain for two to four years. It's very difficult. The governments can't take steps when a new government comes in after two or four years; they come in after one year. But if such policies or strategies can develop our country, for us to make process, these [policies and strategy] should not be touched by any government. If this happens, then we can make progress. (2007-lhr8, my translation)

This statement succinctly sums up the dilemma of high-velocity politics and policy making that confronts industrialists in Pakistan, as in many countries, when policies and strategies for industrial promotion are placed on the table for debate each time a government changes.

What is hoped to be the final emergence of sustained democratic government in Pakistan, along with an increasingly assertive civil society and increasingly powerful political parties, has maintained a politics in which a large portion of state authority and its associated rents are up for grabs by interest groups articulated in the political process. Such elite and popular access to state power is a far cry from the management of the economy under the first two decades of

[58] Jillani 2012.

Pakistan's independence, in which the state both enabled and directed an organized and concentrated private sector in the pursuit of industrialization. The political agitations against the Ayub regime, Bhutto's populist governance, Zia ul Haq's Islamist rule, and hybrid governments in the 1990s all took their toll on the ability of the state to direct development autonomously in concert with industrial production. In a way, Pakistan's political economy from the end of the Ayub era has been a distilled and dramatic version of similar processes that were occurring in India, where the state was no longer able or particularly willing to protect industrial promotion programs politically. The contemporary Pakistani state is now a great deal less willing and less able to perform industrial governance in a manner that systematically supports industrial development.

Industrial Governance and Military, Inc.

One distinctive feature of the Pakistani polity is the dominance of the military as a state within a state. A number of excellent books on the Pakistani military have emphasized its history, its ethnic makeup, its institutional culture, its self-understanding as the guardians of a national mission, its capacity to fight war and conduct insurgency, and the nature of its interventions in national politics.[59] The army is the most studied – some might even say *overstudied* – institution in Pakistan, and perspectives on it differ widely. Yet one point of agreement is that the army is a deeply centripetal institution: one that has a national scope and innate tendencies toward centralization, political order, and institutional continuity.[60] Might the military provide the industrial governance lacking in other sources of politics, by providing stability for investments under its purview?

This is plausible because of the military's significant involvement in the economy. Ayesha Siddiqa's celebrated analysis of the intersection between the military and business, or "milbus," defines the concept as "military capital that is used for the personal benefit of the military fraternity, especially the officer cadre, but is neither recorded nor part of the defense budget."[61] She estimates the total scale of milbus to be approximately $20 billion, which represents just above 10 percent of

---

[59] Nawaz 2008; Shah 2011, 2014; Fair 2014; Wilkinson 2015.
[60] Lieven 2011, 161–203.   [61] Siddiqa 2007, 1.

Pakistan's GDP in 2007 – significant, but not overwhelming. Further, many of the Pakistani military's economic activities involve land acquisition for defense housing projects for serving and retired officers, infrastructure and logistics projects, and education facilities at primary, secondary, and tertiary levels. This portion of milbus is fairly far afield from the concerns of manufacturing.

More relevant to our current purposes, a portion of the milbus complex is represented by the productive assets of military foundations – the Fauji Foundation, the Army Welfare Trust, the Shaheen Foundation, and the Bahria Foundation – which Siddiqa reports had assets of $169 million, $862 million, $34.1 million, and $69 million, respectively.[62] These foundations represent the military's direct involvement in the private sector economy, including in manufacturing. It is possible that military foundation support might structure production, at least with enterprises and in sectors under their purview. Looking a little closer, however, this is unlikely to be hugely significant, for two reasons. First, the investments of the military foundations constitute a small fraction of total private sector investment, which was $17.5 billion in 2007. Second, there are certain commonalities in the economic activities of military foundations. The direct and associated investments of the Fauji Foundation, for instance, involve two gas companies, two fertilizer companies, two agribusiness concerns, one of the largest cement companies in the country, an oil refinery, a power company, employment services, security services, a university, an investment bank, and a sugar mill.[63] Most of the investments in the Fauji Foundation and the other military trusts are in *rent-thick* sectors.[64] This makes sense: the military certainly has the political and institutional capital to access rents, and these activities provide returns that are stable enough to meet obligations to these funds' members, mostly military pensioners. In short, even though Pakistan's military is involved in Pakistan's economy, milbus is concentrated in activities that rely on the creation and allocation of rents, rather than the direction of factor markets for industry. The military, just like other parts of the state, are thus unlikely to be sources for the durable institutional signals manufacturing requires for investment.

---

[62] Siddiqa 2007, 119–126.   [63] Siddiqa 2007, 120t.
[64] Gandhi and Walton 2012.

Conclusion

In the decade and a half after the attacks of September 11, the Pakistani state has been characterized as weak, even failing; beset on all sides by the Taliban insurgency, separatist movements, the politics of radical Islam, charges of endemic corruption, and strained civil–military relations. But the Pakistani state that emerged from Partition was, within a decade, considered a strong, united one, forged by systemic threats and governed by bureaucratic authoritarian leaders. During this period, Pakistan constructed a statist development framework that was, if anything, more powerful and successful than that of India, with a small, close cohort of industrial capitalists that was allied to the state, in an industrial promotion regime not unlike South Korea's. Challenges to this regime arose from those who were excluded from it, and together these forces – the students and workers of the early PPP, Bengali nationalists, and feudal landlords – destroyed the consensus around statism, leading eventually to policies of liberalization and a dramatically different relationship between the state and the manufacturing economy.

The challenges, opportunities, and meaning of production in this context, and the industrial governance that supports it, will be discussed in Chapter 8. But a look at the rise and then the fall of statism in Pakistan suggests that this trajectory is shared by other countries in the developing world, if not always as dramatically. Most countries felt the compulsions of development and understood the state as the only institution powerful enough to drive the process forward. And nearly as many countries had their regimes of statism challenged, both from within – through the rise of excluded interest groups – and from without, through changes in the international economy. Thus, while the rise and fall of statist government is not a universal process, the comparison between India and a much different state (albeit with similar roots) such as Pakistan shows that it is one that may be widely shared among countries in the developing world.

8 Industrialization after Statism in Pakistan

The contemporary Pakistani industrial economy presents a study in contrasts. There have been significant periods of remarkable growth in production and exports, particularly before the security problems that beset the country as a result of the Taliban insurgency in the late 2010s. Pakistani society, and the middle classes in particular, have been increasingly prosperous, even though human development indicators for the poorest sections of society have remained alarmingly stagnant. This prosperity has translated into demand for goods and services, including for domestic manufacturing products that can compete in price and quality with imports. The emergence of respectable midmarket clothing brands and even a domestic car company presents unparalleled opportunity for Pakistani industrialists. Export markets, though depressed in Europe and North America, have also been important targets of opportunity for Pakistani industry; the raw cotton of the Indus valley is high quality, and Pakistan is close to emerging import markets both to the west, in the Persian Gulf, and to the east of the region, in East and Southeast Asia. Further, the possibility of better relations between India and Pakistan offers the long-term possibility of regional trade in South Asia, as evidenced by queues of trucks kilometers long at the Wagah–Atari border between Indian and Pakistani Punjab.

If the long-term prospects of Pakistani industry show signs of greater opportunity ahead, the environment for industrial production and investment could not be more challenging. Inflation has been an ongoing problem, leading to mass protests of food grain price hikes, but it is also an acute problem when a manufacturer is faced with acquiring raw materials, powering machinery, or retaining skilled workers. The monetary system seems to veer from tight money as a means of fighting inflation to encouraging populist spending and speculation on fixed assets, and regular conflicts among parliament, provincial assemblies, and foreign institutional creditors seem inevitably to

230

lead to policy reversals and nonimplementation. More concretely, domestic and increasingly foreign banks see consumer finance as the real target of opportunity in a country with a growing middle class, yet view manufacturing with some suspicion, as a by-product of political lending and asset nonperformance in the early 1990s. The availability of skilled workers is sharply constrained by underinvestment in education and vocational training, and, as a result, competition for recruiting and retaining good workers is intense.

How do manufacturers cope with these challenges? As I have argued in previous chapters, frameworks of industrial governance must support the industrial production of manufacturing firms. The previous chapter described statist industrial governance of Ayub Khan's "development decade," but argued that economic and political conflict effectively ended statism as a source for industrial governance. Yet there are plausible candidates for industrial governance beyond the central state. In Pakistan as in India, sectoral dynamics emanating from globalization might structure the institutions of industrial production; if this were the case, we would see strategies coalescing by industry. And just as in India, provincial governments might have replaced the power and resources of the central state in structuring industrial production. In the Pakistani context, we would expect that, of the two provinces with significant industry, Punjab under a stable probusiness PML-N government would be more capable of deploying a governance regime and driving firm convergence than Sindh, where ethnic conflict and political violence have become ubiquitous.

I argue instead that the institutions of industrial production are the most clearly evident at the level of the firm, driven by the backgrounds and perspectives of manufacturers. Industrialists with educational backgrounds or work experience abroad are likely to view the world through the lens of cognitive globalization; they thus tend to deploy formal rules in labor management and borrow from formal financial institutions in order to finance production and development. Industrialists who invested in manufacturing after significant work experience in local industries or local markets, by contrast, are likely to adopt a moral economy lens; they tend to avoid banks and instead use family or community capital and reinvested profit to finance production, and use affective institutions to manage labor. The fact that such variation exists in each province and each industry can be taken as evidence that neither provincial governments nor sectoral regimes are driving convergence in firm strategies. By contrast, the "governing firms" approach offers a helpful alternative to understanding industrial governance that is rooted in the social sources of investment in Pakistani society.

Analysis of industrial governance in Pakistan might also suggest the possibility of a wider variation of strategies in the many developing countries that experienced some form of liberalization. Pakistan is closer in character to a number of other emergent economies in Asia and the Middle East with hybrid regimes and struggles with both regional dynamics and international pressures to which India, because of its size and the consolidated nature of its democracy, is somewhat insulated. Many countries outside the original East Asian tigers experienced a sharp downsizing of state capacity due to debt crises in the 1980s, financial crises in the 1990s, and Bretton Woods–imposed structural adjustment policies as a reaction to both. The manufacturing sectors of these countries have, as in Pakistan, had to handle the (albeit selective) retreat of the state from industrial governance during a period when the nature and configurations of political institutions were being renegotiated. In this sense, my empirical discussion of the Pakistani case can serve as bridge for broader analysis of industrial governance in important middle-income countries.

This chapter will proceed as follows. First, I will outline the variation in the backgrounds of manufacturers in Pakistan as a means of motivating the potential alternatives to statism in industrial governance. Then, I will discuss industrial governance and firm strategies with regard to capital and labor. I will outline how statist development first managed industrial credit for Pakistani entrepreneurs and how the collapse of this regime has created challenges for industrial finance. Pakistani manufacturers respond to the challenge of acquiring capital in an increasingly competitive environment quite differently; I document this variation and suggest that its roots lie in the backgrounds and perspectives of industrialists themselves. Second, I will discuss the interventions of the Pakistani state during the Ayub period in structuring labor relations through workers' representation and labor legislation. Persistent attacks on organized labor since the mid-1970s, however, have led trade unions to operate primarily in the public sector. I outline how different Pakistani manufacturers respond to the challenge of recruitment and retention of skilled workers, on the basis of their own perspectives and backgrounds.

Backgrounds and Governing Modes in Pakistani Industry

If firms must operate within institutional frameworks in order to provide the necessary structures for industrial production, then what are the sources of these frameworks? I suggest that at the beginning of Pakistan's development trajectory, the central state structured the relationships among firms and financiers and workers. Yet the fall of statist development has meant that the central government is less able or willing to spend its resources directing these inputs in order to promote industrial firms. But then, where are the sources of industrial governance after statism? Certainly, provincial governments or sectoral dynamics could provide governance for firms within their jurisdictions. Yet my field research has suggested, in Pakistan as in India, that variation in firm strategies within sectors and provinces casts doubt on the power of sectoral or subnational governance to determine outcomes.

I argue instead that in Pakistan, as in India, manufacturers structure their relationships to outside actors through either formal rules or personal networks. These modes of governance in turn arise out of manufacturers' backgrounds and professional experiences. In Pakistan, the bifurcation in the socializing experiences that lead manufacturers into industrial investment and provide them with guidance has been more extreme than in India, because the "old guard" in industry – the national bourgeoisie around Karachi – were more vigorously destabilized by Bhutto's populism than the decline and reinvention of the old Indian industrial houses. As a result, many of those currently in manufacturing either began significant investments in the 1980s or were small-scale actors who achieved greater prominence in an economy less dominated by a closed industrial elite. There have been several different routes to industry, which must be investigated and assessed.

Cognitive Globalization and Governance by Formal Rules

Most industrialists devoted to constructing a framework of institutions that formalize and regularize practices of their firm toward suppliers, customers, workers, and financiers tend to do so out of a commitment to technocratic, globalized ways of doing business. Such commitments can result from certain types of elite education or formative professional experiences. A knitwear manufacturer from Lahore was a graduate instructor in economics and an elite civil servant in the Police Service of Pakistan for nine years before being obliged to leave for political reasons. He then served as a corporate director in one of the main textile groups for twelve years before leaving first to receive an executive education course at Harvard and then to start his own firm in 1988 (2007-lhr7).

A major pharmaceutical manufacturer traveled to the United States for an undergraduate engineering degree and worked to put himself through college over six years. He subsequently worked for multi-national companies as an industrial engineer. He credits this experience with giving him the discipline for his second career as an industrialist in the pharmaceutical sector: "If I look back ... [our company] is a model company in this country now, and one of the reasons is that my work habits [and] work ethics were laid in all those jobs I did in the U.S." (2007-khi22). Foreign education and elite professional training are thus important formative experiences.

Similarly, substantive ties or professional opportunities with U.S. or European markets and industries would similarly impart a preference for the formal and the rule-based in production structures. A relatively small auto parts manufacturer worked in a Gujranwalla forging plant before going to Britain for his master's degree in engineering and then working there for a Canadian firm; he established manufacturing units both in Gujranwalla and in the north of England and spends half the year in each of these companies and has founded a business association for Asian Britons in a northern city (2007-grw2). A manufacturer of denim fabric in Karachi started current production in the 1990s, after NAFTA, when denim mills in the United States were closing down. In order to respond to the rise in demand in the Asian market, my respondent – who received an engineering degree at the Ohio State University – traveled throughout the American South and selected equipment and a novel denim-manufacturing technique from mills in Georgia and the Carolinas (2007-khi8).

Third, from the 1980s and 1990s, the Pakistani government encouraged successful professionals and entrepreneurs who had amassed capital while working in the Persian Gulf states to reinvest in Pakistan. A successful physician who amassed a small fortune in savings as a pediatrician in Kuwait established a firm in Lahore manufacturing intravenous solutions in response to the Zia regime call for foreign entrepreneurs to return to the country and invest (2007-lhr5). Another major pharmaceutical manufacturer entered the industry after working as a banker in the Middle East (2007-lhr10). A garment manufacturer in Karachi, from a *muhajir* family and whose father had worked for the State Bank, took the Central Superior Services Examination but rather than enter the civil services, he worked in Saudi Arabia for global banking institutions. He collected capital and entered garment manufacturing in Pakistan in 1988, when the market showed signs of growth (2007-khi7). And a firm that manufactures fabric and garments was established by an ethnic Punjabi who immigrated to the Gulf and became a Bahraini national and a manufacturer of perfume, but encouraged his children to invest in Pakistan in the 1990s; the family maintains close ties between Pakistani and Bahraini investments (2007-lhr16). Politics and business in the Gulf might be thought of as filled with patronage as in South Asia, yet the successes of skilled and professional South Asian expatriates in the Gulf have been predicated on technocratic relationships with economic and social actors, in contrast with the internal political economy of the region.

Finally, older firms with more traditional practices might be transformed by the accession of a new, more technically trained generation to the firm's leadership. A respondent in Lahore from an established and conservative drugs manufacturing firm received his undergraduate education at the elite, private Lahore University of Management Sciences (LUMS) and executive education in the United States that led him to change the practices and strategies of his half-century-old firm when he became its managing director (2007-lhr13). In an auto parts manufacturing business, the two generations work in two separate manufacturing units that operate under very different structures of production; my respondent, educated in the United States, has increasingly focused on components for motorcycles for the rising Pakistani middle class, while his uncle continues the traditional business of producing components for tractors (2007-lhr23). Generational transitions are often awkward experiences for multigenerational firms; they can lead to changes in firm governance when the next generation has assumptions and perspectives that are at variance with their predecessors'.

Moral Economy and Governance by Personal Networks

For manufacturers who govern their firms by personal networks, by contrast, deep and sustained involvement with the embedded norms of local and regional markets in Pakistan provide the defining experiences that carry over into how industrial production is organized. This is perhaps most clearly demonstrated by traders – in textiles or drugs or auto parts – who invest in industrial production when the margins in merchandise trade become too thin. Textile manufacturers in Faisalabad, a well-known textile hub with the country's largest yarn market, tended to follow this route to manufacturing; one of the largest manufacturing groups in the city was founded by a yarn trading family in 1960 (2007-fsb1). More recently a dyeing and printing firm was established when a fabric trader could not ensure uniform quality in his traded goods (2007-fsb2). A manufacturer of drug formulations in Lahore started his career as a pharmaceutical trader among the South Asian expatriate community in Zambia and Zimbabwe, before establishing a wholesale business and then eventually a manufacturing plant in Pakistan (2007-lhr15).

Another pharmaceutical manufacturer in Karachi started pharmaceutical trading by transporting icepacks by bicycle from the wholesale market to a pharmacy. This trade led to more orders and eventually the import trade via a TELEX machine. He commenced domestic production in formulations when the government encouraged leading importers to enter into industry in the mid-1980s (2007-khi13). Trading tends to require relational skills and particular knowledge of different corners of the market and the habits of characters within them, skills and knowledge that can be deeply useful in arranging capital, managing workers, and forming working bonds with other businesses.

Other important sources of entrepreneurial capital and experience that might lead to structuring production by personal networks are agriculture and agriprocessing. One of my respondents was a member of a successful farming family in northern Punjab; his brother is active in provincial politics. He established a mill for edible oils and then two spinning mills (2007-lhr8). Another textile industrialist is also from a Punjabi landed family deeply committed to politics – first with the Muslim League and the Unionist Party and then with Nawaz Sharif's party, the PML-N. He started managing spinning mills when a sleeping partnership with one of Pakistan's biggest industrial groups went sour and they bought out their partners (2007-lhr30). Another textile manufacturing firm transitioned into the industry from packaging and marketing foodstuffs for the middle class in Karachi (2007-khi10). The patterns of patronage and mutual obligation that characterize life in the fields and farms of Pakistan can translate into frames for organizing capital and labor in manufacturing.

Last, another important source of inspiration for governance through personal networks are those who served as employees, foremen, and managers for the older mills and other conglomerates in Pakistan under statism, often working themselves up from the factory floor and thus being intimately familiar with the mechanisms of labor management and control. A large Faisalabad fabric producer – called the *baba*, or "old man," of Faisalabad textiles – worked for a long time as a foreman and then general manager for a large textile mill in Lahore; in 1979, he established his own business producing woven cloth on power looms to sell back to large companies. He has since invested, using retained earnings, in newer technology and diversified into stitching and warehousing (2007-fsb5). After decades working as a supervisory employee in a steel unit within Nawaz Sharif's industrial group, a manufacturer of sheet metal automotive components established his own manufacturing unit (2007-lhr24). Employees, foremen, and line managers tend to have a much closer relationship to the actual production processes and thus are less likely to move away from such processes into more general rules and institutions; they are also more likely to have built up capital over a longer period and thus have retained a more organic notion of growth than what is usual in a world of bank lending.

Such variation in the personal sources of industrial investment in Pakistan has inspired significant variation in how manufacturing is organized in industrial firms. In the next two sections, I will describe the challenges emerging from the retreat of statism in industrial financing and labor management, and how manufacturers have formulated strategies to cope with these challenges. Through this survey into the mechanisms of investment, I suggest that the backgrounds and perspectives of manufacturers can serve as a useful lens through which we might understand the sources of and variation within these strategies.

The Acquisition of Finance

Industrial finance followed the state's strategic imperatives in terms of industrial development.[1] The import-substitution regime that was set

[1] Jalal 1990; Nawaz 2008, 92–121.

in place soon after independence and solidified in the 1950s served several purposes simultaneously. It theoretically decreased imports and thus saved foreign exchange for military expenditure, while providing employment for migrants to Pakistan – most of them clustering around Karachi – and jump-starting economic growth and thus conferring legitimacy on the new state.[2] Yet the difficulty faced by state industrial promoters is that there were virtually no industrial capacity, little capital, and few industrial entrepreneurs in Pakistan at independence.

The Pakistani state's solution to this dilemma – the deliberate creation of an industrial bourgeoisie – built institutionalized cooperation between industrial capitalists and state planners and laid the foundation for structures of industrial finance.[3] Once the state provided the start-up capital for many of the (Karachi-based) industrial investments by the *muhajir* entrepreneurs who made up the first generation of industrialists, the provision of long-term finance ensured the viability of these enterprises. Development finance institutions such as the Pakistan Industrial Credit and Investment Corporation PICIC, an isomorph to ICICI, established in 1957 with World Bank assistance, channeled resources from the state directly to industry, with commercial banks playing a subsidiary role in providing running capital for day-to-day operations.[4] The availability of these loans during the 1960s is considered to be the defining factor in the level of both investment and profitability for the first generation of Pakistani industrialists.[5] Further, development finance agencies such as PICIC and the PIFC were primarily responsible for channeling the resources from foreign aid and the foreign exchange receipts from the export of Pakistani cotton and jute to domestic industrial investment, albeit at the expense of encouraging domestic savings.[6] Thus the state established structures and institutions for financing industry that took much of the risk out of investment for Pakistan's new manufacturers.

In the 1970s and 1980s, however, political instability and market-friendly reforms effectively tied the state's hands in ensuring long-term capital for industry. The United States temporarily suspended foreign aid to both India and Pakistan after the 1965 War. Political crisis and

---

[2] For more on state formation and legitimacy, see Zamindar 2007.
[3] Khan 1999; Papanek 1967, 184–225.   [4] Khan 1999, 16–18.
[5] Amjad 1976.   [6] Mahmood 1997.

conflict between East and West Pakistan in the early 1970s eventually led to the independence of Bangladesh, which meant among many other things the loss of revenues from East Bengal's jute exports. Zulfiqar Ali Bhutto, first under martial law after Yahya Khan's resignation in 1971 and under a democratic government after the 1973 elections, restored some political stability, but in so doing radically altered political alignments against extant industrial capital, thus further endangering the structures of statist industrial finance.

Bhutto's populist agenda, relatively silent on the matter of implementing land reform, was nonetheless particularly evident in a series of high-profile nationalizations, including that of banks along with petroleum distribution and shipping, in 1974. Such policies were an outcome of a government seemingly not very interested in matters of development, yet bound by commitments laid out in their election manifesto.[7] Moreover, Bhutto's major political task consisted in holding together his diverse and fragile coalition, a coalition that included Sindhi landowners, Punjabi cultivators, and urban public sector workers and traders, but did not include the Karachi-based industrial elite. Therefore, as with Indira Gandhi's contemporaneous populism, the political focus on the banking sector was on expanding access to credit for farmers, and thus weakening the deep links formed in the 1960s between finance and industry.

During the Zia era, policy reversals and moderations took away the sharp edge from Bhutto's populism and generally started the country on the road to market reform. Yet two other aspects of the economy during this period widened the cognitive bridge between finance and industry. First, labor migration to the Gulf and remittances became a larger part of the financial economy, yet remittance capital remained largely beyond the remit of the formal financial sector.[8]

Second and relatedly, Zia encouraged the development of Islamic banking as part of the wider program of Islamization in the country, thus further diluting the concentration of capital available to development finance. The introduction of Islamic banking, on which more later, can present a fundamental transformation from a classical capitalist economy to one in which the owners of capital are subjected to the same risk of profit and loss as direct investors. In Pakistan under Zia, the introduction of Islamic banks was more modest, but by 1981, all of

[7] Gustavson 1976.   [8] Arnold and Shah 1984.

the main specialized credit institutions converted assets and liabilities to "profit-and-loss sharing" to eliminate interest, which automatically meant that investments would have to be made in much more explicit rates of return, which implicitly privileged shorter-term trades over the riskier and longer-term industrial investments.[9] The impact of the Bhutto years and the Zia regime was thus effectively to dismantle the structures that channeled capital through specialist agencies toward long-term industrial projects.

The last two decades in Pakistan have seen a radical liberalization in banking and finance. Nawaz Sharif's first government in 1990 privatized the banking system and subsequent governments liberalized interest rates and introduced markets for securities; there is some evidence that such liberalization mobilized savings.[10] The privatization of commercial banks and the introduction of foreign banks in Pakistan increased the suppliers of capital in the country, but ironically it also decreased the variety of activities in which this capital could be invested. Liberalized banking institutions were obligated to invest in areas in which short-term returns were more likely to be realized, such as consumer finance, housing, trading, utilities, and real estate. In this context, manufacturing industry is not attractive enough to receive preferential attention in increasingly competitive capital markets.

Further, the politically motivated lending that accompanied first the nationalization and then the privatization of the commercial banking sector led to major defaults by some big corporate groups, which structurally increased the perceived risk of lending to industry. As an independent banking consultant explained, the reforms in the late 1980s and early 1990s meant a professionalization of the boards and management of the major banks and financial institutions, but such professionalization has led banks to struggle to ameliorate balance sheets by offering out newer loans at higher exchange rates (2007-lhr28). Modern orthodoxies of liberalized finance foreclose the possibility of privileging manufacturing and focus on maximizing the returns to bank depositors and investors. In the mid-2000s, increases in the interest spread – and thus the high interest rates that were a major concern for firms in my interview sample – were caused in part by the proliferation of fixed-interest deposit schemes that were issued as part of increased competi-

---

[9] Khan and Mirakhor 1990.   [10] Khan and Hasan 1998.

tion for scarce capital.[11] Between 2006 and 2007, when I conducted
fieldwork, the real interest rate rose from 6.8 to 14.2 percent between
2006 and 2007, with commercial rates of lending roughly 6.5 percent
higher than that.[12] In other words, the financial market was privileging
creditors at the expense of the borrowers and thus investors of capital.

Further, macroeconomic policy during the Musharraf years was seen
as favoring creditors, especially investors in financial institutions, over
debtors. A medical solutions manufacturer in Lahore expressed what
was a generally common sentiment among manufacturers I interviewed
during this period. He said:

The government has the justification of taking the interest rate from 5 percent
to 14 percent, to promote industrialization? You bring down the interest rate
to increase productivity. That is what our economic managers need to
understand. But they are obsessed with the syndrome of [Central Board of
Revenue]... the government wants money, so that the exchequer is full.
I keep arguing with the government functionaries, saying look at the balance
sheet of the banks... If you look at the balance-sheets of the banks, they are
fabulous, they're bulging with profits. From where are those profits coming?
From those guinea pigs, those who have invested money in the industry.
Industry is starving... I think there needs to be a balanced sort of situation,
where the industry makes good profits, and the banks must be curtailed.
(2007-lhr5)

A textile manufacturer in Karachi echoed the sentiment, focusing on
the unpredictability of the costs of capital and government responses in
relation to it:

When Musharraf was saying yes to everything [in the Global War on Terror],
the money was flowing in. The interest rate was 2 percent, and everyone
invested in textiles because of the low cost of capital. In 2004, rates jumped
from 4 percent to 9 percent within nine months, which is not a sensible jump.
The SBI governor said, "you should have forecasted it." Someone asked,
"Madam, what should we have forecasted? A 5–10 percent increase, or a
100 percent increase?" Where in the world does this happen? (2007-khi14)

This perspective reflects what is, in effect, a distributional fight among
groups of capitalists between the returns to entrepreneurial risk and the
interest returns to the holders of capital, now institutionalized in banks
and other financial institutions.

---

[11] Khwaja and Din 2007.   [12] World Development Indicators 2015.

A manufacturer characterized the overseas Pakistani creditors operating in Pakistan in similarly unflattering terms: "They are the stock exchange breed; they are being given everything free. They make their profit and then go away. They don't invest – build a factory, employ people – they just make a profit and go back to Dubai or Malaysia. People go into real estate, not industry" (2007-khi6).

The liberalization of finance in Pakistan has important implications for the financing of industry. The state no longer expends resources or power to create a framework for financing industrial development. But industry nonetheless requires financing, and it must compete with investments from consumer finance to utilities in order to receive loans. How do manufacturers in contemporary Pakistan secure financing?

In the following, I demonstrate that manufacturers in Pakistan pursue a variety of different strategies in securing finance for their investments. For those who structure production by formal rules, acquiring financing entails building working relationships with and/ or leveraging sources of institutional finance as a means of achieving capital for the longest term and at the most reasonable rates. For those who structure production through personal networks, however, financial institutions are generally to be avoided and financing instead largely is obtained from personal, family, or community assets and the reinvestment of profits. Islamic banking is complicated: it represents a clear commitment to the personal and relational in the financing of industry, but within a framework that is very formal and institutional.

Financing Firms through Formal Rules

For firms that rely on formal rules and institutions to decrease their uncertainty in industrial investment, the sudden and dramatic increases in interest rates in the mid-2000s presented a problem, but one that did not shake their faith in the notion of industrial development through largely bank debt. Most manufacturers of this kind have established "standard" debt–equity ratios, all of which are greater than 1; most fall into the "2 to 1" ratio formula, or one-third equity to two-thirds debt, and in some cases even higher (2007-lhr12; 2007-lhr31; 2007-khi05). One garment manufacturer in Lahore started his knitwear unit with $200,000 of his own capital and $550,000 of loans from banks (2007-lhr7). Older firms mention a transition from developmental finance institutions to commercial banks, as the former became increasingly uninterested in industrial lending; PICIC was recently purchased by a consortium of Gulf investors (2007-lhr22). The increase in interest rates did not seem to decrease the quantum of everyday lending, but it has changed the calculations made by firms regarding the timing of expansion. One textile manufacturer from Karachi lending from both Habib Bank and Citibank mentioned how "there was expansion, at 3 percent [interest], but now it is too expensive" (2007-khi6). Yet, many Pakistani firms had to suffer through this period because of recent expansions. One textile firm, responding to increases in demand, had established another factory: "We hold a 60–40 ratio with the banks: Habib Bank, Muslim Commercial Bank, National Bank of Pakistan... The problem is that the second unit was expensive and now the interest rate is higher, we feel the pain" (2007-lhr31).

Other firms employed a number of strategies to decrease the cost of borrowing through diversification. This included, first, arbitraging interest rates between domestic and multinational banks. One garment manufacturer relies on foreign-currency-denominated loans, trading interest rate for exchange rate volatility, even while sourcing capital machinery from abroad: "As the interest rate went up, we've done offshore financing. There is the risk of [changes in] the exchange rate, but the dollar- and yen-based financing is much cheaper now. We bought Japanese machinery through [the State Bank of Pakistan]'s branch in Tokyo" (2007-lhr26). Another textile manufacturer took out fixed-rate "LIBOR-plus" loans – this was years before the LIBOR fixing scandal – through foreign banks such as ABN-AMRO and Citibank that were expanding their operations in Pakistan (2007-khi14).

The stock market did not seem a viable source of extra capital, according to respondents. One mentioned equity sales in the Karachi Stock Exchange without referring to it as a source of capital: "We offloaded part of our equity to the public through the stock market. The price goes up and down, but factory stays the same. The stock is trading, but we get no new capital. We are giving dividends regularly, not like other companies" (2007-khi8). Yet some have funded major expansions through investment and equity markets. A major auto components manufacturer has raised capital by investing in various ventures – including real estate – and in the course of an expansion into the OEM business is seeking first private equity and then an IPO (2007-khi5). A large textile manufacturer in Lahore balanced the two main sources of finance; he mentioned that he was balancing lenders, meaning banks, with sponsors, meaning new investors (2007-lhr6).

Financing Firms through Personal Networks

For firms that structure production through personal networks, however, financial institutions are too distant to form any real bonds with, as their actions are driven by the imperatives of the market rather than affective relationships. Public offerings are similarly not appealing to these respondents because of the decrease in ownership and control they imply. In Pakistan, a number of my respondents said point-blank that they did not take out loans or completely paid them off (2007-grw01, 2007-grw03, 2007-khi09, 2007-khi12, 2007-khi23, 2007-lhr20, 2007-lhr22, 2007-khi25). Others relied on banks only for operating capital: "We use our own equity, and get only running capital from the banks" (2007-lhr8).

Instead of institutional finance, most of these firms grow by ploughing profits back into the business, growing organically and without oversight from loan administrators, thus blurring the boundary between the wealth of the family and the wealth of the company. This profit reinvestment model is also appealing because it represents self-reliance and the concrete evidence of toil. One said, "We are *khudi* (self-) financing, we ended all bank loans" (2007-khi2008). A Lahore manufacturer said, "I grow on a self-basis *[sic]*: no long-term loans, only working capital. All capital expenses from my own finance" (2007-lhr9). One respondent explained how the business was developed first from legacy capital and then from self-generation: "When we started the business in 1990, I used the land and machines kept by my father, and since then it's based on profits. Expansion has come from my own turnovers" (2007-khi09).

Some Pakistani industrialists refer to taking out loans as an experience not to be repeated. A pharmaceutical manufacturer said: "In the 1980s, I took out a bank loan; that was not very good. I finished off, never again. Islamic banking has prohibitions on interest; Islamic banking should be there" (2007-khi16). And, as we will see in greater detail later, a number of the entrepreneurs I interviewed cited their faith as determining their attitudes toward finance. One said very clearly, "Allah is my main financier; all property is Allah's" (2007-lhr24). Another manufacturer, who had grown up in Bahrain, had instituted a no-debt policy according to his religious beliefs: "We are completely self-financed, I'm against *riba* [interest]. I don't believe in it [because of our] religion – I convinced the family to stay away from banks. Whatever profits we make, we reinvest most into the company" (2007-lhr16). The proscriptions against *riba*, or usury, in Islam make a portion of Pakistani society very uneasy about the operations of modern finance. Yet the penetration of Islamic banking, particularly using capital from the Gulf, has made inroads on this belief, particularly among those who have until now avoided bank lending.

Islamic Banking

Islamic banking has become popular in Pakistan partly to respond to the needs of pious sections of society to take advantage of the goods of a banking system while also conforming to religious practices. Yet because Islamic banks, such as the ubiquitous Bank al-Falah, owned by Emirati investors, have to compete in a larger capital market – and with Pakistani commercial and international banks offering Islamic banking – the returns on deposits and loans approximate market rates. This convergence worries some of my respondents, including this auto components manufacturer:

We are mostly self-financed. We are a religiously inclined family so we avoid loans, and interest. Islamic banking is coming in, so even people like us, who never took a loan, are getting encouraged to get involved. I'm personally not convinced that it is as Islamic, but the board has decided and we have done a few *mudharaba* (profit sharing) projects with them. It is working out, but I'm not satisfied personally. It's evolving and better than the traditional banking we had before, and I have hope it will evolve to be the true Islamic banking, But it's too young, you know? So it will take time, and we will learn from the market. (2007-lhr23)

Others are less concerned: "In 1998, we shifted to Islamic banking, which is not interest-based, for loans over 4–5 years... This is an inside vision, you follow Islam" (2007-fsb1). Another mentioned Islamic banking as a solution to the endemic distrust of formal institutions that has depressed industrial investment: "Islamic banking is the solution; if there is confidence, people will invest and we can get back" (2007-khi6). Yet the convergent properties of Islamic banking can make it seem to be an institution that enables those with particular ethical qualms about debt to participate in mainstream finance without a guilty conscience.

Perhaps the most revealing aspect of Islamic finance is the care that bankers take to screen their clients and form relationships that are dictated by norms other than the market. An interview with an official in a domestic Islamic bank emphasized the common values of the bank and their profit-sharing clients. The key to success in this business is to know about and form relationships with businesses, even at the expense of some paternalism: "We won't give you money for the sake of giving money; we need to understand how the money is being used" (2007-khi17). Thus, Islamic business is a way to embed financial institutions in moral economy networks, even though its transformation of the concepts of debt and finance cuts across some of the more settled distinctions of utilizing or avoiding finance.

Industrialists in Pakistan are divided on how to respond to the volatility of Pakistan's capital and credit markets, which have, if anything, become increasingly more uncertain as a result of inflation, rupee depreciation, and macroeconomic instability. For many manufacturers whose understanding of industrial production relies on explicit norms and dependence on formal market exchange, strategies must involve arbitrage among different sets of domestic and global institutions. For others who understand governance as operating through personal networks, the initial use of family and personal capital, the practices of reinvestment of profits, and the newer institution of Islamic finance as a way to embed credit markets in personal connections are more acceptable. Both modes of acquiring industrial capital for investment can "work," but they do so in divergent directions, thus challenging the notion that financial market institutions might provide the cohesion that the state cannot.

The Recruitment and Retention of Workers

As a result of both lack of ideological commitments to socialism and the relative newness of industrial capacity, Pakistani labor institutions in the decades after partition differed from those in India. The relative stability in labor management afforded to industrialists during the era of statist development was obtained by the coercive mechanisms of the Pakistani state, particularly after the 1958 declaration of martial law. Despite waves of strike activity in the 1950s and 1960s, union activity was suppressed and strikes broken by police action. Pakistan arguably never developed the quasi-corporatist relationships that were formed through the party affiliation of Indian trade unions. But changes in the 1970s and 1980s did create new and different challenges of labor management for contemporary Pakistani industrialists.

The Pakistani working class in the 1950s was largely a product of Partition, in which millions of poor Muslim peasants particularly from North India were compelled to leave their homes and farms and migrated to Karachi. Their agricultural roots now foreclosed, *mohajirs* without capital sought industrial work and competed in an environment of high unemployment.[13] Further, the nature of life and work in industrial Karachi in the 1950s, with a deep lack of adequate housing and basic social services, provided a material platform on which trade unionism was established. Between 1953 and 1957, there were 250 strikes, in which more than 200,000 workers participated.[14]

In response, Ayub Khan's military government replaced the (preindependence) Industrial Disputes Act with an Industrial Disputes Ordinance of 1959, which radically constricted the capacity of workers to bargain collectively or form trade unions and subjected disputes to compulsory adjudication, often through military courts.[15] In the industrial enterprises of the 1960s, concentrated mainly around Karachi, jobbers responsible for ethnically homogeneous work gangs conducted day-to-day shop floor labor management, particularly in relation to Balochi and Pakhtun workers.[16] Christopher Candland characterizes the evolution of the trade union movement in Pakistan as fragmented through policies of military governments and factory-level regimes imposed from above.[17] Hamza Alavi has characterized trade union "activism" in Pakistan as essentially creating legal intermediation between workers and a state-led bureaucratic system of labor arbitration.[18] State intervention, both regulatory and coercive, was thus at the very center of Pakistani labor relations.

The 1970s provided a sharp break from admittedly coercive but largely predictable capital–labor relations in the period of statist development. Factory workers were part of the mass movement that forced Ayub Khan from power. One result of mass mobilization was a more

---

[13] Keddie 1957, 577–579.   [14] Keddie 1957, 569–576; Ali 2005, 86.
[15] Amjad 2001, 72–76.   [16] Ali 2005, 88–89.   [17] Candland 2007, 36–41.
[18] Alavi, cited in Ali 2005, 96n.

liberal Labor Relations Ordinance in 1969, which revitalized trade unionism even as arrests of labor leaders and activists continued.[19] Yet the destabilization of the 1971 war, the growing militancy of labor, and the reimposition of political authority by Bhutto led to a confrontation between labor and the state in June 1972, when the police fired on first striking workers and then a funeral procession of those killed by police, leaving more than a dozen dead and scores wounded.[20] This event – and the reactions to it by the PPP government, the various unions, and other political actors – presaged increasing ethnic tensions that would erupt in systemic violence in Karachi.[21] The Zia ul Haq regime outlawed strikes and demonstrations under martial law between 1977 and 1985, severely curtailed trade union activities, and deployed state violence against workers, as in the Colony Textile Mills in Ismailabad, where thirteen striking workers were killed by the police.[22] And in the democratic interregnum of the 1990s, rival PPP and PML-N governments imposed structural adjustment and privatization, with fragmented trade union organizations unable to alter the pace of neoliberal reform.[23]

The contemporary labor force in Pakistan, as a result of both the assault of union organization and the withdrawal of state expenditure in implementing labor regulation, is deeply underinstitutionalized, with the hollowing out of systems that allowed for – albeit coercive – predictability on the shop floor.[24] In relation to the Pakistani textile industry, Candland characterizes the status of workers as trending toward "labor disorganization."[25] The efforts of organized labor, meanwhile, are fully focusing on preventing retrenchment as a result of privatization in government-owned companies such as utilities; in an interview I conducted with a leader of the Lahore-based Pakistan Workers' Federation (PWF), he acknowledged the problems facing private sector industrial labor, particularly in the textile industry – the use of contract labor, bad working conditions in some locations, the victimization of union activists, and the nonapplication of social security – but emphasized that the PWF's activism is mostly on behalf of workers in government bodies such as the Water and Power

---

[19] Ali 2005, 87–88.   [20] Ali 2005, 87–93.   [21] Ibid., 94–101.
[22] Candland 2007, 46–47.   [23] Ibid., 118–123.
[24] In 2007, the governments of Punjab and Sindh had both suspended labor inspection, citing resource constraints (2007-lhr34).
[25] Candland 2007, 146–151.

Development Authority (2007-lhr34). At the same time, informal mechanisms of organization in tight markets for skilled labor present difficulties for manufacturers who might want more institutionalized mechanisms. The director of a large spinning group explained at length:

Labor wasn't an issue a year or so back; but as industry is booming, labor has more bargaining power. Labor is a very important ingredient: there are several general rules of the game. There's a price. I generally feel that our units are overstaffed, but you don't want to get yourself into a dispute with the labor unless you feel you need to make significant changes – if it's minor, you deal with it. There's a spokesperson – every year there's a bonus, but generally, the area – the mills around you – determines the bonus. To avoid problems, you have to pay regardless of how you are performing. (2007-lhr26)

Such a system might broadly determine wages, but cannot intervene in terms of training, recruitment, retention, or maintaining productivity; this manufacturer went on to mention that yearly attrition for industrial workers was at 25–30 percent, which was not unrepresentative of industry in Pakistan. In other industries in Pakistan, attrition can also be motivated by the desire to move into work perceived as higher status. In the auto components industry, for instance, many skilled workers are being lured away from the industry toward "cleaner," more clerical work because of the discomfort of working in a foundry and the increasing opportunity for working in the garment industry or low-end service work (2007-khi9).

The "disorganization" of industrial labor in contemporary Pakistan presents some unexpected challenges for industrialists. Manufacturers can no long rely on the old legal labor regime and "pocket" unions to maintain communications with workers; they are substantially without broader institutional support in the recruitment, retention, and monitoring of workers. How do manufacturers create and implement a labor management regime in this context? I argue that some, who structure their production through formal rules, tend to new frameworks of institutionalized norms and incentives that exist inside the firm. Others, who structure production by personal networks, focus on building and renewing affective relationships between the *saith* and his workers, as a means of both commitment and monitoring.

Managing Workers through Formal Rules

For those committed to governance by formal rules, labor recruitment, management, and retention need to be handled more formally and systematically, in such a way as to lessen arbitrariness and the personal involvement of the entrepreneur. In fact, one Lahore textile industrialist said, "Here is an observation: if the owner walks into the operation of manufacturing … if he interferes, the firm suffers" (2007-lhr1). Another manufacturer, a former bureaucrat, in-contracted human resources experts as a way of establishing systems of labor management: "I spent a lot of money getting expatriates to do training, but then some stay and others go. And then I need to train the entire chain" (2007-lhr7). Pakistani manufacturers focus on the government's inability to provide vocational training, and how it hampers their ability to establish more formalized systems for labor management, complete with training:

We are trying to convert [from contract] to salaried workers – this is a problem because it is difficult to get people to work on salaries in stitching; it's very difficult. So for that, we are opening our own vocational training school and getting fresh operators, high school graduates. It is difficult because frankly the government should be doing this work, training them in basic skills – it does take a lot of money and time. (2007-lhr16)

In some cases, this means reaching out beyond the firm to proximate institutions. One components manufacturer who trained in postgraduate computer-assisted engineering in England and has maintained ties there is trying to establish a system of recruitment based on institutions of higher education: "Now, I'm trying to make relationships with universities: I will go to the principals of the surrounding technical colleges and ask them for their best students so we can get them in their final year with offers" (2007-grw2).

A large mill owner has also focused on the issue of limited vocational training, as well as the provision of a social wage as a means of retaining workers:

Most [of our] units have in-house training, expertise. The government is doing something: it is establishing a textile college in Faisalabad. But there's a lot more to be done – the quality is low. Some employees have been here from the very beginning – oldest employees have been with us for three–four decades. People join and stay a part of the company. We have an internal HR department... We bridge the gap between social requirements and what's available, such as medical insurance coverage. (2007-lhr4)

And an emphasis on equity is also very important. A pharmaceutical manufacturer in Pakistan emphasized the importance of equity and fairness, and creating institutions that could guarantee these values:

In my experience, [Pakistani workers] are very good – if you train them, pay them above market wage, give them good conditions, hold them accountable, they're outstanding workers, very loyal. In our cafeteria, we serve the same food, same tables, same water for everyone. (2007-khi22)

Many of my respondents mentioned the provision of services as a means of supplementing wages and thereby producing loyalty, which represented recognition that labor markets were tight and workers, especially those skilled and trained, needed additional incentives to be productive and remain in their current positions. A components manufacturer presented a fuller picture of how he is trying to induce the workers to invest in the company:

We provide them housing; all our facilities have housing, facilities, subsidized food, free medical, a free uniform for the different departments. But we are planning many more welfare projects. We are considering a housing society; [a worker] will be given a housing plot after a while [from the provident fund] and then he wants to keep it, sell it, make a house on it – not just monthly, yearly bonuses, we want to give them a house – a luxury for the class of people I am mentioning to you. (2007-lhr23)

More generally, the imposition of rules and institutions – from establishing nonwage incentives to providing formal vocational training – creates the sense of stability not provided by labor market institutions.

Managing Workers through Personal Networks

Other manufacturers are similarly disposed to construct strategies that utilize personal and cultural connections to recruit, retain, and manage workers. An industrialist in Faisalabad whose operations included weaving and finishing power loom cloth stressed personal connections as well, even though employment is on contract terms:

We have three hundred workers on temporary, contract basis, from local areas – the villages. They go back for fifteen days. They are *kisan-log* [peasant-folk] and hand goods craftsmen. *Log ke sath* [with the people], we are involved as a family, *khudi* [ourselves]... You learn directly the feelings/psyche of labor. (2007-fsb3)

The owner of another large mill employing three thousand people – based in Karachi but with industrial units in Punjab – uses the family idiom and discusses welfare in terms of moral responsibility:

Thank God, recruitment and retention is OK with us. We hold on to our employees. In our office, everyone has, at minimum, [been] working for 10 years, and there are third generation employees. To retain them, we treat them like a family. This is not an issue of salaries... When they have an issue of hospital care, I give them a slip saying it will all be free. A worker [who] was crossing the road, he died in an accident, and we took care of the family. This was a very poor family, so we gave them a sewing machine so they can stitch at home and start making money. When someone dies, how will the children survive? We do it because it is right. (2007-khi14).

In this instance, in the language and thus presumably the self-understanding of the employer, the provision of services represents a set of moral obligations rather than supplements on wages that might act as an incentive toward greater productivity.

The use of contractors presents a means to monitor labor. One textile industrialist mentioned the practice in these terms: "The supervisor, he brings people ... it's his responsibility to fulfill our labor requirements" (2007-lhr6). Fewer respondents in Pakistan talked explicitly and openly about contract hiring practices, but the necessity for surveillance and knowledge of workers can lead either jobbers or the *saith* himself to be focused on (subjective) personal qualities rather than formal qualifications in labor management. One rather severe and paternalistic garment exporter in Lahore approached recruitment in this manner: "I am fussy in selection: I look at an applicant's education, family background, integrity, and check whether [the] person is lucky or unlucky" (2007-lhr9).

Echoing the scheme labor of Tamil Nadu discussed in Chapter 5, there are instances when gender and cultural tropes are used as a means of labor control. An auto components manufacturer from Lahore only hires an all-woman workforce for his auto electronics assembly line:

One thing very unique about my production facility is that its 100 percent female, to resolve the cultural issues, and I must say it's one of the best production lines I've ever seen in electronics... Basically, women are more dexterous than men and they can do repetitive jobs without getting mentally antagonized. And thirdly, they have the unique capacity that they can work and talk together... Historically, they have been doing stitching and knitting but now they can do assembly work and still talk and do it. We actually observed that the men and the boys we had on the production line after a while got very frustrated and disturbed, so we thought of moving them out. (2007-lhr14)

During the interview, I bristled at this respondent's blanket generalizations. I thought at the time that it was a not-so-subtle form of patriarchal control of labor, as young women have subordinate social and political power in Pakistan. Given the ideational correlates to that power structure, it would be hard to see possibilities for assertiveness, particularly among high school dropouts. While conceding the inherent patriarchy involved, the industrialist in question had established a culturally productive framework around these workers: they all were from the neighborhood near the factory and were picked up and dropped by bus, and the "process control and staff management" are handled by the industrialist's wife, the HR manager. They receive a fixed salary plus overtime (2007-lhr23). It is also hard to see how these women would be employed on better terms or conditions than this.

Relations between business and labor in contemporary Pakistan are fraught by both the shortage of skilled labor and the decline to obscurity of those institutions that had presented a viable if also largely coercive system of state-enforced labor management. Since the state is both unwilling and unable to expend resources to revitalize the labor management regime, some manufacturers manage labor through the affective relationships and embedded structures that serve as mechanisms for recruitment, retention, and monitoring. Others take recourse to formal rules and explicit institutions – including formal courses of vocational training and provision of productivity-enabling social services – as a means to recruit, anchor, and oversee workers.

Conclusion

Dual regimes of labor management echo differences in the financing of industrial investment and represent a Pakistani industrial community that is divided on how to respond to the retreat of the state from industrial governance. In this sense, Pakistan has mirrored closely the

Indian experience of the end of statist development, even though Pakistan and India represented two very different regimes of state-directed development. From the perspective of understanding the changing role of the state in the industrial experiences of developing countries, the Indian experience might thus be a little remote. In Chapters 7 and 8, I have included an extended analysis of the Pakistani state and the strategies of Pakistani industrialists as a "mirror case," to suggest the applicability of insights on industrial governance after statism within a wider universe of developing countries, within which Pakistan is arguably more representative.

Conclusion

Development after Statism in South Asia

This book has focused on industrial firms in India and in Pakistan, and how they manage to structure production since the retreat of the state. For many in South Asia, as in the United States, the state has come to be seen as an obstacle to progress, a parasite on productive economic activity properly managed by the free market. The call from certain libertarians and business leaders in the United States and South Asia is for the state to get out of the way. Yet, for South Asian manufacturers, the irritations of an arcane inspection regime and too-rigid labor laws pale in comparison to what the state does not govern: the cost of energy, the access to medium-term finance, the availability of skilled workers. We are left with a situation in which the state has neither the capacity nor the inclination to direct key factor markets and structure the industrial economy in the service of development, as it did during Nehruvian era or Ayub Khan's regime.

As it applies to South Asian industry, market libertarianism – a belief that the state should stay out of the economy – rests on two fallacies. First, some might argue that there is, absent the state, a set of market institutions that can more naturally create economywide order and stability. In South Asia, at least, we have not seen the rise of new, powerful national institutions that have regulated or coordinated industrial production after the retreating state. Others might argue that institutional retreat might actually be good for business, in that it created natural entrepreneurs who can take advantage of arbitrage and opportunities to turn profits quickly. This may indeed be the case for those who trade, but manufacturing is different. Investments take years to translate into production and returns on that investment, as factories are built, workers are recruited and trained, capital machinery is integrated into the production process, and networks of suppliers and customers are established. These institutional arrangements constitute a necessary framework for industrialization.

For any developing country with a history of nationalist struggle against colonial powers, a priority of any state was to govern the economy in such a way as to transform its orientation to the production of higher value goods and thereby raise standards of living for the population. In the mid-twentieth century, industrialization was understood to be the driving force for this economic and social transformation. For all their differences, Pakistani and Indian leaders agreed on the political importance of industrialization. Thus the economic planners who controlled the state in both Pakistan and India channeled resources and political capital into establishing and maintaining structures that provided a stable context for industrial investment.

The state in both India and Pakistan directed long-term patient capital through developmental finance toward industrial investments. In India, the party affiliation of trade unions and a framework of labor legislation maintained institutionalized communication between workers and managers in organized sector factories. In Pakistan, where unions were more independent and capital–labor relations more divisive, the existence of unions in the private sector still maintained systems of representation and credible bargaining. For a manufacturing firm during this period, state power ensured industrial governance. And importantly, "state-directed development," to use Atul Kohli's term, served as the preeminent model for how we have come to understand later industrialization, in which powerful autonomous state structures govern the circumstances within which industrial investment can be deployed.

These commitments of the state were predicated on a set of political principles that held until the 1980s. In both countries as in others, a combination of the rise of demand groups and political competition, declines in industrial productivity due to underinvestment and labor militancy, and a changing international environment all contributed to the dismantling of the structures of statist development; after liberalization, a new political economy of rent allocation has precluded the state from expending resources to structure industrial investment.

As a result, the state in either country is unable and unwilling credibly to put and keep in place institutions to direct factor markets and thus structure the context for investment in manufacturing, or, in other words, govern the industrial economy. Further, patterns of firm strategies make it rather difficult to argue that subnational governments, sectoral agencies, or the institutions of global markets have fully replaced the state in providing industrial governance. Firms in the same

Indian state or Pakistani province and within the same industry exhibit wildly different practices in the acquisition of finance, the recruitment and retention of workers, and even the engagement with international markets. Such variation suggests that subnational states, sectoral frameworks and global markets do not provide the credible signals necessary to establish and enforce a "Gujarati" or "Punjabi" model of industrial capitalism, or indeed structures that might enable the auto components or pharmaceutical firms to operate within a common set of institutions.

Instead, I contend that the institutions of industrial production are most readily apparent at the firm level. In the absence of credible cues from the external environment, industrialists – the owners, directors, and managers of manufacturing firms – take recourse to their own backgrounds, values, and experiences in establishing durable relationships to the firm's main interlocutors in order to make investments more certain. I argue that two general categories of backgrounds and experiences led industrialists to understand the economy as either a set of rather formal institutional practices or crosscutting networks of personal ties. These two ways of perceiving the nature and ends of industrial economy lead to production being structured in two remarkably different ways.

Industrialists with educations and work experiences that would predispose them to think in a technocratic, rule-bound manner about confronting the challenges of the chaotic economy would tend to structure production through the establishment and application of sets of clear and transparent institutions. These would serve both as a way to incentivize greater productivity internally and as a signal to other actors such as banks and clients of the seriousness of the enterprise. Structural characteristics at the firm level, such as larger size and greater integration into global markets, serve to complement rather than to constrain the perspectives of manufacturers.

Structuring production by formal rules entails a certain commitment to the principles of market arbitrage in the acquisition of finance. It also means certain practices in the management of "human resources," including incentive-based pay, formal training systems, establishment of in-house union representation, and provision of social services as mechanisms for recruitment and retention. Firms that are structured through formal rules are also more likely to engage with the international economy through the governing structures of global value chains, in which major multinational buyers set the terms of production. In this way, rules-driven manufacturers can internalize in microcosmic form the formal institutions that normally pervade entire economies in industrialized countries.[1]

For those whose backgrounds and experiences include prolonged exposure to the practices of local markets for retail or intermediate products – who might trade in auto components, yarn, or fabric or cultivate raw materials before they invest in industrial enterprise – the Indian or Pakistani economy seems to be a dense web of culturally embedded ties, in which practices may be determined through many previous associations in an otherwise low-trust context. For those who structure their production through personal networks, financing is generally pursued through a combination of family/community capital and the reinvestment of profits. Such embeddedness limits exposure to the fluctuating official cost of credit and maintains personal control over the use of this capital for specific investments.

These firms also tend to manage workers through a deeply familial idiom, either extending paternalistic ties to their workforce themselves or hiring labor contractors to serve as often-coethnic interlocutors between management and workers on the line. Further, firms that arrange production through personal networks tend to spurn the governance frameworks of major multinational buyers and interact instead with the multitude of smaller importers and intermediate agents that link Indian and Pakistani manufacturers with niches in international markets, including the less regulated markets of the developing world. Firms that structure production through personal networks do not seek to transcend but rather embrace the "connectedness" that constitutes market exchange in South Asian economies, using personal ties to other actors as a source of reciprocity, obligation, and trust.

The specific sources, patterns, and mechanisms of variation in firm-level institutional strategies suggest that the most common frame in comparative political economy, that of national models of capitalism, may not be a useful one for understanding industrialization after statism in the developing world, in South Asia and beyond. Neither state institutions nor sectoral regimes have replaced the old developmental state model in providing industrial governance to firms. Rather,

---

[1] I thank Meg Rithmire for her framing of this point.

in India and Pakistan at least, firms have sought to structure their production through forming institutional relationships with capital and labor. The notion of firms as governance actors – as institution makers rather than takers – might be unfamiliar, but it presents a new possibility for industrial governance in debates that have thus far precluded actors other than states or market institutions. Thus, the "governing firms" approach presents a novel lens through which we might understand the inner institutional architecture of industrial development.

The firm level is also a key but hitherto neglected vantage point from which to examine the influences of the state, region, or sector on industrial development. Firms are, after all, where the rubber meets the road in manufacturing. Convergence of firm strategies within provinces would suggest industrial governance at the level of the province; sectoral convergence would similarly suggest sectoral governance. In exploring the patterns and mechanisms of industrial governance in India, Tamil Nadu stands out as a state with distinctive, relatively convergent patterns of financing and labor management; these findings stand in common with other recent research that suggests a Tamil subnationalism and distinctive politics of representation.[2] Similarly, firms in the automotive sector are relatively distinctive in their approach to capital and labor, for reasons that were discussed in greater length in Chapter 6. The research in this book suggests, however, that the state of Tamil Nadu and the automotive sector are exceptions rather than the rule, and the broader lack of convergence among industrial firms in South Asia is a meaningful challenge to the ways we have tended to explain the political economy of industrial development.

Locating Industrial Governance beyond South Asia

Moving beyond the subcontinent, the approach of this book can serve as an important starting point in a search for industrial governance in different regional contexts. Countries as disparate as Argentina and Indonesia have experienced versions of liberalization and economic reform that have redefined the role of the state in relation to the industrial economy. States throughout the developing world have faced pressures from emerging constituencies that have challenged

[2] Agarwala 2013; Singh 2016.

previous commitments to industrialization during the import-substitution era. I contend that firm-level analysis of economic governance might be an important means by which we might understand these changing dynamics beyond the Indian subcontinent.

Latin America

The liberalization experience in Latin America has been dramatic; it has been accompanied in the most extreme examples by deindustrialization, regime change, and party system collapse. During the heyday of statism in the region, the state's role in encouraging industrialization centered on, first, autarkic state-led industrialization and, second, strategic state-led alliances with multinational corporations and domestic industry that would allow for industrial peace, technology transfer, and development of domestic and export markets; Peter Evans has characterized these regimes "dependent development."[3] They were at the very heart of deepening ISI toward capital and producer goods, which entailed added investment, conflicts with workers over distributing the spoils, and the emergence of "bureaucratic authoritarianism" in key countries at the industrial frontier in the region: Brazil, Chile, Argentina, and Uruguay.[4] The debt crises of the 1980s dashed the promise of deepening investment and moving to the next stage of industrialization through state-directed loans from petrodollar-rich private banks. The decade-long process of adjustment and, for some countries, the formulation of industrial trajectories were embedded in political maneuvering among governments, firms, and popular sectors in a context where the state was no longer the apex of economic decision making.

The political support among industrialists for these neoliberal reforms in countries such as Brazil was not particularly coherent or consistent over time, echoing the South Asian cases in which business could not be understood as having consistent and obvious interests in relation to the state. Peter Kingstone, writing about the political preferences of Brazilian industrialists over the 1980s and 1990s, has noted that business rallied around political leaders such as Fernando Cardoso who could promise policy consistency. At a more micro-level, manufacturers could be incorporated in the formation of business–government coalitions

[3] Hirschman 1968; Evans 1979; Gereffi 1982; Bennett and Sharpe 1985.
[4] O'Donnell 1988.

capable of establishing nuanced reform programs that could minimize the downsides of adjustment.[5] Sebastian Etchemendy has argued that the variation in the institutional outcomes of economic liberalization in Latin America – among Brazilian statism, Argentinian corporatism, and the greater market orientation of Chile and Peru – was a product of the type of regime during critical phases of adjustment and, more crucially here, the strength and organization of business and labor interests. In his telling, the state implements different forms of compensation to business (including "ISI insiders") and labor depending on the complexities of interactions between industrialists and government actors at the level of sectors or even firms.[6]

Yet firms have also been important governance actors, acting alone and in concert. Ben Ross Schneider has argued that policy inputs from strong business associations in Mexico and Chile enabled the relative success of economic reform in the 1980s and 1990s.[7] In a recent article, Schneider argues that the persistence of the traditional corporate agglomeration – the *grupo* – in increasingly liberalized Latin America is an institutional response to an environment in which volatility and market imperfections are rampant, stock markets underdeveloped, and thus institutional uncertainty high: *grupo* governance, with family ownership, diversification, and "blockholding," was able to deliver access to long-term capital, specific market information, and policy making.[8]

Other forms of firm-level institutional structures have also emerged in the region. The proliferation of *maquiladores* on Mexico's border with the United States was enabled by the creation of NAFTA, and thus can be seen as a creature of changes in international political economy. Yet the operation of industrial production in some of the most violent regions of contemporary Mexico requires governance arrangements that emerge from particular forms of expatriate capital, indigenous (or "third culture") labor management, and alliances with the state at the local level that can ensure basic protections of property. Thus, in a regional form of development in both international and domestic senses, research at the firm level might help us to anatomize the institutional arrangements and mechanisms that stand behind new forms of production. Domestic industrial firms and business

---

[5] Kingstone 1999.   [6] Etchemendy 2011.   [7] Schneider 2004.
[8] Schneider 2008.

associations are dynamic political and social actors whose interventions are crucial for structuring production in the uncertain economies of postliberalization Latin America.

The Middle East and North Africa

The greater Middle East is a heterogeneous region, at one point drawn together by Ottoman rule from western North Africa northeast to the Anatolian peninsula and east to the Gulf monarchies and the Arabic-speaking *mashreq*. But it was divided by European imperialism, carving states out of a previously more fluid structure of Ottoman rule and thus forming both the contemporary map of the region and the stage for regional internal conflict. Postwar Arab nationalist mobilizations in all but the most conservative monarchies yielded largely authoritarian regimes that were nevertheless committed to economic transformation through state-directed industrialization. The nonrentier states of the Middle East and North Africa suffered the contractions of the 1970s; these led to policies of liberalization and structural adjustment that represented the largest challenge to the state as the paramount governing power in society, until the Arab Spring of 2011.[9]

Scholars have argued that firms and their dynamic relationships to state structures have modified differences in the responses to these shocks. Melani Cammett argued that the differences in the private sector responses to trade liberalization in Tunisia and Morocco stemmed from the fact that industrial firms in the former remained disorganized and distant from the state, while the latter maintained internal cohesion and close business–state relations. Cammett argued that policy formulation in Morocco benefited from the perspectives of the "self-made men" of the export apparel sector who were eager to oppose the ISI era, inward-looking "fat-cat" elites by embracing global integration.[10] In Egypt, the Arabic-speaking Middle East's biggest economy, structural adjustment policies imposed in 1991 by the Mubarak government were largely inconclusive, haphazard, and disjointed because of the social structures created by nationalist mobilization that included the state, the military, and big industrial actors.[11] Labor struggles, central in the buildup to the Arab Spring,

---

[9] For a good overview, see Richards and Waterbury 2008.   [10] Cammett 2007.
[11] Harik 1997; Waterbury 1983.

resulted from a shop floor "moral economy" dynamics whereby the state's liberalization policies threatened established relationships between capital and labor.[12] Any understanding of the political economy dynamics in Egypt and elsewhere in the Middle East thus requires an appreciation of dynamics within the sphere of economic production, in a context where the role of the state in governing the economy has substantially changed.

Turkey is an interesting case; its precocious state formation and its state-directed but private-sector-implicated development trajectory make it more readily comparable to cases in East or South Asia than other countries in the Arab Middle East. David Waldner argued that Turkey lagged behind South Korea and Taiwan in industrial development because the former had higher levels of elite conflict, necessitating broader coalitions that received side payments from the state (what he terms "precocious Keynesianism") and thus diminishing the capacity of the economy to capture gains from higher productivity.[13] The state's intervention in the economy and the close relationships between the Kemalist state and the Istanbul-based industrial elite that dominated Turkey's economy throughout the period of high statism are well documented, as well as the ways that debt crises and liberalizing policy responses undermined these ties and transformed the state's role in the industrial economy.[14]

Cihan Tugal has argued that a potential Islamist challenge to the secular order at this moment of crisis has instead been absorbed through "a passive revolution" into capitalist production, facilitated by the Islamist ruling party the AKP.[15] Part of Turkey's economic dynamism is due to the export success of "Anatolian tiger" manufacturing clusters in cities such as Denezili, bolstered by coreligious ties to Sufi *tariqas* and representing disaggregated production though personal networks, persisting alongside the more traditional large-scale manufacturing firms supported by the retreating Kemalist establishment.[16] Thus in the greater Middle East, in vastly different contexts, understanding political economy after economic reform and now political transformation means understanding that the

---

[12] Posusney 1997; Shehata 2003.
[13] Waldner 1999. For an alternative account of social coalitions in Turkish development, see Naseemullah and Arnold 2015.
[14] Keydar 1987; Arcanli and Rodrik 1990.   [15] Tugal 2009.
[16] Demir et al. 2004.

interests, motivations, political affiliations, and even shop floor
dynamics are vitally important.

I have presented this brief overview of the nature and mechanisms of
production in postliberalization Latin America and the Middle East
not to argue at all that the same dynamics occur in these cases as in
South Asia; this book does not set out a universal framework. Rather,
it was meant to highlight three of this book's features that I believe
have broad applicability to the study of political economy. First,
economic liberalization, while a complex process that has varied significantly between and within regions, does reframe the capacities and
inclinations of the state in directing and promoting industrial development. The extant state-directed approaches to understanding industrial
development must at the very least contend with the significance of
these changes before framing national models of capitalism.

Second and relatedly, many of the new institutional dynamics of
industrial capitalism are best understood when we start our analysis at
the level of the firm. The application of labor and capital in processes
that turn raw materials into higher value intermediate or finished
goods actually occurs in mills, factories, workshops, and other industrial units in manufacturing. Yet the firm is embedded in institutional
structures that are activated when manufacturers regularly engage with
government regulators, local politicians, bankers, union bosses, suppliers, or buying agents for multinationals. These institutional structures are much easier to perceive from the firm level than from the
office of a bureaucrat in the national government. What is lost in
parsimony is made up for in accuracy, as we can analyze both the
patterns and the mechanisms of industrial investment after statism.

Third, it introduces industrialists as potential governance actors.
We tend to understand economic actors as simply driven by the
straightforward maximization of profits, and as a result we are
willing to frame them as chess pieces in a game played by states
over industrialization. I argue here that this perspective misses a lot.
Manufacturers must arrange and sustain a great number of relationships for cotton to be made into thread and fabric, or basic chemicals formulated into statins to treat high cholesterol levels. When
these core relationships are wholly determined by the state's sticks
and carrots, as in statist development, manufacturers are indeed
institution takers: they might choose the design of their products
or the locations to market them, but they have little autonomy over

the sources of capital or the nature of relations between workers and management. In the context of economies after liberalization, however, a diverse array of different actors acts to form and sustain these relationships in the service of production: bureaucrats involved in industrial promotion, certainly, but also agents of global markets, trade unions, political parties, social movements, civil society, management consultants, and so on. Manufacturers indeed represent just one group of actors, but the political economy of development has continued to view them as institution takers. I would argue that incorporating industrialists as governance actors in their own right will lead to a fuller picture of the institutional politics of the industrial economy, in South Asia and beyond.

The State after Statism in South Asia

This investigation into industrial investment after statism has involved long discussions of the state's changing roles in the industrial economy through the process of liberalization. But what might such an investigation mean for the state in the broader politics of South Asia? The transformation of the state from the powerful director of a coherent program of industrial development to a lead actor in a game of rent allocation has entailed a profound shift in the ways that Indians and Pakistanis view the state.

The reform and revitalization of state structures are often thought of as a natural next step after market reform; after we dismantle rotting structures, we aim to construct new and durable ones in their place. And yet, the revitalization of state institutions is a much more politically salient and contentious project than the reforms "by stealth" of the 1990s and 2000s. Anticorruption movements have exploded into prominence in cities and towns all over India and Pakistan, and channeled into new political parties representing the aspirant middle class. Could this decade herald a new progressive politics dedicated to reform of the state?

The firm-level accounts in this book have presented the different responses of members of the industrial bourgeoisie to the absence of effective state governance over the industrial economy. While these individuals are not particularly representative of society at large, I contend that the two categories of reactions outlined above reflect a broader division in social reactions to limited state capacity in South

Asia. These broader reactions – *centripetal* and *centrifugal* politics – constitute the often-implicit political conflict over the nature of the state and may prove decisive over its future.[17] In the following, I will describe how the centrifugal–centripetal division frames Indian democratic politics around the future of state power and the continual conflict between democratic and authoritarian politics in Pakistan.

The Future of the Indian State

Significant episodes in the contentious politics of India over the last decade have involved corruption, seen by many as a systemic disease of the body politic. Corruption, and its perceived impact in frustrating the ambition of middle-class Indians who "follow the rules" – fueled the 2011 mass campaign led by the neo-Gandhian activist Anna Hazare for a Jana Lokpal, a committee of civil society elites that could prosecute elected officials for malfeasance. It has also motivated the formation of the Aam Admi [common man] Party, led by a civil society activist, now Delhi Chief Minister Arvind Kejriwal, which has established an all-India platform for transparency and good governance. There is a widespread discontent, at least among middle-class Indians, over the state's incapacity; many trace this incapacity to the capture of state interests for particular purposes, and ultimately to the corruption of politicians and their clients.

In January 2013, an episode at the normally genteel Jaipur Literary Festival highlighted some of these emergent politics. Ashis Nandy, noted social psychologist and public intellectual, delivered remarks in the panel discussion "The Republic of Ideas" that indicated that the most *visible* corruption in contemporary India was conducted by politicians among the Scheduled Castes, Scheduled Tribes, and the OBCs, groups facing structural discrimination and, until recently, de facto excluded from democratic politics. Nandy argued that the forward castes and elites in India had been operating under a *safarish*, or "you scratch my back," system for decades, and the ability of those rising up from disadvantage to enjoy the goods of the state through political distribution was an equalizing force, even though such

---

[17] I use Lieven's (2011) terms here, but this distinction has family resemblances to Partha Chatterjee's famous formulation of the divisions between civil society and political society in Indian democracy. See Chatterjee 2001; 2004.

activities were seen as corrupt. Upon hearing of these remarks, a Rajasthan state legislator appeared at the festival demanding the arrest of Nandy under the Scheduled Caste and Scheduled Tribes Acts, which outlaws backward caste discrimination. Nandy, in a written statement, clarified his comments:

> I endorsed the statement of Tarun Tejpal, Editor of *Tehelka*, that corruption in India is an equalizing force. I do believe that a zero corruption society in India will be a despotic society. I also said that if people like me or [fellow panelist and Oxford don] Richard Sorabjee want to be corrupt, I shall possibly send his son to Harvard giving him a fellowship and he can send my daughter to Oxford. No one will think it to be corruption. Indeed, it will look like supporting talent. But when Dalits, tribals and the OBCs are corrupt, it looks very corrupt indeed. However, this second corruption equalizes. It gives them access to their entitlements. And so, as long as this equation persists, I have hope for the Republic.[18]

Ashis Nandy's comments and his subsequent arrest, eventually stayed by the Supreme Court, highlight the contradiction of democratic politics in a thoroughly unequal society and a state that does not, indeed cannot, govern according to the ideal of Weberian bureaucratic authority.

The dual forms of corruption characterized by Nandy run as a leitmotif through the history of political economy and economic development in India. The initial structural investments of the Indian state in supporting industrialists disproportionately favored those individuals and communities in privileged positions in society capable of capturing such largesse. "Native" industrialists largely had backgrounds with the wealth and connections to invest in large-scale enterprise, and those who took over the enterprises left behind by departing expatriate capital were professional accountants and engineers. The directors of firms in the position to receive industrial licenses and export quotas were able to speak in the same language – often quite literally – as bank executives and elite bureaucrats; these commonalities replicated at the level of firm relationships the elite consensus between the Nehruvian state and industrial capital that undergirded statist development.

Yet the breakdown of statist development in the 1970s occurred precisely because of the political importance of those in society – the movement of OBC cultivators led by Chaudhry Charan Singh, for

---

[18] NDTV News 2013.

example – whose rise had been stunted by the elitism and urban bias of state structures. Such demand groups understood their goal as gaining the power to control a state apparatus that could distribute resources toward their communities and interests, and away from the industrial elite. Increasing electoral competition and the rise of regional parties as indispensable coalition partners have made distribution of resources and rents to clients the main goal of access to state power. Policies such as the extension of "reserved places" at universities and in the public sector to OBCs in 1990 further added to the frustrations among middle-class, forward caste individuals, who argue that the goods of the state such as education are parceled out to particular constituencies rather than decided on merit; such frustrations and perceived reverse political exclusion are thought to be behind the rise of the Hindu Right in the 1990s.[19] Thus, challenges to state autonomy, ethnic and class antagonisms, and increasingly competitive democratic politics reinforce each other.

In conventional perspectives of industrial development, the absence of the state's governance of the economy is a suboptimal situation; policy makers as well as academics see state power as necessary for industrial upgrading and continuing competitiveness. Business interests in India and beyond have been calling for a set of "second-generation" reforms that would empower autonomous public institutions that could structure, enable, and support the now more market-ized economy. But such talk of these reforms assumes a consensus over what constitutes appropriate governance and the importance of autonomous institutions. It is a fundamental contention of this book that such a consensus does not exist. Rather, the division among industrialists on how firms should be governed reflects a broader division over whether the autonomous state should be reempowered.

From the formal rules perspective, the reinvigoration of powerful, autonomous state institutions with a technocratic ethos would be a welcome respite from the chaos of the modern economy. There is a large and growing constituency, especially within middle-class Indian society, for limiting the scope of India's democracy by empowering agencies of the state with constitutional protections and thus shielding from the rough-and-tumble of political competition.

---

[19] Jaffrelot 1999, 411–446.

One such explicitly constitutional agency, the Supreme Court, has become increasingly interventionist in many different spheres of governance. In the 2000s, the Court placed the Ministry of Environment and Forests under its oversight and has steadily been increasing its power and autonomy through mechanisms such as public interest litigation (PIL), calling public officials to appear before the Court, with the implicit threat of contempt charges. The superior judiciary regularly passes judgements and issues orders in areas as diverse as cycle-rickshaw regulation in Delhi and the appropriateness of the arrest of a social psychologist in Rajasthan, often with little justification beyond consonance with their own technocratic worldviews.[20] For many in Indian society who feel themselves disadvantaged by the perceived corruption in Indian politics, the state needs to be buttressed by a multiplicity of autonomous institutions able to use immense discretionary power to enforce the rules beyond democratic oversight. The proposed Jana Lokpal, for example, places real limits on democracy and represent a tendency toward *centripetal politics*, or a reversion to rule by the center that characterized early Congress party politics in combination with an autonomous civil service. For the sake of "good governance," many in India would place restrictions on the power of democratically elected politicians to distribute resources and favors. This constituency has the most to gain from support of strengthening and reforming autonomous state institutions in order to direct the economy in technocratic fashion.

The personal networks perspective, however, has a different affective relationship to the state. Those who entered business through trading, farming, or employment in local companies tend to have more faith in the durability and reliability of personal networks – including those that involve local political elites – than in the authoritarian and distant institutions of the central state. There is a wide cross section of (newly middle-class) Indian society naturally suspicious of the very state agencies that might have excluded them in favor of entrenched elites of the statist development era.

The 2007 Bollywood product *Guru*, directed by Mani Ratnam and starring Abhishek Bachchan and Aishwarya Rai, was made as a *film à clef* of the founder of India's largest industrial conglomerate, who is represented as a Horatio Alger figure who challenged the entrenched

[20] For more on this argument, see Mate 2010.

interests of the cotton textile mills through nylon manufacturing. In a speech in court when he is charged with corruption, the eponymous main character says:

I came to Bombay with two shirts, a wife and a brother-in-law. I thought, "I'll do business." But when I came here, I saw that all the doors were closed. If they opened, they only opened for the rich. They were the doors made by the government. They either opened with a bribe or a kick. I did both. Where I had to kick, I kicked. Where you wanted me to salute, I saluted. And today you ask why does this man kick so much, why does he salute so much.

In response to rules written to facilitate exclusion, aspirant groups in India – like the Gurukant Desai character in the film – acted to build relationships and extend their personal spheres outward to encapsulate not just families but also workers, business associates, bureaucratic agents, and even politicians. Economic and social success became dependent on these relationships and not on the power of the state to enforce the rules. For these formerly excluded groups, the state thus becomes less a source of governance and more a source of rents and resources. This vision of Indian society and the state represents *centrifugal politics*, in which regional parties, state and local politics, and the personal relationships among economic and political actors constitute Indian politics. For those committed to this perspective, any increase in the power of authoritarian, centralized, and democratically unaccountable state institutions represents a threat to the working arrangements and relationships that enable economic activity and social life.

There is a natural conflict between centripetal and centrifugal politics in India, and between different sections of aspirant middle class society, based on fundamentally different understandings of the place of the state in society. As with much of the politics in South Asia, this conflict is more implicit than expressed as a major cleavage around which electoral politics are mobilized. But when it comes to the implementation of policies and the expenditure of resources, political and popular pressures for and against reform and empowerment of state institutions often end in stalemate and discontent. The size and power of the state are, in other words, a deep if sublimated point of contention among different sections of Indian society.

The Future of the Pakistani Democracy

The conflict between centripetal and centrifugal politics *is* more formally expressed, as a conflict between democratic and authoritarian ruling models, in Pakistan's hybrid democracy. In early January 2013, Dr. Tahirul Qadri, the leader of the religious organization Minhaj-ul-Quran International, marched from Lahore to Islamabad with tens of thousands of supporters – he had originally claimed 4 million would join him in the capital – to call for a "revolution" against the perceived widespread corruption of the PPP-coalition government. During the middle of Qadri's three-day rally, the Supreme Court of Pakistan demanded the arrest of Prime Minister Raja Pervez Ashraf relating to corruption charges when he was energy minister, and many commentators saw the timing as evidence that Qadri was coordinating his protest with efforts by the Supreme Court against the PPP government, possibly with the implicit backing of the military.[21] In the autumn of 2014, Qadri and Imran Khan, the head of the Pakistan Tehreek-e-Insaaf, established a months-long protest in the capital demanding the resignation of the allegedly corrupt PML-N government, which had been elected months before in Pakistan's first peaceful transfer of power in its history. This protest was again thought to be supported by elements of the military elite displeased with Nawaz Sharif's policies toward India and the treatment of the former president and army chief Pervez Musharraf.[22] The Qadri and Imran Khan agitations place in stark contrast the differences between the technocratic, anticorruption governance rhetoric favored by some of the more authoritarian institutions and the "connected politics" of democratic rule by, in effect, a group of regional parties.

Such a difference lies at the very heart of Pakistan's authoritarian legacies. For Generals Iskander Mirza and Ayub Khan in 1958, the imposition of martial law was the result of the failure of civilian parliamentary politics to rise above parochial interests to provide national unity and political order. The military as the quintessentially centripetal institution in Pakistani politics feared that the centrifugal influences of provincial politicians in general, and the populous and restive Bengalis in particular, would tear the country apart.[23] The Ayub Khan era was characterized not just by industrial development

[21] Walsh 2013.   [22] Jaffrelot 2014.   [23] Nawaz 2008, 122–191.

but also by rule by technocrats and the suppression of party competition through a depoliticizing system of "Basic Democracy." The two other long-lasting military dictatorships in Pakistani history also made use of self-consciously technocratic rule, and often used local and municipal government as a means to constrain the influence of provincial politicians. General Zia ul Haq outlawed political parties and established a Majlis-e-Shoora of scholars, ulema, professionals, and business that served as a government of technocrats between 1980 and 1984, while General Pervez Musharraf appointed Shaukat Aziz as finance minister in 1999 and prime minister in 2004 largely for his credentials as a former executive vice president at Citibank.

In episodes of democratic rule, however, powerful regional and sectional interests become more prominent. In the 1970s after the independence of Bangladesh, Zulfiqar Ali Bhutto formed an uneasy coalition of Sindhi landed elites and urban popular classes. In the 1990s, Benazir Bhutto's PPP coalition competed for political power against an emergent bloc of rich Punjabi farmers and business elites led by Mian Nawaz Sharif's PML-N. After the reversion to democratic rule in 2008, President Asif Ali Zardari oversaw a national coalition government that included the PPP, the PML-N splinter and former Musarraf-backed party the PML-Q (now the PML), the Karachi-based *mohajir* MQM, and the Pakhtun nationalist ANP, parties with vastly different, even conflicting interests at provincial and municipal levels; activists affiliated with the ANP and the MQM are regularly involved in targeted killings against one another in Karachi. After the transformative 2013 elections, the government at the center was dominated by the PML-N with a traditional base in Punjab, but with each of the provinces governed by a different political party or coalition. Democratic politics are thus deeply centrifugal, privileging provincial and local interests that aggregate themselves into provincial and national governments that maintain their coherence through the distribution of rents to a wide array of clients.

The division between perspectives informed by formal rules and by personal networks thus reflects a broader division in Pakistani society between supporting centralizing, technocratic institutions of authoritarian governance or the deeply parochial interests of democratic politics. Not a few of my respondents had explicit ties to provincial politics (2007-lhr8; 2007-lhr30). Others, meanwhile, had military or central civil service backgrounds (2007-lhr14; 2007-lhr7). Yet since the state's fall from its original roles in the governance of the economy during the Ayub era, the industrial economy has not been effectively governed by the state even during periods of military rule.

During my field research in Pakistan in 2007, Musharraf was still in power, and technocratic policy-makers such as Shaukat Aziz privileged the owners of credit over borrowers and were generally unmoved by industrialists' concerns over the cost of credit, energy, and other inputs. Yet the different responses by industrialists to the resulting uncertainty reflect dueling pressures either to empower or to bypass authoritarian state structures, and thus are deeply inflected by politics. For those in Pakistani society enamored with technocratic solutions provided by centralizing and often-unaccountable aspects of state power – those supporting centripetal politics, in other words – are more likely to support continuing centralization and ultimately the continued emphasis of bureaucratic authoritarian inflections in Pakistani politics. For those who bypass state power and rely instead on the personal networks that often overlap with local and provincial politics, the state must become a resource for social and economic uplift not through disciplinary governance but through the provision of resources and rents to client groups. Thus, different conceptions of the nature and ends of economic development and the state have serious impact on whether Pakistan will become a consolidated democracy like India or remain a state with powerful authoritarian legacies.

Whither the South Asian State

For three decades after independence from colonial rule, the state was the central actor in Indian and Pakistani development. And yet, in the political economy of industrial development, at least, the state has been steadily slipping from its paramount position, unable and politically unwilling to govern the industrial economy after the process of liberalization. In this context, I have argued that industrialists create and maintain frameworks of institutional certainty for their own firms, and they do so either through personal networks or by formal rules. These two styles of production succeed in structuring industrial production after statism, even though they challenge our expectations of the coherence of national models of industrial capitalism, in South Asia and beyond. These institutional responses reflect two broader perspectives on the nature and ends of economic activity, and the place of the state, in South Asia. Can the state reform itself or be empowered with the resources and authority to govern the economy? This is not self-evident, but rather a matter of the ideational perspectives and political actions of individual economic actors, working in concert. This book has provided a lens through which some of those dynamics might be more clearly understood.

Finally, this book sounds a cautionary note regarding the capacity of either India or Pakistan to achieve the economic transformation that we saw first in South Korea and Taiwan and then in China. As I have argued, industrial production can occur without the governance of the state, through the building of institutions at the firm level. But these institutional successes are very local and thus disjointed; structural change in developing economies has always required coordination at a much greater scale. Absent the state as a governing actor in the industrial economy, it is not entirely apparent where the sources of such coordination are located, casting some doubt on the long-term viability of industrialization as a vehicle for the long-term economic transformation. But without industrial development, where can tens of millions of workers in India or Pakistan find employment with dignity? As we continue to think about development and transformational economic change in the twenty-first century, the previously assumed and recently ignored role of industry in that project needs to be brought into much sharper analytical and empirical focus.

Statistical Models

Chapters four and five of this book, on financing and labor management in India, presented firm-level patterns with regard to the potential forms of industrial governance. In this appendix, I present the results of regression analyses of various institutional factors – state, sector and various firm-level characteristics – on patterns of financing and labor management at the firm level. The purpose of these analyses is not to provide a comprehensive explanatory model for debt-capital ratios or the proportion of non-wage costs in total labor costs, but rather to compare the power of these various explanations against one another.

For these analyses, I use ordinary least squares regression with robust errors and quantile (median) regression with bootstrapped standard errors. Median regression is more robust to outlier cases and more agnostic to non-parametric features of the data. The fact that both analyses produce similar outcomes adds a certain amount of confidence to the results. In addition to the independent variables mentioned in the chapters, I use two other control variables in both analyses relating to firm ownership: "private" indicates private limited firms, with the reference category being public companies, and "group" refers to companies that are members of a corporate group, with the reference category being standalone firms. For the models relating to labor, I include a third control: 'Directors to Salaries Ratio,' the ratio of directors' compensation to workers' salaries.

The Acquisition of Finance

For the OLS model on finance, I regress several categories of independent variables on the log of debt-capital ratios plus one. Table A-1 reports the results of the analysis.

The OLS regression shows that the proxy for manufacturers' backgrounds, age cohort group, is significant as is firm size in almost all categories. Export orientation categories are more ambiguous.

Table A-1: *OLS Regression on Log Debt–Capital Ratios*

		Coefficient	Standard Error
Ownership	Private	.210***	.025
	Group	.010	.015
States	Delhi & Haryana	.015	.017
	Maharashtra	.016	.015
	Tamil Nadu	.077***	.021
	Gujarat	−.025	.018
	West Bengal	−.001	.019
Sectors	Textiles	.101***	.016
	Garments	.017	.029
	Automotive	.014	.021
	Pharmaceuticals	−.011	.022
Age Cohort	Before 1950	.179***	.025
	1951–1970	.095***	.021
	After 1991	−.044***	.011
Export Percent	Below 24	.016	.013
	25–49	.060**	.022
	50–74	.037	.026
	75–100	.051	.027
Size Categories	1	.508***	.031
	2	.371***	.024
	3	.245***	.022
	4	.139***	.022
	5	.065**	.023
	7	.012	.028
	8	−.134***	.026
	9	−.152***	.027
	10	−.286***	.024
Constant		.420***	.089
	R^2	.20	
	N	8332	

Measures for significance:

*** : $p<.0001$

** : $p<.001$

* : $p<.05$

In regional categories, only Tamil Nadu is significant and in sectoral categories, only textiles are significant.

Happily, the median regression model allows us to dispense with the log due to a feature of quantile regression is its robustness to outliers, making interpretation a little more straightforward. Table A2 records these results.

The quantile regression shows less support for regional and sectoral explanations, with the exception of textiles (the automotive sector is just beyond conventional levels of significance at .06); differences are not surprising given the differences between the median of an indicator and the mean of that indicator's log. Yet firm-level indicators are significant: firms established before 1950 are associated with one and a half as much debt as firms established in the 1970s and 1980s, and those established after liberalization are associated with 40 percent less debt in relation to capital, all else equal. The size categories are even more dramatic: the largest firms are associated with seven times as much debt as the reference category. This is perhaps not surprising given that large firms have greater capacity to borrow. Export quartiles are mostly significant, in expected directions.

Labor Management

For the OLS model on labor management, I regress several categories of independent variables on the proportion of non-wage in total labor costs. I fit two models, the first including the full sample and the second including only those firms where non-wage portion of total factor cost does not equal zero; the latter fully discounts the unknown number of cases in which the firm simply recorded the same number for both values. Table A-3 reports the results of the analysis.

The outcomes are largely similar for the two models in all categories except for firm size and exports; we would expect this, as the exclusion of firms with no recorded non-wage labor costs would disproportionately exclude smaller, domestic firms, with other categories expected to be uncorrelated. For labor management, several states are significant, but only Tamil Nadu in a positive direction: the presence of a negative sign indicates that firms in the state have on average lower non-wage labor costs and thus presumably less committed to formal mechanisms of retention and/or the state's regulatory regimes. Of the sectors, only automotives proved significant, with a positive sign.

Table A-2: *Median Regression on Debt-Capital Ratios*

		Coefficient	S.E.
Ownership	Private	.102	.087
	Group	−.102	.054
States	Delhi & Haryana	−.028	.030
	Maharashtra	.030	.059
	Tamil Nadu	.074	.056
	Gujarat	−.028	.040
	West Bengal	−.028	.085
Sectors	Textiles	1.057***	.148
	Garments	.333	.250
	Automotive	.502	.271
	Pharmaceuticals	>.0001	.081
Age Cohort	Before 1950	1.547***	.424
	1951–1970	.872**	.285
	After 1991	−.417***	.059
Export Percent	Below 24	.420***	.106
	25–49	1.025***	.291
	50–74	.486	.291
	75–100	.479*	.237
Size Categories	1	7.467***	.744
	2	3.972***	.296
	3	2.454***	.213
	4	1.280***	.143
	5	.570**	.173
	7	−.218	.148
	8	−.622***	.155
.150	9	−.652***	.150
	10	−.652***	.144
Constant		1.098***	.140
	Pseudo R^2		.02
	N		8331

Measures for significance:

*** : $p<.0001$

** : $p<.001$

* : $p<.05$

Table A-3: *OLS Regression on Non-Wage Proportion of Total Labor Cost*

		(1)		(2)	
		Coefficient	S.E.	Coeffecient	S.E.
Ownership	Private	−.003	.004	−.007	.004
	Group	.012***	.003	.009**	.003
States	Delhi & Haryana	−.016***	.004	−.015***	.004
	Maharashtra	−.010**	.003	−.006	.004
	Tamil Nadu	.027***	.005	.030***	.005
	Gujarat	−.014**	.005	−.008	.005
	West Bengal	.010	.006	.017**	.006
Sectors	Textiles	−.002	.004	−.006	.004
	Garments	.011	.008	.049	.009
	Automotive	.017***	.004	.062**	.004
	Pharmaceuticals	−.001	.005	−.008	.005
Age Cohort	Before 1950	.069***	.007	.062**	.003
	1951–1970	.056***	.006	.049***	.006
	After 1991	−.013***	.003	−.009***	.007
Export Percent	Below 24	.007*	.003	−.009**	.003
	25–49	.009*	.005	−.007	.004
	50–74	.003	.005	−.014**	.004
	75–100	.003	.005	−.011*	.005
Size Categories	1	.010	.006	−.005	.006
	2	.010*	.005	−.004	.005
	3	.009	.005	−.005	.005
	4	.008	.005	−.005	.005
	5	.007	.006	−.002	.006
	7	−.0002	.007	.017*	.008
	8	−.025**	.007	.022*	.009
	9	−.053***	.009	.025	.015
	10	−.065***	.015	.056	.030
	Directors to Salaries ratio	−.079***	.007	−.93***	.011
Constant		.129***	.005	.162***	.005
	R^2	.134		R^2	.11
	N	6538		N	5493

Measures for significance:

*** : $p<.0001$

** : $p<.001$

* : $p<.05$

Table A-4: *Median Regression on Non-Wage Proportion of Total Labor Cost*

		(1)		(2)	
		Coefficient	S.E.	Coeffecient	S.E.
Ownership	Private	−.0001	.002	−.003	.004
	Group	.022***	.002	.018***	.002
States	Delhi & Haryana	−.014***	.003	−.015***	.004
	Maharashtra	−.017**	.003	−.014***	.003
	Tamil Nadu	.023***	.004	.026***	.004
	Gujarat	−.017**	.004	−.013**	.004
	West Bengal	.010	.006	.001	.005
Sectors	Textiles	−.007**	.003	−.010**	.003
	Garments	.005	.005	.002	.007
	Automotive	.018***	.004	.004***	.004
	Pharmaceuticals	−.006	.003	.004	.004
Age Cohort	Before 1950	.047***	.007	.440**	.006
	1951–1970	.038***	.005	.326***	.004
	After 1991	−.013***	.002	−.013***	.002
Export Percent	Below 24	.013***	.003	.0003	.002
	25–49	.017**	.004	.004	.004
	50–74	.013	.003	−.002	.005
	75–100	.014	.007	.004	.005
Size Categories	1	.007	.006	−.003	.005
	2	.014**	.004	.004	.004
	3	.011	.005	.003	.005
	4	.013**	.004	.004	.004
	5	.007	.005	−.0009	.005
	7	−.012	.008	.012	.005
	8	−.040**	.007	.014*	.007
	9	−.083***	.005	.016*	.011
	10	−.094***	.008	.018	.033
Directors to Salaries ratio		−.067***	.007	−.073***	.008
Constant		.115***	.004	.139	.003
		Psuedo R^2	.118	Psuedo R^2	.069
		N	6538	N	5493

Measures for significance:
*** : p<.0001
** : p<.01
* : p<.05

Of the firm-level characteristics, only firm age cohort is systematically significant. Interestingly, export percentages are only significant at lower levels of export and firm size at the smaller categories and size is only significant for smaller firms. The control for the ratio of directors' remuneration to salaries is significant but has modest effects, with the shift of .01 in the ratio associated with a less than one percent shift in non-wage proportions of labor costs, all else equal.

Results for the median regression are presented in table A4.

The median regression broadly affirms the results of the OLS regression for both models. Several regional indicators are significant, but all but Tamil Nadu exhibit negative signs. The automotive sector is significant. Age cohort is statistically and substantively significant: firms established before 1950 and between 1950 and 1970 are associated with five and four percent more in non-wage costs than firms established between 1970 and 1990, with much higher effects in the smaller sample. Size becomes statistically and substantively significant at lower levels: the last two size categories are associated with a decrease of nine and ten percent in non-wage costs in the first model.

List of Interviews

The following is a list of interviews, grouped mostly by industry, with non-confidential information about the respondents. For each firm-based interview, I include information on the location of the interview (most often the head office of the firm), the firm's product categories and its rough size, measured in annual sales turnover, converted to US dollars.[1] For interviews, with other industry officials or experts, I report their occupation or the organization they represent.

Respondents not affiliated to an industry

2007-lhr3	Rep., Lahore Chamber of Commerce and Industry, Feb. 8.
2007-fsb4	Rep., Faisalabad Chamber of Commerce and Industry, Feb. 23.
2007-skt1	Rep., Sialkot Chamber of Commerce and Industry, March 8.
2007-lhr28	Independent banker and investment advisor, Lahore, March 9.
2007-lhr29	Rep., Al-Falah (Islamic) Bank, Lahore, March 9.
2007-lhr34	Rep., Pakistan Workers Federation. March 11.
2007-khi1	Rep., Karachi Chamber of Commerce and Industry, April 2.
2007-khi2	Independent academic, Karachi, April 2.
2007-khi17	Rep., Meezan (Islamic) Bank, April 20.
2007-khi21	Stock brokerage, Karachi, April 25.
2007-chn11	Journalist, *the Hindu*, Chennai, Dec. 3.
2007- chn 12	Journalist, *Frontline*, Chennai, Dec. 3.
2007- chn 13	Journalist, *Hindu Business Line*, Chennai, Dec. 3.
2007- chn 14	Journalist, *Hindu Business Line*, Chennai, Dec. 3.
2008-coi1	Rep., Southern Indian Mills Association, Coimbatore, March 24.
2008-coi6	Independent trade unionist, Coimbatore, March 27.
2008-adb2	Rep., Ahmedabad Textile Mills Association, April 8.
2008-sur2	Rep., South Gujarat Chamber of Commerce and Industry, Surat, April 15.

---

[1] For firms not willing to divulge their turnover figures, I have categorized them as small, medium or large based on other information, such as number of employees.

Textiles

2007-lhr1	Yarn manufacturer, Lahore, Feb. 2 (medium).
2007-lhr2	Rep., All-Pakistan Textile Manufacturers' Association, Feb 3.
2007-lhr4	Yarn manufacturer, Lahore, Feb. 9 (large).
2007-lhr6	Yarn, fabric and apparel manufacturer, Lahore, Feb. 10 ($350 million).
2007-lhr7	Knitwear manufacturer, Lahore, Feb. 12 ($22 million).
2007-lhr8	Yarn manufacturer, Lahore, Feb. 13 (medium).
2007-lhr9	Knitwear manufacturer, Lahore, Feb. 13 (medium).
2007-lhr16	Apparel manufacturer, Lahore, Feb. 24 (medium).
2007-fsb1	Yarn, fabric manufacturer and processor, Faisalabad, Feb., 22 (large).
2007-fsb2	Fabric manufacturer and processor, Faisalabad, Feb. 22 (medium).
2007-fsb3	Fabric manufacturer, Faisalabad, Feb. 22 (small).
2007-fsb5	Fabric and apparel manufacturer, Faisalabad, Feb. 23 ($65 million).
2007-lhr21	Yarn manufacturer, Lahore, March 2 ($35 million).
2007-lhr22	Synthetic yarn and knitwear manufacturer, March 2 (medium).
2007-lhr25	Yarn manufacturer, Lahore, March 6 (medium).
2007-lhr26	Yarn manufacturer, Lahore, March 6 (large).
2007-lhr30	Yarn manufacturer, Lahore, March 10 (medium).
2007-lhr31	Yarn manufacturer, Lahore, March 10 (medium).
2007-khi6	Yarn manufacturer, Karachi, April 10 (large).
2007-khi7	Apparel manufacturer, Karachi, April 10 (medium).
2007-khi8	Denim fabric manufacturer, Karachi, April 11 (large).
2007-khi10	Fabric manufacturer and processor, Karachi, April 13 (medium).
2007-khi11	Embroidered fabric manufacturer, Karachi, April 16 (small).
2007-khi14	Yarn manufacturer, Karachi, April 18 (medium).
2007-khi18	Yarn manufacturer, Karachi, April 23 (medium).
2007-khi19	Denim garment manufacturer, April 23 (medium).
2007-del2	Yarn manufacturer, Delhi, Sept 29 ($1 billion).
2007-del3	Rep., North Indian Textile Manufacturers' Association, Sept. 29.
2007-del4	Knitwear manufacturer, Delhi, Sept. 28 ($148.5 million).
2007-del6	Garment manufacturer and exporter, Delhi, Oct. 3 (medium).
2007-del8	Fashion designer/garment manufacturer, Delhi, Oct. 5 ($500,000).
2007-del9	Rep., Confederation of Indian Textile Industry, Delhi, Oct. 6.
2007-del12	Composite textile manufacturer, Delhi, Oct. 10 ($250 million).

(cont.)

2007-del15	Yarn manufacturer, Delhi, Oct. 15 ($6.25 million).
2007-del20	Composite textile manufacturer, Delhi, Oct. 19 ($500 million).
2007-del22	Garment manufacturer, Delhi, Oct. 20 ($375,000).
2007-del23	Rep., Okhla Garment and Textile Cluster, Delhi, Oct. 22.
2007-del24	Yarn, knitwear manufacturer and processor, Delhi NCR, Oct. 23 (large).
2007-del25	Yarn manufacturer, Delhi, Oct. 24 (6.75 million).
2007-del27	Garment manufacturer and exporter, Delhi, Oct. 26 ($6 million +).
2007-del28	Yarn manufacturer, Delhi, Oct. 30 ($38 million).
2007-del29	Knitwear manufacturer and exporter, Delhi, Oct. 30 (medium).
2007-del31	Garment manufacturer and exporter, Delhi NCR, Oct. 31 (large).
2007-del33	Garment manufacturer and exporter, Delhi NCR, Nov. 3 ($5 million).
2007-del36	Yarn and denim fabric manufacturer, Delhi, Nov. 8 ($6 million).
2007-del38	Garment manufacturer and exporter, Delhi NCR, Nov. 13 ($5 million).
2007-del39	Garment manufacturer, Delhi, Delhi, Nov. 13 ($3 million).
2007-del41	Rep., Apparel Export Promotion Council, Delhi NCR, Nov. 16.
2007-del42	Another Rep., Apparel Export Promotion Council, Delhi NCR, Nov. 16.
2007-del46	Fabric manufacturer, Delhi, Dec. 12 (medium).
2008-lud1	Yarn manufacturer, Ludhiana, Jan. 10 ($50 million).
2008-lud2	Yarn manufacturer, Ludhiana, Jan. 10 ($75 million).
2008-lud3	Yarn and fabric manufacturer, Ludhiana, Jan 10 (large).
2008-cdg3	Yarn and knitted fabric manufacturer, Chandigarh, Jan. 11 (large).
2008-cdg4	Yarn manufacturer, Chandigarh, Jan. 11 ($20 million).
2008-mmb3	Garment manufacturer and exporter, Mumbai, Feb 1 (medium).
2008-mmb5	Rep., Clothing Manufacturers Association of India, Mumbai, Feb. 4.
2008-mmb8	Garment manufacturer and exporter, Mumbai, Feb 8 ($3 million).
2008-mmb9	Fabric and linens manufacturer, Mumbai, Feb 11 (medium).
2008-mmb10	Yarn manufacturer and exporter, Mumbai, Feb 12 (medium).

(cont.)

2008-mmb12	Rep., Mumbai Millowners Association, Feb. 14.
2008-mmb13	Composite textile manufacturer, Mumbai, Feb 21 ($100 million).
2008-mmb14	Furnishings manufacturer, Mumbai, Feb 22 ($11 million).
2008-mmb15	Rep., Powerloom Development and Export Promotion Council, Mumbai, Feb. 23.
2008-mmb16	Consultant and observer, synthetic textiles industry, Mumbai, Feb. 25.
2008-mmb17	Rep., Synthetic and Rayon Textiles Export Promotion Council, Mumbai, Feb. 26.
2008-mmb18	Fabric manufacturer, Mumbai, Feb 26 ($1.5 million).
2008-mmb19	Viscose / Cellulose fiber manufacturer, Mumbai, Feb. 27 (v. large).
2008-mmb20	Synthetic yarn producer, Mumbai, Feb. 28 ($12 million).
2008-mmb21	Composite textile manufacturer, Mumbai, Feb 29 (large).
2008-mmb22	Fabric manufacturer, Mumbai, March 1 (small).
2008-mmb26	Polyester fiber manufacturer, Mumbai, March 4 ($3 billion).
2008-mmb27	Fabric manufacturer, Bhiwandi, Distt. Thane, March 5 ($500,000).
2008-mmb28	Fabric manufacturer, Bhiwandi, Distt. Thane, March 5 ($750,000).
2008-mmb29	Rep., Cotton Textiles Export Promotion Council (TEXPROCIL), Mumbai, March 6.
2008-mmb31	Fabric and garment manufacturer, Mumbai ($12.5 million).
2008-mmb32	Yarn manufacturer, Mumbai, March 11 ($32.5 million).
2008-mmb33	Composite textile manufacturer, Mumbai, March 12 (large but sick).
2008-mmb34	Textiles trader and printer, Mumbai, March 20 ($500,000).
2008-coi1	Rep., Southern Indian Mills Association, Coimbatore, March 24.
2008-coi2	Yarn manufacturer, Coimbatore, March 24 ($62.5 million).
2008-coi3	Yarn and hosiery manufacturer, Coimbatore, March 25 ($15 million).
2008-coi4	Composite textile manufacturer, Coimbatore, March 25 ($25 million).
2008-trp1	Rep., Tiruppur Exporters Association, March 26.
2008-trp2	Garment manufacturer and exporter, Tiruppur, March 26 ($2.5 million).
2008-trp3	Garment manufacturer and exporter, Tiruppur, March 26 (small).

(*cont.*)

2008-trp4	Garment manufacturer and exporter, Tiruppur, March 26 (large).
2008-coi5	Yarn and denim fabric manufacturer, Coimbatore, March 27 (large).
2008-trp5	Fabric and linens manufacturer, Tiruppur, March 27 ($10 million).
2008-coi7	Yarn manufacturers, Coimbatore, March 28 (large).
2008-coi8	Yarn manufacturers, Coimbatore, March 28 ($14 million).
2008-mmb35	Fabric and apparel manufacturers, Mumbai, April 1 ($125 million).
2008-mmb36	Denim fabric manufacturer, Mumbai, April 1 (medium).
2008-mmb38	Composite textile manufacturer, Mumbai, April 3 ($150 million).
2008-adb1	Yarn and knitted fabric manufacturer, Ahmedabad, April 7 (medium).
2008-adb2	Rep., Ahmedabad Textile Mills Association, April 8.
2008-adb3	Garment manufacturer and exporter, Ahmedabad, April 8 ($6.25 million).
2008-adb7	Composite textile manufacturer, Ahmedabad ($62.5 million).
2008-adb8	Textile printing designer, Ahmedabad, April 10 ($5 million).
2008-sur1	Synthetic yarn manufacturer, Surat, April 14 ($29.8 million).
2008-sur2	Synthetic yarn manufacturer, Surat, April 14 ($2.5 million).
2008-sur4	Yarn manufacturer, Surat, April 16 (medium).
2008-sur5	Yarn and fabric manufacturers and processors, Surat, April 17 ($62.5 million).
2008-sur7	Synthetic composite textile manufacturer, Surat, April 18 (large).
2008-mmb41	Embroidery designer and fabric processor, Mumbai, April 23 ($5.5 million).
2008-mmb57	Composite woolen manufacturer, Mumbai, May 8 (large).
2008-del50	Handloom and apparel manufacturer, Delhi, May 17 ($50 million+).

Automotive[2]

2007-lhr12	Rubber molding components manufacturer, Lahore, Feb. 16 (medium).
2007-lhr14	Electrical components manufacturer, Lahore, Feb 20 (medium).
2007-lhr23	Composite system component manufacturer, March 3 (large).
2007-lhr24	Sheet metal components manufacturer, Lahore, March 3 (small).
2007-grw1	Sheet metal components manufacturer, Gujranwalla, March 5 ($2.5 million).
2007-grw2	Rubber molding and seet metal components, Gujranwalla, March 5 (small)
2007-grw3	Sheet metal components manufacturer, Lahore, March 5 (micro).
2007-lhr27	Machining-based manufacturers, Lahore, March 7 (13.3 million).
2007-skt2	Surgical instruments manufacturer, Sialkot, March 8 (large).
2007-skt3	Surgical instruments manufacturer, Sialkot, March 8 (medium).
2007-lhr33	OEM tractor manufacturer, Lahore, March 14 ($183 million).
2007-khi5	OEM car and components manufacturer, Karachi, April 9 (large) .
2007-khi9	Casting components manufacturer, Karachi, April 12 (medium).
2007-khi12	Sheet metal components manufacturer, Karachi, April 17 (small).
2007-khi23	Complex system components manufacturer, Karachi, April 26 (large).
2007-khi24	OEM/ MNC joint venture motorcycle manufacturer, Karachi, April 27 (large).
2007-del5	Sheet metal componemt capital machinery manufacturer, Delhi, Oct. 1 (medium).
2007-del16	Electrical components manufacturer, Delhi NCR, Oct. 17 (medium).
2007-del17 & 18	Rubber molding components manufacturer, Delhi NCR, Oct. 17 ($750,000).

---

[2] "exp" refers to interviews conducted at the Indian Auto Expo 2008. For these interviews, I report where the firm is based, as all the interviews were conducted at the Pragati Maidan Exhibition Grounds, in New Delhi.

(cont.)

2007-del21	Pistons and auto systems manufacturer, Delhi, Oct. 19 (medium).
2007-del26	Suspension systems manufacturer, Delhi NCR, Oct. 25 (medium).
2007-del30	Complex systems manufacturer, Delhi, Oct. 31 (large).
2007-del34	Fuel solutions and auto components manufacturer, Delhi, Nov. 5 ($123 million).
2007-del35	Rep., Automotive Component Manufacturers Association of India, Delhi, Nov. 7.
2007-del37	Clutch systems manufacturer, Delhi, Nov. 12 (medium).
2007-del40	Complex system component manufacturer, Delhi NCR, Nov. 15 (large).
2007-del43	Injection mollding components manufacturer, Delhi, Nov. 16 (medium).
2007-chn3	Foundry components manufacturer, Chennai, Nov. 21 (medium).
2007-chn4	Forgining components manufacturer, Chennai, Nov. 22 (large).
2007-chn5	Casting components manufacturer, Chennai, Nov. 23 ($5 million).
2007-chn8	Brakes and die-casting components, Chennai, Nov. 28 (large - part of OEM group).
2007-chn9	Sheet metal components manufacturer, Chennai, Nov. 29 (medium).
2007-chn10	Complex systems conglomerate, Chennai, Nov. 30 ($2.3 billion).
2007-chn15	Complex systems conglomerate, Chennai, Dec. 5 (large).
2007-chn16	Ring system component manufacturer, Chennai, Dec. 5 ($12 million).
2007-del44	Rep., Society for Indian Automotive Manufacturers, Delhi, Nov. 10.
2007-del47	Gear manufacturer, Delhi, Dec. 13 ($10 million).
2008-exp1	Trailer manufacturer from Delhi, Jan. 14 ($12.5 million).
2008-exp2	Harvester and trailer manufacturer from Ludhiana, Jan. 14 (large).
2008-exp3	Auto rickshaw assembler from Delhi, Jan. 14 (medium).
2008-exp4	Plastic gear and components manufacturer from Jallandar, Jan. 14 (small).
2008-exp5	Tractor components manufacturer from Ludhiana, Jan. 14 (medium).

(cont.)

2008-exp6	Deisel engine valves manufacturer from Rajkot, Jan. 14 (medium).
2008-exp7	Plastic gears manufacturer from Delhi, Jan. 14 (medium).
2008-exp8	Water pumps manufacturer from Jallandar, Jan. 14 ($1.5 million).
2008-exp9	Wiring manufacturer and assember from Delhi, Jan. 14 (small).
2008-exp10	Lighting systems manufacturer from Delhi, Jan. 14 (large).
2008-exp11	Instrument cluster manufacturer from Coimbatore, Jan. 14 ($145.75 million).
2008-exp12	Axle and other component manufacturer from Delhi, Jan. 14 (small).
2008-exp13	Starter motor manufacturer from Delhi, Jan. 15 (medium).
2008-exp14	Rep. from multinational subsidiary, Jan. 15.
2008-exp15	Complex systems manufacturer from Ludhiana, Jan. 15 ($50 million).
2008-exp16	Deisel engine and complex systems manufacturer from Pune, Jan. 15 ($300 million).
2008-exp17	Mirrors and car seats manufacturer from Delhi, Jan. 15 (large).
2008-exp18	Engine bearings manufacturer from Agra, Jan. 15 ($12.5 million).
2008-exp19	Shock absorber and springs manufacturer from Delhi, Jan. 15 (small).
2008-exp20	Vacuum manufacturer from Coimbatore, Jan. 15 ($50 million).
2008-exp21	Spring and sheet metal components manufacturer from Delhi, Jan. 15 ($50 million).
2008-exp22	Sheet mental components manufacturer from Delhi, Jan. 15 (large).
2008-coi7	Components manufacturer, Coimbatore, March 28 (medium).
2008-adb4	Lubricants manufacturer, Ahmedabad, April 8 ($750,000).
2008-sur6	Textile engineering and machine manufacturer, Surat, April 17 (medium) .
2008-mmb40	Gear manufacturer and trader, Mumbai, April 23 ($1 million).
2008-mmb42	Components manufacturer, Mumbai, April 24 ($1.75 million).
2008-mmb43	OEM Car and truck manufacturer, Mumbai, April 25 ($8.2 billion).
2008-pun1	Foundry components manufacturer, Pune, April 29 (medium).
2008-pun2	Carburettor manufacturer, Pune, April 29 ($13.75 million).
2008-pun3	Sheet metal press components manufacturer, Pune, April 29 ($52.5 million).

(cont.)

2008-pun4	Sheet metal components manufacturer, Pune, April 30 ($100 million - out of business).
2008-pun5	OEM Motocycle and scooter manufacturer, Pune, April 30 ($2.1 billion).
2008-pun6	Small assemblies manufacturer, Pune, April 30 ($14 million).
2008-pun7	Components manufacturer, Pune, April 30 ($25 million).
2008-mmb46	OEM tractor and SUV manufacturer, Mumbai, May 6 ($2 billion).

Pharmaceuticals

2007-lhr5	Medical solutions (drip) manufacturer, Lahore, Feb. 9 (medium).
2007-lhr10	Licensed drugs manufacturer, Lahore, Feb. 14 ($25 million).
2007-lhr13	Licensed drugs munufacturer, Lahore, Feb. 19 ($16.7 million).
2007-lhr15	Off-patent drugs manufacturer, Lahore, Feb 20 (medium).
2007-lhr17 & 18	Licensed drugs manufacturer, Lahore, Feb. 28 (large).
2007-lhr19	Off-patent drugs manufacturer, Lahore, Feb 28 ($1.6 million +).
2007-lhr20	Off-patent drugs manufacturer, Lahore, Feb 20 (medium).
2007-lhr32	Off-patent drugs manufacturer, Lahore, Lahore, March 3 (medium).
2007-khi3	Reps., Multinational subsidiary, Karachi, April 6.
2007-khi4	Licensed and off-patent drugs manufacturer, April 6 ($40 million).
2007-khi13	Off-patent drugs manufacturer, Karachi, April 18 (medium).
2007-khi15	Off-patent drugs manufacturer, Karachi, April 18 (small).
2007-khi16	Off-patent drugs manufacturer, Karachi, April 19 ($16.7 million).
2007-khi20	Pharmaceutical engineer and manufacturer, Karachi, April 24 ($300,000).
2007-khi25	Off-patent drugs manufacturer, Karachi, April 24 (small).
2007-khi22	Licensed drugs manufacturer and exporter, Karachi, April 26 ($67 million).
2007-del1	Rep., Indian Drug Manufacturers' Association, Delhi, Sept. 25.
2007-del7	Off-patent drugs manufacturer, Delhi, Oct. 4 (small).
2007-del10	Off-patent drugs manufacturer, Delhi, Oct. 8 ($3 million).
2007-del11	Off-patent drugs manufacturer, Delhi, Oct. 9 ($250,000).
2007-del13	Off-patent and third-party drugs manufacturer, Delhi, Oct. 12 ($2.5 million).
2007-del14	Skin-care products manufacturer, Delhi, Oct. 12 ($6 million).
2007-del19	Off-patent drugs manufacturer, Delhi, Oct. 24 ($25 million).
2007-del32	Off-patent drugs manufacturer and trader, Delhi, Nov. 1 (medium).
2007-chn1	Off-patent drugs manufacturer, Chennai, Nov. 19 ($11.75 million).
2007-chn2	Off-patent drugs manufacturer, Chennai, Nov. 20 ($44.5 million).
2007-chn6	Off-patent drugs manufacturer, Chennai, Nov. 26 ($5.5 million).

(cont.)

2007-chn7	Off-patent drugs contract manufacturer, Chennai, Nov. 27 ($4.5 million).
2007-chn11	Off-patent drugs and medical equipment manufacturer, Chennai, Nov. 30 ($50 million).
2007-del45	Research molecules, API and drugs manufacturer, Delhi, Dec. 1 ($1.35 billion).
2007-del48	Off-patent drugs manufacturer and trader, Delhi, Dec. 14 ($250,000).
2007-del49	Vaccine and drug manufacturer, Delhi, Dec. 15 (large).
2008-cdg1	API and drugs manufacturer, Chandigarh, Jan. 9 ($200 million).
2008-cdg2	Off-patent drugs manufacturer, Chandigarh, Jan. 14 (small).
2008-mmb1	API manufacturer, Mumbai, Jan. 30 ($80 million).
2008-mmb2	Ayurvedic drugs manufacturer, Mumbai, Jan. 31 (medium).
2008-mmb4	Research molecules, API and drugs manufacturer, Mumbai, Feb. 4 ($1 billion).
2008-mmb6	Research molecules, API and drugs manufacturer, Mumbai, Feb. 6 ($1 billion).
2008-mmb7	Active pharmaceutical ingredients manufacturer, Mumbai, Feb. 7 (medium).
2008-mmb11	Off-patent drugs manufacturer and trader, Mumbai, Feb. 13 ($6.3 million).
2008-mmb24	Off-patent drugs contract manufacturer, Mumbai, March 3 ($3 million).
2008-mmb25	Vaccine and bio-tech manufacturer and researcher, Mumbai, March 4 (medium).
2008-mmb30	Off-patent and bio-tech manufacturer, Mumbai, March 7 ($175 million).
2008-mmb37	Off-patent drugs manufacturer, Mumbai, April 1 ($2.5 million).
2008-adb5	Off-patent drugs manufacturer, Ahmedabad, April 9 ($3 million).
2008-adb6	Off-patent drugs manufacturer, Ahmedabad, April 9 ($2.5 million).
2008-adb9	API and off-patent drugs manufacturer, Ahmedabad, April 10 ($175 million).
2008-adb10	Research molecules, API and drugs manufacturer, Ahmedabad, Feb. 11 ($175 million).
2008-mmb39	API, drug and medical equipment manufacturer, Mumbai, April 22 ($650 million).
2008-mmb44	Former mg. director, state-owned API enterprise, Mumbai, May 3 ($12.5 million).

(cont.)

2008-mmb45	Licensed drugs and API manufacturer, Mumbai, May 5 ($21 million).
2008-del51	Off-patent drugs manufacturer and exporter, Delhi, May 20 ($9 million +).

Pre-dissertation interviews

2006-mmb1	Principal advisor to the Confed. of Indian Industry, Mumbai, July 13.
2006-mmb2	Rep., Thane Small Scale Industries Association, Thane, July 14.
2006-mmb3	Rep., Society for Innovation and Entrepreneurship, IIT Mumbai, July 17.
2006-mmb4	Entrepreneural Cell (student organization), IIT Mumbai, July 17.
2006-mmb5	Independent journalist, Mumbai, July 18.
2006-mmb6	Rep., Powerloom Development and Export Council, Mumbai, July 18.
2006-mmb7	Rep., Maharasthra Economic Development Council, Mumbai, July 19.
2006-mmb8	Powerloom Manufacturer, Mumbai, July 19.
2006-mmb9	Academic, Indhira Gandhi Institute of Development Studies, July 19.
2006-mmb10	Journalist, July 21.
2006-mmb11	Academic, Tata Institute of Social Sciences, July 21.
2006-mmb12	Rep., Center for Industrial Trade Unions, Mumbai, July 22.
2006-mmb13	Academic, Mumbai University, July 23.
2006-mmb14	Rep., Mumbai Millowners' Association, July 5.
2006-mmb15	Academic, Center for Policy Research, July 27.

References

Abdelal, Rawi, Yoshiko M. Herrera, Alastair Iain Johnston, and Rose McDermott. 2006. "Identity as a Variable." *Perspectives on Politics* 4 No. 4: 695–711.

Acemoglu, Daron and James Robinson. 2012. *Why Nations Fail*. New York: Crown.

Adelman, Irma. 1969. *Practical Approaches to Economic Planning: Korea's Second Five Year Plan*. Baltimore, MD: Johns Hopkins University Press.

Adler, Emmanuel. 1997. "Seizing the Middle Ground: Constructivism in World Politics." *European Journal of International Relations* 3 No. 3: 319–363.

Agarwala, Rina. 2013. *Informal Labor, Formal Politics, and Dignified Discontent in India*. New York: Cambridge University Press.

Aggarwal, Vinod. 2013. "Bilaternal Trade Agreements in the Asia-Pacific." In *Bilaternal Trade Agreements in the Asia-Pacific* (Aggarwal and Urata, eds.). Abingdon: Routledge.

    1987. *International Debt Threat*. Berkeley, CA: Institute of International Studies.

    1985. *Liberal Protectionism: The International Politics of the Organized Textile Trade*. Berkeley: University of California Press.

Ahmad, Mushtaq. 2001. *Nawaz Sharif: The Politics of Business*. Karachi: Royal Book Company.

Ahmed, Nezar Syed. 1991. *The Origins of Muslim Consciousness in India*. Westport, CT: Praeger Greenwood.

Alavi, Hamza. 1983. "Class and the State." In *Pakistan: The Roots of Dictatorship* (Gardezi and Rashid, eds.). London: Zed Books.

    1972. "The State in Post-Colonial Societies." *New Left Review* 74 No. 1: 59–81.

Albert, Michel. 1991. *Capitalism against Capitalism*. London: Whurr.

Ali, Kamran Asdar. 2005. "The Strength of the Streets Meets the Strength of the State." *International Journal of Middle East Studies* 37 No. 1 (Feb.): 83–107.

Allen, Franklin, Rajesh Chakrabarti, Sankar De, Jun Qian, and Meijun Qian. 2006. "Financing Firms in India." Policy Research Working Paper 3975, The World Bank, August.

Amable, Bruno. 2003. *The Diversity of Modern Capitalism*. New York: Oxford University Press.

Amjad, Ali. 2001. *Labor Legislation and Trade Unions in India and Pakistan*. Karachi: Oxford University Press.

Amjad, Rashid. 1983. "Industrial Concentration and Economic Power." In *Pakistan: The Roots of Dictatorship* (Gardezi and Rashid, eds.). London: Zed Books.

  1982. *Private Industrial Investment in Pakistan*. Cambridge: Cambridge University Press.

  1976. "Industrial Concentration and Economic Power in Pakistan." *Pakistan Economic and Social Review* 14 No. 1: 211–261.

  1976. "A Study of Investment Behavior in Pakistan, 1962–1970." *Pakistan Development Review* 15 No. 2: 134–153.

Amsden, Alice. 1989. *Asia's Next Giant*. New York: Oxford University Press.

Anbarasan, Ethirajan. 2012. "Chinese Factories Turn to Bangladesh as Labour Costs Rise." *BBC News*, August 29.

Ansell, Ben and David Samuels. 2010. *Inequality and Democratization*. Cambridge: Cambridge University Press.

Arcanli, Tosun and Dani Rodrik. 1990. "An Overview of Turkey's Experience with Economic Liberalization and Structural Adjustment." *World Development* 18 No. 10 (October): 1343–1350.

Arnold, Caroline. 2010. "Where the Low Road and the High Road Meet: Flexible Employment in Global Value Chains." *Journal of Contemporary Asia* 40 No. 4: 612–637.

  2006. "Claims on the Common." Doctoral Dissertation, University of California, Berkeley.

Arnold, Fred and Nasra Shah. 1984. "Asian Labor Migration to the Middle East." *International Migration Review* 18 (Summer): 294–318.

Ashar, Sandeep. 2014. "Maharashtra CM Devendra Fadnavis Told to Rethink Farm Power Dole, Free Drugs." *Indian Express*, November 2.

Athreye, Suma and Sandeep Kapur. 2006. "Industrial Concentration in a Liberalizing Economy: A Study of Manufacturing." *Journal of Development Studies* 42 No. 6: 981–999.

Bagchi, A. K. 2000. *Private Investment in India, 1900–1939*. London: Taylor & Francis.

  1985. "Transition from Indian to British Indian Systems of Money and Banking, 1800–1850." *Modern Asian Studies* 19 (April): 501–519.

Barber, Benjamin. 1995. *Jihad vs. McWorld*. New York: Ballantine.

Bardhan, Pranab. 2011. "A Democratic Malaise?" Presented at *Developing an Agenda for Urbanization in India*, Delhi, March 24.

  1984. *The Political Economy of Development in India*. Delhi: Oxford University Press.

Bardhan, Pranab and Dilip Mookherjee. 2000. "Capture and Governance at Local and National Levels." *American Economic Review* 90 No. 2: 135–139.

Barnwal, Bijay Kumar. 2000. *Economic Reforms and Policy Change: A Case Study of the Indian Drug Industry*. Delhi: Classical Publishing Company.

Bates, Robert. 1981. *Markets and States in Tropical Africa*. Berkeley: University of California Press.

BBC News. 2012. "India Orders Probe into Walmart Lobbying." *BBC News*, December 12.

Bennett, Douglas and Kenneth Sharpe. 1985. *Transnational Corporations vs. the State*. Princeton, NJ: Princeton University Press.

Bennett-Jones, Owen. 2002. *Pakistan: The Eye of the Storm*. New Haven, CT: Yale University Press.

Berman, Sheri. 2006. *The Primacy of Politics*. Cambridge: Cambridge University Press.

Bhagwati, Jagdish. 1993. *Freeing the Economy: India in Transition*. Oxford: Oxford University Press.

    1989. *Protectionism*. Cambridge, MA: MIT Press.

Bhagwati, Jagdish and T. N. Srinivasan. 1978. "Shadow Prices for Project Selection in the Presence of Distortions: Effective Rates of Protection and Domestic Resource Costs." *Journal of Political Economy* 86 (Feb.): 97–116.

Birla, Ritu. 2008. *Stages of Capital*. Durham, NC: Duke University Press.

Blyth, Mark. 2002. *Great Transformations*. Cambridge: Cambridge University Press.

Booth, William James. 1994. "On the Idea of the Moral Economy." *American Political Science Review* 88: 653–667.

Braconier, Henrik, Guiseppe Nicoletti, and Ben Westmore. 2014. "Policy Challenges for the Next 50 Years." *OECD Economic Policy Papers*, No. 9.

Breman, Jan. 1999a. "The Study of Industrial Labor in Post-Colonial India – the Formal Sector." *Contributions to Indian Sociology* 33 (February): 1–41.

    1999b. "The Study of Industrial Labor in Post-Colonial India – the Informal Sector." *Contributions to Indian Sociology* 33 (February): 407–431.

    1996. *Footloose Labour: Working in India's Informal Economy*. Cambridge: Cambridge University Press.

Breman, Jan and Parthiv Shah. 2004. *Working in the Mill No More*. Delhi: Oxford University Press.

Burki, Shahid Javed. 2007. *Changing Perceptions, Altered Reality: Pakistan's Economy under Musharraf*. Karachi: Oxford University Press.

    1980. *Pakistan under Bhutto, 1971–1977*. London: MacMillan.

1974. "Politics of Economic Decision-Making during the Bhutto Period." *Asian Survey* 14 (December): 1126–1140.

Bussell, Jennifer. 2012. *Corruption and Reform in India* (Cambridge: Cambridge University Press)

Cammett, Melani. 2007. *Globalization and Business Politics in Arab North Africa: A Comparative Perspective*. New York: Cambridge University Press.

Campbell, John. 1998. "Institutional Analysis and the Role of Ideas in Political Economy." *Theory and Society* 27: 377–409.

Candland, Christopher. 2007. *Labor, Democratization and Development in India and Pakistan*. Abingdon: Routledge.

2001. "The Costs of Incorporation: Labor Institutions, Industrial Restructuring and new Trade Union Strategies." In *The Politics of Labor in a Global Age* (Candland and Sil, eds.). New York: Oxford University Press.

1997. "Congress Decline and Party Pluralism in India." *Journal of International Affairs* 51: 19–35.

Cardoso, Enrique and Enzo Faletto. 1979. *Dependency and Development in Latin America*. Berkeley: University of California Press.

Carney, Michael, Eric Gedajlovic, and Xiaohua Yang. 2009. "Varieties of Asian Capitalism." *Asua Pacific Journal of Management* 26 No. 3: 361–380.

Cawthorne, Pamela. 1995. "Of Networks and Markets: The Rise and Rise of a South Indian Town, the Example of Tiruppur's Knitwear Industry." *World Development* 23 No. 1: 43–56.

Chakrabarty, Bidyut. 1992. "Jawaharlal Nehru and Planning." *Modern Asian Studies* 26: 275–287.

Chakravarty, Sukhamoy. 1993. *Development Planning: The Indian Experience*. Delhi: Oxford University Press.

Chandavarkar, Rajnarayan. 1999. "Questions of Class: The General Strikes in Bombay." *Contributions to Indian Sociology* 33 (February): 210–211.

1998. *Imperial Power and Popular Politics*. Cambridge: Cambridge University Press.

1994. *The Origins of Industrial Capitalism*. Cambridge: Cambridge University Press.

1981. "Workers' Politics and the Mill Districts in Bombay between the Wars." *Modern Asian Studies* 15: 603–647.

Chandra, Bipan. 1966. *The Rise and Growth of Economic Nationalism in India*. Delhi: People's Publishing House.

Chandra, Kanchan. 2006. "Counting Heads: A Theory of Voter and Elite Behavior in Patronage Democracies." In *Patrons, Clients and*

Policies (Kitschelt and Wilkinson, eds.). Cambridge: Cambridge University Press.

2004. *Why Ethnic Parties Succeed: Patronage and Ethnic Head Counts in India.* New York: Cambridge University Press.

Chandrasekhar, C. P. and Jayanti Ghosh. 2002. *The Market That Failed.* Delhi: Left Word Books.

Chari, Sharad. 2004. *Fraternal Capital.* Stanford, CA: Stanford University Press.

2000. "The Agrarian Origins of the Knitwear Industrial Cluster in Tiruppur, India." *World Development* 28: 579–599.

Chatterjee, Elizabeth. 2015. "Underpowered: Electricity Policy and the State in India, 1991–2014." Doctoral Dissertation, the University of Oxford.

Chatterjee, Partha. 2004. *The Politics of the Governed.* New York: Columbia University Press.

2001. "On Civil and Political Society in Post-Colonial Democracies." In *Civil Society: History and Possibilities* (Kaviraj, ed.). Cambridge: Cambridge University Press.

Chaudhry, Kiren Aziz. 1997. *The Price of Wealth.* Ithaca, NY: Cornell University Press.

1993. "The Myths of the Market and the Common History of Late Developers." *Politics and Society* 21: 245–274.

Chhibber, Pradeep. 1999. *Democracy without Associations.* Ann Arbor, MI: University of Michigan Press.

Chhibber, Pradeep and Irfan Nooruddin. 2010. "Making India's 'Known-to' Democracy Work: Associations and the Power of Connectedness." Presented at "Six Decades of Indian Democracy," Brown University, May 6–9.

2008. "Unstable Politics: Fiscal Space and Electoral Volatility in Indian States." *Comparative Political Studies* 41: 1073–1075.

Chhibber, Pradeep and Ken Kollman. 2004. *The Formation of National Party Systems.* Princeton, NJ: Princeton University Press.

Chhibber, Pradeep and Sumit Majumdar. 1999. "Foreign Ownership and Profitability: Property Rights, Control, and the Performance of Firms in Indian Industry." *The Journal of Law and Economics* 42 No. 1: 209–238.

1998. "State as Investor and State as Owner: Consequences for Firm Performance in India." *Economic Development and Cultural Change* 46 No. 3: 561–580.

Chibber, Vivek. 2003. *Locked in Place.* Princeton, NJ: Princeton University Press.

Chossudovsky, Michel. 1993. "India under IMF Rule." *Economic and Political Weekly* 28 No. 10: 385–387.

Chua, Amy. 2003. *World on Fire*. New York: Random House.

Coase, Ronald. 1937. "The Theory of the Firm." *Economica* 4: 386–405.

Corbridge, Stuart. 2002. "The Continuing Struggle for India's Jharkhand." *Commonwealth & Comparative Politics* 40 (January): 55–71.

Cross, Jamie. 2014. *Dream Zones: Anticipating Capitalism and Development in India*. London: Pluto Press.

——— 2010. "Neoliberalism as Unexceptional." *Critique of Anthropology* 30: 355–373.

——— 2009. "From Dreams to Discontent: Educated Young Men and the Politics of Work in a Special Economic Zone in Andhra Pradesh." *Contributions to Indian Sociology* 43: 351–379.

Crouch, Colin, Martin Schröder, and Helmut Voelzkow. 2009. "Regional and Sectoral Varieties of Capitalism." *Economy and Society* 38 No. 4: 654–678.

Das, Gurcharan. 2000. *India Unbound*. Delhi: Penguin India.

Damodaran, Harish. 2008. *India's New Capitalists*. Delhi: Permanent Black.

Darden, Keith. 2009. *Neoliberalism and Its Rivals: The Formation of International Institutions among the Post-Soviet States*. Cambridge: Cambridge University Press.

Dasgupta, Biplab. 1999. "Patent Lies and Latent Danger." *Economic and Political Weekly* 34 No. 16–17: 979–993.

D'Costa, Anthony. 1995. "The Restructuring of the Indian Automobile Industry: Indian State and Japanese Capital." *World Development* 23 No. 3 (March): 497–498.

D'Monte, Darryl. 2002. *Ripping the Fabric: The Decline of Mumbai and Its Mills*. Delhi: Oxford University Press.

De Neve, Gert and Grace Carswell. 2011. "NREGA and the Return to Identity Politics in Western Tamil Nadu, India." *Forum for Development Studies* 38: 205–211.

Demir, Omer, Mustafa Acar, and Metin Toprak. 2004. "Anatolian Tigers or Islamic Capital: Prospects and Challenges." *Middle East Studies* 40 (November): 166–188.

Denoon, David. 1998. "Cycles of Economic Liberalization, 1966–1996." *Comparative Politics* 31: 43–60.

Dhawan, Rajat, Gautam Swaroop, and Adil Zainulbhai. 2012. "Fulfilling the Promise of India's Manufacturing Sector." *McKinsey Insights*, March. www.mckinsey.com/insights/operations/fulfilling_the_promise_of_indias_manufacturing_sector, accessed April 19, 2014.

DiMaggio, Paul and Walter Powell. 1991. "Introduction" In *The New Institutionalism in Organizational Analysis* (Powell and DiMaggio, eds.). Chicago: University of Chicago Press, 1–40.

1983. "The Iron Cage Revisited." *American Sociological Review* 48: 147–160.

Doner, Richard. 2009. *Politics of Uneven Development.* Cambridge: Cambridge University Press.

Doner, Richard, Brian Ritchie, and Dan Slater. 2005. "Systematic Vulnerability and the Origins of Developmental States: Northeast and Southeast Asia in Comparative Perspective." *International Organization* 59: 337–361.

Dwivedi, Ranjit. 1997. "People's Movements in Environmental Politics: A Critical Analysis of the Narmada Bachao Andolan." Working Paper No. 242, Institute of Social Studies, March. repub.eur.nl/res/pub/18981/wp242.pdf.

Easterly, William. 2000. "The Middle Class Consensus and Economic Development." World Bank Policy Research Paper 2346.

Eaton, Kent. 2001. "Decentralization, Democratization, and Liberalization." *Journal of Latin American Studies* 33: 1–28.

Economic and Political Weekly. 1968. "New Vistas for ICICI." *Economic and Political Weekly* 3 No. 11 (March 16), 444.

1968b. "Ayub Regime Challenged from Within." *Economic & Political Weekly* 3 (November 30).

1967. "Another Role for ICICI." *Economic and Political Weekly* 2 No. 11 (March 18): 544.

1966. "India's Biggest Investment Banker." *Economic and Political Weekly* 1 No. 5 (September 17): 182–183.

Economist Intelligence Unit. 2014. *Country Commerce Report: India.* New York: Economist Intelligence Unit.

Esposito, Bruce. 1974. "The Politics of Agrarian Reform in Pakistan." *Asian Survey* 14 (May): 229–438.

Etchemendy, Sebastian. 2011. *Models of Economic Liberalization.* Cambridge: Cambridge University Press.

Evans, Peter. 1995. *Embedded Autonomy.* Princeton, NJ: Princeton University Press.

1979. *Dependent Development: The Alliance of Multinational, State and Local Capital in Brazil.* Princeton, NJ: Princeton University Press.

Fair, Christine. 2014. *Fighting to the End.* Oxford: Oxford University Press.

Federation of Indian Chambers of Commerce and Industry. 2013. *India Risk Survey.* Delhi: Federation of Indian Chambers of Commerce and Industry.

Felix, David. 1990. "Latin America's Debt Crisis." *World Policy Journal* 7: 733–771.

Finnemore, Martha and Kathryn Sikkink. 2001. "Taking Stock: The Constructivist Research Program in International Relations and Comparative Politics." *Annual Review of Political Science* 4: 391–416.

Fiss, Peter and Paul Hirsch. 2005. "The Discourse of Globalization." *American Sociological Review* 70 (February): 29–52.

Fligstein, Neil. 2001. *The Architecture of Markets*. Princeton, NJ: Princeton University Press.

Fourcade, Marion. 2009. *Economists and Societies*. Princeton, NJ: Princeton University Press.

Frankel, Francine. 2005. *India's Political Economy, 1947–2004: The Gradual Revolution*. Delhi: Oxford University Press.

Frieden, Jeffrey and Ronald Rogowski. 1996. "The Impact of the International Economy on National Policies." In *Internationalization and Domestic Policies* (Keohane and Milner, eds.). Cambridge: Cambridge University Press, 3–24.

Friedman, Thomas. 1999. *The Lexus and the Olive Tree*. New York: Ferrar, Strauss & Giroux.

Fukuyama, Francis. 1992. *The End of History and the Last Man*. New York: Free Press.

Fuller, Douglas. 2016. *Paper Tigers, Hidden Dragons: The Political Economy of Technological Development in China*. Oxford: Oxford University Press.

    2014. "Chip Design in China and India." *Technological Forecasting & Social Change* 81 No. 1: 1–10.

Gandhi, Aditi and Michael Walton. 2012. "Where Do India's Billionaires Get Their Wealth?" *Economic and Political Weekly* 47 No. 40: 10–14.

Gaur, Ajai S. and Vikas Kumar. 2009. "International Diversification, Business Group Affiliation and Firm Performance: Empirical Evidence from India." *British Journal of Management* 20 No. 2: 172–186.

Gereffi, Gary. 1982. *The Pharmaceutical Industry and Dependency in the Third World*. Princeton, NJ: Princeton University Press.

Gereffi, Gary, John Humphreys, and Timothy Sturgeon. 2005. "The Governance of Global Value Chains." *Review of International Political Economy* 12: 78–104.

Gerschenkron, Alexander. 1962. *Economic Backwardness in Historical Perspective*. Cambridge, MA: Harvard University Press.

Gilpin, Robert. 1975. *The Multinational Corporation: The Political Economy of Foreign Direct Investment*. New York: Basic Books.

Goldberg, Pinelopi. 2010. "Intellectual Property Rights Protection in Developing Countries: The Case of Pharmceuticals." *Journal of the European Economic Association* 8 No. 2–3: 326–353.

Goldberg, Penelopi, Amit Khandelwal, Nina Pavcnik, and Petia Topalova. 2010. "Imported Intermediate Inputs and Domestic Product Growth: Evidence from India." *The Quarterly Journal of Economics* 125 No. 4: 1727–1767.

Goswami, Manu. 2004. *Producing India: From Colonial Economy to National Space*. Chicago: University of Chicago Press.

Goswami, Omkar. 1989. "Sahibs, Babus and Banias: Changes in Industrial Control in India, 1918–50." *Journal of Asian Studies* 48 (May): 289–309.

Gould, William. 2011. *Bureaucracy, Community and Influence in India*. Abingdon: Routledge.

Gourevitch, Philip. 1986. *Politics in Hard Times*. Ithaca, NY: Cornell University Press.

1978. "The Second Image Reversed: The International Sources of Domestic Politics." *International Organization* 32 No. 4: 881–912.

Govindarajan, Vijay and Ravi Ramamurti. 2011. "Reverse Innovation, Emerging Markets and Global Strategy." *Global Strategy Journal* 1 No. 3–4: 191–205.

Government of India. 2010. POSCO Committee Report, Ministry of Environment and Forests, Government of India. http://moef.nic.in/downloads/public-information/report-committee-posco.pdf, accessed December 22, 2012.

1961. *Third Five Year Plan*. New Delhi: Planning Commission.

1956. *Second Five Year Plan*. New Delhi: The Planning Commission.

Government of India Labor Bureau. 2010a. *Statistics of Factories, 2010*. Simla and Chandigarh: Government of India Labor Bureau.

2010b. *Indian Labor Yearbook, 2009 and 2010*. Simla and Chandigarh: Government of India Labor Bureau.

1956. *Statistics of Factories, 1955 and 1956*. Delhi: Government of India Labour Bureau.

Government of Pakistan. 1970. *Reports of the Advisory Panels for the Fourth Five Year Plan 1970–75*. Vol. I. Islamabad: Planning Commission, Government of Pakistan.

Granta. 2010. "How to Write about Pakistan." *Granta* 112 (September).

Grare, Frederic. 2006. "Pakistan: The Resurgence of Baluch Nationalism." Carnegie Papers No. 65, Carnegie Endowment for International Peace, January.

Greif, Avner. 2006. *Institutions and the Path to the Modern Economy*. Cambridge: Cambridge University Press.

Grieco, Joseph. 1984. *Between Dependency and Autonomy*. Berkeley: University of California Press.

Gunder Frank, Andre. 1966. "The Development of Underdevelopment." *Monthly Review* 18 (September).

Gupta, Akhil and K. Sivaramakrishnan. 2010. "Introduction to the State in India after Liberalization." In *The State in India after Liberalization* (Gupta and Sivaramakrishnan, eds.). Abingdon: Routledge.

Gustavson, W. Eric. 1976. "Economic Problems of Pakistan under Bhutto." *Asian Survey* 16 (April): 365–367.

Haan, Arjan de. 1999. "The Badli System in Industrial Labor Recruitment." *Contributions to Indian Sociology* 33 (February): 271–301.

Habermas, Jurgen. 1975. *Legitimation Crisis*. Boston: Beacon Press.

Habib, Irfan. 1975. "Colonization of the Indian Economy, 1757–1900." *Social Scientist* 3: 23–53.

Hacker, Jacob. 2004. "Privatizing Risk without Privatizing the Welfare State." *American Political Science Review* 98: 243–260.

Haggard, Stephan. 1990. *Pathways from the Periphery*. Ithaca, NY: Cornell University Press.

Haley, Usha and George Haley. 2008. "Subsidies and the China Price." *Harvard Business Review*, June 23.

Hall, Peter. 1986. *Governing the Economy*. Oxford: Oxford University Press.

Hall, Peter and David Soskice. 2001. "An Introduction to the Varieties of Capitalism." In *Varieties of Capitalism* (Hall and Soskice, eds.). Oxford: Oxford University Press.

Hancké, Bob, Martin Rhodes, and Mark Thatcher. 2007. "Introduction." In *Beyond Varieties of Capitalism: Conflict, Contradiction and Complementarities in the European Economy* (Hancké and Thatcher, eds.). Oxford: Oxford University Press.

Hanson, A. H. 1966. *The Process of Planning*. Oxford: Oxford University Press.

Hanson, Stephen. 2010. *Post-Imperial Democracies*. Cambridge: Cambridge University Press.

Haqqani, Husain. 2005. *Pakistan: Between Mosque and Military*. Washington, DC: The Carnegie Endowment.

Harik, Illiya. 1997. *Economic Policy Reform in Egypt*. Gainesville: University of Florida Press.

Harriss-White, Barbara. 2003. *India Working: Essays of Economy and Society*. Cambridge: Cambridge University Press.

Harriss-White, Barbara, with Muhammad Ali Jan and Asha Amirali. 2015. "Malgudi on the Move." Presented at "The Political Economy of Development in India" – Thirty Years On, All Soul's College Oxford, March 19.

Haynes, Douglas. 2001. "Artisan Cloth-Producers and the Emergence of Powerloom Manufacture in Western India 1920–1950." *Past and Present* 172: 170–198.

Held, David, Athony McGrew, David Goldblatt, and Jonathan Perraton. 1999. *Global Transformations*. Stanford, CA: Stanford University Press.

Hellman, Joel S., Geraint Jones, and Daniel Kaufmann. 2000. "Seize the State, Seize the Day: State Capture, Corruption and Influence in Transition." World Bank Policy Research Working Paper 2444 .

Helmke, Gretchen and Steven Levitsky. 2004. "Informal Institutions and Comparative Politics: A Research Agenda." *Perspectives on Politics* 2 No. 4: 725–740.

Herbst, Jeffrey. 2000. *States and Power in Africa: Comparative Lessons in Authority and Control*. Princeton, NJ: Princeton University Press.

Herrera, Yoshiko. 2005. *Imagined Economies: The Sources of Russian Regionalism*. Cambridge: Cambridge University Press.

Herrigel, Gary. 1996. *Industrial Constructions*. Cambridge: Cambridge University Press.

Herring, Ronald. 1999. "Embedded Particularism: India's Failed Developmental State." In *The Developmental State* (Woo-Cumings, ed.). Ithaca, NY: Cornell University Press.

1979. "Zulfikar Ali Bhutto and 'the Eradication of Feudalism' in Pakistan." *Comparative Studies of Society and History* 21 (October): 519–557.

Hischman, Albert. 1968. "The Political Economy of Import-Substituting Industrialization in Ltin America." *The Quarterly Journal of Economics* 82 No. 1: 1–32.

Holmstrom, Mark. 1984. *Industry and Inequality: The Social Anthropology of Indian Labor*. Cambridge: Cambridge University Press.

1976. *South Indian Factory Workers*. Cambridge: Cambridge University Press.

Huang Yasheng. 1994. "Information, Bureaucracy and Economic Reforms in China and the Soviet Union." *World Politics* 47 (October): 102–134.

Humphrey, John. 2003. "Globalization and Supply Chain Networks: The Auto Industry in Brazil and India." *Global Networks* 3 (April).

India International Center. 1986. *Monetary Policy: Review of the Sukhamoy Chakravarty Report*. New Delhi: India International Center.

Jackson, Robert H. and Carl G. Rosberg. 1982. "Why Africa's Weak States Persist: The Empirical and the Juridical in Statehood." *World Politics* 35 No. 1: 1–24.

Jaffrelot, Christophe. 2015. *Saffron Modernity in India*. London: Hurst Publishers.

2014. "Painted into a Corner." *Indian Express*, August 20.

1999. *The Hindu Nationalist Movement and Indian Politics*. New York: Columbia University Press.

Jain, Sunil. 2006. "Competition Issues for Transportation Sectors." In *A Functional Competition Policy for India* (Mehta, ed.). New Delhi: Academic Foundation.

Jalal, Ayesha. 1995. *Democracy and Authoritarianism in South Asia.* Cambridge: Cambridge University Press.

1990. *The State of Martial Rule.* Cambridge: Cambridge University Press.

1985. *The Sole Spokesman.* Cambridge: Cambridge University Press.

Jenkins, Rob. 2004. "Labor Policy and the Second Generation of Economic Reform in India." *India Review* 3 (October): 333–363.

1999. *Democratic Politics and Economic Reform in India.* Cambridge: Cambridge University Press.

Jillani, Shahzeb. 2012. "Pakistan's Economy at a Crossroads." *BBC News,* June 3.

Johnson, Chalmers. 1995. *Japan: Who Governs?* New York: W. W. Norton.

1982. *MITI and the Japanese Miracle.* Stanford, CA: Stanford University Press.

Joshi, Gopal. 2002. "Overview of Competitiveness, Productivity and Job Quality in South Asian Garment Industry." In *The Garment Industry in South Asia* (Joshi, ed.). New Delhi: International Labour Organization.

Joshi, P. C. 1967. "Export Policy for the Fourth Plan." *Economic and Political Weekly* 2 (February): 309–318.

Kannappan, Subbiah. 1962. "The Gandhian Model of Unionism in a Developing Economy: The TLA in India." *Industrial and Labor Relations Review* 16 (October): 86–110.

Kapur, Devesh. 2004. "Ideas and Economic Liberalization." *India Review* 3: 373–377.

Kapur, Devesh, John Lewis, and Richard Webb. 1997. *The World Bank: Its First Half-Century.* Washington, DC: The Brookings Institution.

Keddie, Nikki. 1957. "Labor Problems in Pakistan." *Journal of Asian Studies* 16 (August): 577–579.

Keyder, Caglar. 1987. *State and Class in Turkey.* London: Verso.

Khan, Ashfaque and Lubna Hasan. 1998. "Financial Liberalization, Savings and Economic Developiment in Pakistan." *Economic Development and Cultural Change* 46 (April): 581–597.

Khan, Mohsin S. and Abbas Mirakhor. 1990. "Islamic Banking: Experiences in the Islamic Republic of Iran and in Pakistan." *Economic Development and Cultural Change* 38 (January): 365–369.

Khan, Mushtaq. 1999. "The Political Economy of Industrial Policy in Pakistan." Working paper. SOAS, University of London.

Khwaja, M. Idrees and Musleh ud Din. 2007. "Determinants of Interest Spread in Pakistan." *Pakistan Development Review* 46 (Summer): 129–143.

Kingstone, Peter. 1999. *Crafting Coalitions for Reform*. State College: Penn State Press.

Kochanek, Stanley. 1986. "Regulation and Liberalization Theology in India." *Asian Survey* 26: 1284–1308.

1983. *Interest Groups and Development*. Karachi: Oxford University Press.

1974. *Business and Politics in India*. Berkeley: University of California Press.

1968. *The Congress Party of India*. Princeton, NJ: Princeton University Press.

Kohli, Atul. 2011. *Poverty amid Plenty in the New India*. Cambridge: Cambridge University Press.

2006a. "Politics of Economic Growth in India, 1980–2005. Part I. The 1980s."*Economic and Political Weekly* 41 No. 3: 1251–1259.

2006b. "Politics of Economic Growth in India, 1980–2005. Part II. The 1990s and Beyond." *Economic and Political Weekly* 41 No. 14: 1361–1370.

2004. *State-Directed Development*. Cambridge: Cambridge University Press.

1990. *Democracy and Discontent*. Cambridge: Cambridge University Press.

1989. "Politics of Economic Liberalization in India." *World Development* 17 No. 3: 305–328.

Kothari, Rajni. 1964. "The Congress 'System' in India." *Asian Survey* 4 No. 12 (December): 1161–1173.

Kreuger, Anne. 1974. "The Political Economy of the Rent-Seeking Society." *American Economic Review* 64 (June): 291–303.

Krishnan, Viswanathan. 1996. "Indian Automotive Industry: Opportunities and Challenges Posed by Recent Developments." IMVP Working Papers, Massachusetts Institute of Technology.

Kumar, K. Ram and N. S. Vageesh. 2003. "State Bank of India to Focus More on Term Loans, Recovery." *Hindu Business Line*, March 24.

Kumarappa, J. C. 1951. *Gandhian Economic Thought*. Bombay: Vora.

Kurth, James. 1979. "The Political Consequences of the Product Cycle: Industrial History and Political Outcomes." *International Organization* 33 No. 1: 1–34.

Lake, David. 2009. "Open Economy Politics." *Review of International Organizations* 4 No. 3: 219–244.

Lal, Deepak. 1985. *The Poverty of Development Economics*. Cambridge, MA: Harvard University Press.

Lala, R. M. 1993. *Beyond the Last Blue Mountain*. Delhi: Penguin Books.

Lane, David. 2005. "Emerging Varieties of Capitalism in Former State Socialist Societies." *Competition and Change* 9 No. 3: 227–247.

Lanjouw, Jean. 1998. "The Introduction of Pharmaceutical Product Patents in India: 'Heartless Exploitation of the Poor and Suffering'?" Discussion Paper No. 775, Economic Growth Center, Yale University.

Leadbeater, Simon. 1993. *The Politics of Textiles: The Indian Cotton Mill Industry and the Legacy of Swadeshi, 1900–1985.* New Delhi: Sage.

Levien, Michael. 2013. "The Politics of Dispossession: Theorizing India's Land Wars." *Politics & Society* 41: 351–394.

——— 2012. "The Land Question: Special Economic Zones and the Political Economy of Dispossession in India." *Journal of Peasant Studies* 39: 933–969.

——— 2011. "Special Economic Zones and Accumulation by Dispossession in India." *Journal of Agrarian Change* 11 (October): 454–483.

Levy, Jonah. 2006. "The State Also Rises." In *The State after Statism* (Levy, ed). Cambridge, MA: Harvard University Press.

Lewis, W. Arthur. 1954. "Economic Development with Unlimited Supplies of Labor." *The Manchester School* 22 No. 2 (May): 139–191.

Lieven, Anatol. 2011. *Pakistan: A Hard Country.* London: Allen Lane.

List, Friedrich. 1856. *National System of Political Economy* (G. A. Matile, trans.). Philadelphia: Lippincott.

Litvack, Jennie, Junaid Ahmed, and Richard Bird, *Rethinking Decentralization in Developing Countries.* Washington, DC: World Bank, 1998.

Locke, Richard M. 1995. *Remaking the Italian Economy.* Ithaca, NY: Cornell University Press.

MacGregor, James. 2012. *No Ancient Wisdom, No Followers.* Westport, CT: Prospecta Press.

Magnier, Mark. 2012. "India's Power Outage Puts Its Superpower Dreams in a New Light." *Los Angeles Times*, August 1. http://articles.latimes.com/2012/aug/01/ world/la-fg-india-blackouts-20120801, accessed August 20, 2012.

Mahmood, Azhar. 1997. "The Role of Foreign Aid in the Economic Development of Pakistan, 1960–61 to 1994–5." *Pakistan Economic and Social Review* 15 (Summer): 57–90.

Majumdar, Sumit K. and Pradeep Chhibber. 1999. "Capital Structure and Performance: Evidence from a Transition Economy on an Aspect of Corporate Governance." *Public Choice* 98 No. 3–4: 287–305.

Mangla, Akshay. 2013. "Rights for the Voiceless." Doctoral Dissertation, MIT.

March, James and Johan Olsen. (1984). "The New Institutionalism." *American Political Science Review* 78: 734–749.

Mares, Isabella. 2003. *The Politics of Social Risk.* New York: Cambridge University.

Martin, Lee R. 1956. "Report of the Land Tenure Situation in India and Pakistan." *Journal of Farm Economics* 38 (May): 438–447.

Mate, Manoj. 2010. "The Variable Power of Courts: The Expansion of the Power of the Supreme Court of India in Fundamental Rights and Governance Decisions." Doctoral Dissertation, University of California, Berkeley.

Maurer, Noel, Armando Razo, and Stephen Haber. 2003. *The Politics of Property Rights*. Cambridge: Cambridge University Press.

McCartney, Matthew. 2012. *Pakistan – the Political Economy of Growth, Stagnation and the State – 1951–2008*. Abingdon: Routledge.

2010. *Political Economy, Growth and Liberalisation in India, 1991–2008*. Abingdon: Routledge.

2009. *India: The Political Economy of Growth, Stagnation and the State – 1951–2007*. Abingdon: Routledge.

McMahon, Robert. 1994. *The Cold War on the Periphery*. New York: Columbia University Press.

McNeill, Donald. 2006. "Clinton in Deal to Cut AIDS Treatment Costs." *New York Times*, January 12.

2002. "New List of Safe Drugs, Despite Industry Lobby." *New York Times*, March 21.

Mehrotra, N. N. 1987. "Indian Patents Act, Paris Convention and Self-Reliance." *Economic & Political Weekly* 24 (August 22).

Mehta, Pratap Bhanu. 2012. "Age of Sleaze." *Indian Express*, April 25.

Mehta, Pratap Bhanu and Devesh Kapur. 2007. *Public Institutions in India: Performance and Design*. Delhi: Oxford University Press.

Miles, Tom. 2014. "WTO Failure Points to Fragmented Future for Global Trade." *Reuters*, August 14.

Milner, Helen and Robert Keohane. 1996. "Internationalization and Domestic Politics: An Introduction." In *Internationalization and Domestic Politics* (Keohane and Milner, eds.). Cambridge: Cambridge University Press.

Mizruchi, Mark. 2013. *The Fracturing of the American Corporate Elite*. Cambridge, MA: Harvard University Press.

Mody, Ashok, Anusha Nath and Michael Walton. 2011. "Cources of Profits in India: Business Dynamism or Advantages of Entrenchments." In *India Policy Forum*, Vol. 7 (Bery, Bosworth and Panagariya, eds.). Delhi: Sage.

Moreau, Ron. 2007. "Where Jihad Lives Now." *Newsweek*, October 20.

Morris, Morris D. 1983. "The Growth of Large-Scale Industry." In *The Cambridge Economic History of India*, Vol. 2 (Dharma Kumar, ed.). Cambridge: Cambridge University Press.

Mukherji, Rahul. 2014. "Ideas, Interests, and the Tipping Point: Economic Change in India." *Review of International Political Economy* 20 No. 2: 363–389.

2013. *Globalization and Deregulation.* New Delhi: Oxford University Press.

Murali, Kanta. 2010. "Economic Liberalization, Sub-National Politics and Private Investment in India." Doctoral Dissertation, Princeton University,

Myrdal, Gunnar. 1968. *Asian Dilemma: Enquiry into the Poverty of Nations.* New York: The Twentieth Century Fund.

Narain, Arohini, Chetan Tolia, Raveendra Chitoor and Richa Vyas. 2013. "Creating a Corporate Advantage: The Case of the Tata Group." *Harvard Business Review*, February 15.

Naseemullah, Adnan. 2013. "Mosaics of Manufacture: Understanding Industrial Variation in South Asia." *Studies in Comparative International Development* 48 (March): 23–50.

Naseemullah, Adnan and Caroline Arnold. 2015. "The Politics of Developmental State Persistence." *Studies in Comparative International Development* 50 (March): 121–142.

Nawaz, Shuja. 2008. *Crossed Swords: Pakistan, Its Army and the Wars Within.* Oxford: Oxford University Press.

Nayar, Baldev Raj. 2009. *The Myth of the Shrinking State.* Delhi: Oxford University Press.

Nayar, Baldev Raj and T. V. Paul. 2003. *India and the World Order: Searching for Great Power Status.* Cambridge: Cambridge University Press.

NDTV News. 2013. "Ashis Nandy Clarifies, Says He Was Misinterpreted." *NDTV News*, January 28.

2011. "Tamil Nadu Polls: AIADMK Offers Laptop, Mixies, Gold for Mangalsutra." *NDTV News*, March 24.

Nichter, Simeon and Lara Goldmark. 2009. "Small Firm Growth in Developing Countries." *World Development* 37: 1453–1465.

Nölke, Andreas and Arjan Vliegenthart. 2009. "Enlarging the Varieties of Capitalism: The Emergence of Dependent Market Economies in East Central Europe." *World Politics* 61 No. 4: 670–702.

North, Douglass. 1991. "Institutions." *Journal of Economic Perspectives* 5 No. 1: 97–112.

1990. *Institutions, Institutional Change and Economic Performance.* Cambridge: Cambridge University Press.

North, Douglass and Barry Weingast. 1989. "Constitutions and Commitment: The Evolution of Institutions Governing Public Choice in Seventeenth-Century England." *The Journal of Economic History* 49: 803–832.

Nooruddin, Irfan. 2011. *Coalition Politics and Economic Development: Credibility and the Strength of Weak Governments.* Cambridge: Cambridge University Press.

O'Donnell, Guillermo. 1988. *Bureaucratic Authoritarianism.* Berkeley, CA: The University of California Press.

O'Neill, Jim. 2011. "The World Needs Better Global Economic BRICs." *Goldman Sachs Global Economic Papers* 66 (November).

Ohmae, Kenichi. 1995. *The End of the Nation State.* London: Harper Collins.

Okada, Aya. 2004. "Skills Development and Inter-Firm Learning Linkages under Globalization: Lessons from the Indian Automobile Industry." *World Development* 32 (July): 1265–1288.

Olson, Mancur. 1993. "Dictatorship, Democracy, and Development." *American Political Science Review* 87 No. 3: 567–576.

Ornati, Oscar. 1957. "Problems of Indian Trade Unionism." *Annals of the American Academy of Social and Political Science* 310 No. 1: 151–161.

Ostermann, Susan. 2015. "Rule of Law against the Odds: Legal Knowledge, Poverty and Compliance along the India-Nepal Border." Doctoral Dissertation, University of California, Berkeley.

Ostrom, Elinor. 1990. *Governing the Commons.* Cambridge: Cambridge University Press.

Papanek, Gustav. 1967. *Pakistan's Development: Social Goals and Private Incentives.* Cambridge, MA: Harvard University Press.

Parekh, H. T. 1980. *ICICI, 1955–1979: The Story of a Development Bank.* Mumbai: Industrial Credit and Investment Corporation of India.

Patel, Sujata. 1987. *The Making of Industrial Relations: The Ahmedabad Textile Industry 1918–1939.* Delhi: Oxford University Press.

Patnaik, Prabhat. 2012. "The Contrast Could Not Have Been Sharper." *Pragoti*, September 19. www.pragoti.in/node/4769.

Paul, T.V. 2014. *The Warrior State.* Delhi: Random House India.

Pierson, Paul. 2004. *Politics in Time.* Princeton, NJ: Princeton University Press.

Pingle, Vibha. 1999. *Rethinking the Developmental State.* New York: Palgrave Macmillan.

Piore, Michael and Charles Sabel. 1982. *The Second Industrial Divide.* New York: Basic Books.

Polanyi, Karl. 2001 [1944]. *The Great Transformation.* Boston: Beacon Press.

Posusney, Marsha Pripstein. 1997. *Labor and the State in Egypt, 1952–1994: Workers, Unions and Economic Restructuring.* New York: Columbia University Press.

Przeworski, Adam and Henry Teune. 1970. *The Logic of Comparative Social Enquiry.* New York: Wiley-Interscience.

Rafi Khan, Shahrukh. 2004. *Pakistan under Musharraf, 1999–2002: Economic Reform and Political Change*. Lahore: Vangard Press.

Raj, K. N. 1948. *The Monetary Policy of the Reserve Bank of India*. Mumbai: National Information and Publications.

Ramamurti, Ravi. 2009. "Why Study Emerging-Market Multinationals?" In *Emerging Multinationals from Emerging Markets* (Ramamurti and Singh, eds.). Cambridge: Cambridge University Press.

Ramaswamy, E. A. 1994. *The Rayon Spinners: The Strategic Management of Industrial Relations*. Delhi: Oxford University Press.

1977. *The Worker and His Union*. Columbia, MO: South Asia Books.

Ramaswamy, Kannan. 2012. "Reliance Industries: An Indian Family Business Comes of Age in Global Energy and Petrochemicals." *Harvard Business Review*, October 4.

Ramaswamy, Uma. 1983. *Work, Union and Community*. Delhi: Oxford University Press.

Ray, R. K. 1979. *Industrialization in India: Growth and Conflict in the Private Corporate Sector, 1914–1947*. Delhi: Oxford University Press.

Reddy, C. D. and N. Vishal Gupta. 2013. "Contract Research and Manufacturing Services (CRAMS) and its Present Status in India." *Asian Journal of Pharmaceutical and Clinical Research* 6 No. 2: 33–37.

Revri, Chamanlal. 1972. *The Indian Trade Union Movement, 1880–1947*. Delhi: Orient Longman.

Richards, Alan and John Waterbury.2008. *Political Economy of the Middle East*. Boulder, CO: Westview Press.

Rodrik, Dani. 2011. *The Globalization Paradox: Democracy and the Future of the World Economy*. New York: W. W. Norton.

Rondinelli, Dennis, John Nellis, and Shabbir Cheema, "Decentralization in Developing Countries." World Bank Staff Working Paper 581, 1983.

Roosa, John. 2001. "Passive Revolution Meets Peasant Revolution." *Journal of Peasant Studies* 28 No. 4: 57–94.

Rosenstein-Rodan, Paul. 1961. "International Aid for Underdeveloped Countries." *Review of Economics and Statistics* 43: 107–138.

Rostow, Dankwart. 1970. "Transitions to Democracy: Towards a Dynamic Model." *Comparative Politics* 2 No. 3: 337–363.

Rothermund, Deitmar 2002. *An Economic History of India: From Pre-Colonial Times to 1991*. Abingdon: Routledge.

Roy, Tirthankar. 2012. *India in the World Eeconomy*. Cambridge: Cambridge University Press.

1998. "Development or Distortion? 'Powerlooms in India', 1950–1997." *Economic and Political Weekly* 33 (April 18).

Rudolph, Lloyd and Susanne Rudolph. 2006. *Post-Modern Gandhi and Other Essays*. Chicago: University of Chicago Press.

1987. *In Pursuit of Laxmi*. Chicago: University of Chicago Press.

1967. *The Modernity of Tradition*. Chicago: University of Chicago Press.

Rudolph, Matthew. 2002. "The Diversity of Convergence: State Authority, Economic Governance, and the Politics of Securities Finance in India and China." Doctoral Dissertation, Cornell University.

Ruggie, John Gerard. 1982. "International Regimes, Transactions and Change: Embedded Liberalism in the Postwar Economic Order." *International Organization* 36 (March): 379–415.

Sabel, Charles. 1989. "Flexible Specialisation and the Re-Emergence of Regional Economies." In *Reversing Industrial Decline* (Hirst and Zeitlin, eds.). Oxford: Berg, pp. 17–70.

Sabel, Charles and Jonathan Zeitlin. 1985. "Historical Alternatives to Mass Production: Politics, Markets and Technology in Nineteenth-Century Industrialization." *Past and Present* 108: 133–176.

Sachs, Jeffrey, Nirupam Bajpai, and Ananthi Ramiah. 2002. "Understanding Regional Economic Growth in India." *Asian Economic Papers* 1: 32–62.

Saez, Lawrence and Crystal Chang. 2009. "The Political Economy of Global Firms from India and China." *Contemporary Politics* 15 No.3: 265–286.

Sainath, P. 2010. "Farm Suicides: A Twelve Year Saga." *The Hindu*, January 25.

Sayeed, Asad. 1995. "Political Alignments, the State and Industrial Policy in Pakistan." Doctoral Dissertation, the University of Cambridge,

Sayeed, Khalid. 1975. "How Radical Is the Pakistan People's Party." *Pacific Affairs* 48 (Spring).

1961. "Pakistan's Basic Democracy." *Middle East Journal* 15 (Summer): 249–263.

Schamis, Hector. 2002. *Reforming the State: The Politics of Privatization in Latin America and Europe*. Ann Arbor: University of Michigan Press.

Schmidt, Vivien. 2009. "Putting the Political Back into Political Economy by Bringing the State Back In Yet Again." *World Politics* 61 No. 3: 516–546.

Schmitz, Hubert and Khalid Nadvi. 1999. "Clustering and Industrialization: Introduction." *World Development* 27: 1503–14.

Schneider, Ben Ross. 2009. "Hierarchical Market Economies and Varieties of Capitalism in Latin America." *Journal of Latin American Studies* 41 No. 03: 553–575.

2008. "Economic Liberalization and Corporate Governance." *Comparative Politics* 40: 379–397.

2004. *Business Politics and the State in Twentieth-Century Latin America*. Cambridge: Cambridge University Press.

Schonfield, Andrew. 1965. *Modern Capitalism*. Oxford: Oxford University Press.

Scott, James. 1977. *The Moral Economy of the Peasant*. New Haven, CT: Yale University Press.

Sen, Kunal and Sabyasachi Kar 2014. "Boom or Bust? A Political Economy Reading of India's Growth Experience, 1993–2013." *Economic and Political Weekly* 49 No. 50: 40–52.

Shadlen, Ken. 2005. "Exchanging Development for Market Access." *Review of International Political Economy* 12 No. 5: 750–775.

Shafer, Michael. 1994. *Winners and Losers*. Ithaca, NY: Cornell University Press.

Shah, Alpa. 2010. *In the Shadows of the State*. Durham, NC: Duke University Press.

Shah, Aqil. 2014. *The Army and Democracy*. Cambridge, MA: Harvard University Press.

2011. "Getting the Military out of Pakistani Politics." *Foreign Affairs* 90 No. 3 (May–June): 69–82.

Shaheed, Zafar. 2007. *The Labor Movement in Pakistan*. Karachi: Oxford University Press.

Shankar, Uday. 1982. "Recent Trends in the Indian Economy." *Social Scientist* 10 No. 1: 32–39.

Shehata, Samer. 2003. "In the Basha's House: The Organizational Culture of an Egyptian Public-Sector Enterprise." *International Journal of Middle Eastern Studies* 35 (February): 103–132.

Sheth, N. R. 1968. *The Social Framework of an Indian Factory*. Manchester: Manchester University Press.

Siddiqa, Ayesha. 2007. *Military, Inc.: Inside Pakistan's Military Economy*. London: Pluto Press.

Singh, Nirvarkar. 2010. "The Trillion Dollar Question." *Indian Express*, December 19.

Singh, Prerna. 2016. *How Solidarity Works for Welfare: Subnationalism and Social Development in India*. Cambridge: Cambridge University Press.

Singh, Tarlok. 1969. *Towards an Integrated Society*. Westport, CT: Greenwood.

Sinha, Aseema. 2016. *Globalizing India: How Global Rules and Markets Are Shaping India's Rise to Power*. Cambridge: Cambridge University Press.

2010. "An Institutional Perspective on the Post-Liberalization State in India." In *The State in India after Liberalization* (Gupta and Sivaramakrishnan, eds.) Abingdon: Routledge.

2007. "Global Linkages and Domestic Politics: Trade Reform and Institution Building in India in Comparative Perspective." *Comparative Political Studies* 40 No. 10: 1183–1210.

2005. *The Regional Roots of Developmental Politics in India: The Divided Leviathan*. Bloomington: Indiana University Press.

2005. "Understanding the Rise and Transformation of Business Collective Action in India." *Business and Politics* 7: 1–35.

Snyder, Richard. 2001. "The Sub-National Comparative Method." *Studies in Comparative International Development* 36: 93–110.

Srinivasan, T. N. 2006. "China, India and the World Economy." *Economic and Political Weekly* 41 (August 26): 3716–3727.

Srinivasulu, K. 1996. "1985 Textile Policy and Handloom Industry: Policy, Promises and Performance." *Economic & Political Weekly* 31 (December 7).

Staniland, Paul. 2012. "Insurgents, States and Wartime Political Orders." *Perspectives on Politics* 10 No. 3 (June): 243–264.

Stern, Robert. 2001. *Democracy and Dictatorship in South Asia*. Westport, CT: Praeger.

Strange, Susan. 1996. *The Retreat of the State*. Cambridge: Cambridge University Press.

Streeck, Wolfgang and Kathleen Thelen. 2005. "Introduction: Institutional Change in Advanced Political Economies." In *Beyond Continuity* (Streeck and Thelen, eds.). Oxford: Oxford University.

Sud, Nikita. 2009. "The Indian State in a Liberalizing Landscape." *Development and Change* 40, no. 4: 645–665.

Sundar, Nandini. 2006. "Bastar, Maoism and the Salwa Judum." *Economic and Political Weekly* 41 (July): 3187–3192.

Sutton, John. 2005. "The Globalization Process: Auto-Component Supply Chains in China and India." ABCDE World Bank Conference on Development Economics.

Swenson, Peter. 2002. *Capitalists against Markets*. Oxford: Oxford University Press.

Tarrow, Sidney. 2010. "The Strategy of Paired Comparison: Toward a Theory of Practice." *Comparative Political Studies* 43 No. 2: 230–259.

Teece, David, Richard Rumelt, Giovanni Dosi and Sidney Winter. 1994. "Understanding Corporate Coherence: Theory and Evidence." *Journal of Economic Behavior and Organization* 23 No. 1: 1–30.

Teitelbaum, Emmanuel. 2010. "Mobilizing Restraint: Economic Reform and the Politics of Industrial Protest in South Asia." *World Politics* 62: 676–713.

2006. "Was the Indian Labor Movement Ever Co-Opted?" *Modern Asian Studies* 38 No. 4.

Tewari, Meenu. 1999. "Successful Adjustment in Indian Industry: The Case of Ludhiana's Woolen Knitwear Industry." *World Development* 27 (September): 1651–1671.

Thachil, Tariq. 2010. "Do Policies Matter in Indian Elections?" Center for the Advanced Study of India, University Pennsylvania, April 26.

Thakurdas, Purshottamdas et al. 1945. *A Brief Memorandum Outlining a Plan of Economic Development for India*. Bombay, January.

Thompson, E. P. 1971. "The Moral Economy of the English Crowd in the Eighteenth Century." *Past and Present* 50: 76–136.

Thakurdas, Purushottamdas (ed.) 1945. *A Brief Memorandum Outlining a Plan of Economic Development for India*, London: Penguin.

Tillin, Louise. 2013. *Remapping India*. London: Hurst.

    2011. "Questioning Borders: Social Movements, Political Parties and the Creation of New States in India." *Pacific Affairs* 84 (March): 67–87.

Times of India. 2011. "Strike at Maruti Suzuki's Manesar Plant Ends; 64 Workers to be Taken Back." *Times of India*, October 21.

Tomlinson, B. R. 1993. *The Economy of Modern India, 1860–1970*. Cambridge: Cambridge University Press.

    1982. "The Political Economy of the Raj: The Decline of Colonialism." *Journal of Economic History* 42 No. 1: 133–137.

    1981. "Colonial Firms and the Decline of Colonialism in Eastern India, 1914–1947." *Modern Asian Studies* 15: 455–486.

    1979. "Britain and the Indian Currency Crisis, 1930–32." *Economic History Review* 32: 88–99.

Topalova, Petia. 2004. *Overview of the Indian Corporate Sector: 1989–2002*. International Monetary Fund Working Paper No. 04–64.

Torri, Michelguglielmo. 1975. "Factional Politics and Economic Policy: The Case of India's Bank Nationalization." *Asian Survey* 15: 1077–1096.

Tudor, Maya. 2013. *The Promise of Power*. Cambridge: Cambridge University Press.

Tudor, Maya and Adam Ziegfeld. 2010. "Subnational Democratization in India." *Nuffield College Working Papers on Politics*, June.

Tugal, Cihan. 2009. *Passive Revolution: Absorbing the Islamic Challenge to Capitalism*. Stanford, CA: Stanford University Press.

Uppal, Yogesh. 2009. "The Disadvantaged Incumbents: Estimating Incumbency Effects in Indian State Legislatures." *Public Choice* 138: 9–27.

Varshney, Ashutosh. 2012. "Man with a Plan." *Indian Express*, December 14.

    2011. "Has Urban India Arrived?" *Indian Express*, August 25.

    2002. *Ethnic Conflict and Civil Life*. New Haven, CT: Yale University Press.

    1995. *Democracy, Development and the Countryside*. New York: Cambridge University Press.

    1984. "The Political Economy of Slow Growth in India." *Economic & Political Weekly* 19 (September 1): 1511–1517.

Venkataramani, Raja. 1990. *Japan Enters Indian Industry: The Maruti-Suzuki Joint Venture*. Delhi: Radiant.

Vitols, Sigurt. 2001. "Varieties of Corporate Governance: Comparing Germany and the UK." In *Varieties of Capitalism* (Hall and Soskice, eds.). Oxford: Oxford University Press, 337–359.

Vogel, Steven. 1996. *Freer Markets, More Rules*. Ithaca, NY: Cornell University Press.

Vu, Tuong. 2010. *Paths to Development in Asia*. Cambridge: Cambridge University Press.

Wade, Robert. 1996. "Globalization and Its Limits: Reports of the Death of the National Economy are Greatly Exaggerated." In *National Diversity and Global Capitalism* (Berger and Dore, eds.). Ithaca, NY: Cornell University Press: 60–88.

1990. *Governing the Market: Economic Theory and the Role of Government in East Asian Industrialization*. Princeton, NJ: Princeton University Press.

Waldner, David. 1999. *State Building and Late Development*. Ithaca, NY: Cornell University Press.

Walsh, Declan. 2013. "Internal Forces Besiege Pakistan Ahead of Voting." *New York Times*, January 15.

Walton, Michael. 2015. "India's Gilded Age?" Presented at 'The Political Economy of Development in India' – Thirty Years On, All Soul's College Oxford, March 19.

Waterbury, John. 1983. *The Egypt of Nasser and Sadat: Political Economy of Two Regimes*. Princeton, NJ: Princeton University Press.

Wazirat, Shahida. 2002. *The Rise and Fall of Industrial Productivity in Pakistan*. Oxford: Oxford University Press.

Weber, Max. 2002 [1905]. *Protestant Ethic and the Spirit of Capitalism* (Baehr and Wells, trans.). London: Penguin.

Weiner, Myron. 1986. "The Political Economy of Industrial Growth in India." *World Politics* 38 (July): 596–610.

1982. "International Migration and Development: Indians in the Persian Gulf." *Population and Development Review* 8 (March): 1–36.

1972. *Party Politics in India*. Port Washington, NY: Kennikat Press.

1967. *Party Building in the New Nation*. Chicago: University of Chicago Press.

Weiss, Anita. 1991. *Culture, Class and Development in Pakistan*. Lahore: Vangard Books.

White, Lawrence. 1974. "Pakistan's Industrial Families: The Extent, Causes, and Effects of Economic Power." *Journal of Development Studies* 10: 10.

Wilkinson, Steven. 2015. *Army and Nation*. Cambridge, MA: Harvard University Press.

2006. "Explaining Changing Party-Voter Linkages in India." In *Patrons, Clients and Policies* (Kitschelt and Wilkinson, eds.). Cambridge: Cambridge University Press.

Williamson, Oliver. 1985. *The Economic Institutions of Capitalism.* New York: The Free Press.

Womack, James, Daniel Jones, and Daniel Roos. 1990. *The Machine that Changed the World.* New York: Scribner.

Wong, Joseph. 1994. *Healthy Democracies.* Ithaca, NY: Cornell University Press.

Woo-Cummings, Meredith. 1991. *Race to the Swift: State and Finance in Korean Industrialization.* New York: Columbia University Press.

World Development Indicators. 2015. Databank.worldbank.org.

World Bank. 1997. *World Development Report: The State in a Changing World.* Washington, DC: World Bank.

Yardley, James. 2011. "In India, Dynamism Wrestles with Dysfunction." *New York Times,* June 8.

Yi, Matthew. 2001. "Compassion before Profit in AIDS War." *San Francisco Chronicle,* March 26.

Yong, Tan Tai. 2005. *The Garrison State: The Military, Government and Society in Colonial Punjab, 1849–1947.* Delhi: Sage.

Zachariah, Ben. 2005. *Developing India: An Intellectual and Social History, 1930–1950.* Delhi: Oxford University Press.

Zaidi, S. Akbar. 2005. *Issues in Pakistan's Economy.* Oxford: Oxford University Press.

Zamindar, Vazira. 2007. *The Long Partition and the Making of Modern South Asia.* New York: Columbia University Press.

Ziegfeld, Adam. 2012. "Coalition Government and Party System Change: Explaining the Rise of Regional Political Parties in India." *Comparative Politics* 45: 69–87.

Zysman, John. 1994. "How Institutions Create Historically Rooted Trajectories of Growth." *Industrial and Corporate Change* 3: 243–283.

Index

CPSIA information can be obtained
at www.ICGtesting.com
Printed in the USA
LVOW10*1718070317
526430LV00012B/171/P

9 781107 158634